# The P
# STARR FAITHFULL

# The Passing of
# STARR FAITHFULL

JONATHAN GOODMAN

*For John —*

*a true*

*friend. Jon*

*October '97*

THE KENT STATE UNIVERSITY PRESS

*Kent, Ohio, and London, England*

Previously published in Great Britain by Judy Piatkus (Publishers) Ltd.,
copyright Jonathan Goodman, 1990.


*Library of Congress Cataloging-in-Publication Data*

Goodman, Jonathan.
The passing of Starr Faithfull / Jonathan Goodman.
p.     cm.
Originally published: Great Britain : J. Piatkus, c1990.
Includes index.
ISBN 0-87338-541-1 (pbk. : alk. paper) ⊚
1. Faithfull, Starr, 1906–1931—Death and burial.
2. Celebrities—United States—Death.
3. Celebrities—England—Death. I. Title.
CT275.F3714G66   1996
973.91'092—dc20
[B]                                        95-38202


British Library Cataloging-in-Publication data are available.

For Moray Watson –
fine actor; firm friend

I was much too far out all my life
And not waving but drowning.
                    *Stevie Smith*

Picture the outline of a dog that, facing left, is jumping, but only just, over three twigs laid end to end. Its front legs, one hidden by the other, are doubled under its jaw; its hind legs, one hidden by the other, are stretched back; its tail is stiff with expectation – because the animal is almost within snapping range of a chop that is unaccountably dangled from the tip of a willow-branch.

And now imagine that the branch is the borough of New York City called Manhattan; that the chop is another of the boroughs, Staten Island; and that the dog is Long Island. The dog's jaw is the borough of Brooklyn, and the rest of its head, together with the extended front leg, is the borough of Queens. Its neck and collarbone are parts of Nassau County, and the eastern remainder, tail and all, is Suffolk County. The twigs are actually slender islets underlining Long Island.

The western islet of the three, which is called Long Beach, measures nine miles from tip to tip, and, at most, a mile from shore to shore; bridges, one for the Long Island Rail Road, span Reynolds Channel, the sliver of Atlantic that makes Long Beach a separated bit of Nassau County. Just to the west of the centre of Long Beach, twenty-five residential thoroughfares run, perfectly parallel, from the edge of the channel to the edge of the southern, sandy shore; as if that immaculate tectonic tidiness were not enough, the thoroughfares are alternately designated as streets and avenues, and each is called after a different State of the Union.

The eleventh block from the east is Minnesota Avenue.

On Monday, 8 June 1931, the corpse of a young woman was found nestled in the moist sand at the foot of Minnesota Avenue. Her life was going to be ransacked in the hope of explaining its unnatural end. Hundreds of reporters would, between them, write millions of words about what one of the best of them would describe as 'this mystery with the wonderful name'.

The wonderful name was Starr Faithfull.

*

The spell of fine, sometimes sweltering weather had been interrupted the day before, Sunday, when the average of the temperatures recorded in Battery Park, the southern tip of Manhattan, was 64°F – three points below normal for 7 June. At about ten in the morning, a heavy grey blanket of cloud had drooped low enough to make fog in many places, mist in most others – but still, there was a long queue throughout the day for the express elevator towards the 102nd, 'observatory' floor of the Empire State Building, the tallest building in the world, which had been open for little more than a month, and by mid-afternoon 25,000 people had groped their way across Brooklyn to the Floyd Bennett airfield and passed through entrances beside which were notices, 'LOW CEILING = NO FLYING. SORRY FOLKS.'

The fog was worst over the sea – worst of all in the Lower Bay, which extends to the Narrows between Staten Island and Brooklyn, the opening to New York Harbour. One after another, five incoming liners glided at snail's pace along Ambrose Channel, the main shipping lane curving across the Lower Bay (though the channel's pinpointer, the Ambrose Lightship, was 7½ nautical miles[1] south of Long Beach, the wailing of the liners' sirens may have been just about audible to visitors there: some 20,000 of them, far fewer than was usual on a summer Sunday), and, slower still, into the harbour. Four of the five glided, even more slowly, to the piers of their respective lines, jutting into the Hudson River from the west side of Manhattan, arriving only a few hours late; but the master of the fifth vessel, the White Star Line's *Adriatic,* from Liverpool, hearing the harbour pilot's comment that the Statue of Liberty was somewhere close by on the port side, but himself seeing no sign of that imposing monument, straightway decided to stop engines and drop anchor till the morning. (It may be that, following the sinking of the White Star Line's allegedly unsinkable *Titanic,* nineteen years before, masters of that line were given instructions towards avoiding collision that were stricter than those given to masters of other lines.)

If any of the *Adriatic*'s passengers were pleased when told the news, considering a ninth night aboard a bonus, even they must have sided with the incommoded majority at eight in the evening, when, all of a sudden, gale-force winds, accompanying thunder and lightning, put severe strain on the ship's stabilisers – and must have

---

1. The American nautical mile is 6080 feet (2026 ⅔ yards), slightly shorter than the British Admiralty Measured Mile.

made a number of the crew members uneasy as to the adequacy of the anchor. At first, the eye of the storm was over Staten Island, where, as the wind blew the fog away, it caused patches of deeper darkness by snapping overhead electricity cables, many of which fluttered across roads, spitting sparks; some consequently alarmed motorists braked so suddenly that they stalled their engines, and some of those motorists opened their bonnets to tinker in the pouring rain, which made matters worse, while some motorists in the ensuing traffic jams, low on petrol but not daring to switch off their overheating engines, ran out of petrol – and so, by half-past eight, most of the roads were clogged. At about the same time, the electricity-supplying Edison Company, perturbed by a radio news-flash that the south-eastern area of the island, the most exposed part of it, was littered with live wires, and unable to check the accuracy of the report by telephoning the area manager because his telephone wire was down, cut off the supply there.

The storm was, by then, churning the water in the Lower Bay; tossing waves high up the beaches on Long Island's southern shores. At the Brooklyn seaside resort called, though it isn't an island, Coney Island, most of the emergency-squad policemen who should have been on night-duty were resting, as during the day they had been distributed among posses on behalf of the one-Sunday-each-summer Clean Up Coney campaign against pedlars on the Boardwalk, women bathers who let their shoulder straps slip, and small boys wearing back-to-front underpants rather than swimming costumes. That meant that when two crowded pleasure boats were seen bobbing helplessly in the surf, there were only enough emergency-squad men to render assistance to one of them. While that was being done (by shooting a lifeline to the boat and hauling it to shallow water), a dozen or so brave non-policemen swam to the other boat and rescued those passengers who couldn't swim.

The storm caused no such specific excitements that night at any of the seaside resorts of Brooklyn or Queens to the east of Coney Island and within ten miles of it. Nor at Long Beach, slightly farther on.

By half-past ten, the storm was spent. Speaking of Long Beach, the rest of the night was fine; just occasionally, wisps of cloud veiled the small moon.

Beachcombers, they called themselves, the men who, early every summer Monday morning, left their mean homes in Long Beach and walked along the islet's southern shore, always staring at the off-white sand, every so often pausing to pierce it with the pointed sticks they had brought with them, and sometimes stooping to pick something up, either for instant pocketing or for appraisal. Most of the men were unemployed; some of those had been put out of work as a result of the economic depression that, gathering throughout the 1920s, had been made irresistible by the stock-market crash in the last October of that decade. Ignoring the flotsam that conventional beachcombers consider, they searched for things that weekend visitors had not meant to leave behind: coins that had fallen from the pockets of clothes bundled as pillows, bottles that had not been drained of alcohol (which for eleven years now, since the passing of the 'nobly experimental' Volstead Act, was supposed to be Prohibited), and divers others articles, many of a nature that made it less surprising that they had been left on the beach than that they had been brought there in the first place.

The pickings were poor on the morning of Monday, 8 June. The fog had kept the number of Sunday trippers down; the waves curled by the storm had tumbled almost to the end of the sand, scouring it more efficiently than any tide. Although Daniel Moriarity was always ahead of the rest of the westbound beachcombers, he had collected only a few paltry things when, having trudged for over a mile, he came abreast of New York Avenue, the first of the State-named thoroughfares. Wondering whether or not to continue, he glanced at the dainty Bulova wristwatch that had become his on a previous Monday morning. Probably because the watch was not as water-resistant as Bulova had guaranteed it to be, it was none too reliable. Six-thirty, it said. Or near enough, Daniel thought. He reckoned that he had a good fifteen minutes to spare before he needed to make for the municipal waste-dump where he worked. He trudged on, meaning to go a further half-mile to the right-turn into Nevada Avenue, the last of the State-named thoroughfares. Over-stuffed gulls and gannets clattered up from the sand as he approached them, flapped around, croaking from the effort, till he had passed, then tumbled back to the self-same pecking places. The sun, warm on his back (the temperature was already up to the mid-sixties), stretched his shadow far in front of him.

He passed New Hampshire Street, and his shadow started to climb the rocky breakwater that ran for a hundred yards across the beach from near the slight embankment at the foot of Minnesota Avenue. It was only then that his gaze — tutored since several summers ago to stay steeply diagonal to the sand, darting left and right but never far forward — encompassed a large, sprawled object in the lee of the breakwater. Though sea-birds and sparrows engrossed the chamfered top of the breakwater, some resting, some tapping at rocks dyed bottle-green by lichen, there were no birds in the closer vicinity of the object. Daniel's first impression was that a bath towel, or something of the sort, had snagged on a lump of driftwood. Not till he was so close to the object as to be looking down at it did he realise − or, to contradict that word in his subsequent statement, *accept* − that it was the supine body of a young woman.

He knew that she was dead. He knelt beside her but did not touch her skin. All that he did while he knelt beside her was to pull her frock down over her left leg, which had been exposed. She was wearing silk stockings. No shoes. Her frock was of soft untwilled silk printed with a paisley design, most of it only dark blue and white but with additional colours, red and green, on the long sleeves, which, from halfway down, were cut as four ruffles, each of the three lower ones cupped within the one above; the frock had a black patent-leather belt; the neckline was a simple curve, quite high. Daniel Moriarity may have noticed that she was not wearing a wristwatch; no jewellery at all. Her fingernails, which were not long, were varnished scarlet, and the varnish was unmarred. She had been beautiful. Though there were many small cuts and grazes and bruises on her face, and though her dark hair was bedraggled, filthy with sand, she was still beautiful.

Rather than shouting to the two nearest beachcombers, Daniel ran to them. Their names were Patrick Fairbanks and George Evans. They were closer to the sea, both of them shunning the clearly-furrowed course he had taken, and each staying well away from the other, for neither wanted to spark an argument, perhaps even a fight, over who had seen a bit of treasure first. They came together as Daniel approached, his progress clumsy now because the sand here was still drenched and puddle-pocked. He panted words that, though not making a sentence, were intriguing enough to cause Fairbanks and Evans to follow him as, without looking to see if they were following, he retraced his steps.

The three beachcombers stood near the body for a while. The hollows impressed by their boots were not as deep as the hollow that fitted tight to the edges of the body: a sign even surer than the scattering of sand on the body that it had lain on the beach during at least part of the flow and all of the ebb of the last high tide, about twelve-thirty that morning − the sea had brushed the sand first one way, then the other, leaving tilted brims around anything that would not budge.

5

Going by a snapshot of George Evans, he was still in his teens — certainly a lot younger than Daniel Moriarity and Patrick Fairbanks, who, going by snaps of them, were in their thirties. Evans, either deputed by his elders or volunteering, ran off the beach to search for a policeman. By the time he returned with one, Patrolman O'Connor, the tableau was altered, enlarged: Daniel, concerned that the fact that he had found a corpse might not be considered a valid excuse for being late to work, had dashed off to the waste-dump — but other beachcombers had joined Patrick, as had a woman resident of New Hampshire Street, distracted from walking her Scottie along the front. Patrolman O'Connor was almost immediately perplexed. He believed that, having established that there *was* a body on the shore and that it was dead, textbook-correct procedure so far, the next right thing for him to do was to guard the scene till reinforcements arrived — which was all very well except that he somehow had to summon those reinforcements. Perhaps his perplexity showed. Anyway, the woman with the dog provided a solution to O'Connor's conundrum, by offering to use the phone in her house on his behalf. He gave her the number of the Long Beach police station; he may also have told her what to say. As soon as she had gone, he got some of the remaining onlookers to help him carry the body farther up the beach. There was no practical reason for the removal: the tide would not start to flow till early in the afternoon.

It has been noted by occupational psychologists that when 'lone workers' (including, one supposes, occupational psychologists) are suddenly thrust into situations to which they are unaccustomed, they tend to invent things to do, simply for the sake of doing *something*: they confuse motion with action. That appears to be the only explanation for what O'Connor did, which was not merely unnecessary but also a breaking of one of the basic rules of police work.

The message phoned by the woman with the dog was relayed through other wires, eventually to a house in the village of Hempstead, some eight miles north of Long Beach. The house was the residence of Harold King, the inspector in charge of the detective bureau of the Nassau County Police Department.

That police department (the NCPD for short) had existed for only six years. In April 1925, the county's Board of Supervisors, having agreed that most of the autonomous district police forces should be replaced by a combined force, had appointed Abram Skidmore, a police official in other parts of New York State since the 1890s, to carry out the rationalisation. The headquarters of the department were in the small, neat town of Mineola, the county seat − for the first few months in the basement, nicknamed 'the dug-out', of the Old County Courthouse, then in the annex to the New Courthouse, on the other, east side of Franklin Avenue, and then, from the summer of 1930, in a bespoke building next to the Old Courthouse, constructed of similar honey-coloured stone, and also fronted by a lawn. There was an underground tunnel between the police headquarters and the Old County Courthouse.

The first batch of recruits, fifty-five of them, had all been deputy sheriffs in the county; after choosing a captain, two sergeants (Harold King, who had been the deputy sheriff at Hempstead for five years, was one), and a fingerprint man, Skidmore assigned eleven of the others as motorcycle patrolmen and the rest as foot patrolmen; two months later, by which time fifty more men had been taken on, ten of the original foot patrolmen were made detectives, under the command of Harold King, who was soon afterwards promoted to the rank of inspector. By the summer of 1931, the force numbered more than three hundred. Skidmore, needing to explain the rapidly-risen, still rising expenditure to the Board of Supervisors, cited three increases: in population (just over 200,000 in 1925, just over 300,000 in 1931), in the volume of motorised road traffic, and in the amount of crime (most of that resulting from Prohibition: possession of alcohol; visible, smellable or analysable signs that a person had imbibed; offences committed under the influence of drink; the operation of a distillery, brewery or speakeasy; the transporting of quantities of liquor − specially prevalent on the central east-west roads of Nassau County, for secluded harbours on the east of Long Island were favoured by rum-runners as places of disembarkation of cargo ordered by bootleggers in New York City) − and, a further reason, the fact that several of the districts that had originally been outside the NCPD's jurisdiction were now within it.

Among the still-exceptional districts, Long Beach was most in need of fairly efficient and reasonably honest policing. More people lived on the island than in the rest of such districts put together. On fine summer days, or summer days that started fine, the island was crowded with trippers, nearly all attracted only by the southern sandy shore − and whatever the season, whatever the forecast or actual weather, many visitors were attracted only by unnatural amenities, all contravening Prohibition, some flouting gambling laws, and some employing whores described as hostesses. According to a campaigning group of 'dry' residents (who probably preferred guessing the worst to doing arithmetic), there were three times as many speakeasies and 'wet' hotels than there had been licensed premises till Prohibition. Every so often, the police carried out a raid – once or twice without warning – but there are strong indications that Commissioner Morris Grossman[1] and the men he had promoted to be his immediate subordinates, far from wishing to trouble the bootleggers, were keen to warrant their indebtedness. A few members of the force were called detectives, but they were really only officers excused from wearing uniform; if any of them successfully investigated anything, that was a bonus, publicised by Grossman as proof that his selection procedure (actually no more procedural than going eeny-meeny-miney-mo between men who toadied to him) was considerably better than perfect. Once the detective bureau of the Nassau County Police Department was functioning, an arrangement was made whereby it *could* be called upon by the police forces of Long Beach and other districts outside the department's jurisdiction, to give assistance in a wide range of circumstances – and *had* to lead the investigation of all cases of unnatural death.

Therefore, when the woman with the dog phoned the Long Beach police station, what happened was this: a switchboard operator, having listened to her, transferred her to a Sergeant O'Halloran, who told her to repeat the message, and then, she having rung off, repeated it to another policeman – who, as well as arranging for the Acting Coroner, a local doctor named Nathan Ginsberg, to go and

---

1. Who had been appointed by the Mayor of Long Beach, Frank Frankel – who had been elected with the assistance of Vannie Higgins, a flamboyant racketeer whose gang of bootleggers was specially active in the Long Island boroughs of New York City. On 15 March 1931, the *New York Times* reported the arrest of a small-time hoodlum named Meyer Feinman for the murder of Alfred Medrisch, a former member of Vannie Higgins's gang; at the time of the murder, the Nassau County Police were looking for Medrisch to testify against Higgins in a case of rum-running at Long Beach. The report notes that 'Medrisch came into public attention shortly after the Long Beach elections of 1929. With others, he was accused of having gone to that city to vote for Mayor Frank Frankel and Councilmen Eugene Blumenthal and Develan Smith. At the trial, at which he testified for the State, he said that "perhaps 100 to 200" had done so. Eleven were arrested, one was convicted – later receiving a suspended sentence – and the others were acquitted. Medrisch was said to have done the recruiting in pool rooms about the city.'

It is nice to know that Morris Grossman was forced to resign as Commissioner in 1935; after being out of work for two years, he was taken on as an attendant in the Long Beach City Court; in 1943, when he was fifty-five, he died from a heart attack.

look at the body (and, presumably, despatching one or more officers to reinforce or relieve Patrolman O'Connor), rang the NCPD headquarters at Mineola and left a 'call-out order' with the communications bureau − whence a message was passed, just along a corridor, to one of the forty members of the detective bureau − and he (*a*, noting that the time was 8.30; *b*, knowing that Inspector King was supposed to start work at nine but, being a stickler for punctuality, would arrive ten minutes early; *c*, reckoning that though the inspector drove his car as excitingly as he must have driven motor-bikes when, prior to becoming a deputy sheriff, he had been a despatch rider in the wartime army, it took him at least three minutes to drive the two miles north from Hempstead; and *d*, sure that if he let the message from Long Beach languish for twenty minutes, or meanwhile took action off his own bat, the inspector would reprimand him in that ice-cold way of his) phoned the inspector at home. The message seems to have been amended during its travels. King was told, or thought he heard, that 'the body of an unidentified male adult, badly decomposed, had washed up on the sand on the ocean-front at the foot of Wisconsin Avenue, Long Beach'.[1] He gave the phoning detective instructions, telling him that the results of them were to be apparent at 9.10 on the dot.

And they *were*. At that time, King, having driven to Mineola and spent twenty minutes at his desk, returned to his car, which, as there were no parking restrictions on Franklin Avenue, he had parked outside the police headquarters. He was, as usual, physically immaculate: his dark hair, brushed diagonally back from a centre parting, was shaved so close at the greying sides that there it glittered like iron filings; never mind that the day promised to be humid, he wore a three-piece suit − discreetly checked, the double-breasting of the jacket tending to hide his plumpness. Waiting by his car were two detectives, Joseph Culkin and Thomas Shanley, and a freelance photographer, Milton Kreuscher, draped with equipment. Behind the car was a black van, its cabin crammed with three black-suited men − Joseph Macken, proprietor of an undertaking firm in the town called Rockville Centre (that word for some reason spelt in that unAmerican way), and two of his workers. Macken could be excused if vexation marred his practised solemnity, for he had come the five miles from his morgue, driving faster than was seemly to his trade so as to arrive before the deadline-time he had been given over

---

1. Unless otherwise stated, all quoted material in this book is taken either from official records or from newspaper reports.

the phone – only to be told by the waiting detectives that he would have to drive all the way back, as Rockville Centre was about halfway between Mineola and the place which the caller, in his haste to carry out all of Inspector King's instructions, had neglected to say was the eventual destination. King, having ordered Detective Shanley to drive the car, a Hudson Great Eight, sat in the front passenger seat; Detective Culkin and Milton Kreuscher sat, uncomfortably because of the latter's paraphernalia, in the back. The car and the van proceeded to Long Beach.

It was about half-past nine when the investigators, the photographer, and the undertakers – the two employed ones lugging a wickerwork shell – plodded through the sand to where the body had been re-laid.

The tableau was altered, enlarged. Some of the first spectators had left; considerably more had arrived. Patrick Fairbanks and George Evans were still present. There was at least one uniformed policeman; also a Long Beach detective, Sergeant Thomas Walsh. Dr Nathan Ginsberg, who had touched only a wrist of the body, stood on the outskirts of the crowd, using his little attaché case, unopened since he had driven from his place of general practice, as an easel for the writing of something in a notebook or on a bill pad. Two fully-dressed members of the Long Beach life-patrol stood on either side of the body, appearing to be protective of it; one of them, Thomas Cusick, having noticed that 'the dead girl's lips were parted in a half-smile,' had thought that 'it gave her an expression of utter peacefulness (but the 'half-smile' may have been the *rictus sardonicus* that is a common effect of the temporary stiffening of jaw muscles after death). I cannot tell whether the woman with the dog (whose respective names may have been Constance Callaway and Angus; different names appear in different reports), having made the phone call and returned to tell Patrolman O'Connor that she had done so, was still, more than two hours later, on the shore. Nor do I know whether O'Connor had been relieved or reinforced; if reinforced, then King, learning from him or by chance of the altering of the body's situation – which must have caused King to utter an oh-no-not-again sort of sigh with regard to the Keystone Kopishness of the local force – got him to point out the original situation.

One, two, or all three of the Nassau County detectives may have walked to the water-line, beachcombing discriminately; there seems to be no indication as to whether or not such routine searching was done: certainly, nothing was found. The detectives shooed space around the body, and while they (the undertakers too), peered at the body, Milton Kreuscher, who had already taken some pictures, took others. Then, after a nod from King, Joseph Macken and his helpers lifted the body into the shell, the floor of which was covered with greaseproof paper, carried it up the beach, slid it into the van, and drove off. King and his men lingered no more than a few minutes longer; before they left, King must have reminded the local detective and the local doctor of the slight contributions each had to make to the paperwork of the death. By ten o'clock, everyone had gone from the stretch of tousled sand; birds were back, most of them pecking at morsels that the footprints had squeezed from safety, some zigzagging overhead, and the rest, the artful ones, pottering along the breakwater, ready to descend on movements in the sand that the busy birds, because of their busyness, had failed to notice.

By the time the police car turned into the back yard of Macken's Morgue, Rockville Centre, the undertakers had dragged the shell from the black van, carried it through the tradesmen's entrance, and emptied the contents, grease-proof paper and all, on to a custom-built side-table, wide enough to accommodate two queuing bodies and still leave good margins and a decent space down the middle, which stood near one of the white-tiled walls of the windowless but brightly lit room. The room's centrepiece was so recent a replacement of a plain, marble-topped bench that the latter was tucked into a corner, ready for removal by a scrap dealer; the replacing contraption had been brand-named 'The Triple Miracle' by its specialising manufacturer, for its steel working surface was said to be unstainable, its plumbing uncloggable, and its swan-necked (patent pending) spotlight unshockable. To most people entering Macken's Morgue who had never been in any morgue, wonderment at The Triple Miracle, or curiosity in anything else, would have been delayed till the shock of the smell of the place – a breathtaking blending of the sickly-sweet scent of formaldehyde with the smells of neat household disinfectant and ammonia – had diminished.

King and his men stood with their backs to The Triple Miracle (but, respectful of Joseph Macken's pride in his new acquisition, did not loll against it) while Macken's helpers undressed the body brought from the beach. As the paisley frock was damp, which had made it cling, the men may have expected to see that the breasts were bare. They were large; still firm; the nipples were nearly an inch and a half in diameter; the pigmentation of them was accentuated by the dead-white of the surrounding skin. The men, perhaps unsurprised by the absence of a brassiere, were surely surprised, more or less, by the absence of panties. There were no underclothes at all — only a glossy, cream-coloured suspender-girdle, the four shiny clips of which were secured to the silk stockings. Either there was a slight ladder leaning to the seam of each of the stockings before they were unclipped and rolled from the legs by the undertakers or one or both of the ladders, neither noticed till the following day, resulted from the removal of the stockings. There was no indication on the suspender-girdle of the company that had made or sold it. There was, however, a label gummed inside the nape of the frock, claiming that the garment had been 'fashioned exclusively' for Lord & Taylor, purveyors of dry goods. Since that company had not yet branched out from its department store in midtown Manhattan (on Fifth Avenue, two blocks south of the New York Public Library), here was a possible clue — so far, the only one — towards the identity of the dead woman.

Using the discarded sheet of greaseproof paper as wrapping, one of the detectives made a parcel of the frock, its black patent-leather belt, the suspender-girdle, the stockings. King told Macken that he would phone him about the autopsy. The detectives and the photographer drove back to Mineola.

For most of the period from whatever the time was when the detectives entered the police headquarters (well before midday) until about three in the afternoon, they caught up on work connected with other cases — but King arranged, over the phone, for Dr Algernon Warinner, a neighbour of his in Hempstead, to conduct an autopsy, and then rang Joseph Macken (King may also have spoken to a reporter for the *Nassau Daily Review* who augmented his wages by acting as a 'stringer' for a New York evening paper); Detective Culkin looked at missing-person reports from other forces, and either he or Detective Shanley stencilled a rudimentary description of the dead woman, ran off copies of it, popped most of them into envelopes ready-addressed to other forces, and put those in the evening-post basket.

Neither King nor either of his detective-subordinates thought for a moment that the case might pose problems. With a bit of luck, the body would be identified — meaning that the case file, its contents weighing less than the manila, could go, via the civilian records-clerk, to the document store in the basement. If there was no such luck, well, never mind — the file would remain within the precincts of the detectives bureau for a year or so, tucked away with other tucked-away files in a drawer marked *AC*, standing for *Awaiting*

*Completion*, and would then go, evasive of the records clerk, down to the basement. With variations, that either/or way of disposing of certain case files was followed in just about every police force – was one of the host of dodges that helped police statisticians, lacking computers in aid of manipulation, to conjure respectable-looking annual success rates.

At ten past three, when King, Culkin and Shanley re-entered Macken's Morgue, the body had been lifted from the side table and laid on The Triple Miracle, and Dr Warinner – jacket off, shirtsleeves rolled, a long rubber apron on – had already made some formal estimates and observations, and dictated them to Henry Inderdohnen, the undertaker deputed to act as both labourer and note-taker: 'female, apparently 21 years of age, 5 feet 6 inches, weight 135lbs, reddish brown hair, blue eyes ...' As soon as the official audience was settled, the doctor began examining in what he considered was in earnest: he found and counted discolorations and bruises on different parts of the body, observed that the cheeks and forehead had 'a bluish red appearance', detected stiffening from rigor mortis in the hips and knees, and noted when he turned the body on to its left side that blood-tinged fluid ran from the left nostril (but, supposing that he also turned the body on to its right side, either did not notice fluid running from the right nostril or noticed it but neglected to dictate a comment to Inderdohnen); having cut open the torso, he saw

a quantity of approximately one half pint of cherry-red bloody fluid free in the pertenial [*sic:* peritoneal] cavity, and collected in pelvis and flank. Exploration of the abdominal cavity ... revealed two small lacerations, one inch in length, and five small ones, one quarter inch in length, on the dome of the liver, on the right side, high under the diaphragm ... The lungs are greyish red in colour and containing throughout air. On sectioning of lung, it presents a bright red colour, and red froth exudes from the cut surface.

There is no record of the duration of the autopsy. The typed report, based on Inderdohnen's scribblings, fits easily on one side of a quarto sheet of paper. Whoever the typist was, he or she needed more practice, appears to have been dyslexic, and was certainly unlucky at guessing. Anyone reading the report must think sympathetically of Dr Warinner's patients, for all three of the alternative explanations for the absence of corrections indicate that he was a deficient physician: the explanations are that he didn't bother to check what had been typed, that he did but failed to see

13

anything wrong with it, or that he spotted the errors but let them pass. At the very start of the report, the date of the autopsy is given as the 9th rather than the 8th of June; it is clear what 'rigid mortis' ought to be, but some thought is needed towards deciphering 'conjtava' as 'conjunctiva' (the membrane covering the front of the eyeball and the inner surface of the lid); the worst error is the typing of 'shown as' instead of 'show no' in the sentence, 'External genitalia shown as evidence of injury'; since it is safe to say that no parts of the woman's legs were above her hip, the sentence 'There are 17 discolorations or minor bruises on lower legs below the hip' leaves one uncertain as to whether the counted marks were over the whole of the legs or only below the *knees*; and as for the sentence, 'Chest cavity on each side contain a large quantity, nearly a pint of clear fluid,' one cannot make out whether there was nearly a pint on each side or nearly a pint altogether. The report is simply a listing of appearances. Dr Warinner must have drawn conclusions from some of them, individually or in combination, but he uttered nothing more opinionative in his commentary to Inderdohnen than the estimates of age, height and weight. He must, before leaving the morgue, have told Inspector King that, in his opinion, the woman had died from drowning, and that — again in his opinion — none of the appearances that he had observed on or in the body was suggestive of foul play.

The detectives returned to Mineola. One of them phoned the office of the coroner's court at Lynbrook, a town within strolling distance of Rockville Centre, and said that, no hurry, arrangements had to be made for an inquest into the cause of death, which was drowning, of a presently unidentified female.

That, it seemed, was just about that.

Peculiarly, considering that Harold King's memory was generally enviable, when the inquest, admittedly long-delayed, was eventually held, and the coroner asked him what time it was when Stanley E. (for Edward) Faithfull arrived at the Nassau County Police Headquarters on Monday, 8 June, he replied: 'About eleven o'clock that night, if I am not mistaken.' He was excessively mistaken. The mistake is made more peculiar by the fact that, at about eleven o'clock that night, he and several other men were leaving Macken's Morgue, having spent the past two and a half hours there as a result of Stanley Faithfull's visit.

Faithfull, who actually arrived at the police headquarters shortly after six o'clock, looked older than his age, which was fifty-one. The illusion was all to do with his head: the unnaturally tall dome of it would have been naked on top if he had not let the grey, almost white hair at the temples grow into long strands that, when brushed up and across from each side, and with the overlapping ends smarmed with pomade, drew attention to his baldness; he had to wear spectacles, and chose to wear black-framed ones, the lenses perfectly circular and so large that his dark-pupilled eyes, though not small, seemed to be; his moustache, swagged from between his nostrils to the edges of his straight lips, was dark, perhaps from a dye; one of King's first impressions of him, that he was 'dour and flinty', seems to have been belied by the deep-etched lines, apparently smile-lines, that curved towards his pointed chin. He was of medium height, thin, straight-backed; it is hard to visualise him wearing casual clothes – or, indeed, wearing only the trousers of one of his three-piece suits, all of heavy material, striped, and obviously, from the way they sagged, bought off the peg – but that may be because press photographs of him during the following weeks were either posed or taken when he was going to or coming from formal meetings. Though he tended, as King said, to 'rattle on', he chose his words and spoke them precisely. There was what some Americans think of as Englishness in the tone of his voice. The Englishness, if it was really that, may have been inherited.

Introducing himself to King, he stressed the double L of his surname. And, straightway coming to the reason for his visit, he referred to his elder step-daughter, saying that her Christian name was Starr – spelt S T A *double R*.

Two days earlier, late in the evening of Saturday, 6 June, he had called at the police station on Charles Street, which runs south-west to the Hudson River, in the Greenwich Village district of downtown Manhattan, and after a tiff with the uniformed policeman manning the front desk, because he refused to say why he wished to speak to a detective in private, was taken to an interview room by Detective Jeremiah Ahearn. He gave Ahearn his name, stressing the double L, and his address – an apartment of a house on St Luke's Place, which is a little more than a quarter of a mile south of Charles Street and roughly parallel with a single block of it. Without waiting for Ahearn, a slow writer, to finish writing the address, he told him that what he was about to say was to be treated in confidence: as much as he and his wife wanted the help of the New York Police Department, they dreaded the thought of the least publicity. Ahearn, having completed the address, ostentatiously jabbed a dot on the end of it and peered at his watch – sign language saying that he had heard the proviso but was giving no promises.

Without more ado, Faithfull revealed that his elder step-daughter, Starr (with two Rs), who was twenty-five, had left the family apartment at 9.30 a.m. on the previous day, Friday, carrying no more cash than three dollars, two of which he had just given her so that she could have her hair waved, which was the sole specific reason she had given for going out, and had still – some thirty-six hours later – not returned. He said that he, his wife, and his younger step-daughter had 'spent the [Friday] night in restless anxiety'. Today, he and his wife (no mention of his younger step-daughter) had racked their brains for some innocent explanation for Starr's absence. They had been unable to think of anyone who might be able to throw light on the mystery, for she was 'a rather private person' – so far as they were aware, she had no close friends in Manhattan. Faithfull explained that for the past year he, being 'between proper employments', had worked as a salesman, on a commission-only basis, for the Airian Products Corporation, makers of pneumatic mattresses, whose offices were on the thirty-seventh floor of the Woolworth Building,[1] at the southern end of Broadway. He said that, during the day, feeling that there was no one else he could turn to, he had gone to the offices and talked to George Perry, the manager of the firm, whom he had known for ten years, and that Perry had 'ordered' him to inform the police of Starr's disappearance. He had delayed doing so because, having walked home and told his wife what Perry had said, she had 'expressed deep concern that a report to the police might cause undue publicity', and he had 'understood her disquiet'.

If Ahearn did not understand why the Faithfulls, man and wife, were so anxious to avoid publicity, he was either too polite or not interested enough to ask for an explanation. He asked if Starr had ever 'gone missing' before. Never, Faithfull said – she had never stayed out later than midnight. Might she have gone to some speakeasy and drunk herself into a stupor? 'Starr never drinks,' Faithfull snapped. 'There wouldn't be any sense in looking there.' Ahearn snapped back that there had to be somewhere or someone she might have taken it into her head to visit, and Faithfull, having

---

1. Opened in 1913 (remotely by President Woodrow Wilson – who, sitting at his desk in the White House, pressed a button that signalled the switching on of all 86,000 bulbs in the cathedralesque building), it remained the tallest skyscraper in the world till 1930, when the Chrysler Building was completed.

thought for a minute, said that all he could think of was that she had a few friends and a larger number of relatives in Boston, Massachusetts — but added that she, being very particular about her appearance, was most unlikely to have gone to Boston, even on the spur of the moment, without having had her hair waved, and that that would have left her with nothing like enough cash to cover the fare, whether by train, bus or steamer, for the journey of more than two hundred miles. He further added that she did not have a bank account.

Ahearn, who may have begun to feel that Faithfull was determined to keep Starr's disappearance mysterious, asked if she always went to the same hairdresser. Faithfull said that he didn't know: his wife would, however — she and Starr were like *that* (he clenched a fist), as mutually confiding and gossipy as a mother and daughter could be.

He gave Ahearn a photograph of Starr; answered a string of one- or two-word questions about her physique, colouring, etc.; stated, when asked the formal question, that she was Protestant; itemised her outerwear when she had left home on the Friday morning — small black hat, black coat with fur collar; black gloves; paisley-design dress, predominantly dark blue and white, with ruffled sleeves; tan-coloured stockings; black shoes made by Katz — and said that all of the clothes had been bought from Lord & Taylor. (Ahearn surely recalled that the previous day had been a scorcher — at 9.30 a.m. the temperature in Manhattan was 71°F, and the cloudless sky gave clear warning of 80s in the afternoon — yet he did not express surprise either at the number of garments or at the unseasonableness of one of them, the fur-collared coat. Perhaps he was, like most detectives, a lover of lists for lists' sake and therefore so delighted with the length of the list of garments that he was dazzled from wondering why it *was* so long, let alone noticing an apparent peculiarity about it. There are other possible explanations: tiredness because, this being a weekend, he was working a double shift, or a treating of his task as being junior-clerical, for the majority of missing person reports turned out to be false alarms. The inexplicable thing is this — that, so far as I can tell, no one who subsequently saw the list was at all perplexed by it.)

Faithfull told Ahearn something of Starr's antecedents, and in doing so referred to some of his wife's, his other step-daughter's, and his own. Unfortunately, the detective's notes of this part of the interview are lost. Though one can be confident that Faithfull carefully omitted to mention certain events, as well as the cause of certain others that he may have mentioned, there is no way of knowing which salient details he left out simply by oversight or what unimportant matters he included. There would have been some of both. These are the relevant details he had no reason not to disclose:

On 5 March 1904, at a church in Boston, Helen MacGregor Pierce, a native of the town of Andover in upstate Massachusetts, was married to Frank Wyman II, a man of about her own age, who in the early twenties, had come east from his parental home in St Louis, Missouri, to attend Harvard University, across the Charles River from Boston, and having graduated as Bachelor of Arts with the class of 1900, was employed by one of the many firms of investment brokers in the city. Helen's family line was long by American standards. She was proud of that; she knew the genealogy by heart, made sentimental journeys to places in New England where ancestors had dwelt, and treasured petty mementoes as provenances of her pride. It was a wistful pride, because her father, a recipient equally with his brother and sister of their father's considerable estate, had put all of his one-third share into a business venture that had foundered, and, contemptuous of business ever after, had left no estate to speak of. His wife had died while Helen was being courted by Frank Wyman; Helen and her older brother, her only sibling, had decided between themselves what each should have of their mother's belongings, agreeing the distribution democratically by taking turns at choosing between things that were clearly of little or no value and apparently valuable things whose appearance was deceptive. The most hallucinatory of the latter, taken by Helen, was a bijou summer-house, mortgaged to the hilt, at Centerville, on Cape Cod, the part of Massachusetts that pokes out, then up, then partway back, like a finger beckoning the Atlantic towards Boston Bay. The mortgaged house, with its paltry contents augmented by the rest of Helen's share of her mother's assets, was her sole dowry. Frank Wyman's disappointment at that would have been alleviated by cheque wedding presents from some of Helen's wealthy aunts, uncles and cousins.

Within a year of the marriage, the couple moved a thousand miles west, to Chicago. There, Wyman worked for a finance company in the Loop, the business district bounded by the elevated railroad; they lived in a rented house in the suburb of Evanston, north along the shore of Lake Michigan.

The first of the Wymans' two children, both of them daughters, was born at Evanston on Saturday, 27 January 1906. Prior to the birth, Helen, her husband acquiescing, had decided that the child, whether a boy or a girl, would be christened Starr. That was a name that had been passed down in her family, being given to a female or, despite its prettiness, a male member of each generation – in hers to her brother (who by 1931, presumably by industriousness rather than from inheritance, was well to do – living, alone except for servants, in a corner-house on Boston's Beacon Hill, a very snooty neighbourhood, almost entirely inhabited by the city's 'old rich', generally known as Brahmins). The new Starr soon had a pet-name: Bamby.

Within a year of their becoming parents, Frank and Helen Wyman returned, with Starr, to the east, and settled in the quiet New Jersey town of Montclair, a dozen miles from the Hudson River, the estuary of which separates the so-called Garden State from Manhattan. The reason for the move to Montclair cannot also have been the reason for the move from Chicago; it may be that Wyman lost his job in the finance house and, unable to find another in Chicago, answered advertisements in eastern newspapers, ever more desperately until, as happened, he was engaged as an executive vice-president of a firm of sub-contracting manufacturers in Montclair that was so small that comparatively few of its employees can have had unpresidential job titles. Hoping, at first, that some better job would turn up, he rented a small, furnished apartment; though even he must have accepted after, say, two years that his hope was forlorn, he continued to rent the temporary accommodation for eight more.

With increasing frequency during those eight years, and for ever longer periods, he was left to look after himself. Once Starr had progressed from toddling to walking, Helen took her on trips to Massachusetts. The journey was tiring but uncomplicated – a bus from Montclair to Manhattan, a train from Pennsylvania Station, at West Thirty-Fourth Street and Eighth Avenue, or from Grand Central, eight blocks uptown, between Park and Lexington Avenues on East Forty-Second Street. The trips always included visits to Boston, where Starr – a plump little girl with reddish-brown hair (Titian, Helen insisted), precocious but polite – was shown off to relatives. Even if Helen could have afforded the cost of a hotel, she would still have stayed with relatives – not only because, as she wrote in a post-visit thank-you letter to one of them, a cousin, Mrs Martha Peters, 'family ties are precious to me ... being away from you [all] is a cause of sadness,' but also because they never embarrassed her by pretending that she was not to be pitied, and always gave her leave-taking gifts of cash. Each winter, she arranged for the house at Centerville to be let throughout the summer, using the proceeds to keep up payments on the mortgage and to cover the annual bill for local taxes on the property. In the spring and fall she stayed with Starr in the house for varying lengths of time, respectively to prepare it and to tidy up and check the contents against the inventory. Often, when the weather was fine, a couple called Parkinson, year-long residents of Centerville, escorted Starr to Weduaquet Lake, just up the road, or to West Hyannisport, and there she learned to swim.

The Wymans' second child was born on 5 August 1911. Helen was in Boston at the time; Frank may have taken time off so as to be there too; Starr, who was now five, was looked after by relatives till her mother was better. Though the new baby was given the first name of Elizabeth, she was never called by it or by any of its diminutives, but was known by her middle name of Tucker, which was the surname of a dead branch of the family tree and a middle name of one of Helen's aunts – the mother of her cousin Martha. Saying that Elizabeth was known as Tucker is not sufficient: when she was able to write, and later, when she had also mastered the rudiments of spelling, she wrote 'Tucker' as 'Tooka', and at the age of ten or so, perhaps envious of her sister's lovely name, she began calling herself Sylvia. There are no sure indications that Tucker (let us stick to that name, ignoring her misspelling and attempted replacement of it) was ever jealous of Starr, or vice versa. But, of course, jealousy is the most easily disguised of the Seven Sins – and the artfulness of some of the forms of disguise may even deceive the sinners themselves. The infant Starr's beauty was unblemished. The conventionality of the infant Tucker's prettiness was marred in a strange way. Her hair (straighter than her sister's – being, in the main, a shade darker, the reddish tints were barely noticeable) had a patch of white, the size of a waistcoat button, exactly over the centre of her forehead. Helen at first – upset when she heard or read of a superstition that such patches were the Devil's finger-marks – and then Tucker herself once she became careful of her looks, tried to hide the white by dabbing it with dyes (but none quite matched the surrounding hair, and, in any event, twice-daily dabbings were needed to colour the stippling at the roots) and by combing covering quiffs and fringes (but none stayed in place without the unsightly aid of umpteen grips). One of the sisters' few mutual childhood friends subsequently recalled that 'Starr, over-sensitive herself, was always troubled by Tucker's sensitivity in certain respects, her white patch of hair especially; that difficulty appeared to be Starr's chief worry'.

When the time approached for Starr to be educated, Martha Peters invited half a dozen of the other wealthy relatives to tea, and, saying that she was sure they all knew what she was going to suggest, surprised them by suggesting a clubbing together so that poor Helen would be spared the humiliation of having to send Starr to a non-fee-paying school or the responsibility of finding the means to keep the child at a good school. The suggestion, which didn't sound terribly expensive, was accepted unanimously. Starr was enrolled at Miss Julia Park's School on Chestnut Hill in Brookline, the western suburb of Boston in which several of the relatives, including the Peters, lived. According to some sources, Starr was a boarder, but there is a good deal of circumstantial evidence that she was a day-girl. If so, she almost certainly lived *en famille* with relatives, perhaps with different ones at different times. Certainly, she spent some school vacations with various relatives. The fact that none of her term-reports seems to have survived may mean that they were sent, not to Helen, but to whichever of the contributing relatives acted as collector from the others and payer of Miss Park. There are reasons (which will appear) for believing that the following recollections of Starr by a former classmate refer to her last four years at the school, from when she was eleven:

> [She was] a moody girl, noted for her remarkably erudite conversation and her habit of reading books far beyond her age. She read prodigiously of the heaviest tomes and kept a complete record in her diary of her impressions, claiming she intended, some day, to write a book, and she would then appreciate this daily record of all her reactions, experiences and conclusions on life in general. She grew more and more sensitive about her personal and family affairs; once, she suddenly broke off acquaintanceship with two chums because, she explained, 'they were too curious about my family affairs'.

Starr left Miss Julia Park's School at the end of the spring term, 1921, spent the next three months at the holiday home of a related family, as did Helen and Tucker, and on the last day of September travelled to Lowell, Massachusetts – thirty-odd miles north of Boston, close to the border with New Hampshire – to be 'finished' at the exclusive Rogers Hall School. Since one doesn't know how strict a regimen was enforced by the headmistress, Miss Olive Parsons, and the teaching staff, nor how the frequency and gravity of Starr's disobediences compared with those of other girls, no conclusion can be drawn from the 'large number' of de-merits she received — for, among other repetitive lapses, being noisy after lights-out, missing breakfast (which may have been because she was trying to slim: she always, to her way of thinking, had weight problems), curtailing an evening study-hour for the purpose of washing her hair (and, though this wasn't mentioned in the indictment, perming it; round about this time, she was sacrificing her beauty to fashion by crimping her hair into tight curls, swagged on the left, almost to her eyebrow, like a bead curtain). Her grades midway through her second year at Rogers Hall were *A* in art, *B* in accounts, French, and physical training (she probably got *A* in PT in her first year, when she collected almost twice as many marks for swimming as the runner-up; for some reason, thereafter, she never swam or even sunbathed), and *C* in English history, English literature, English themes,[1] physiology, and scripture.

Starr reached the age of eighteen in January 1924. She was five months from graduating. She did not return to Rogers Hall after the Christmas holiday. It was a sudden decision; the tuition fee for the new term had been paid, and the relatives got a refund of $105.44. The least wealthy and the begrudgingly generous of them would have been pleased that Starr's education had unexpectedly ended — for, over the years (particularly the last eight or nine, since Tucker, coming of school-age, had had *her* bills paid too), the acceptance of Martha Peter's suggestion had grown very expensive indeed. There is no record of how much it cost to keep Starr at Miss Park's school (or of the total for Tucker, who also attended that school, till she was twelve, and then spent two years at the School of the Museum of Fine Arts, Boston), but the cost of Starr's twenty-seven months at Rogers Hall was, taking the refund into account, $5904.64. The bill for 1923 included $1000 for tuition and $50 for bed (inexplicably, there is no mention of board), $43 pocket-money, and $889.47 reimbursement to Helen of payments made on behalf of Starr ($715.38 for clothes[2]).

---

1. A teacher-friend has explained to me that 'English themes' are simply short essays that a pupil writes for his or her 'English class', in the vain hope that it will teach the child to write good prose. Since the early 1940s, it has gone under the name of 'Language Arts' — can you believe it?
2. An extraordinarily large amount. Here are some garment prices, taken at random from advertisements for Boston and Manhattan department stores (including, among the latter, Lord & Taylor) in 1923: satin coat, $39.75; shantung-silk suit, $30.00; organdie frock, $24.50; woollen jumper, $9.75; batiste blouse, $10.00; piqué skirt, $6.95; women's boots, $15.00, and shoes, $11.50. Supposing that Helen was

In August 1918, seventeen months after the US declaration of war on Germany, Frank Wyman had gone to Paris to serve as a kind of liaison officer with the Foyer du Soldat, an organisation similar to the Young Men's Christian Association. Returning in October 1919, nearly a year after the Armistice, he had taken a job with the YMCA in Boston, eking out the small salary by selling municipal bonds on commission. Either before his return or soon afterwards, Helen and their daughters had moved into a house in Brookline, 9 Park Street, which was owned by one of the relatives. Frank had found digs in Boston.

On 26 May 1924, in the courthouse at Dedham,[1] the town contiguous to the south-west of Boston, Helen was granted a decree of divorce on the grounds of desertion. Later in the day, she celebrated in public with a man who had been her friend for over a year, but with whom, till Judge Joseph McColle had swallowed the last morsel of her tale of how Frank's increasingly lengthy absences at home had culminated in his complete desertion of her and their children, she had been careful in public to seem no more than casually friendly.

Her friend was Stanley E. Faithfull.

He had, as a baby, been British. Whether his mother was British born and bred is made doubtful by her forenames, Maria Wilhelmina Despard, and her maiden-name of Grantoff. In the *occupation of father* box on the certificate of Stanley's birth on 27 October 1879, Alfred Williams Faithfull ('Williams' suggestive of ancestral

---

unaware that Starr had given up swimming and sunbathing, she might have bought her a bathing costume and could have chosen from two at $12.95; a one-piece in silk taffeta or a two-piece in poplin, 'with flounce effect (both supplied with the indispensable combination)'.

1. The venue, three years before, of the trial of Nicola Sacco and Bartolomeo Vanzetti for the murder during a payroll robbery of a cashier, Frederick Parmenter, and a guard, Alessandro Berardelli. Both were found guilty and were sentenced to death. Their lawyers, an ever-changing pack, used legal stragems to postpone the executions; meanwhile, throughout the civilised world, protestors chanted that Sacco and Vanzetti had been framed and condemned because they were Italian immigrants, or because they were anarchists, or both. The executions were carried out, six years late, in 1927. In 1977, by which time there were many Italian-Americans of voting age living in Massachusetts, the Governor of the State, a Greek-American named Michael Dukakis, declared 23 August, the anniversary of the executions, to be 'Nicola Sacco and Bartolomeo Vanzetti Memorial Day'. He forestalled a question that was otherwise bound to be asked by saying that he 'took no stand' on whether the two men he had decided to honour by naming a day after them were guilty or innocent of the murder of the two men whose names had slipped his mind for the moment.

Welshness) is called 'a Gentleman' — which means that he was not gainfully employed when his son's birth was registered (a full seven weeks after the event), either because he did not need to work or because he was out of work, had no firm offer of a job, and was unqualified by study or practise to claim a particular trade. The former explanation seems to be ruled out by the family's address: 15 Stockwell Park Road, a two-up, two-down semi-detached house of grey brick in Lambeth, a part of South London in which no one who could have afforded to live elsewhere would have chosen to live.

In 1882, or thereabouts, the family — Alfred and Maria, their first child, Claude Augustus, who was a couple of years older than Stanley, and Stanley himself — emigrated to America. If they disembarked at Manhattan, they trekked a thousand miles west, to the town of Decorah, Iowa, where there was an English colony; Alfred got a job in a paper mill. Maria, pregnant en route, gave birth to a third child, another son, Reginald Percy. In 1884, Maria gave birth to a daughter, named Evalina. That same year, the family moved three hundred miles farther west, to the small manufacturing city of Sioux Falls, South Dakota, where Alfred worked menially for a carriage-maker, and Claude, Stanley and, eventually, Reginald attended a grade school. Five years in Sioux Falls were followed by about as many in the larger manufacturing city of Minneapolis, two hundred miles to the north-east, in Minnesota. There, Alfred went from job to job, one of his places of work being an iron foundry, another a warehouse for linseed oil. Stanley had not finished high school when the family made their last, and longest, overland journey — to Los Angeles, in Southern California. There is not a scrap of information as to how Alfred filled the time till his retirement.

Three members of the family, perhaps four, remained in Los Angeles for the rest of their lives. By 1931, Alfred and Maria were dead, and so was Evalina, who does not seem to have married; Claude was a teacher at a polytechnic institute in the city; Reginald was a dairyman in Honolulu, Hawaii.

Stanley did not attend a school in Los Angeles; as he would have been about fourteen when the family moved there, he almost certainly began working then. In 1897, when he was seventeen, he did not merely leave home but separated himself from it by near enough as many miles as he could go without becoming an expatriate. As soon as he reached his destination, which was Boston, he sought out Charles S. Fellows, a distant relative who had emigrated from England some ten years before, when he was in his early twenties, and was now an apparently successful middleman in the grain business, fixing deals between farmers and East Coast wholesalers and taking a cut from both. Fellows got Stanley a bookkeeping job with Phipps & Tarbell, a firm of grain jobbers in Boston, and within six months Stanley was given a raise to $25 a week; he supplemented his daytime earnings − and became familiar with suburbs other than Lower Mills, where he had digs (close to the Neponset River, on the farther bank of which was a place called, not uniquely, Montclair) − by doing an evening job, touting books of an improving nature door to door.

After a year, he left Phipps & Tarbell and joined the American Cereal Company as senior salesman in Vermont. He cannot have been much outnumbered, if at all, by junior salesmen, for the small state − running, hilly most of the way, from the western side of the northern boundary of Massachusetts to Canada − was sparsely populated, mostly by cereal farmers. He stuck out the coals-to-Newcastle, or ice-to-Alaska, job for nine months, then offered himself back to Phipps & Tarbell − who reinstated him, giving him ten dollars a week more than he was getting when he left. His second period with the firm was no longer than his first; meanwhile, he prepared to set up in business on his own. He finished with Phipps & Tarbell on the last Saturday of 1899, and on the following Monday, the first day of the new century, became, all alone, Stanley E. Faithfull & Co., Grain Jobbers and Commission Merchants, with an address for mail (perhaps accommodation too − if not a properly rented cubby-hole, then a sparing by Charles Fellows of space in his suite on the third floor) in the Boston Chamber of Commerce Building. He was not yet twenty-one.

There is a tale, said to be true, of an ever-resting actor who stared blankly when a dole-man suggested that he should seek other work, and then exclaimed, 'What, and give up show business?' Stanley seems to have been almost as dedicated, but to the general condition of self-employment. Though he never earned more per annum as his own boss than he would have done if he had stayed with Phipps & Tarbell, working only conscientiously during far fewer hours, bored at times but never fearful, there were thirteen of those annums. It appears that either excessive pride postponed his admission of defeat or he persevered for too long because he believed that the longer he persevered, the closer he came to making a crock-of-gold kind of deal. When you have learned more about him, you will, I think, credit the latter explanation.

Stanley's claim that he was a company in the grain business was not much more of an exaggeration than Miss Margaret Butterfield's claim that she was the proprietress of an employment agency specialising in the provision of part-time secretarial assistance to private individuals. Hers was an almost entirely personal service; on the rare occasions when she was deluged with as many as three concurrent commissions, she tried to get the commissioners' assent to her apportioning of her time so that, by going without meal-breaks, she could do part of each part-time job each day – only if the assent was not unanimous did she act as an agent, by scouting out stand-ins for herself from among her lady friends. As well as working in other people's homes – in some, not only secretarially but also as a baby-sitter or locum governess – she did typing in her own home, an apartment of a house on Beaufort Road, in the Jamaica Plain suburb of Boston.

Stanley had been self-employed for four or five years when he first met Miss Butterfield. The meeting was brief, to do with business: he, unable to type (he subsequently taught himself), asked her to do some typing for him; she agreed, quoting a price – which he probably tried to haggle down – and told him when the work would be ready for collection. There were similar meetings over the following months. Gradually, a friendship developed; the friendship blossomed into a romance. On 2 September 1907, the couple were married in the village of Darien, Connecticut, on the northern shore of Long Island Sound. The marriage licence states that both parties were thirty-four. As you may already have reckoned up, Stanley was only twenty-seven. It seems less likely that he lied about his age to spare his intended's blushes than that he had added half a dozen years to his twenty when he took up grain-jobbing and had felt that he had to stay just as ostensibly older ever since.

Married, Margaret kept on working; and she continued to call herself – or, at any rate, to be called by long-standing clients – Miss Butterfield. Among those clients were members of two of Boston's most exalted families, the Peabodys[1] and the Saltonstalls. The Peabodys were so attached to Miss Butterfield that they permitted her and Stanley to spend vacations at a lodge on the family estate at Ipswich, north of Boston; the dowager Mrs Peabody posthumously signified her special attachment to Miss Butterfield by leaving her a legacy of $10,000. In 1931, Mrs Richard N.

---

1. Peabody was a common name in Massachusetts. The Peabodys who employed Miss Butterfield do not seem to have been related to the Peabodys who will be mentioned later.

Saltonstall, who was by then the dowager in *her* family, recalled that 'Miss Butterfield was a lovely, cultured, widely esteemed gentlewoman. She worked as my confidential secretary and as governess for my son Leverett, now speaker of the Massachusetts House of Representatives. After she married Mr Faithfull ... we were always happy to help her, for the Faithfulls had no money. But I do remember distinctly that they were devoted to each other. I think Faithfull was some sort of a small manufacturer.'

Clearly, in the last sentence of her recollection Mrs Saltonstall was speaking of some time after the spring of 1913, when Stanley, having given up both self-employment and the grain business, joined the 150-strong Avery Chemical Company as treasurer and general manager − at a salary, so he afterwards said, of $150 a week. If he did earn that much, then − taking into account Miss Butterfield's earnings and the fact that they were paying comparatively little rent for their home, the top floor of a two-floor house on Winthrop Road, in Brookline − Mrs Saltonstall's comment that 'the Faithfulls had no money' probably referred to their situation after the spring of 1917, round about the time of the US declaration of war on Germany. That was when Stanley left the Avery Chemical Company, having received a promise of financial backing from the Hollister White investment firm, and set up two companies in the same premises − the administrative offices at 40 Central Street, in the business district of Boston, and the production plants occupying a building previously leased by a wholesale butcher at Mansfield, some twenty miles south of the city. Stanley was named president of both the Atlantic Chemical Company and the Lactic Chemical Company, but as the multifarious products of both companies were made by a combined force of versatile workers (forty at most), his double presidency took up only a singularly presidential amount of time. If the setting up of two companies was not meant to facilitate ingenious accounting, the reason had something to do with some uncommon intention − which may, just conceivably, have been honest.

Many of the products attributed to the Atlantic company were derivatives of the sulphate, chrome-alum, for use by, among others, photographers and tanners. All of the fewer products attributed to the Lactic company were derivatives of edible lactose, obtained from sour milk or whey, and, apart from one called only Lacto (an Ovaltine sort of drink), had brand-names that included the president's surname: for instance, Faithfull Baking Powder, Lactic Faithful, Cream of Lactate Faithfull, and Lactic Faithfull De Luxe.

27

The idea of using chrome-alum and edible lactose respectively as the bases of lots of products in several markets was not Stanley's but that of a young chemist, Harold Whitman, who presented the idea to Stanley, apparently with no hope of a reward greater than employment by him; in any event, Whitman was the first recruit, taken on as 'chief chemist' – and paid wages – while the building at Mansfield was being made ready. According to Stanley, he himself owned half of the ordinary shares in both companies and, unequally spread between them, preferential shares with a face-value of $15,000.

In the spring of 1921, the shares in the Atlantic company became worthless. As soon as the debts and assets of the entire operation had been assigned to that company, and immediately 'purchased' by the Lactic company, the Atlantic company went out of business. Stanley sought funds to keep the Lactic company going, but within months that company was also declared bankrupt. A newspaper reporter who questioned former employees heard no unkind words about Stanley: 'He was,' said one, 'a real human being. He was unpretentious – not high-hat. He treated his men well – perhaps too well for his own good.'

For Stanley, himself unemployed, this was the worst period of his life so far. During the previous year, he and his wife had moved to an even smaller apartment; it was in Sutherland Road, one of a number of Scottish-named thoroughfares on the western edge of Brookline. Soon after the move, Miss Butterfield had started complaining of aches and pains; they had continued, become more severe, but still she had put off seeking medical help. When she at last did so, she was found to be suffering from cancer. Perhaps not then but following her death a few months later, on 26 January 1922, cancer was discovered in her brain, breast, liver and lungs. Mrs Richard N. Saltonstall paid all of the accumulation of medical bills. Whereas that is certain, there is only equivocal evidence that she also paid for the interment in Mount Auburn Cemetery, to the north of Brookline, and for a memorial stone. The widower inherited all of his wife's estate, which, including the legacy from the dowager Mrs Peabody, was worth more than $20,000.

There is no record of how, or roughly when, Stanley Faithfull and Helen Wyman first met. The fact that they were residents of Brookline (Park Street, where Helen lived from round about 1919, was half a mile east of Winthrop Road, twice as far from Sutherland Road) supports the possibility that they were introduced at a social or community gathering; another possibility, wholly unsupported, is that Miss Butterfield was partially employed by one of Helen's rich relatives in the neighbourhood, and Stanley visited the relative's house when Helen was also visiting. I can see no reason for doubting her recollection that they had been 'on close friendly terms for over a year' by the time of her divorce from Frank Wyman, in May 1924. (In June 1931, a reporter for the *Boston Post* carefully pretended not to suggest that 'a young woman bookkeeper who on many occasions accompanied Faithfull on drives to Mansfield, when he was known as president of a chemical company there,' may have been Helen in a clerical disguise. Since the reporter could easily have found out if his guess was right or wrong, but did not do so, he presumably lacked confidence in it.)

A few months after Frank Wyman had − to use an expression that was common then − gone into the discard, Helen made public her acceptance of Stanley's proposal of marriage. She and her daughters had already moved into a different apartment − at 53 Grove Street, on the south-western edge of Boston. Stanley had moved out of the apartment in Winthrop Road. Till the wedding, he lived at, or was permitted to have mail delivered to, 17 Pinckney Street, on Beacon Hill. It is unclear whether the wedding, on Saturday, 7 February 1925, was performed by a curate of the Harvard Congregational Church in that church or in some unconsecrated place. Just as there had been a delay in recording Stanley's birth, in England, forty-five years before, there was a delay − till Friday the thirteenth of the following month − in recording his marriage to Helen. He gave his true age. Though he had been unemployed for nearly four years, since the liquidation of the business in Mansfield, he described himself as 'Merchant'. Helen gave her age as forty-one, and said that she had no occupation. Starr (who had left Rogers Hall thirteen months before) and Tucker (who would end her shorter education in the summer) chose to be known as Faithfull as soon as their mother was legally entitled to that name.

If an affidavit sworn by Stanley is to be believed, the daughters very nearly became orphans on the last Saturday of July 1925, when the car he was driving, with Helen beside him, skidded on an unkempt road in the countryside west of Boston, and ended up in a ditch. He, by the grace of God, suffered only slight bruising, but Helen − so she swore too − received physical injuries that remained painful for a considerable time and never quite recovered from the shock. He instituted an action for damages from the State of Massachusetts. The action dragged on for nearly six years, till the middle of April 1931, when Helen was awarded $4062.

The usual law's delays may have been augmented by geographic difficulties in getting the opposing parties together. In September 1925, so shortly after the accident that Helen must still have been wearing one or two band-aids for a healing purpose, the recently-constituted family moved from Massachusetts to New Jersey – to 528 Ridgewood Road, a neat, timber-faced house, its central entrance sheltered by a canopy supported by corkscrew pillars, the whole place small enough to be overhung by a lopsided ancient oak, in the town of West Orange. If Helen had been at all sentimental about her first marriage, she would have been sentimental about the location of the new home, for West Orange is only a couple of miles from Montclair.

Two financial transactions – one by Helen, the other, immediately afterwards, by Stanley – may have been unconnected: she had taken out a second mortgage, for $2000, on the house at Centerville that she had struggled for twenty years to retain, dreaming of the day when it would be truly hers. Then he had taken out a mortgage to buy the house at West Orange, the purchase-price of which was $22,500. When the family had been living there for no more than nine months, he took out a second mortgage. And so, by the summer of 1926, Stanley – unemployed, the husband of a woman with no occupation, the step-father of two daughters who had never worked and who, so far as one can tell, had neither of them seriously considered getting a job – was, as chancellor of the family exchequer, lumbered with four mortgage-repayment demands per month. And, of course, he had to find the money to pay other bills, some just as regular, that carried a powerful threat, stated or politely implied, of unpleasant consequences if they were not paid soon; and he had to sort other bills into those written all in black ink, uncomplicated by dunning annotations, that could be tossed into the waste-paper bin, those that deserved second thoughts, but not just now, and those that definitely required a responding note – apologising for the absence of an enclosure or requesting a receipt for an enclosed cheque that he, being absent-minded or in such a hurry to settle up, had forgotten to enclose. He managed to keep the wolves from the door of 528 Ridgewood Road for just over four years.

Starting in the spring of 1926, he busied himself, often in Manhattan, with preparations for the launch of an organisation that, despite the name chosen for it, the Dunbar Molasses Company, was intended to make and market products that had lactic acid in them. Ninety thousand dollars was to be put up by a syndicate of New York 'money men', and he was to put up $10,000; as the venture was his idea, the first $20,000 of net profit were to be split equally between the syndicate and himself. A man named Jake Kaplan was to be president, and he, Stanley, was to be vice-president, with an annual salary of $15,000. In the late summer of 1926, the syndicate pulled out of the deal, and Stanley sued the members, claiming damages of $75,000 for alleged breach of contract. Five years on, the action was still unresolved.

At noon on Thursday, 1 July 1926, Starr Faithfull, who was then twenty, was a tourist-class passenger on the Cunard liner, the *California*, as it slipped away from Pier 54, at the western end of Thirteenth Street, Manhattan, for a nine-week cruise around the Mediterranean. At the embarkation, she knew no one on board. She was not attached to a party. She was not chaperoned. Stanley would have had to pay the bill in advance, and sufficiently in advance for his cheque to be cleared; Starr would have bought especial things to wear (excepting a bathing costume), and may have bought some of them from stores that either did not provide credit facilities or, having been bitten more than once by the Faithfulls, were shy of their account-custom; and Starr must have been given pocket-money. Previously, she had gone on pleasure-trips, always accompanied, within the eastern United States. The Mediterranean cruise was her first ocean-going holiday. She went on six more such holidays during the following fifty months, till November 1930. Apart from a cruise to the West Indies, late in 1927, the destination of all of the subsequent trips was Great Britain: first, in June 1927, for an escorted tour of the country, starting in Scotland and travelling south by charabanc, eventually to London – and then, four times, simply to be in London. [1]

At the end of October 1929, when Starr came home after her third long stay in London, home was still 528 Ridgewood Road, West Orange. If she had arrived a day or so later, it would not have been. On 1 November, the family moved out, leaving all the furniture – even Helen's heirlooms – behind. The four of them went to Manhattan, but not to one address: Helen and her daughters moved into a furnished apartment at 35 West Ninth Street, while Stanley booked in at a residential hotel, the Albert, which was a stroll away, at the corner of East Eleventh Street and University Place. Long afterwards, when Helen was asked why Stanley had not shared the

---

1. The tourist class transatlantic return fare was $175 (£35).

apartment, she explained – to the satisfaction of the enquirer, who appears to have been easily satisfied – that 'his business plans were very uncertain; he expected to be away that winter and was holding them in abeyance. We were going to take two apartments – we just kept waiting to see what he was going to do.' She also said that she had 'spent several nights in the Albert Hotel' – but as she added that 'Starr stayed with me there,' the purpose of the overnight stays seems to have had nothing to do with Stanley's conjugal rights and is therefore obscure.

On Stanley's behalf, George Munther, an estate agent in West Orange, rented the forsaken house, furnished, to a family named Glass. Each month, he collected $150 from them and sent a cheque for $135 to Stanley. The cheques were cashed at the head office of the Brooklyn National Bank – near Van Brunt Street, where Stanley had scrounged space in an office as the National Headquarters of both the Amerlic Products Corporation and the Lactate Corporation, for both of which he was trying, but with no success at all, to find starting capital. George Munther posted the last of the cheques in September 1930. That month, the mortgages on the house were foreclosed, and the title-deed – in the name of Helen L.C. Faithfull (the initials are inexplicable) – passed to the single mortgagee. The house, put up at auction, was knocked down to Mr Munther for $13,000.

Having done rather well out of his Faithfull-related transactions, he was probably only too glad to accept Stanley's offer to pay him for storing the family furniture – and he may not have been too upset when, following the removal of the furniture, Stanley expressed mystification at his request for payment, saying that, unless his own memory was at fault (which it wasn't), there was nothing in writing about the storage arrangement, and adding that he wished there were, so that he might counter-claim because of water-staining of certain valuable items. (One valuable item – perhaps the *most* valuable of Helen's heirlooms – was separated from the family furniture directly after the period of storage, in June 1930. Stanley arranged for the item, a vast sideboard, to be delivered to Alban Baumann's antique shop at 451 Hudson Street, Greenwich Village, having talked the shopkeeper into displaying it for sale on a commission basis, and provided a plywood sign that he had taken considerable trouble to paint, to the extent of giving a blue shadow effect to the red, Gothic-style letters that made the message: 'For Sale. Old English Sideboard. Made for Alanson Tucker, Derry, New Hampshire, 1800. $1000.' The sideboard stayed in the shop for nine months. The conspicuous disappearance of it then may mean that it had been bought or that Mr Baumann, cramped for room, had informed Stanley, in writing, that he intended to charge for storage.)

George Perry's recollection confirmed Stanley's, that they had got to know each other in 1920 or '21. Neither seems to have said how or where that happened, nor whether they had kept in touch over the years till the late spring of 1930. Perry was then the manager of the Airian Products Corporation, makers of pneumatic mattresses, whose offices were in the Woolworth Building. He was living at 9 St Luke's Place, Greenwich Village. Stanley called on him and, after getting a negative response to his offer of shares in the embryonic Amerlic and Lactate Corporations, admitted that 'he was destitute and needed some sort of a job to keep him going'. Perry took him on as an unsalaried salesman. And when Stanley spoke of his 'double outgoings' — because he was staying at a hotel, his dependents in an apartment — Perry, happening to know that a fair-sized apartment was vacant in a house three doors from where he lived, said that he would make enquiries about it. A man of his word in that respect, he passed on what he had learned, and the upshot was that the Faithfulls were domestically re-united in the top-floor apartment of 12 St Luke's Place.

Manhattan had plenty of thoroughfares that were beautiful or gracious or quaint or squalid; but few that were pretty. St Luke's Place may have been the prettiest of the few. Much of the prettiness was due to the fact that, for nearly all of its slight length, little more than a hundred yards, there were buildings on one side, the northern, only: there was a building, the Hudson Park branch of the New York Public Library, on the south-eastern corner, at Seventh Avenue, but the rest of the southern side *was* Hudson Park — a rectangle of neglected grass, with one or two trees, that had been a cemetery of Trinity Parish till 1898. There was a nice vista to the west: directly across the main Hudson Street (on which, a quarter of a mile uptown, Albert Baumann tried to sell antiques). Leroy Street led, descending all of its short way, to the Hudson River, and, if the weather was clear, you could see the far side of the river, buildings on the New Jersey shore. There were eighteen houses, side by side, in St Luke's Place; they were numbered from the west: and as the thirteenth was, not to tempt providence, called 12½, the end-house, opposite the library, was No. 17. The houses, built in the early 1850s, were much of a muchness, the most eye-catching difference between some and the others being that the tawny-red brickwork of their facades had been painted in different colours. The style was Italianate.

Each house had four floors. There was a half-basement, its area railed with wrought iron at the sidewalk, and a stoop of ten steps, also railed, ascended to the main entrance – double, glass-panelled doors within a porch that was flanked by Corinthian pillars, and on either side of which were the tall and slim windows of the parlour floor. Halfway down the hall, to the right, was the start of a wide staircase (the banister ornate, topped with polished mahogany) to the upper floors, each composed of two large rooms, one at the front, the other at the back (looking out, across gardens, to the back of the houses in Morton Street, about twenty yards away), and two small rooms, one at the front, the other, windowless, between the large rooms, and a bathroom and a kitchen. The houses had flat roofs, accessible through trap-doors above the top landings; not all of the houses had foldaway ladders to the trap-doors, but No. 12 did.

Most people who knew only one thing about St Luke's Place knew that No.6 was the family home, the residence, of James J. Walker, Mayor of New York since 1925, and a man of diverse unpolitical talents, one being as a writer of the lyrics of pop songs, including 'Will You Love Me in December as You Do in May?' which was his signature-tune when he campaigned on his own behalf or in aid of fellow Democrats. His nickname, 'Gentleman Jimmy', alluded, not to any refinement of character, for he was quite as corrupt as Mayors of New York were expected to be, but to his ostentatious apparel.[1] In 1930, Walker was the Place's only notable resident, but back in 1922, when he was minority leader of the State Senate, he had had three literarily-notable neighbours: Theodore Dreiser, who had the parlour floor of No. 16; the poet, Marianne Moore, living with her mother in the basement of No. 14 (and working part-time in the library across the road), and Sherwood Anderson, occupying part of the parlour floor of No.12.

The Faithfulls' domestic reunification, due to the auspices of George Perry, had got no farther than their wondering how to dispose of George Munther's emptied tea-chests, when Stanley became a grass-widower again. They moved into the top-floor

---

1. Some years after his forced resignation as Mayor in 1932, Hudson Park was renamed James J. Walker Park. Now, cemented over, it is abandoned to basketball. The standard-lamps erected on either side of the stoop of No. 6 while Walker was supposed to be running the city have come to be called 'The Mayor's Lamps'.

apartment of 12 St Luke's Place about a week before 22 June 1930, when Helen and Tucker, for the first time as well as Starr, set sail for London, England. Perhaps a month had passed, certainly no more, since Stanley had told George Perry that he was destitute.

As Stanley was as busy as a bee — what with trying to find backers, or just one, for what he called his 'Brooklyn-based ventures', pursuing the legal actions against the State of Massachusetts (with mounting optimism) and the syndicate that had pulled out of financing the Dunbar Molasses Company (with increasing pessimism), and touting pneumatic mattresses from store to store — he may have hired a handyman to get the apartment shipshape before the womenfolk returned. If so, and if he did not delay the hiring for longer than five months, the handyman would not have needed to rush to meet the deadline, which was at the end of November.

That was just over six months ago.

A day in the April of those months had been red-lettered by the arrival of a cheque from the State of Massachusetts. After each member of the family had used some of the $4062 in a celebratory way (and though Starr had wanted to use considerably more of it for yet another visit to London), whatever was left had gone towards paying bills that simply had to be paid — only towards. Stanley, having taken a break from trying to sell pneumatic mattresses, had tried, tried again, but had been no more successful in breaking down the stiff sales-resistance, largely founded on the fear that the mattresses' pneumatism was pervious to punctures — that sleepers on them, if at all sharp, risked going bump in the night. Neither Starr nor Tucker, neither of whom had ever worked, had recently done so. Neither Helen, herself still wholly leisured, nor Stanley, unsalaried for a decade, had pestered either of the girls to look for a job. Never.

'*Never*,' Stanley Faithfull insisted, noticing how Detective Jeremiah Ahearn was looking at him. That slight exchange — a quizzical or baffled look, a stressed repetition of a word — may not have come quite at the end of the interview on the night of Saturday, 6 June. But if not at the end, then close to it — close to the time when Ahearn, worried that he had been delayed for so long from more important tasks, slapped his notebook shut and stood up, indicating that Faithfull should follow suit. While walking with him to the door of the police station, he remarked that he would be passing the case to the Bureau of Missing Persons at the New York Police

Headquarters, adding that no action would be taken till Monday morning, and advising Faithfull to try not to worry – he wouldn't be surprised if Starr's disappearance was explained, relievingly to her loved and loving ones, before Monday.

At ten o'clock on Monday morning (which, if Daniel Moriarity's Bulova watch was right, was three and a half hours after the discovery of the body at Long Beach), Stanley Faithfull turned up at the New York Police Headquarters . He was directed upstairs and to the end of a long, dimly-lit corridor, where Detective Sergeant Thomas Gannon of the Bureau of Missing Persons, waiting for him, showed him into an interview room. Gannon had received the report from Detective Ahearn. He may have read more than the opening lines of descriptive data.

Faithfull said that his elder step-daughter was still missing, having left home three mornings ago. He said that he was sure she was not with friends because he had got in touch with everyone the family knew. He said (while Gannon took 'keyword notes') that 'Starr was a model girl; had never been away from home, shunned men, had no reason for going away, and he could give no explanation nor account as to her disappearance. She had always been carefully and zealously watched over by the family and had never been away from home a night in her life before. He said that she hardly ever drank, and then only a little. She couldn't carry her liquor well.' Gannon asked him how he knew that, and 'he said he had tested her out and found that a couple of drinks were too much for her'. (By this time, Gannon was 'much impressed' but also 'slightly concerned that so few avenues seemed worth exploring': 'He had me in such a frame of mind that I thought we had better be looking in churches rather than in the speakies or the gayer spots of the town.')

Subsequently, Faithfull confirmed Gannon's recollection of the early part of their conversation. But his version of the rest of it differed from the detective's in several respects.

According to Gannon, he, intrigued by something he had seen in Ahearn's report, asked Faithfull, 'Why did you classify her as "poor mentally"?' and was told, 'Because of the fits of depression and melancholia with which she is occasionally afflicted.' But according to Faithfull, he had said nothing to Ahearn that should have made him think that Starr was 'poor mentally', and if Gannon had asked him to explain the term, he would, in the first place, have retorted that Ahearn had misquoted him, and, in the second, have said that the question was therefore redundant.

According to Gannon, it was only because Faithfull said that Starr was occasionally afflicted with fits of depression and melancholia that he, Gannon, said, 'Well, then, if that's the case, maybe we had better have a look at Bellevue Hospital.' But according to Faithfull, the trip to that hospital, spreading south along the bank of the East River from the end of Thirty-Fourth Street, came about because

> Detective Gannon said he had looked through the list of all persons reported to his bureau, and that no person had been involved in any accident or was reported unidentified, with the exception of one person at the Bellevue Hospital, who was not positively identified on the records by name ... He suggested, and I acquiesced, that we ... see the person in question.
>
> We went to Bellevue Hospital, and there learned that the person in question had been identified and had left the hospital.
>
> Detective Gannon then made the suggestion that in view of the fact that we were at the hospital, and that at Bellevue Hospital a great majority of people who had suffered accidents might be found, it might be well for us to go into what he described as a receiving ward, and see if Starr might be among those in that ward. We therefore went into this receiving ward; I walked through, I think, two rooms – there may have been more – and I said there was no one resembling Starr there, and then left with Detective Gannon.

According to Gannon, the tour of the receiving wards was at Faithfull's suggestion, he having recalled that 'a friend of his had become drunk once and had been badly beaten up; he had been placed in a psychopathic ward at Bellevue under a fictitious name, and it was some time before his family could locate him'.

There was a brief jibing of the subsequent accounts: the two men left the hospital and walked down First Avenue, Faithfull meanwhile saying that he would get in touch with some friends in Massachusetts in the hope that one or more of them had seen or heard from Starr since Friday morning. He agreed to return to the police headquarters at three o'clock.

But at the corner of Third Street, as they were about to part, Gannon to continue down First Avenue, Faithfull to walk west to St Luke's Place, the latter asked a question – 'apropos of nothing,' according to the detective; prompted by a comment from the detective, according to Faithfull:

'Do you know how long it will take a body to come to the surface in a drowning case?'

37

Gannon ('confused for a moment') replied, 'It's too early to think of that idea. Why do you ask that?'

'I'm merely curious,' Faithfull replied – and asked the question again.

Gannon told him that 'there was no established rule, that it varied in every individual case. It was generally accepted that it required nine days but it might be accomplished in only six hours.'

Faithfull did not get in touch with any friends in Massachusetts. Nor did he keep the three o'clock appointment at the police headquarters.

Some time between four and five, he rang Detective Sergeant Gannon. He made no apology for missing the appointment, gave no explanation as to why he had not turned up, did not say what had prevented him from phoning at least an hour earlier, to cancel or postpone the appointment. He was speaking from the Woolworth Building – so close by that, but for the intervention of City Hall, Gannon could have looked through the window of the Bureau of Missing Persons and seen him using the phone in George Perry's office. Faithfull's subsequent account of what followed near enough matched that of Gannon:

> I told Detective Gannon over the telephone that I had just been shown a newspaper clipping, in which there was a report of the finding of some person in Long Beach; that from the printed description I was not positive as to whether or not the body reported could be that of Starr, but that I felt an investigation should be made by myself to determine as to whether or not it was or was not Starr, and asked him if he could ascertain for me as to where I should go for the purpose of making identification, if it turned out to be Starr, asking him to call me back at the number I gave him as quickly as possible.
>
> In a few minutes he called me back again, and told me that I should go to Mineola, and that there would be police officers in the police headquarters there, awaiting my arrival. Both in this later conversation with Detective Gannon and in my first conversation with him, I particularly called his attention to the fact that I wished absolutely no publicity given to anything said by either of us, particularly no mention should be made to any newspaper.

Presumably, it was George Perry who had spotted the report. The fact that he had taken the trouble to clip it from the newspaper suggests that he had spotted it prior to Faithfull's arrival in his office. If that is so, then it appears that he was expecting a visit from Faithfull. Perry's connecting of a report of 'the finding of some person in Long Beach' with the disappearance of Faithfull's elder step-daughter seems too contemptuous of probability to be called a hunch. Blackening the mystery of how he came by the wild surmise, researchers who have scoured extant afternoon editions of New York papers of Monday, 8 June 1931, have failed to find a report of the find at Long Beach.

Before leaving Perry, Faithfull asked a small favour – required because there was no telephone in his apartment. Perry said yes, of course: after work, he would pop into 12 St Luke's Place, three doors from his own home, to let Helen Faithfull know what was happening.

Faithfull walked or was transported uptown to Pennsylvania Station, and there boarded a train of the Long Island Rail Road which, after stopping at Brooklyn, Jamaica (in the borough of Queens), New Hyde Park (just inside Nassau County) and Merillon Avenue, arrived at Mineola. The journey took just over half an hour. Turning right outside the small but busy station, he walked the few steps to the southern end of the Boulevard, crossed Old Country Road, and, now on Franklin Avenue, walked a few steps along it, still on the right, to the Nassau County Police Headquarters. As you know, he arrived there soon after six.

Much happened in the next couple of hours. One catches glimpses, no more than that, of some of the happenings; one only knows of others, not all of the others, because of things that happened as a result of them.

Called from the detective bureau by a uniformed receptionist, Inspector Harold King had a brief conversation with Faithfull, and then, telling him to follow – and nodding to the receptionist that it was all right for the visitor to be behind the PUBLIC ACCESS PROHIBITED sign – walked part of the way back along the corridor to a small room, the walls of which were hidden, floor to ceiling, by box-shelves, all crammed with stuff that was or might turn out to be what King called 'material of evidential relevance to in-process investigations'. As the shelf space was replete, stuff that had arrived lately was stowed in motley containers stacked against the shelves that faced the door. An electric bulb hung from the centre of the ceiling; the light from it, directed down by a shade of green glass, illuminated a plain-wood table, the only piece of furniture in the room.

The top of the table was overlapped by a sheet of greaseproof paper, grey-lined where folds had been smoothed away, and hillocked at one end because King had, perhaps fastidiously, tucked a suspender-girdle and a pair of stockings out of sight. A paisley-design frock, all of the buttons done up, a belt fastened around it, was laid tidily on the paper. King had intended to ask Faithfull if he recognised the frock, but there was no need. Faithfull reached out both of his hands and pressed his fingers on the hem. 'It's Starr's,' he murmured. 'You're sure?' King asked. 'Quite sure. She hasn't had it long. It came from Lord and Taylor, I believe.'

King took Faithfull back to the entrance hall; left him for a few minutes. There was nowhere for him to sit. Then King drove him to Macken's Morgue. For all one knows, neither man said a word during the journey.

Joseph Macken had gone home, leaving Henry Inderdohnen in charge. The body that had been brought from the beach that morning, and examined by Dr Algernon Warinner that afternoon, was on the side-table, covered from head to toes with a sheet of heavy white linen. Inderdohnen indicated it. King motioned Faithfull into the space between the table and The Triple Miracle, then nodded to Inderdohnen, who, using both hands, made a neat fold of the top of the sheet, just enough to reveal the face. King:

'Faithfull looked at her very carefully, and he didn't turn a hair. Finally, he just touched her lightly on the forehead and said "You poor girl."'

King required a more formal statement of identification than that. 'Is it your daughter?' he asked.

Faithfull nodded.

King repeated the question.

'Yes, it is she,' Faithfull said.

Before folding the top of the sheet back, Inderdohnen, who probably had a small glossary of Right Things to Say, said, 'She favours you, sir.'

Not curtly, it seems, Faithfull said, 'She is my *step*-daughter.'

Then, according to King, 'He turned right round, looked at the caskets in the mortuary, and said he wanted the cheapest one he could get.'

If that is true, then Inderdohnen, trained and trusted by Joseph Macken, would have quoted a price, taking care not to use the word competitive.

King drove Faithfull back to Mineola.

At the start of the journey, King was contented. He may have been thinking that he could have what for him would be an early night; may have been wondering what his wife would be giving him for supper. The body had a name. Some time soon, he and his friend Algernon Warinner would say a few words at an inquest, and the jury, acting on Coroner Edward Neu's intructions, would attribute Starr Faithfull's demise to accident or suicide – or, unable to decide one way or the other, would return an open verdict, less officially but just as effectively closing the case. There was a bit of paperwork to be done before he knocked off, but that shouldn't take long.

By the end of the journey – which, if King drove as fast as he usually did, lasted about five minutes – he was no longer contented. Though Faithfull was subsequently asked thousands of questions by dozens of people, he was never asked what passed between himself and King during the drive – and he never volunteered that information. As for King, he made no reference to the return journey in the short report of Faithfull's Monday-night visit to Nassau County that he wrote hurriedly next day, and all that he ever said about it in public was this:

'While proceeding from the direction of Rockville Centre, Faithfull and I had some little conversation about the general situation.' (Once I have told you that he went on to say that that conversation did not include the slightest reference to events following Starr's disappearance from home, your guess as to what he meant by 'the general situation' is as good as mine.) 'Shortly thereafter, Faithfull expressed the opinion that the girl had been murdered. From his expression by word of mouth, he was very emphatic in that conviction.'

No matter how emphatically the conviction was expressed, King's contentment would have remained almost intact, allayed only by slight irritation with his ranting passenger, if Faithfull had not said something that impressed King as being either grounds for suspecting murder or a reason for making absolutely sure that murder was ruled out. The latter possibility seems remote: if Faithfull, in insisting that his unexplained conviction be taken seriously, had dropped the names of prominent persons who might make trouble for King if it were not, there is little likelihood that King would have been impressed. (Supposing that Faithfull had dropped the name of his near-neighbour, the Mayor – recklessly, for their residential proximity had not acquainted them – King, a guardian of one of the most Republican parts of the State, might have *hoped* for the Democratic Walker's intervention, believing that local detestation of Walker was so strong that he himself would, simply by oppositional comparison, be seen as a local hero.)

Almost certainly, then, Faithfull stated a ground, an impressive one, for believing that his step-daughter had been murdered.

There is no information as to whether King, having driven back to Mineola, dropped Faithfull at the railway station or took him into the police headquarters for further questioning and then saw him off the premises, leaving him to walk to the station. Wherever, whenever, they parted, Faithfull promised or warned that he would return next morning. He may or may not have gathered that King was impressed.

That King was greatly impressed is shown by his actions once Faithfull was out of the way. Since King, like most detectives, believed himself to be a cut above uniformed policemen – and since he was the autocratic head of a detective bureau that he was trying to make virtually autonomous – it is safe to say that the first of his actions went against the grain. He conferred with the senior uniformed duty-officer, Captain Theodore Green, who, the minute he twigged that King's purpose in calling the conference was to share the buck for a contemplated action, phoned an off-duty captain, Emil Morse, summoning him to be a party to the buck-sharing. As soon as Green and Morse were in agreement that King should do so, he phoned Dr Otto Schultze, the Medical Assistant to the District Attorney of New York County (the name applied to Manhattan as a judicial district), at his home in Brookville, Nassau County.

Schultze's contract only prohibited him from accepting freelance assignments that might result in conflict of interest, and he had been hired by the Nassau County Police Department on several occasions during the past six years – never, though, to conduct a second autopsy on a body, which was what King now asked him to do. Considering that Schultze had conducted no more than a handful of second autopsies among the ten thousand autopsies that he claimed to have performed since he had qualified as a forensic pathologist near the start of the century, he must have expressed curiosity at the assignment – and King must have given an explanation of some kind. In any event, Schultze said that he would be at Macken's Morgue by half-past eight.

King then made other phone calls. At least four: to Henry Inderdohnen, to Dr Algernon Warinner, to a professional stenographer named Nathan Birchall, and to someone at the Long Beach police station.

\*

Meanwhile, Faithfull had travelled back to Manhattan. It was still daylight — therefore, some time before 8.26 — when he reached the end of Seventh Avenue and crossed West Houston Street to the northern tip of Varick Street. There he encountered George Perry — who, so he afterwards stated,

...had decided to meet him and walk home with him and warn him against a large group of newspaper reporters that had gathered outside 12 St Luke's Place. I met him at the corner of Varick Street and on the way to the house the first words Faithfull uttered were, 'That was she and it is murder.' He kept insisting that it was murder and appeared excited. I advised him to say nothing to the newspaper reporters and to keep still. He agreed that this was sound advice. Upon leaving him at the doorstep of his home, I started away to my own home, 9 St Luke's Place, but noticed on looking back that he was expounding his views and theories to the reporters there assembled. I turned back and went up the stairs of the stoop and almost bodily pushed him in the house, pleading with him to keep still and say nothing. I then retraced my steps to my home.

We know that Faithfull was a fast talker — but still, considering how much he rattled off to the reporters while Perry was proceeding no more than twenty yards west, then the same distance back, and then ascending the stoop of No. 12 (which, admittedly, may have necessitated some pushing and shoving), Perry must have been a slow walker.

Next day, particular reports of the alfresco press conference uniquely attributed certain comments to Faithfull. The uniqueness is clear proof of inventiveness. The credible rest of the reports, unanimously corroborating one another, often word-for-word, can be presented in the form of a play-script of a street scene:

PERRY *exits towards No. 9.*

*Simultaneously*, FAITHFULL *climbs the stoop of No. 12; he is followed by the* REPORTERS, *each shouting a different question; reaching the top, he turns and addresses them.*

FAITHFULL: I have just returned from Nassau County, where I positively identified a dead body found at Long Beach as my step-daughter, Miss Starr Faithfull — two Rs in Starr, two Ls in Faithfull. She was her normal self when she left here last Friday morning. She was accustomed to going for a daily walk. She graduated from Rogers Hall School in Lowell, Massachusetts, where she was captain of the swimming team. Her prowess as a swimmer is hard to reconcile with the idea that her death was due to accidental drowning.

A REPORTER: Was she acquainted with anyone at Long Beach?

FAITHFULL: No. So far as I am aware, she never went to Long Beach in her life.

A REPORTER: Did she have any love-affairs?

FAITHFULL: Absolutely not. She had a few casual boy-friends. I have been in touch with men with whom she occasionally corresponded. She had a few cultured friends in this city and in Boston whom she frequently visited. Otherwise, she spent her time reading, shopping, and attending the theatre. She wrote exceedingly well – so well that I often urged her to pursue a literary career.

A REPORTER (*taking a shot in the dark*): What about diaries?

FAITHFULL: I destroyed them.

ALL OF THE REPORTERS *babble questions about* the *diaries.*

FAITHFULL (*changing the subject*): Starr was a light-hearted, happy, tranquil-minded girl. She was perfectly happy on the Thursday night before her disappearance. She spent that night at home.

A REPORTER: Is there any chance she committed suicide?

FAITHFULL: Absolutely not. She had no reason to. If any of you print anything reflecting on the memory of my step-daughter, I'll bring suit. You will tell me your names, if you please – also the names of your papers.

ALL OF THE REPORTERS *do so.*

PERRY *returns; he 'almost bodily' pushes* FAITHFULL *into the front hall and closes the door behind him, then retraces his steps to his home.* ALL OF THE REPORTERS *exeunt.* FAITHFULL *climbs the two flights of stairs to the top apartment; presuming that* HELEN *and* TUCKER FAITHFULL *are there – presuming, too, that he has not managed to get a message to them since his visit to Macken's Morgue – he tells them the bad news.*

Two things are perplexing: Perry's decision to meet Faithfull (for no other reason, so he said, than to warn him that reporters were gathered on his doorstep), and the cause of that gathering.

When Perry first left his house and headed east along St Luke's Place, he may have stopped for a minute to speak to the reporters, and been told that Faithfull was on his way back from Mineola – *but he already knew that.* He had received a phone call from Faithfull and arranged to meet him. If that were not so, how could he have known *where* to meet him? He could have guessed – or been told by the reporters – that Faithfull was returning to Manhattan on the Long Island Rail Road, but he could not know whether Faithfull, having arrived at Pennsylvania Station, would board a subway train or a bus to the vicinity of St Luke's Place, or hail a cab (which would take one of several routes, some to the western end of the Place, some to its eastern end), or walk (if he came out of Pennsylvania Station on its western side, he would walk down Eighth Avenue, continue down Hudson Street, and enter the Place from the west; if he came out of the station on its eastern side, he would walk down Seventh Avenue and, two blocks from the start of Varick Street, enter the Place from the east). As you know, he in fact walked down Seventh Avenue – all the way down, *passing St Luke's Place*, passing Clarkson Street, and crossing West Houston Street to Varick Street, where Perry was waiting. They must have arranged to meet there.

According to Perry's statement, as they walked towards St Luke's Place he advised Faithfull 'to say nothing to the newspaper reporters and to keep still'. Faithfull, while replying that that was sound advice, had no intention of following it. Let us give Perry the benefit of the doubt. When he made his statement, he quite forgot to mention that he had 'decided to meet' Faithfull at the corner of Varick Street, not on the offchance that the latter would absent-mindedly take a long-cut home, but because Faithfull, phoning him before leaving Mineola or after arriving at Pennsylvania Station, had requested the meeting, saying roughly when and exactly where but not why – and had neither asked whether men who might be suspected of being reporters were littering the stoop of No.12 nor been told so by Perry off the cuff. Faithfull did not express surprise when Perry told him about the reporters. Although, during the past couple of days, he had given the impression that he was fearful of publicity, he did not appear to be alarmed or angry or even irritated. Those negative facts, coupled with a subsequent positive one, that he was *determined* to talk to the reporters, corroborate other evidence – evidence so strong that it hardly needs corroboration – that Faithfull was the instigator of the gathering of reporters.

The other evidence is based upon Sherlock Holmes's dictum (admittedly, not infallible) that 'when you have eliminated the impossible, whatever is left, however improbable, must be the truth'. Who else but Faithfull could have, and might have, informed various organs of the New York press (at least half a dozen of them, ranging from the staid *Times* and *Herald Tribune* to the sensationalist *Mirror* and *World-Telegram*) that *a* he had travelled to Nassau County and identified a corpse as being that of his step-daughter Starr, *b* he was convinced that she had not committed suicide or met her death by accident, ergo that she had been murdered, *c* he was on his way back to Manhattan, *d* he lived at 12 St Luke's Place? Certainly not Inspector King or either of the police captains, Green and Morse, who shared a self-protective keenness to keep the second autopsy secret from anyone not involved in it, at any rate until the results of the examination were known. If a subordinate policeman had overheard or been privy to either King's post-identification discussion with Faithfull or his conference with the captains, any temptation to pass the story to the press would have been resisted, for the source of the published story would have been disclosed by a simple, single-suspect investigation. George Littleworth, the crime reporter for the local paper, the *Nassau Daily Review*, may have dropped in at the police headquarters during the early evening; if so, he may have spoken to King (with whom he was friendly; he too lived in the village of Hempstead), and King may, mistakenly trusting, have confided in him — but Littleworth was the stringer for only one New York daily paper, the *News*. None of the persons phoned by King with regard to the second autopsy (or, as he always insisted on calling it, 'the *continuation* of the autopsy') received from him as much information as the papers must have been given.

That leaves Faithfull and nobody else.

We don't know how long he waited for a train at Mineola Station. If he had just missed one, he had nearly half an hour to spare. Even if he had to get change in nickels from the booking clerk — even if, in the absence of a Manhattan phone book by the public call-box in the waiting room, he needed to quiz a directory-assistance operator before ringing various news-rooms — he was back on the platform within ten minutes, probably lighting a cigarette, and certainly starting to think out what and, as important, what not to say to the reporters who would be gathered on his doorstep when he got home.

He cannot have got home, in the company of George Perry, much before the sunset time of 8.26.

By that time, the gathering was complete at Macken's Morgue. There was, in fact, one member more than the expected eight: Joseph Macken, who presumably had been phoned by Henry Inderdohnen. It is hard to make out which section of the gathering — workers or witnesses — he belonged to: perhaps neither, but present solely for the pleasure of seeing The Triple Miracle being used appreciatively by the celebrated Dr Otto Schultze. Inderdohnen assisted Schultze, and Nathan Birchall, sitting near on a bentwood chair, took down the doctor's commentary in shorthand. Seated on other, farther bentwood chairs, four of the witnesses — King, the pair of captains, and Detective Sergeant Thomas Walsh, representing the Long Beach Police Department — stared uncomprehendingly straight ahead, and the fifth, Dr Algernon

Warinner, looked and listened as if with professional interest. The typed report of his observations some five hours before had run to about forty lines. Birchall's typing of Schultze's commentary – far neater, the spelling, even of the complicated medical words, immaculate – would run to about 250 lines on a dozen pages.

Supposing that there was a coffee-break during the second autopsy, Schultze peered and probed and commented for two and a half hours, starting on the dot of 8.30 and ending at 11.10.

Meanwhile, reporters gathered in the back yard. So far as one can tell, they were, though latterly worried about meeting copy-times, well-behaved. Some of them had been at St Luke's Place; they had phoned through their notes of what Stanley Faithfull had said and been ordered to hasten to Nassau County to find out what the police had to say. Others, given copies of colleagues' notes, had received the same order. All of them had travelled – some by train, some by car, some by cab – to the police headquarters. The first arriving there had been at first bemused, for the uniformed receptionist, asked to produce the senior duty-officer, had replied that that officer was not on the premises. But the receptionist, not wanting the reporters to think that Captain Green had gone AWOL, had wiped away their bemusement by saying where he was, adding that Inspector King and Captain Morse were also there. The reporters had scampered out, en route to Rockville Centre.

There is no information as to whether or not Schultze read Warinner's report, or spoke to him other than socially, before he began the second autopsy – or, indeed, during the coffee-break, if there was one, or immediately afterwards, while Nathan Birchall waited, notepad still open in one hand, pencil still held in the other, in case Schultze wished to amend or augment his commentary. Schultze, the forensically-specialising pathologist, may have preferred not to know what had been observed by a country doctor with rudimentary knowledge and slight experience of general pathology – but, if so, he should have made one exception, that being Warinner's observation of rigor mortis, the presence or absence of which can be ascertained as reliably by someone with no medical qualifications as by someone with many.

Warinner had noted that rigor mortis was 'not present in arms or neck, but present in hips and knees'. Schultze noted that it was 'still well developed in the muscles of the lower jaw, and in both lower extremities, but absent in both upper extremities, with the exception of the fingers of the right hand, where it was just disappearing'. That statement was surely partly opinionative: the phrases 'still well developed' and 'just disappearing' indicate that Schultze took it for granted that the rigor was wearing off. He could only have known that for certain if he had been told that the rigor had been more apparent during the day – yet no one apart from Warinner seems to have noticed *any* rigor, and he had noticed less (or rather, its presence in fewer parts of the body) than did Schultze. I shall return to this point in a subsequent chapter.

The fact that Warinner had noted that 'the palm surfaces of the hands and feet were corrugated as if exposed to water a long time', whereas Schultze said nothing about those parts of the body other than that rigor was present in the fingers of the right hand and that 'the fingernails showed a very brilliant scarlet-red manicure stain', suggests that the corrugation (known colloquially in forensic circles as 'washerwoman's wrinkle') had faded since the afternoon. Warinner had also noted that, presumably as an effect of lengthy contact with water or friction from a rough material such as sand, or both, there was 'softening of the superficial skin over the posterial aspect of the right arm for a distance of 7 inches from the shoulder [and] a similar appearance over the right buttock, where the superficial skin could be wiped off'. Schultze, as well as observing those appearances, noted that 'the epidermis has become loosened and is abraided in an area two inches vertical by one and a quarter inches transverse on the posterior surface of the left arm near the shoulder'.

Unlike Warinner, Schultze observed post-mortem hypostases (livid stains, caused by the settling of still blood in dependent parts of a body, which usually start to appear within an hour or two of death, become marked within about eight hours, and remain unless the body's position is altered): 'the hypostases were well marked over the back of the neck and both shoulders.'

Schultze spotted far more outward marks indicative of recent injury than Warinner had – well over a hundred. He described them variously as fine red spots, abrasions, discolorations, swellings, scratch marks, reddish marks, bluish marks, bluish-red marks, oval marks with reddish outlines, haemorrhages in the skin and subcutaneous fat, contusions, and depressions in the true skin. The forehead and chin were peppered with fine red spots, both cheeks were discoloured and slightly swollen, there were scratches on the right temple, a discoloured abrasion stretched down the bridge of the nose, and the throat showed reddish marks and scratches, the most noticeable of the latter being on the right side – 'passing from above the sternocleidomastoid muscle and toward the front, and measuring two and a half inches in length by one-half inch in width'. (During his examination of the head and neck, Schultze looked in the mouth: 'All teeth were present and sound with the exception of the right upper lateral incisor, which showed a fine cavity underneath the gum.') There were 31 bluish-red marks on the right arm, none larger than an inch by half an inch, and 'all showing haemorrhage beneath the skin in the subcutaneous fat'; there was just one bluish mark and an abrasion, both slight, on the left arm. ('The axillae [armpits] had been recently shaved.') For a reason that will appear, Schultze's comments on the torso must be given verbatim:

> On the right side of the chest there is a bluish-red mark, one and a half inches transverse and one inch vertical, and located with the inner margin two inches to the right of the middle line, with the subcutaneous tissue and also the true skin infiltrated with blood.
>
> Also on the right side of the chest, from the armpit downwards for a distance of eight inches, there are numerous fine haemorrhages in the skin, with bluish-red discolorations in an area eight inches in length and in the widest part four inches transverse, with the underlying skin and subcutaneous fat infiltrated with blood.
>
> In the middle of the back, along the left side of the lower dorsal spine, and one inch to the left of it, there are six depressions in the skin.

On the right leg, including the thigh, were three bluish-red marks, a reddish mark, and, just below the knee, 'an area of contusions two inches vertically by two inches transverse'; all of those marks were accompanied by haemorrhages. The front and external surfaces of the right knee 'showed four spots up to three-quarters of an inch in size'. There were seven similar spots on the front of the left leg.

As Warinner had not imagined, following the first autopsy, that there would be a second, he must, if he was at all neat, have done some sewing where he had opened the abdominal cavity. Schultze undid that work. He noted that, although the lungs had been cut by Warinner, blood remained in the left ventricle of the heart and in the inferior vena cava (one of the large veins by which blood is returned to the right atrium of the heart). He scooped respective samples into test-tubes and handed them to Inderdohnen for wiping, corking, and labelling. Examining, first, the right lung, he observed, in addition to what Warinner had,

> ...a line of haemorrhage underneath the pleura and in the tissue beneath, like a haemorrhagic infarction [dead tissue resulting from

obstruction of the circulation], about one inch long, bluish, and extending about an inch towards the root of the lung, which organ is distended.

Then:

The bronchi of the lung contain fine, gritty particles, not visible, but palpable.
On scraping with a knife, the lung delivers a very light-coloured froth that easily runs off the surface of the knife, and a froth of large bubbles. From the froth, very fine, gritty sand-particles can be separated on the palm of the hand.

Similarly, upon probing the branches of the bronchi of the *left* lung, he felt

numerous fine grains of sand. When sectioned, the lung delivers an almost colourless froth with large bubbles which when rubbed between the hands discloses fine particles of sand.

Cutting open the trachea (windpipe), he observed 'a column of sand about one inch in thickness adherent to the posterior wall'.

Till Schultze, commenting, had spoken of the sand, Warinner, his rump become numb from the uncushioned bentwood chair, had not felt too embarrassed; may even have once or twice enjoyed smugness. For, after all, the big-city, full-time, long-experienced pathologist had found nothing that he himself had not found. Well, nothing except the cavitied tooth, the stubbled armpits. Nothing important. Schultze had simply been more detailed, more precise — had pronounced impressive medical words more surely, as if he knew how to spell them too. But then he had found the sand — and then another lot — another — yet another. Enough, it sounded, to build a castle. Warinner knew that the finding of the sand was important. In all probability, so did King and Sergeant Walsh. The presence of the sand in the lungs strongly supported the strong assumption that Starr Faithfull had died by drowning. As it was virtually inconceivable that she had swallowed or breathed in *dry* sand — and as, when the head of a corpse is submerged in water, some of the water may enter the upper air passages but *none* will enter the lungs (and therefore neither will be distended as the result of residual air being 'cramped', and there will be little or no frothing) — there was virtually no doubt that she had drowned. Less surely, the presence of the sand in the lungs indicated that she had died in shallow water. That indication, linked with the fact that her body had been discovered on a sandy beach, seemed to mean that she had died close to that beach, where the water was specked with sand swirled from the bed not far below − or that she had died *on* the beach, probably unconscious before dying, oblivious of a tide rising over her.

Schultze did not take samples of the sandy froth in the lungs. He did, however, cut out the pancreas and the stomach, and, having noted that 'the stomach contents consist of some food particles and very thin, watery material, without distinct odour', placed both organs in a glass jar.

Using callipers, he measured various components of the heart. In his opinion, the valves and the pericardium (the conical sac of membrane that encloses the heart and the roots of the great blood vessels) were normal. Both the gall bladder and the spleen were filled with fluid blood. Turning to the liver, he observed

> six transverse tears through the [enclosing] capsule over the posterior superior part of the right lobe, and running about one-eighth inch into the liver tissue, without haemorrhage. The rest of the liver is deeply stained with blood. Normal in size.

The kidneys, also normal in size, were deeply congested. In his examination of the genital organs, Schultze found that

> the vulva [the opening] and the hair of the vulva contain a lot of sand. The ostium vaginae when distended [is] three-quarters inch in diameter with fimbriated [fringing] remnants showing previous deflorescence. The absence of hymen [the fold of membrane partly closing the orifice of the vagina], with very minute remnants, is especially marked in the posterior and left posterior quadrant. Sand is also in the lower part of the vagina. The left ovary is converted into a cyst about one and a half inches in diameter; the right ovary contains a cyst about one inch in diameter. [1] The uterine blood-vessels are congested, but the uterus is normal.

Having completed the autopsy and cleaned himself up, Schultze spoke to King. He said that he would take the samples home with

1. Some writers on the case, all speaking of only one ovarian cyst, have stated that it would have prevented Starr Faithfull from having children. The likelihood is that, as often happens, an early writer made the statement, and subsequent writers, accepting his word, copied him. A leading present-day obstetrician and gynaecologist comments: 'The cysts could have been luteal cysts, which are physiological, or they could have been follicular cysts, which are associated with temporary absence of ovulation. They are not permanent impediments to becoming pregnant.'

him. First thing in the morning, before going to his office in Manhattan, he would deliver them to Dr Alexander Gettler, who, as well as being Professor of Chemistry at New York University, was the chief toxicologist to the Medical Examiner of New York City. He would stress that the results of their analysis were required urgently.

He told the inspector that there was no doubt that Starr Faithfull had died by drowning.

It was about half-past eleven when the men left the morgue. Schultze, carrying the samples in the battered black bag of the tools of his trade, led the untidy procession along the wide corridor to the back yard, and Henry Inderdohnen brought up the rear, locking doors behind him and turning off all of the lights apart from a small one, cupped by a shade of translucent yellow porcelain, which was fixed to the outside wall beside the back door, lighting a bell-push and a tacked postcard that gave Joseph Macken's home address and phone number for the information of prospective customers or delivery men who got no reply to their ringing of the bell.

The minute Schultze emerged, he was recognised by some of the reporters, who crowded around him, questioning, and were hastily joined by the rest. They all heard him say that he had established death from drowning, and most of them understood him to say that some of the numerous injuries to the body had been inflicted pre-mortem. MacGregor Bond, representing the *New York World-Telegram*, later wrote a confirming memo at the request of that paper's city editor:

[Dr Schultze] told me that bruises on the body, autopsy proved, were received before death. None of them sufficiently serious to have caused death. Might have been received during a struggle, according to the doctor's opinion.

While Schultze engrossed the reporters' attention, the four policemen got into two cars — King and the captains in one, Walsh in the other — and drove away. Nathan Birchall also drove away.

And so did Dr Algernon Warinner. If any of the reporters noticed him, they assumed that he was either a fifth policeman or a supernumerary nobody. Not at the start of the case nor ever after was Warinner given his small due as the performer of the first autopsy. Indeed, no writer seems to have gathered that there *was* a first autopsy, considered an end of the medical matters as soon as it was done. King's statement that Schultze 'continued' the autopsy on the Monday night was taken to mean that there was one elongated transaction, carried out in two instalments.

The reporters, pressed for copy time, did not prolong the questioning of Schultze. Even before he had got into his car, stowing his bag on the passenger seat, they were hurrying from the yard – their progress briefly obstructed by Joseph Macken, handing out colourful advertisement leaflets – and making for public phones that they had thoughtfully spotted on their way to the morgue.

Macken and Inderdohnen were the last to leave. The night must have been the most exciting of their purposely unexciting professional lives. They would not have believed it possible that they were in for a greater, daytime excitement in a few days' time.

## 2

**E**lvin Edwards, the District Attorney of Nassau County, did not enjoy reading books, least of all ones on the law since he had been forced to read lots of those before graduating from the New York Law School in 1905. Though a room in his nice house at Freeport, just east of Rockville Centre, was known as The Library, much of its wall-space was bare, and most of the books on the few shelves were of an uplifting nature, left to him by his father, who was a clergyman, or prettily leather-spined, bought on that account alone by his wife Lydia, or tales of derring-do that had been bought by or as presents for his sons, Elvin Junior and Donald, both of whom did enjoy reading books.

But he loved newspapers. He was the local newsagent's best customer, having him always deliver the *Nassau Daily Review* and several of the New York papers, and sometimes, whenever he had done or said something that seemed to him worthy of wide reportage, the rest of them too. When approached by feature writers running short of subjects for Men of Our Time series, he invariably shook his head against co-operation, saying in a rueful tone, 'I've had character sketches written about me before,' and, having glanced to make sure that the writer had his pad and pencil handy, went on to explain what the previous writers should have written. And yet, despite his unintended assistance, the pen-portraits hardly varied. This representative of them, by Earl Sparling, appeared in the *New York World-Telegram* in the early summer of 1931:

### He has Drawing-Room Manners, but Obtains Convictions of Gangsters

Elvin N. Edwards has been District Attorney of probably the tallest-hatted county in America for six years. Nassau County is filled with millionaires and with people who like to act as if they were. It is a county where any famous name is apt to bob up on a jury. Even J. Pierpont Morgan [financier, art-collector, and owner of many properties, one at

Matinicock Point, Glen Cove, on the northern shore of Nassau County]
was a grand juryman a year or two ago. What complicates things is that
Nassau County is also something of a natural playground for racketmen
from Brooklyn and Manhattan, if they can ever dig in long enough to get
organised. The racketeers look longingly at Nassau County, a place made
for the landing of contraband liquors and for the operation of convivial
rustic hot spots.

For fifteen years, nine of them as an assistant district attorney, Elvin
Edwards has occupied a front trench in the war of the millionaires to keep
out the mobmen.

He is a wide, short, grey-haired, neatly tailored chap of forty-nine, at
home in a score of princely county homes ...

Several criminal cases recently have been, if a pun is permissible, sore
trials in Nassau.

There was the Long Beach case in which it developed, if anyone didn't
know it, that booze for Manhattan and Brooklyn speakeasies was being
shorthauled from the Nassau County shores. That wasn't so bad, for
even in Nassau County booze is booze, although sometimes it is
champagne. But the ugly part of it was a suspicion, and a formal
allegation by indictment, that Vannie Higgins, a notorious Brooklyn
character, was implicated[1] ...

District Attorney Edwards ... has indicated to his assistants that New
York gangdom will take Nassau only over his dead body. He has a
tailored antipathy for gangsters, symbolised by his exhibit room. The
exhibit room is a result of the drive against 'nuisances' he started two
years ago. On the walls of the exhibit room – really the office of his
mannered young chief assistant, Martin W. Littleton, Jr. – hang
blackjacks, clubs, brassknucks, revolvers, automatics, sawed-off
shotguns, tins of opium, bottles of poisonous liquor, etc. All were
obtained in raids of 'public nuisances', about 75 per cent of which were
speakeasies. During the first year of his drive against 'nuisances' he
raided more than 200 Nassau County joints. He obtained 192
convictions. To date, he has closed from 300 to 400 places.

On March 27, 1930, the District Attorney explained publicly to the
Hollis Republican Club that he personally was a wet and that he only
raided places selling liquor that should be raided whether there was
Prohibition or not.

Nassau County, after all, is a civilised, cultured region. It is a county
where citizens have complained against the noise of outboard motor-
boats and where the District Attorney, to allow the gentry to sleep, once
ordered all airplanes to cease flying in summer at 11 p.m.

During the last week of May 1931, the Freeport newsagent
supplied Edwards with more papers than ever before: not only all of

1. This case was mentioned in the footnote on page 8.

the New York ones, but some from other East Coast cities – perhaps even a few from farther afield. On none of the days was Edwards disappointed with any of the papers for failing to mention him. His suddenly wide celebrity arose from his prosecution, in the court at Mineola, of Francis Crowley, a twenty-year-old psychopath (summed up by a reporter for the *New York Times* as 'undersized, underchinned, underwitted'), whose self-given nickname, Two-Gun, was derived from what seems to have been a fact that, from soon after he took to wearing long trousers, he used them to conceal two automatics, one strapped to each leg just above the sock. The charge was the murder of a Nassau County police patrolman, Fred Hirsch, who, suspecting that the driver of a maroon Ford sedan parked on a dirt-road in woods near Freeport was Crowley – wanted for questioning in regard to the murder of a 'taxi dancer' by Rudolph Duringer, a friend of Crowley's, at Yonkers, north of Manhattan – had asked him for his driver's licence, and been killed by at least one of six bullets fired by Crowley from one of his two guns. A couple of days later, on 7 May 1931, Crowley, his moll, and Duringer were ambushed in an apartment on West Ninetieth Street, Manhattan. Not much was left of the apartment after some of the posse of policemen, eventually 300 of them, had fired more than 700 bullets and an unestimated number of tear-gas bombs at and into it, and Crowley, suffering from four slight wounds, and his companions, both physically unscathed but shell-shocked, were brought out to cheers from members of the public, reckoned to be 15,000-strong by then, who had been allowed to watch 'The Siege on West Ninetieth Street'. After receiving first-aid at Bellevue Hospital, Crowley was driven, under heavy guard, to Nassau Hospital in Mineola. Even in those days, before the American legal system got bogged down in a mess of technicalities, Elvin Edwards' alacrity in dealing with Crowley was astounding. All in the space of three weeks from the arrest, he marshalled the evidence and sub-poenaed the witnesses against Crowley, brought him to trial in the New Courthouse, gave the prosecution witnesses the cues for what he had rehearsed them to say, asked just one or two questions, each in a tone of expectant disbelief, of each of the few defence witnesses, and, speaking in a 'drawing-room voice', briefly addressed the jury. There were still two days left of May when Crowley, his wounds still patched, was sentenced to die in the electric chair at Sing Sing. He smirked.[1]

1. The execution – delayed because Crowley was needed to give evidence at the re-trial of a man convicted of an armed robbery that he, Crowley, claimed to have

At breakfast on Tuesday, 9 June, when Elvin Edwards, having said grace and thanked the black maidservant Martha for pouring his coffee, looked at the front page of whichever paper was topmost on the regular-sized pile of them, he saw a report of happenings in Nassau County that were news to him. Shoving that paper aside, he looked at the others and, without needing to open any of them, found similar reports, all with the name 'Starr Faithfull' in their headlines, most making reference to Inspector Harold King, and none saying a single reminding word about who the District Attorney of Nassau County was. Forgoing his usual second cup of coffee, he drove to the Old Courthouse in Mineola and hurried to his office on the second floor, arriving there before his secretary. Using the private line, he rang the detective bureau at the police headquarters and, not asking to speak to Inspector King, not even asking if he was present, told whoever he spoke to that he wished to see the inspector 'as a matter of urgency'.

Despite his long overtime on the previous night, King got to work no later than his usual ten-minutes-early. A fat manila envelope, dabbed with sealing wax, was already on his desk. Nathan Birchall, conscientious too, had stayed up to type Dr Schultze's report, with two carbon-copies, and had delivered the package on his way to his own office. Also on the desk, placed there by a junior detective, was a stapled sheaf of newspaper cuttings. The sheaf was bulky this morning − far bulkier than recent ones, since the morning after the

---

committed (the claim was not believed by the second jury) − was carrried out on 21 January 1932. During the ambush, Crowley had written 'a letter to the world at large' which read, in part, 'Underneath my coat will lay a weary kind heart what wouldn't harm anything. I hadn't nothing else to do. That's why I went around bumping off cops ... When I die put a lily in my hand − let the boys know how they'll look.' Though that request went unfulfilled, a subsequent one, made a moment before the hood was placed over his shaven head − 'Give my love to mother' − was fulfilled by the prison warden to the best of his ability. He sent Crowley's love to the woman 'baby-farmer' who, finding him on her doorstep when he was a month old, had fostered him. (Incidentally, Rudolph Duringer, whose murder of a 'taxi dancer' was the indirect cause of the murder of Patrolman Fred Hirsch, also died in the electric chair at Sing Sing.)

The 1939 movie, *Angels With Dirty Faces*, is said to have been suggested by the Crowley case: the tough-guy character played by James Cagney bears certain resemblances to Crowley, and an all-hell-let-loose scene is reminiscent of The Siege on West Ninetieth Street.

Crowley trial. And, tucked under a triangular corner of the blotting pad, was a memo slip with the urgent message, timed at 08.40, from the District Attorney.

King, who had expected the summons but not so soon, guessed that its early arrival meant that Edwards was peeved. He should, he may have admitted to himself, have informed the DA of the drowning case without being asked — if not before Stanley Faithfull's visit, then before Faithfull had left. The mystery is why he had not done so. Whatever the reason, which may have been, quite simply, forgetfulness, he now saw it as he believed Edwards would see it, as a sign of frailty, as a cause for questioning whether he was up to his job — and so he was determined to tell Edwards an excuse rather than confess to him whatever the reason was. As he walked through the underground tunnel to the Old Courthouse, carrying in a cardboard folder the top copy of both Warinner's and Schultze's reports, he rehearsed the words of the excuse. The excuse was this: that, never mind Stanley Faithfull's insistence that his step-daughter had been murdered, he, King, had no doubt, none at all, that the girl had committed suicide or met her death by accident — either way, of no formal interest to the District Attorney. His decision (backed up by the two captains) to arrange a second autopsy, though maybe seeming to show that he accepted the possibility of foul play, was actually taken because he was a firm believer (as he knew Mr Edwards was) in making assurance double sure.

It seems unlikely that Edwards, made intuitive of wiliness by his experience as a cross-examiner, was taken in. If his peevishness had dwindled since breakfast-time, he may have expressed acceptance of what King said, but in such a way, so over-politely, as to make King embarrassedly aware that the expressed acceptance veiled utter disbelief. All that is known about the conversation in the closed room, which lasted some forty-five minutes, till a quarter to ten, is that King mentioned that Stanley Faithfull was returning to Mineola that morning, and that Edwards ordered him to go at once to the railway station to meet Faithfull off the train, whichever one it was, and bring him directly to the Old Courthouse. Edwards may have softened the order by pointing out that, as King was the only person who was sure to recognise Faithfull, he was the only person who could be sent on the errand, but King would still have believed that he was being put in his place.

He did as he had been told. As it turned out, he did not have to wait, seething the while, for long. Faithfull had left home at about a quarter past nine. Nodding but saying nothing to a morning shift of reporters (and quite disregarding a sprinkling of spectators, one of whom, an elderly woman wearing a sort of cowboy hat, a flower-patterned frock and carpet-slippers, had a toy duck on a lead[1]), he had made his way, trailed by some of the reporters, to Pennsylvania Station, and, leaving the reporters at the barrier, boarded the 9.40 train to Mineola, which arrived there at 10.16. King met him on the patch of wasteland beside the platform and took him to see the District Attorney.

The interviewing of Faithfull, which lasted, with a few breaks, for about three hours, was divided into three parts. At first, for over an hour, he was questioned and coaxed along by Edwards; there was no stenographer present, and neither Edwards nor King, he apparently silent throughout, took written notes. Then Edwards, politely excusing himself, went into the adjoining office, that which was a kind of Black Museum, its walls hung with trophies of Edwards' 'war against nuisances', to confer with the occupant, Martin Littleton, who, though not officially the *chief* assistant district attorney, was the one Edwards was most reliant upon.

Littleton looked inappropriate to the decor. In his early thirties, tall and darkly handsome, he was exquisitely dressed. His costume today included a light grey, subtly pinstriped, double-breasted suit, obviously bespoke from a good tailor, not the least crease in it that was not intended, a whiter-than-white silk shirt, and a necktie, knotted where it was slimmest, that was polka-dotted with a tiny picture of a tiger, the emblem of Princeton University – which he had left in his freshman year to serve in the navy while America was at war with Germany, and returned to when demobilised. As for accessories, he had a white rosebud in his buttonhole, a white display-hankie, arranged so that the monogram on it was readable, a silver-braceleted silver wristwatch, silver and enamel cufflinks, and a gold signet-ring, which, as it was on the third finger of his left hand, showed that he, though a dandy, was married. Littleton had served under Edwards for two years, since 1929, at which time his curriculum vitae was as follows:

1. Two days later, a woman in New Jersey, envious of the publicity given to the woman with the toy duck, travelled to Manhattan, to St Luke's Place, and (according to the *New York Herald Tribune*) 'mingled with the groups standing in doorways along the entire block. She wore a Russian smock and had a parrot on her shoulder. She lingered to tell reporters about her trained duck that "the Ringlings wanted to buy for their circus".'

I graduated from Columbia Law School and was admitted to the Bar in 1923. I was then associated as a clerk with the firm of Lamar Hardy for about a year, when the firm was dissolved. I then worked with my father[1] who was engaged in the general practise of law at 149 Broadway, Manhattan. I remained with him for a period of about a year or a little more. At that time I went into the legal department of the Sinclair Refining Company, and worked there until the conclusion of what was at that time known as the Teapot Dome Oil Scandal.[2] Upon the conclusion of the Sinclair trials, I returned to my father's office.

Edwards, having engaged Littleton despite his unimpressive c.v., had tried him out as the prosecutor in an open-and-shut case, which Littleton lost. But the disappointing debut was followed by a barely-interrupted run of successes, some in cases in which the verdict could have gone either way. Littleton's style of courtroom advocacy was very different from that of Edwards: he harried unhelpful witnesses, seeking to intimidate them into saying what he wanted them to say, and, in addressing juries, was rarely quieter than stentorian.

When Edwards returned to his office – where, since he had left a few minutes before, Faithfull and King had sat in complete silence – he was followed by Littleton; also by his own secretary. While she took shorthand-notes, Edwards repeated some of the questions he had asked Faithfull and gave him cues to repeat some of his unprompted comments.

1. Marton W. Littleton, Senior. His most celebrated, and probably wealthiest, former client was Harry Kendall Thaw, who, on Monday, 25 June 1906, during the opening performance of *Mamzelle Champagne* in the rooftop theatre of Madison Square Garden, and just after a comedian had sung a ditty called 'I Could Love a Thousand Girls', shot to death Stanford White, the great architect (of, among other buildings in Manhattan, Madison Square Garden), because White, among others, had had an affair with his, Thaw's, beautiful wife Evelyn, *née* Nesbit. No doubt because one or two members of the jury at Thaw's first trial had been suborned, they were unable to reach a verdict. After a re-trial, at which Thaw's leading counsel was Littleton, he was found guilty but insane, and was sent to the State Asylum at Matteawan – but, as he was so rich, not for long.
2. Which resulted from the discovery that, in 1922, Albert B. Fall, Secretary of the Interior in President Harding's cabinet, had leased government-owned oil reserves at Teapot Dome, Wyoming, and Elk Hills, California, respectively to two oil tycoons, Harry F. Sinclair and Edward L. Doheny, and that he had received substantial 'interest-free loans' from both men, neither of whom was famed for generosity. The leases were revoked in 1927; in the same year, Fall was convicted of bribery and sentenced to twelve months' imprisonment and a fine of $100,000. Sinclair and Doheny were acquitted of bribery, but the former was sentenced to nine months' imprisonment and a fine of $1000 for contempt of court. It seems likely that Littleton got the job with the Sinclair Refining Company through nepotism: his father was Harry F. Sinclair's leading trial counsel.

That was not the end of the interviewing, however. King escorted Faithfull to the police headquarters. But it was not King who continued the interviewing. That was done by Littleton, who had followed them across, wearing a grey homburg throughout the short journey. One is perplexed – first, by the fact that the shorthand-noted part of the proceedings, rather than coming at the end, was sandwiched in the middle, and second, by the switch from one venue to another. The only explanation I can think of for the first of those oddities is that Edwards intended the shorthand recapitulation to be the tailpiece of the interview, but Littleton, having listened to the recapitulation, felt that further information was needed from Faithfull. I can think of no explanation for the second oddity.

It is impossible to be sure of the sequence in which Faithfull first referred to particular topics, either as replies to questions or as unprompted comments. The transcript made by Edwards' secretary shows that certain topics arose during the 'Edwards part' of the interviewing; however, there are strong indications that Edwards' recapitulation was incomplete, and that he brought up topics as they came into his mind, not in their original order. When, a long while afterwards, Littleton made written and oral statements about his interviewing of Faithfull, he referred to several topics which had certainly already been raised as if they were fresh, and that casts doubts on the freshness of all but one of other topics that he referred to in the same way. King, present from first to last, subsequently recalled much of what Faithfull had said but little that is helpful towards establishing the sequence. Edwards never spoke explicitly of what had transpired in or, later, out of his presence. All that being so, the most that can be said for the sequence of the following account is that it is possible.

Asked by Edwards, 'Did you have any idea from anything Starr did in the last year or so that she would want to destroy herself?' Faithfull replied, 'Absolutely the contrary. She particularly loved life.'[1]

*Q.* 'Did she have a bad temper?'   *A.* 'No, she did not.'

*Q.* 'Was she generous?' *A.* 'Yes, exceptionally so.'

*Q.* 'Was she lovable to her own folks?' *A.* 'Yes.'

Enlarging on that one-word answer, Faithfull said that Starr's affection was 'not of the expressed kind'. He added, speaking of his

1. All directly-reported questions and answers are from the transcript. It follows, of course, that the topics to which they relate were raised during the 'Edwards part' of the interviewing.

wife and step-daughters: 'The children are not of the kissable kind. I have never seen mother kiss daughter.' He said that Starr and her younger sister Tucker 'got along remarkably well together. They are not physically alike, but one is the equal of the other as far as beauty is concerned.' There was never any jealousy between them 'but I do think that Starr had somewhat of an inferiority complex towards Tucker. It was certainly not resentment.'

Faithfull said that he was sure that Starr had never had 'any close romantic attachments'. He could not recall the name of any man with whom she was friendly in New York. 'When she didn't come home last Friday evening, we got in touch with everybody we thought she might have gone to. The only persons we could think of were some friends of ours named Foster — Nathaniel Foster and his wife. They live over in Washington Square. They were friends of my wife's more than Starr's.'

*Q*. 'Had they seen or heard from her?' *A*. 'I don't think they were in. I don't think we got in touch with them, so we knew she couldn't be there.'

*Q*. 'Had she a habit of going to them sometimes?' *A*. 'Well, she had never been away before a night.'

That, it turned out, was not quite true. Perhaps Faithfull meant that Starr had never spent nights away from home of her own accord. The discrepancy seems to have come to light as an afterthought by Faithfull to his comment that Starr 'could not take liquor':

'There was an episode a little over a year ago. She was meeting a girlfriend at the apartment. We were living in another address in Manhattan then — 35 West Ninth Street. [Or rather, the women of the family were. Faithfull was staying at the nearby Albert Hotel.] She had got to know the girl, Constance Little, when they were fellow-passengers on the *Baltic*, travelling to England, in 1929. She asked me if I would mix up a few drinks for herself and this girl. So I mixed up actually four small cocktails and I diluted them well down, and they were made out of pre-war stuff too. It was pretty nearly the end of what I had. Pre-war gin and pre-war Vermouth — and I added about twenty-five per cent water so as to make them good and mild. The girlfriend did not arrive at the moment she was supposed to, so Starr drank all four of them. The girl then showed up, and the girl said Starr was perfectly all right — did not seem to be under the influence of liquor — but when she was leaving she said she was a little bit worried about Starr because she did not seem to be quite right.'

*Q.* 'Did you have your liquor locked up?' *A.* 'Well, I didn't have it locked up, but I had it hidden, and I kept track of it to see whether or not she got any.

'Anyway, after Constance Little left, Starr left the house and we did not find her until the next day, and then she was at Bellevue Hospital. She was so badly beaten up that it was two weeks before she could come out of the house. Mostly on her face. She had evidently been in a fight with some man because it was some man who left her at Bellevue Hospital under an assumed name. She had been taken from a hotel up around Columbus Circle [at the southwest corner of Central Park, in midtown Manhattan]. He said, "This is my wife, Mary Jones," or something of that sort. I don't know what the name was he used. I don't remember the name of the hotel offhand.'

*Q.* 'Was she raped at that time?' *A.* 'She has no recollection of even leaving the house to this day. She doesn't know a thing that happened to her. I immediately called a doctor and told him I was afraid she had been raped, and he said of course he couldn't tell definitely.'

According to King's recollection, 'There was some talk [in the DA's office] that we would like to get hold of any writings or papers or letters or diaries that she might have had, and Mr Faithfull said at that time that he had burned two diaries of Starr's at her request at some time before in the furnace — in *a* furnace: whether he said at 12 St Luke's Place or somewhere else, I don't remember.'

When asked about events in the week or so before Starr's disappearance on Friday, 5 June, Faithfull spoke of an incident on the previous Friday, 29 May:

'My wife and I were in our apartment. Starr came in at about 5.20 or 5.30 in the afternoon. She said that she had been on the *Franconia*, one of the Cunard liners, which was sailing that day on a voyage to England. The Cunard piers are close to where we live. She said that she had been with Dr George Jameson Carr, the surgeon on the *Franconia*, whom she had known for some years. She had first met him when she was a passenger on a Cunard liner going to England and he was the ship's surgeon. She left the boat about quarter before five.

'She did not appear to be intoxicated. Her clothes were neat and in order. My wife had some talk with her to try to find out what had happened, if anything. Starr said she had met a man named Francis Peabody Hamlin on the *Franconia* and that she had gone to the chief officer's cabin, where there was some little party going on, and

63

she had met two men there. She said she expected to see them again. It is well known that some officials on the liners are mixed up with bootleggers. Possibly she met a couple of bootleggers there in the chief officer's cabin. Hamlin may know who they were. He is a cruise director for Cunard, working from the Boston office. I wrote to him at the weekend, after Starr's disappearance. Cunard's address in Boston is on Tremont Street.

'Some time at the start of the following week − that is, the week beginning 1 June − she went down to get the mail the first thing in the morning. On Thursday, 4 June, she returned to the apartment around six or seven o'clock in the evening − I was away in Boston, so I am not sure of the time, but if I remember correctly, my wife said it was around six or seven o'clock − and said that she had met one of the two men and that she had an appointment to meet him again at 9.45 that evening. She had had probably one drink, possibly two. She was good-natured and seemed perfectly all right. My wife said that she could meet the man only provided she would tell her who he was and where she was going. She said she didn't want to give that information because of the fact that every time she met a man, Tucker eventually got him. She was going to keep a man to herself this time. She said this more or less in a humorous sort of way. And she furthermore said, "Now, I know perfectly well that I must not drink; that in so doing I do pass out" − that is the expression she used − and she said, "You needn't worry. I am perfectly capable of taking care of myself, and I *will* take care of myself."

'As I was away and mother didn't know exactly what to do, she let her go. She came back again about one in the morning and made the observation when she returned that for the first time in her life − which was the truth − she had seen the inside of a speakeasy in New York City. My wife asked her where the speakeasy was, and she said it was near the Times Building − which, I agree, is an inexact address: she might as well have said the United States of America.'

*Q.* 'This was one o'clock in the morning of Friday, 5 June, when your wife had this talk with her?' *A.* 'Yes.'

*Q.* 'What was Starr's mood then, do you know?' *A.* 'She was perfectly all right. Mother was very careful to see how she looked and what condition her hair was in. She wanted to be sure as to whether or not there was any evidence of any petting party, as it is commonly expressed, and she told me she was satisfied by her hair, and one thing and another, and that there had not been anything of that sort. Although the child always would say if there was anything of that sort – always frankly. She seemed to be perfectly all right in every way, shape and manner.

'The next morning, I returned on the boat from Boston and arrived at the house. By the time that I arrived, about eight, my wife had not arisen, and Starr came into our bedroom. She wanted to know if there was anything she could do for me. She was particularly cheerful, particularly bright, and unusually, you might say, sweet in her behaviour. I asked her what she was going to do, and she said she was going uptown to have lunch, and she might have her hair waved. And mother asked her when she could expect her back, and she said, "Well, I may go out again this evening." She said, "I will telegraph." And her mother said, "No, don't telegraph – come back." She said, "All right, I will. I will come back. I know how you feel, you are worried about me all the time, but there is no sense in it. I am perfectly able to take care of myself," and so forth. And she said it, not in the spirit at all of trying to pacify one, don't you know, but with that kind of assurance that made both of us feel more at ease from the standpoint that she was capable of taking care of herself. It was about 9.30 in the morning when she left. And that is the last that we saw her.'

Bewildering as some of Faithfull's statements were, they are no more bewildering than the fact that Edwards did not query them. For instance, Edwards does not seem to have considered it at all peculiar that Starr, having for some reason decided to destroy two diaries (which must have contained very personal entries, otherwise she could simply have dumped them in a garbage-bin), had, instead of destroying them herself, given them to her step-father to burn. Edwards did not even ask Faithfull if he had yielded to the practically irresistible temptation to skip through the diaries before throwing them into a furnace. He did not mention the destroyed diaries, the by-proxy destruction of them, during the shorthand recapitulation. The most glaring example of Edwards' uninquisitiveness is that, though Faithfull spoke time and again of how he and his wife had treated Starr as if she were a child, checking up on where she was going, where she had been, Edwards did not ask whether there was a reason for the mollycoddling, did not ask about the apparent contradiction between the safeguarding of Starr and her several unchaperoned trips to England.

Now we come to the change of scene – from Edwards' large and comfortably furnished office in the Old Courthouse to King's small, utilitarian one in the police headquarters – and to Martin Littleton's continuation of the interviewing. Littleton would have noted gaps in the recapitulation; he may, perhaps while a lowly policeman was bringing coffee or while Faithfull was using the toilet, have asked King what unasked questions had occurred to him. He sat in King's desk chair. There was only one other chair in the office. Faithfull sat on it. King remained standing the whole time – about an hour and a half, starting shortly before noon.

Neither Littleton nor King took written notes; there was no shorthand recapitulation. Too long afterwards, when Littleton had to give an account of the topics raised, he spoke sketchily of all but one of them, for his memory was virtually monopolised by the exceptional topic:

'I asked Mr Faithfull if there were any men or friends in the life of his step-daughter Starr whom he had reason to believe, or who he suspected, might have desired to see her dead.

'Mr Faithfull, in response to that question, stated that there was a matter that he wanted to discuss and bring to our attention, but that it was of an extremely confidential nature, and he wanted it to be understood that it was to be treated as confidential. I told him I would so treat it.

'He proceeded to tell us.'

What he said may not have come as a complete surprise to King. I believe that he had spoken guardedly of the matter, refusing to go into details, the night before – that that was what had persuaded King that a second autopsy was called for.

'Mr Faithfull said that there had been in the life of this girl, for a period of years commencing at a time when she was eleven years of age, a man, a politician, who was related to the family and who lived in Boston. He stated that he and his wife had discovered very, very much later – not until the summer of 1926, when Starr was twenty – that the man's relationship with her had been of the very worst kind, of the most sordid nature, and that by virtue of the circumstances surrounding this contact between Starr as a child and this man, he was of the belief that this man was the logical suspect as her murderer, the type of man who would be inclined to do away with her, or desire to have done away with her.

'*The man's name, he said, was Andrew J. Peters.*'

Littleton had inherited a keen interest in politics from his father, who had served as Borough President of Brooklyn and as a Congressman, and so he recognised the name at once. King had no interest in politics; but simply because he was a policeman, he also recognised the name.

*

Andrew James Peters was born – and still lived – in a white Regency house, 310 South Street, in the part of Boston called Jamaica Plain, immediately south-east of the Brookline district, in April 1872, which means that he was now fifty-nine (and that he had been forty-five in 1917, when Starr was eleven). According to an historian of Boston, Francis Russell,

> The first Peters, a distiller – also named Andrew – arrived in Boston in 1657. Though the Peters endured locally, they were not noted in the history of the province, the Revolution or even the Civil War. Wealth came to the family early in the nineteenth century through Edward Dyer Peters, who in 1811 founded Boston's first wholesale lumber firm, one that exists to this day ...
>
> Like many a dissenting Yankee family, the Peters ... drifted into Episcopalianism. Andrew James was sent to St Paul's School, not, indeed, as fashionable as Groton or St Mark's, but fashionable enough. He entered Harvard with the Class of 1895 ... From the college he went on to the law school, and after receiving his degree joined the law firm of Colonel William Gaston [a former Mayor of Boston and Governor of Massachusetts]. In 1904 and again in 1905 he was elected to the Massachusetts House of Representatives, and after two terms there graduated to two terms in the state senate. His Republican Jamaica Plain district was of singular advantage to him. The minority Democrats voted for him because he was a Democrat; the Yankee Republicans crossed party lines out of ethnic allegiance to his Puritan descent ... In 1906 he took the larger step of running for Congress from an expanded district that included the anonymous streets and massed three-deckers of Forest Hills [south of Jamaica Plain]... In those pre-welfare days it was a district amenable to a candidate of judicious means. Peters was elected and three times re-elected.[1]

In 1910 he married Martha Phillips, a member of one of Boston's oldest and richest families. An ancestor of hers, John Phillips, had been the city's first mayor in 1822. Shortly after the marriage, and as a result of it, Peters' name was included in the Boston *Social Register*. Till 1919, Martha Peters was more often pregnant than not, six times successfully, and each of those times with an outcome that was singular and male; the first son was given both of his father's names, and the following ones were called Alanson Tucker (that second name a middle name of his maternal grandmother), John Phillips, Bradford, Robeson, and David McClure. All but one of Martha's relatives on her side of the family were well to do. The

---

1. *The Knave of Boston & Other Ambiguous Massachusetts Characters*, Quinlan Press, Boston, 1987.

comparatively poor relation was a second cousin, Helen, presently Mrs Frank Wyman.

In 1914 Peters resigned from Congress, having accepted an appointment from President Woodrow Wilson as Assistant Secretary of the Treasury in charge of Customs. In August (the month in which the Great War broke out in Europe) the magazine *Practical Politics* published an article about him which he can have minded only as an affront to his modesty. The accompanying studio-photograph had him looking thoughtfully – not so much so as to furrow the front of his domed, prematurely bald head – at something on the left of the camera; his eyes, small and dark, their brows tufted (in curious contrast to the hair at his temples, which, untouched by grey, looked as if it had been painted on), were spaced well away from his nose, which was thin along the bridge but bulbous around the nostrils; his lips, the top one making a cupid's bow, were very large. The anonymous author of the article began by praising the President, saying that

> he seems to have a faculty for solving any problem that comes before him with dispatch and good judgment.
>
> It didn't take him long to decide who was the best man, from every standpoint, to select for the vacant post in his administration. Andrew J. Peters has for years been one of the big assets the Democratic party has had in Massachusetts. He represents the none too plentiful type of the American Democrat, clean-cut in appearance, eloquent in speech, pleasing in manner, and possessed of great ability. He has been a credit to his district, to the state and to his party. He has won a high place in Congress and by so doing has reflected honour upon those who helped elect him. To enumerate his accomplishments as a public official would require a good-sized volume. Suffice it to say that he has been one of the most faithful and hard-working Democrats in Congress and that he has never betrayed any trust.
>
> He has at various times been mentioned for Governor and as a candidate for Mayor of Boston, but he has shown no inclination whatever to go into any contest.

Peters remained at the Treasury for three years. Then, after a few months' service in the United States section of the International High Commission, he entered the Boston Mayoralty contest as a reform candidate, under the aegis of the city's Good Government Association – which James Michael Curley, the Democrat incumbent Mayor, who was seeking re-election, derided as the Goo-Goos. Though Peters also had the backing of the minority Republicans, in a straight fight, Curley (an Irish-American, and therefore − never mind that he was famous as a crook − assured of the enormous Irish-American vote) would have won hands dɔwn. But two other bosses of the Democratic party in Boston, each as corrupt as Curley, had fallen out with him over the division of loot and were determined to deprive him of the mayoral perks. One was Martin Lomasney, the so-called mahatma of the electorally-important Ward 8, covering the West End of the city. The other was John F. Fitzgerald,[1] the evil dwarf whose tenor rendering of his campaign song, 'Sweet Adeline', had gained him the nickname of Honey Fitz. For all but a couple of the past dozen years, he and Curley had taken turns at being mayor. Exemplifying the corruption under his regimes, cronies whom he had enlisted as road-mending contractors had charged the city for each side of paving stones, many of which the contractors had prised from perfectly good roads, thereby increasing the number of roads that needed mending. Honey Fitz conspired with Lomasney, who ordered two underlings whom he had fixed up with Congressional seats to stand in the 1917 mayoral election. The votes they took from Curley were sufficient to oust him from City Hall − incidentally, so far as Honey Fitz and Lomasney were concerned, to make Andrew J. Peters the Mayor.

There are few exceptions to the rule (applicable to England as well as to America) that persons elected to political office on reform tickets fail to live up to their promises. Mayor Peters was unexceptional. The first of the following quotations regarding him and his four-year term, coming as it does from the memoirs of Michael John Curley,[2] would be hard to excel as an instance of a pot calling a kettle black:

> The wholesale pilfering of the city treasury reached such scandalous proportions in Peters' do-nothing regime that Boston was left in a sorry condition, with a depleted treasury and little of a tangible nature to show for the funds that had disappeared ... The vulturous palace guard who surrounded him made a travesty of the highest political office in Boston ... Although a person of mighty moral muscle and admitted courtliness, he deserved the censure even his friends heaped upon him when they called him 'an innocent dupe for a conscienceless corps of bandits'.

The required confirmation of Curley's comments is provided by Joseph Dineen, a Boston newspaper reporter:

1. The grandfather of, inter alios, President John Fitzgerald Kennedy.
2. *I'd Do It Again*, written with the help of John Henry Cutler; McGraw-Hill, 1949.

> In an anteroom adjoining Peters' office there was a 'bagman' who would deal, dicker or negotiate for almost anything ... Jobs and promotions had price tags on them. Political affiliation meant nothing. Anybody could buy almost anything at the bargain counter. All that was needed was the price ...
>
> Peters was one of the most trusting souls ever placed in a job that required the quick eyes, ears and instincts of an honest poker player among cardsharps. He believed implicitly everything he was told. He signed his name to documents without reading them, and even repeated into a telephone acknowledgments and compliments which his secretariat called to him ... He never took a wrong nickel while in office and a time came when he looked around blinking, bewildered and uncomprehending, not knowing what had happened. He never did figure it out.

Other critics of Mayor Peters, in seeking to explain how he, an experienced politician, failed to notice the blatant corruption at City Hall, have suggested that he was too often elsewhere − that the rats played while the kitten was away. Curley's description of Peters as 'our part-time mayor' seems to have been very nearly justified. A member of half a dozen gentlemen's clubs (including the Somerset − probably the grandest in the country, let alone in Boston), he was a frequenter of all of them, often for long periods during what were supposed to be his working hours. On the other hand, he was creative with excuses for refusing invitations to political clubs, and when forced to put in an appearance at any of them, spent most of an always short time apologising that he could not stay long. He was often away from the city for weeks on end: touring incognito, or horse-riding on the farm at Dover, west of Boston, that his wife had inherited, or, in the summers, cruising in his schooner-yacht from North Haven Island, off the coast of Maine, where he had bought a holiday-home − called a cottage but plenty large enough to accommodate his family and most of his domestic servants throughout the summers, and visiting groups of relatives and friends at different times during them.

In the July of 1919 − which, speaking of most of the United States, was a year of strikes, protests by and on behalf of unemployed ex-servicemen, and bombings by anarchists, many of whom were illegal immigrants from Italy − Boston was practically paralysed for four days by a strike of public transport workers. The mayor was away at the time, cruising somewhere off the coast of Maine − unable to be reached because a forecast of heavy Atlantic fog that he had been given before setting sail, and soon after hearing that the strike was imminent, had proved correct. Meanwhile, one of the mayor's lawyers negotiating with the leaders of the strike composed a heartfelt ditty:

> Our Andy is out on the ocean,
> Our Andy is befogged at sea,
> Our Andy has just got the notion,
> It's a damn good place to be.

When Peters returned to Boston, the streetcars and the trains were running normally again — far more expensively, though, for the strikers' demands for higher wages had been met. He signed the strike-ending agreement, also a few letters that his secretary felt were too important to be rubber-stamped with his signature, and he was briefed on the threat of Boston's becoming the first American city to be hit by a police strike. Then he went back to North Haven Island for a few days.

He took further awaybreaks during the following month, August; but the last of them, which he had planned to extend into September, had to be cut short because, lacking a fog to hide in, he received the news that an action, truly an action, that he had recently visited Boston specially to take, believing that it put an end to all the talk about a police strike, had resulted in an action by the police commissioner that made a strike far more likely and also more justifiable.

Francis Russell[1] itemises the ingredients of the unrest:

There were the policemen themselves — mostly of Irish descent — angry and belligerent, preparing to form a union affiliated with the American Federation of Labor. (The 1914 dollar had in five years sunk [in purchasing power] to forty-seven cents ... A policeman who at the beginning of the war had thought himself reasonably well off with a thousand dollars a year, felt himself impoverished at the war's end. So it was with the Boston police, aggrieved as well by a ten-hour day and a seven-day week.) There was an intransigent police commissioner of the Yankee epigone, Edwin Curtis, who forbade the police any such

---

1. See page 67. Francis Russell has also written a comprehensive account of the police strike: *A City in Terror*, Viking Press, New York, 1975.

Just over a month before the strike in Boston, there had been a police strike in England, chiefly affecting Liverpool and London; in my book *The Killing of Julia Wallace* (revised edition: Headline, London, 1987) which examines the Wallace murder case in Liverpool in 1931, I note repercussions of the strike — one being that, as so many efficient members of the Liverpool force were dismissed, and so many stupid or dishonest men recruited, the force became, and remained for more than a dozen years, sub-standard.

affiliation, insisting with tight-lipped righteousness that a policeman was not an employee but a government official whose impartiality would be compromised by his joining a union. There was a Republican governor, Calvin Coolidge, determined not to act unless he had to, though it was the governor and not the mayor who held the appointment of the police commissioner. And finally there was Mayor Peters, unaware of the extent of his own powers, spending most of the crisis period aboard his yacht.

When, defying Curtis's order, the police organised their union, the commissioner charged the new union's leaders with insubordination and ordered eighteen of them to stand trial. The union countered by warning him that if these men were disciplined the police would strike. Faced with this threat, Peters appointed a Citizens Committee of Thirty-Four to try to find a way out of the impasse, then left for Maine. The committee recommended granting the police a union independent of the American Federation of Labor, with no action to be taken against the union officers. With some reluctance the policemen would probably have accepted the compromise. But Curtis would not. The eighteen had acted in direct violation of his orders. He suspended them. And as he did so, almost the whole Boston police force walked out.

A night of riots, looting and mob violence followed. Before the disturbances ended, eight persons had been killed, twenty-one wounded and at least fifty injured. A third of a million dollars worth of property was either stolen or destroyed, downtown Boston left a shambles.

The violence could have been averted if, as the policemen prepared to leave their posts, the state guard had been sent in to take over. Peters, although he was unaware of the fact, had the authority to call out the state guard units within the Boston area 'if tumult, riot or mob is threatened'. But even when on his quick return from Maine he was informed of this, he hesitated. How could he know for sure whether tumult, riot or mob threatened? First it had to happen.

Governor Coolidge could have called out the state guard before the rioting started. But, as he was cannily aware, any governor who calls out the militia prematurely commits political suicide ...

Only after a night of riot and destruction did Coolidge act. He then called out the six regiments of the state guard. As the guardsmen moved into Boston, another turbulent evening ensued, but by morning the guard was in unchallenged control of the city. Peters, assuming the guard to be his auxiliary police force, was still prepared to negotiate with the union. At this point Coolidge, as the guard's commander-in-chief, brushed Peters aside and took over the Boston Police Department. While guardsmen were moving into the Commonwealth Armory, the governor and the mayor happened to meet there on the stairs. At the sight of Coolidge Peters lunged at him in impotent rage, punching him in the eye. Coolidge did not respond, but for several days he nursed a shiner.

While Coolidge was still nursing his shiner, the police strike foundered, hastened to an end by the fact that the Boston firemen, who had threatened to walk out in support, decided not to, and he (Coolidge, that is) was hailed as a hero by editorialists throughout the land. A sentence of a letter that he – or his surrogate, Henry Long – wrote to Samuel Gompers, the leader of the American Federation of Labor, and which was telegraphed to the news agencies, was seen as a battle-cry against the Red Menace: 'There is no right to strike against the public safety by anybody, anywhere, any time.' Coolidge, practically unknown outside New England before the strike, was all of a sudden a national celebrity. In the following summer, the Republican Convention, meeting in Chicago, nominated Warren Gamaliel Harding for President on the tenth ballot (by arrangement between leading villains of the party who had got together in a suite at the Blackstone Hotel, incidentally but legend-inspiringly filling it with cigar-smoke) – and, unanimously on the first ballot, chose Coolidge as his running-mate. The partnership of Harding, pledged to 'a return to normalcy', and Coolidge, the battle-crying breaker of the police strike, scored a landslide victory over the Democratic candidates, James Cox (governor of the same state, Ohio, which Harding represented in the Senate) and the New Yorker, Franklin Delano Roosevelt, who, though he had served as Assistant Secretary of the Navy for the past seven years, was still only thirty-eight. Harding died in office (suddenly; according to some historians, unnaturally), and was succeeded by Coolidge – who in 1924, fortunate in that most of the crimes committed by Harding's 'Ohio Gang' had either not yet been revealed or were being unravelled, was elected President in his own right, with Charles Gates Dawes[1] as Vice-President. Coolidge's most publicised act during his term as elected President was one of omission: in 1927 he refused to intervene in the general strike of coal-miners. Again fortunate in regard to timing, he vacated the White House one month after assuring Congress that 'the country . . . can anticipate the future with optimism' and ten months before the Wall Street Crash made the Depression apparent

---

1. A retired general who claimed to understand financial reports – and who wrote music (some of it good enough to be played by Fritz Kreisler; one piece, given a lyric beginning 'Many a tear has to fall, but it's all in the game', became a popular song of the early 1950s). From 1929, soon after his term as Vice-President, till 1932, he was US Ambassador to Great Britain (a post occupied by Joseph P. Kennedy, Honey Fitz's son-in-law and John F.'s father, from 1937 till 1940, when, faced with the sack on account of his anti-Britishness, he resigned).

to everyone. In January 1933, on hearing the news that Coolidge was dead, the witty Dorothy Parker enquired, 'How do they know?' Just that. She did not need to add explanation to the joke about the politician who had become President through his being hyped as A Man of Deeds, that estimate based solely on his actually delayed response to the Boston police strike.

Reverting to Peters: soon after his election as Mayor of Boston – too soon for his inadequacies to have become so apparent that other politicians in the State felt that Bostonians had to be protected against the outside chance that his tenure of City Hall would last longer than four years – the Massachusetts legislature passed an Act that prohibited a sitting mayor from seeking re-election. Towards the end of his term, he claimed that the only reason he was not standing again was because he was not allowed to. If he was as honest as he was made out to be, and a bit superstitious, he may have had his fingers crossed when he spoke, not only to excuse himself for a fib but also to cancel out any tempting of a providential rescinding of the Act. Having become the ex-mayor (succeeded by Curley), he dashed back to Maine and, between nautical times, composed a rhyme, 'Reflections Upon Running for Office', which, as well as showing in its first stanza that he was a firm believer of flattery, revealed in its final stanza that his arm was available for twisting if any top Democrats thought of nominating him as governor, tenant of the gold-domed State House on Beacon Hill:

> I've done my job as Mayor
> And they say I've done it well,
> So I'll give up public life
> And rest and play a spell.

> I'll return to private practice,
> The practice of the law,
> And with my little graflex
> I'll literally wage war.

> I may become the president
> Of a small but growing Trust –
> Or I may pull together
> One which recently went bust.

I may take a fling upon the Street
With partners all well-known,
Or maybe run a banking shop
That's really quite my own.

I've chances quite a few
To go out and try my luck
With just enough of gamble in them
To let me test my pluck.

And of course I've done my bit
To keep the Nation going –
So I've no interest at all
In political winds a-blowing –

No, none at all – and yet –
There's the Gold Dome on the hill,
Perhaps a couple of years up there
Would really fill the bill?

He did return to the practice of the law, specialising in estate management. In 1928 he left the firm in which he had been a partner (while mayor, of the sleeping, or at any rate dozing, sort) for many years, and joined with two leading lawyers, Harold L. Clark and Richard E. Keating, in founding a firm, successful from the start, with impressive offices at 1 Federal Street, in the centre of the commercial district. He did join the boards of several banks and trust companies. In 1926 he was appointed president of the Boston Chamber of Commerce.

He remained influential in politics, overtly as a member of the Democratic State Committee, stealthily as an elder statesman of the party, wooed for support or, the next best thing, acquiescence by power-brokers and prospective candidates. Indicating his prestige, at the Democratic Convention in Houston in 1928 he was chosen to make one of the seconding speeches for the nomination of Al Smith, the Governor of New York, as Presidential candidate. (Smith, chosen on the first ballot, was defeated in the election by Herbert Hoover, Coolidge's Secretary of Commerce – or rather, by the Three Ps: Prejudice [he was a Roman Catholic], Prohibition [he believed that the Volstead Act should be repealed], and Prosperity.)

Every so often, journalistic soothsayers predicted that ex-Mayor Peters would stand for election to the US Senate or as Governor of

Massachusetts. He didn't. In 1929 — so the story goes — the Democratic State Committee tentatively chose him as a candidate for the governorship; the chairman phoned him, with the intention of sounding him out, but was told that he was taking his daily nap and could not be disturbed; the message left by the chairman was not passed on, and Peters' lack of response to it was taken to mean that he, for once impolite, could not be bothered to reply. Therefore, his dream of occupying the building with the gold dome on the hill became a reality for the Democrat originally second on the list.

By the summer of 1931 — to be more precise, by 9 June — the Democratic State Committee had asked Peters to organise the collection of funds for the Presidential campaign in the following year. Peters' friend Franklin Delano Roosevelt, now Governor of New York, was already the red-hot favourite to be the Democratic candidate — sure, because Prosperity was a thing of the past, of ousting Herbert Hoover. If Peters collected successfully, Democrats who mattered would insist that his ten years out of public office was ten years too long.

When Stanley Faithfull was in a talkative mood, which he rarely wasn't, it was hard to stop him, hard to get a word in edgeways. Even so, he must have paused — if not for dramatic effect, then to squint enquiringly at the expression on Martin Littleton's face, perhaps at Harold King's as well — after giving the name of Andrew J. Peters. Neither the assistant district attorney nor the detective would have looked the least bit shocked; Littleton had practised, become perfect at, hiding the disconcernment made by witnesses' unexpected answers — of King's small repertoire of expressions made much difference to his face.

According to Littleton's subsequent recollection, Faithfull (having paused) went on to speak of 'an episode which, as he described it, occurred on the night of Tuesday, June 29, 1926, at the Hotel Astor in Manhattan [on Times Square, at the corner of Broadway and West Forty-Fourth Street].

'At that time, Andrew J. Peters was in the city, and had called up the Faithfulls at their home in West Orange, New Jersey, where they were then living, and had asked Mrs Faithfull if he might take Starr to the theatre. She granted her consent, and accordingly Starr went to Manhattan. At this time, Starr Faithfull was twenty years of age. Later that night, Andrew Peters phoned the Faith ↳lls and told them that it was stormy, a bad night, and that it would be awkward or inconvenient for Starr to come home, and wouldn't it be all right if he arranged for her to be put up at the Biltmore Hotel [on Madison Avenue at East Forty-Third Street — about half a mile from the Astor] — that he would secure a room for her and that she could go home in the morning.

'On the following morning Starr returned to West Orange. Her mother had left home earlier that morning to keep a business appointment with Andrew Peters at ten o'clock at the Biltmore Hotel. Faithfull was at home.

'As soon as Starr got into the house, Faithfull, so he told me, noted from her demeanour and appearance that something was wrong. He asked her several questions. From her responses and her general attitude, he concluded that the matter was of a nature that ought to be enquired into by her mother. She was scheduled to leave next day for a two-month trip to Europe, the first of several. In order to distract her mind from whatever had transpired, he kept her busy engaged in packing her trunks and running up and down stairs, as he put it, until her mother arrived home from her mission in New York at noon.

'Then he had a few words with his wife, following which she closeted herself in a room with Starr for a considerable time. Mrs Faithfull came out and explained to Faithfull the sordid relationship that had existed between Starr and Andrew J. Peters from when she was aged eleven. It had consisted of perverted sexual acts. He said that Mrs Faithfull had never known until then that Andrew Peters had taken advantage of Starr. He explained that, until 1925, when he married Mrs Faithfull, Starr had lacked a father's care. Andrew Peters had visited Starr frequently, sometimes when her mother was absent, and, with her mother's consent, had taken her on trips, and her mother had thought that he was displaying paternal instincts. She had never thought otherwise. But now, having spoken to Starr, she knew the truth.

'She knew that, when Starr was eleven years of age, Andrew Peters instructed her by reading to her from books by Havelock Ellis [the English author of, among other books which he published before 1917, six volumes of a series entitled *Studies in the Psychology of Sex*]. By gradual stages, the relationship progressed to physical excitation. Faithfull gave me his general conception of what perverted sexual acts Andrew Peters had indulged in. I am frank to say that, in questioning him on this matter, I used words and language that are less suitable to other occasions. He said that Andrew Peters introduced the child to the practice of sniffing ether or chloroform. Faithfull said that, after hearing of that from Mrs Faithfull, it occurred to him that he had noticed that Starr reacted strongly to the smell of ether; he said that one day he was cleaning some gloves, and Starr smelled the cleaning liquid and said, "Oh, I l-o-v-e that."

'He said that Starr had revealed to her mother that she had spent the night of June 29, 1926, with Andrew Peters at the Hotel Astor – that then, for the first time, he had had natural sexual intercourse with her. It was that fact, he said – the changed way of making love – that accounted for the peculiar demeanour he noted when she returned home next morning.'

In an I-dare-you-to sort of voice, Littleton asked Faithfull to repeat what he had just said. When Faithfull did so, Littleton lost his temper – or, as likely, pretended that he had, intending to intimidate:

'I said to him, "You can't honestly expect me to believe that a girl of twenty, having lived through a sordid relationship as a child and never manifested it to her mother or her step-father or her real father, would become hysterical, excited, nervously overwrought – any of those things – from her first natural act of sexual intercourse." But he said again that that was the fact, and I told him I thought it was crazy, and left the office.'

Eventually returning, Littleton stayed silent for a while, hoping that Faithfull had changed his mind and would say so, and then, the hope unrealised, muttered the supposition that Starr, though traumatised by her new experience at the Hotel Astor, had not cancelled her trip to Europe two days later.

That was correct, Faithfull said. Continuing, he took a roundabout route towards an explanation for Starr's subsequent trips. Littleton: 'He said that while Starr was abroad in the summer of 1926, he and his wife earnestly discussed what was to be done for her so that she might recover from Andrew Peters' treatment of her. He estimated that some $38,000, including $25,000, would represent a fair and reasonable sum for the outlay to which they had been put since the discovery following the Hotel Astor incident. He said that the expenses involved doctors – that they had brought in a Dr Garretson – in an effort to rehabilitate her morally and mentally and spiritually, and it was also necessary to send the girl to England every year, because that was apparently the only thing that would give her mental rest and pleasure.'

After ordering Faithfull to keep quiet for a minute, Littleton asked him what he meant by 'some $38,000, including $25,000'.

Uncharacteristically, Faithfull remained quiet for longer than a minute. When he spoke, it was to say that he could not answer the question directly – only 'in the context of other relevant matters'. Littleton told him 'to go ahead in his own way'.

Several of the relevant matters were wholly or partly concerned with documents of one sort or another. Faithfull had not brought any of the documents with him. He produced them at a later date, having fished them from among others in a folder marked 'AJP'. For the sake of clarity and conciseness, I shall quote from them now.

Faithfull began by explaining something that Littleton should have asked him to explain earlier: the reason for Mrs Faithfull's meeting with Andrew Peters at the Biltmore Hotel on the morning of 30 June 1926. At that time, he said, he and his wife had severe financial worries – particularly about impending bills that had to be paid promptly, else they might lose possession of the house in West Orange – and, at the meeting, Mrs Faithfull discussed those worries with Peters, who promised that, as soon as he got back to Boston, he would see what he could do to help. Faithfull did not say – and Littleton did not enquire – when the meeting had been arranged: whether before, during, or after Peters' phone call to Mrs Faithfull, requesting her consent to his taking Starr to the theatre on the night of 29 June.

Faithfull does not seem to have reminded Littleton that, straightway after the meeting, his wife had returned home, he had expressed concern about Starr, and she had talked with the girl, and then told him what she had been told. Some time later that day, he and his wife composed a letter – typed by him, signed by her – to Andrew Peters.

Dear Andrew,

As I have only a few minutes before the mail is collected I must write very hastily.

The payments on the Orange house during the next six months are as follows:

| | |
|---|---:|
| Taxes to be paid before Sept. 30 | $222.80 |
| Taxes to be paid before Dec. 31 | $219.48 |
| Interest and payment on 2nd Mortgage Aug. 15 | $740.00 |
| Interest and payment on 1st Mortgage Sept. 30 | $603.50 |
| | $1785.78 |

Assessed value – $12,100.00
Actual value – $25,000.00

I find that there are no payments to be made on principal on Centerville [Mrs Faithfull's summer-house on Cape Cod] for a year, and before that time I am sure that either everything will be all right or Centerville will be sold. Two real estate men have stated that they consider the present value of Centerville to be $25,000.00. There is a first mortgage of $6,000 and a second of $2,000, total $8,000.

It was very good to see you this morning.

In his reply, written a week later, Peters carefully stressed that the only help he was able – or willing – to give was as a go-between:

Dear Helen,

Your favour of June 30 is at hand.

I have gone over the matter with George Phillips [one of his wife's brothers] and have tried to get in touch with Starr. [Starr Pierce, Mrs Faithfull's brother. This reference to him, the only one I have seen, suggests that he was not in touch with her but that their rich Boston relatives expected him to show some interest in her welfare.] He was not in the office, however, yesterday but was expected back today. As I told you, it is a matter entirely for them to decide.

It was a pleasure to see you in New York.

I hope Bamby [Starr's pet-name] got off well and is enjoying the trip.

With best wishes,
Sincerely yours,
ANDREW J. PETERS

Presumably, Faithfull told Littleton whether or not the relatives came up with the money to pay the property bills. All one knows is that the bills *were* paid – as were those submitted during the following three years or so – otherwise the Faithfulls would have lost the West Orange house prior to 1930; also the house at Centerville.

Starr returned from her first overseas trip at the end of August 1926. During her two months' absence, had her mother and step-father frequently discussed what she had shockingly revealed on the eve of her departure? Surely they had. During the next two months, did Mrs Faithfull have closeted heart-to-heart talks with Starr? Surely she did.

Mrs Faithfull spent the last few days of October at Centerville, tidying up her house following its summer letting, and then visited relatives in Boston – among them, one supposes, her dearest cousin, Martha Peters. She also visited an old family-friend, Mrs Benjamin Russell. (*Especially from now on, bear in mind that I am not reporting events – only Faithfull's version of events.*) In the course of her conversation with Mrs Russell, Mrs Faithfull – not having intended to speak of what she and her husband had kept to themselves for four months, but suddenly feeling that company in distress would make the sorrow less — spoke of it. Not for one moment did Mrs Faithfull think that the old family-friend would breathe a word to anyone. And so she was surprised when, shortly afterwards, just before she left Boston, Mrs Russell's husband, a stockbroker, invited her to his office and asked her to repeat the accusations against Andrew Peters. She did so — not for one moment thinking that Benjamin Russell would breathe a word to anyone.

A couple of months later, early in January 1927, Mrs Faithfull made another trip to Boston. She phoned Mrs Russell, hoping for an invitation to tea, and was told, much to her surprise, also to her dismay, that Benjamin Russell had mentioned her accusations to his attorney, Charles F. Rowley, a partner of the distinguished firm of Peabody, Brown, Rowley & Storey, and that Rowley, though sceptical of the accusations, would like to meet her. She met him, in his office on State Street, that afternoon. He spoke sternly, warning her that slander was a serious offence, but when she refused to budge, advised her to seek corroborative evidence. Returning to West Orange, she talked things over with her husband, and they decided to hire a private investigator.

He did several jobs for them, two successfully. Visiting the Astor Hotel, he persuaded an under-manager to let him examine the register for 29 June 1926, found entries, one after the other, for 'A. Peters' and 'S. Peters', both said to be residents of Boston, who had been given adjoining rooms, and further persuaded the under-manager to provide a photostat of the page. The names, looking like signatures, and the word 'Boston' were in the same hand, which, compared by the Faithfulls with handwritten parts of letters from Andrew Peters, was clearly his. Mrs Faithfull had recalled that, about six months before the Astor Incident, she had consented to a request from Peters to allow Starr to accompany him to a Broadway musical and to spend the night at the Hotel Richmond on West Forty-Sixth Street, where he was staying. He had told her that he had tried other hotels for a room for Starr, but all were full. The private eye obtained a photostat of one of the Hotel Richmond's register pages for Monday, 18 January 1926, which showed that Peters and Starr had been booked into adjoining rooms, and established that there was no general shortage of hotel accommodation in midtown Manhattan that night.

Some time in February 1927, Mr and Mrs Faithfull and Starr went

on a day-trip to Boston, specially to see Charles Rowley. He talked
to the three of them together, to Mr and Mrs Faithfull out of Starr's
presence, and to Starr alone.

Some time in March, while Mr and Mrs Faithfull were at the
house at Centerville, one or other of them was blessed by
serendipity. In a letter that Faithfull wrote to Rowley on 13 April, he
explained that

> we ... there found a scrapbook which Starr kept in 1923. In it were
> various theatre tickets, programmes and stationery from certain hotels.
>
> With this information we were able to establish dates as to when they
> [Peters and Starr] went to certain hotels, but the man I sent to look up the
> records reports neither Andrew J. Peters nor Starr were registered. When
> I see you next I will show you the scrapbook and we can decide what is the
> best action to take.

Saliently, on one page of the scrapbook Starr had written an
itinerary of her travels with Peters in the summer of 1923, when she
was on holiday from Rogers Hall School. The long duration of those
travels raises four questions, none of which seems to have been
answered: How did Peters explain his absences to his wife, left to
look after their sons and to entertain guests at the summer house on
North Haven Island? As Peters must have asked permission from
Starr's mother for Starr to accompany him on his travels, did she
consent instantly or only after considering whether it was quite
proper for a seventeen-year-old girl to be away, sometimes for
weeks on end, with a middle-aged male in-law? What did Starr say
about her travels with Peters when, as must have happened
afterwards, she talked about them to her mother? Had Mrs Faithfull
completely forgotten Starr's travels with Peters in the summer of
1923 till she read the following account of them in the spring of
1927?

> July 2nd left with AJP for North Haven in the car. Stayed at Portland
> overnight in the Lafayette Hotel. Arrived at North Haven next day.
> [Portland, Maine, is some seventy miles south-west of North Haven, and
> on the most direct route there from Boston.]
>
> Stayed at North Haven about two weeks and four days.
>
> We started for Canada about July 20. Stayed at a small inn somewhere
> around the border line of Maine and Canada. Got to the Chateau
> Frontenac, Quebec, at about six next day. Stayed there two nights.
> Started for White Mountains [New Hampshire] and stayed at the
> Newport House in Vermont overnight. Reached Bretton Woods in the

July 2nd left with for North Haven in the car. Stayed at Portland over night in the Lafayette Hotel. Arrived at North Haven next day.

Stayed at North Haven about two weeks and four days.

We started for Canada about July 20. Stayed at a small inn somewhere around the border line of Maine and Canada. Got to the Chateau Frontenac, Quebec, at about six next day. Stayed there two nights. Started for White Mountains and stayed at the Newport House in Vermont over night. Reached Bretton Woods in the White Mountains next day. Stayed there about three days. Then back to Marblehead.

Started for New York August 21st. Stayed at the Mohican Hotel, New London, over night. Got to New York next evening at about six. Stayed at the Plaza Hotel. Left New York in about five days, for Springfield, Mass. Stayed at the Hotel Kimball in Springfield. Saw Smith College. Next night stayed at the Bancroft in Worcester, Mass. Motored to Marblehead next morning.

Stayed Sunday night at the Biltmore Hotel in Providence. Went to Barnstable next day

*Part of the 'itinerary page'.*

White Mountains next day. Stayed there about three days. Then back to Marblehead.

Started for New York August 21st. Stayed at the Mohican Hotel, New London [Connecticut], overnight. Got to New York next evening at about

83

six. Stayed at the Plaza Hotel [facing Central Park from the south]. Left New York in about five days, for Springfield, Mass. Stayed at the Hotel Kimball in Springfield. Saw Smith College. That night stayed at the Bancroft in Worcester, Mass. Motored to Marblehead next morning [the 29th?].

Stayed Sunday night [2 September?] at the Biltmore Hotel in Providence [Rhode Island, south of Massachusetts]. Went to Barnstable [on Cape Cod,] next day.

Some time before the end of April, either at Rowley's suggestion or off his own bat, Faithfull did a tour of hotels where the private eye had drawn a blank. Masquerading as an investigator for a law firm (Rowley's?), he said that he was compiling a chronology for use in an action for breach of patent and asked to see the registers for the summer of 1923. The perseverance paid off at the Hotel Mohican in New London, where he found confirmation of the note in Starr's scrapbook that she and Peters had stayed there on 21 August.

Faithfull wrote triumphantly to Rowley on the last day of April 1927. By then, the lawyer had put the accusations to Peters – who, himself a lawyer, therefore a dedicated believer in the saying that a person who defends himself has a fool for a client, had asked a lawyer-friend, Alexander Whiteside, to act on his behalf. So far as Faithfull knew, all that Rowley had heard from Whiteside was that 'a full rebutting response [would] follow in due time'. Towards the end of his letter to Rowley, Faithfull urged him to 'retain the initiative' by informing Whiteside of the Hotel Mohican evidence at once:

> In view of the fact that AJP has been spoken to directly, it will give him a sense of security that no further action has been taken, which I feel is dangerous.

Whiteside's 'rebutting response', delivered to Rowley in mid-May, was to the effect that Peters agreed that he and Starr had stayed concurrently at various hotels, sometimes in adjoining rooms, but 'absolutely and categorically' denied misconduct with her, on those occasions or on any others.

There was further correspondence between Rowley and Whiteside, and the latter eventually conceded that Peters, innocent but anxious to protect his stainless reputation, might be willing to make an *ex gratia* payment in tacit acknowledgment of a written assurance that the allegations would not be aired.

The lawyers haggled. In the first week of June, Rowley, rather pleased with himself (and *for* himself, as he was working on a contingency basis − no fee whatever happened, but twenty per cent of any proceeds), told the Faithfulls that he believed that Whiteside would settle for $25,000. [1]

Mrs Faithfull replied on the 11th − or rather, she signed a letter composed and typed by her husband. She reckoned that the ultimate cost of trying to rehabilitate Starr would be greatly in excess of $25,000, and, seeking to justify the arithmetic, claimed that 'the expenses I have been under in the past ... amount easily to $15,000'. Then − maybe not meaning to suggest that Peters should be 'squeezed' by the threat of disclosure of the allegations to his wife − she mentioned, just in passing, that Martha Peters was rich in her own right, well able to afford to pay her husband's 'moral debt'. And then − maybe not meaning to suggest that a collection-box should be shaken at Martha's brothers, William and George Phillips, both tall pillars of society − she went on, as if assuming that Peters had responded to the threat of disclosure of the allegations to his wife by giving her a sanitised account of them:

This matter will be discussed among members of the Phillips family, who will get Martha's version. Therefore it seems to me that somebody should see William and George so that they will know the truth.

Rowley, replying on the 15th, but not to the maybe-unsuggestive bits of the ghost-written letter, was politely incredulous of the rest of it:

In view of the fact that Starr's education for several years was paid for, I find it hard to see how $15,000 has already been expended since the

1. Spring 1990: A 1927 dollar would now have purchasing power of about $7; therefore, $25,000 then would be worth about $175,000 now. (A 1931 dollar would, as a result of the Depression sparked off by the Wall Street Crash, be worth about $8.)

From 1927 till September 1931 (when Britain's suspension of the Gold Standard caused a 24% devaluation of the pound), the £/$ exchange rate was 1 to approximately 4.85. A 1927 pound would now have purchasing power of about £17 (a 1931 pound, about £19.75): very roughly speaking, $25,000 in 1927 would be the equivalent in Britain today of £85,000.

The only estimate of 1927 (and 1931) US earnings relates to production workers. In 1927, the average annual wage was about $1275 ($24.47 a week); by 1931, the average had fallen to about $1075 ($20.64 a week). In terms of current purchasing power, the 1927 wage would be worth about $8800 ($170 a week); the current average annual wage is about £22,000 ($420 a week) − which goes towards showing that few of the above statistics should be taken too seriously.

situation was discovered [a little over a year before] and she has been under treatment, but it may well be that you can show this amount.

Less politely, the lawyer referred to an obstacle raised by Faithfull in a phoned postscript:

One of the difficulties we confront is the statement of Mr Faithful that under no circumstances would any release of any kind be given. I do not see how you can expect any person to pay a substantial sum of money in settlement of a claim of any kind, whether it be a dispute over a horse or a more serious situation such as we are confronted with, without receiving some form of release against future claims arising out of the same matter.

A reply, signed by Mrs Faithfull, went off to Rowley by return of post. Not only did she stick by her husband's guns, but she closed the letter with a new threat − nothing ambiguous about this one:

I have definitely decided that the only thing to do is to take the matter up with the District Attorney here.

Two days later, on the 18th, Faithfull, writing as himself for a change, told Rowley that he 'heartily concurred' in his wife's decision to take the case to the local DA. He threw in another threat: to seek allies among Peters' enemies in his home-city. He gave an or-else deadline − as much to Rowley, whom he seems to have suspected of being a turncoat, as to Whiteside, proxy for Peters:

Mrs Faithfull and I expect to be in Boston in about ten days and until then we do not wish to give a decision as to what we are willing to do. As we have both told you, we are more interested in the moral than the financial aspect of the matter.

Then the punch-line:

We therefore wish to talk the matter over with a few prominent people in Boston who will not be biased in favour of Mr Peters, and then decide what to do.

The punch-line scored a technical KO. Well before the deadline, Whiteside made a firm offer of $25,000, and Faithfull, who must have known all along that he would have to give a release, said that he would. After some bickering between the lawyers − partly because Rowley wanted his cut to be paid direct to him (he did not express fear that if the full sum went to the Faithfulls, he would have the devil's own job getting them to part with twenty per cent of it) — they agreed on *two* releases, one for Starr's signature, the other for the signatures of her mother and step-father. Both releases were signed on the same day, the second of them reading as follows:

### KNOW ALL MEN BY THESE PRESENTS

that we, STANLEY E. FAITHFULL and HELEN MacGREGOR FAITHFULL, wife of said Stanley E. Faithfull, and mother of Starr Faithfull, of West Orange in the State of New Jersey, (said Starr Faithfull being of age and having executed a release of like tenor and effect to this one if not identical in form to Andrew J. Peters hereinafter referred to) for and in consideration of the sum of Twenty Thousand (20,000) Dollars paid to us and to said Starr Faithfull by ANDREW J. PETERS of Boston in the Commonwealth of Massachusetts, the receipt whereof is hereby acknowledged, have remised, released, and forever discharged, and do hereby, for ourselves, our heirs, executors, administrators, and assigns, remise, release, and forever discharge said Andrew J. Peters, his heirs, executors, and administrators, of and from all debts, demands, actions, causes of action, suits, sum and sums of money, controversies, agreements, promises, omissions, variances, damages, and liabilities whatsoever, both in law and equity, which against the said Andrew J. Peters we now have or ever have had from the beginning of the world to the date of these presents.

IN WITNESS WHEREOF, we, the said STANLEY E. FAITHFULL and HELEN MacGREGOR FAITHFULL, have hereunto set our hands and seals, this *30th* day of June, in the year 1927.

STANLEY E. FAITHFULL
HELEN MacGREGOR FAITHFULL

The release forms had arrived at the Faithfulls' home in the nick of time to save a long delay in their completion and return. An hour or so later, Starr left West Orange for Montreal, there to board a Cunard liner, the *Aurania*, for an escorted trip to Scotland and England.

She returned at the start of August — at about which time Faithfull received the settlement-cheque, enclosed with a note from Rowley, pointing out that, 'while made payable to your order, it is in the nature of a payment to you as agent for the benefit of yourself, Mrs Faithfull, and Starr'.

To remind you: that August was of 1927.

Three and three-quarter years went by.

On 4 May 1931 — just over a month before Starr Faithfull's death

– Alexander Whiteside received a phone call from a man who refused to give his name. He said that he represented a news agency, but refused to say which one. He said that he had heard that Andrew J. Peters, ex-Mayor of Boston, had paid a large sum to a young woman, Starr Faithfull, in settlement of a claim she had brought against him. Whiteside interrupted, saying that he had no idea what the man was talking about but that, in any event, he was not prepared to discuss named persons with someone who refused to give his own name, and hung up. Much alarmed, he rang Charles Rowley, told him about the anonymous call, and asked him to find out whether any of the Faithfulls had broken their vow of silence.

It appears that Rowley knew that the Faithfulls had moved from West Orange to Manhattan, that they were now living at 12 St Luke's Place, that they had no phone. He sent a telegram, asking Stanley Faithfull to call him. Faithfull, having done so, took umbrage at the idea, the very idea, that he or his wife or Starr might have been illegally indiscreet – and, flying off the handle, exclaimed a fresh accusation against Peters, adding that he had better watch out. He followed up the phone call with a letter:

> I have talked with Mrs Faithfull about our telephone talk and we are both utterly at a loss to understand how any newspaper has any knowledge of the matter you handled some years ago.
>
> As I told you over the telephone, a matter came up some months ago which has convinced us that AJP made some derogatory [remark] about Mrs Faithfull to his brother-in-law, Mr William Phillips, and we both feel that this must be corrected. Certainly AJP cannot think that we would allow any remarks of his to go unchallenged.
>
> I expect to be in Boston in the next few weeks and will let you know in advance of my going over.

Faithfull told Littleton that, though he *had* been in Boston, and more than once, in the past few weeks, he had not seen Rowley. So far as he knew, Alexander Whiteside had received just the one call from the mystery man. Littleton asked if the man had been in touch with him or any member of his family, and Faithfull, monosyllabic for once, said no.

The session in Inspector King's office ended and the three men returned to the Old Courthouse, where Elvin Edwards, who had meanwhile attended a Rotary lunch, awaited them. Having implored Faithfull please not to interrupt till he had finished, Littleton referred to his pledge of confidentiality, which Edwards indicated that he too would try to honour, and then outlined the confidential information. Faithfull had his say – apparently only to emphasise what he thought was important. Edwards – impressed, excited even, but outwardly only interested – thanked Faithfull for his help, told King to arrange for him to be driven home, and before Faithfull, not wanting to leave, left, asked him to stay at home for the rest of the day, in case his further help was required.

Once Faithfull had been removed, Edwards, no longer hiding his feelings, talked to Littleton. By the time King re-appeared, the attorneys had made a list of jobs that needed to be done at once. There would have been more than two items on the list, but the record of actions taken by King and his men during the rest of the afternoon refers only to those that brought results, and there were only two of those.

One was in regard to Faithfull's statement that, in the spring of the previous year, Starr had been beaten up by an unknown man at a hotel near Columbus Circle.

A detective phoned Bellevue Hospital, and with a speed that nowadays seems incredible, a file, the right file, was found. Ringing back, the finder of the file summarised some of its contents and dictated others:

The name on the admittance card has been changed from Marie Collins to Starr Faithfull. On the night of March 30, 1930 [a Sunday], an ambulance of the Flower Hospital was called to the Hotel St Paul, 40 West Sixtieth Street. The patient was found in room 48, in the presence of a middle-aged man who identified himself to Ambulance Surgeon Galbaski as her husband, Joseph Collins. The admittance card states:

'Brought [to Bellevue] by Flower Hospital ambulance at 10.30 p.m. Noisy and unsteady. Diagnosis: acute alcoholism. Complications: contusions on face, jaw and upper lip. Given medication; went to sleep. next a.m., noisy, crying.'

Attached to the card is a note of a statement made by the patient:

'I was drinking gin as far as I know. This is the first time I have drunk anything for six months. I had nothing until yesterday. I don't know how many I had. I don't remember. I suppose someone knocked me around a bit.'

The card shows that Helen Faithfull, the patient's mother, and her father [sic], Stanley E. Faithfull, came to the hospital on the morning of March 31. A statement by Mr Faithfull is attached:

'Nothing was wrong with her at 2.30 p.m. yesterday. I know of no reason why she was admitted here. I did mix one drink for her. Incidentally, it was pre-war stuff. She never drank outside since she returned from Europe last fall in late October. She has not had one drink outside the house.'

The last entry on the card reads:

'Parents insisted they take her home. She was discharged in their custody.'

While one detective was taking down that information, another was on the phone, seeking information about Francis Peabody Hamlin, the Cunard cruise director whom Starr, so she had told her mother, had met on the liner *Franconia* during the afternoon of Friday, 29 May. In conversation with Hubert Besse, the manager of Cunard's office in Boston, the detective learned that Hamlin was twenty-three; that he had joined the company soon after leaving school; that he was actually an *assistant* cruise director. He had been aboard the *Franconia*, seeing to the needs of passengers from Boston, during a cruise that had ended at Pier 56, Manhattan, on Thursday, 28 May, and would have remained aboard, doing post-cruise chores and helping the colleague who was replacing him, till shortly before five o'clock on the Friday afternoon, when the liner set sail for England. He had then taken a week's holiday – spending some part of it with friends on Cape Cod, the manager believed – and had returned to the office the morning before.

Hamlin stood out in a crowd, the manager said – physically because he was extremely tall, somewhere around six foot six, but also because he was so obviously of good stock. His father, B. Nason Hamlin, a prosperous and respected broker, with offices on State Street, was more widely known as a polo-player. Had the detective not heard of him? Because of the nature of young Hamlin's job, he was often away – and then often far away – from Boston; but between trips he lived with his parents at their fine house, 30 Highland Street, in the town of Dedham. (If the detective had heard of Dedham, it was probably solely in connection with the Sacco-Vanzetti trial; neither he nor any of the other Nassau County investigators knew that Dedham was where Mrs Faithfull had obtained her divorce from Frank Wyman. Indeed, at this stage none of the Nassau County investigators knew of any particular public incident in the lives of the Faithfulls before three of them took that name from the fourth.) Sounding even more impressed by young Hamlin's lineage, the manager said that he had been baptised Francis Peabody in tribute to his maternal grandfather, the General. Now, surely the detective had heard of *him?* Well, General Francis Peabody – who, between themselves had never been a full-time soldier, only a member of the National Guard, a brigadier-general of it from the minute he joined – had, for some forty years, from the late 1870s till the early 1920s, occupied an exalted position in Boston society and in the local Democratic party. Though he was a lawyer by profession – strangely enough, he had, as a youth, been sent to England to get a grounding in the law, and had been called to the Bar at Middle Temple on the eve of his return home – he had devoted most of his time, most of his extraordinary energy, to politics. Chosen as the Democratic candidate in the Boston Mayoralty election of 1895, he had been defeated by the Republican, Edwin Curtis. Twenty-four years later, Curtis, then the Police Commissioner, had, by his intransigence, provoked the police strike – and General Peabody, supportive of his old friend, the incumbent mayor, had assumed command of a battalion of volunteer strike-breakers.

The detective thanked the manager for his help, repeated what he had said at the start, that he trusted that the manager would not mention the call to Francis Peabody Hamlin, rang off, and typed a report from his notes. Some time later in the afternoon, a copy of the report, together with a copy of the report of the information received from Bellevue, was sent across to the DA's office. Elvin Edwards jotted a pair of exclamation-marks against the passages that indicated a possible link – tenuous, via a self-styled general – between a young cruise director and a middle-aged ex-mayor.

Early that day, Dr Otto Schultze, taking an indirect route to his place of work in midtown Manhattan, had stopped off in the grounds of Bellevue, by the Office of the Medical Examiner of New York City, to deliver to Dr Alexander Gettler the organs he had removed from the body of Starr Faithfull; he had outlined his autopsy findings to the toxicologist and asked him to give top priority to the analysis of the organs.

Gettler, who was in his late forties, was a native of Austria. He had been brought to America at the age of five. His parents, while remaining as poor as synagogue mice, imprisoned in the slums of Manhattan's Lower East Side, had somehow managed to support him as a student at City College. He later recalled: 'I thought I was going to teach, but when I finished City, I found that teaching in public schools was too dull. I decided to take more chemistry.' So as to afford a post-graduate course at Columbia University, to the north-west of Central Park, he had sold tickets for a Manhattan-to-Queens ferry from midnight till 8 a.m., six days a week. In 1910, only months after receiving his Master's degree, he had been appointed professor of chemistry at Bellevue, and five years later, by then a Ph.D, he had become the hospital's chief chemist. In 1918, when the Medical Examiner's Office was founded, he had joined Dr Charles Norris, the first Examiner, as his toxicologist. Since then, Gettler reckoned, he had investigated more than 25,000 deaths. Between times, he had done research on radium poisoning (work for which he had been honoured by the American Medical Association in the spring of 1931); and for other cases he had developed two tests – one, using a 'chart of inebriation', for estimating the effects of alcohol; the other, involving measurement of the respective amounts of sodium chloride (common salt) in the two sides of the heart, to establish whether a drowned person had died in fresh or salt water.[1]

Around tea-time on the Tuesday, some ten hours after Schultze's delivering visit to Gettler, he returned to the laboratory, having received a phone call asking him to, and Gettler related his findings and answered Schultze's questions about them:

*First:* There is no doubt that death was due to drowning and that the deceased was drowned in salt water.

Gettler added: 'It would have been impossible for the deceased to have drowned herself, or been criminally drowned, in fresh water, say in a tub, and then to have been tossed into the ocean. She drew salt water into her lungs, and the blood analysis shows that fact.'

*Second:* There is present in the organs a fair amount of Veronal, not enough to cause death, but enough, however, to have caused stupor or at least semi-stupor. The amount of Veronal found in the organs examined was 634.8 milligrams, approximating to 10 grains or two tablets the size of an aspirin pastille.

Gettler added: 'Veronal, a hypnotic drug, is taken to allay nervousness and to induce sleep. It is a drug that spreads quickly throughout the system. A normal does of Veronal is from ten to twenty grains. Death might follow the ingestion of forty grains, and anything above that would certainly be fatal. It is not possible to state definitely in the case in question how long before death the ten grains were taken. One cannot state how long such a dose of the drug would continue to affect a human being, beyond the

1 Research carried out since the 1950s has discredited the Gettler Drowning Test in cases where death has occurred more than twelve hours before.

generalisation that it would be effective for several hours. The drug might have been self-administered or forced on the deceased without her knowledge. Had she taken it unwittingly, the person who administered it would have had to put it in her food, for Veronal has a sour and metallic taste which cannot escape detection.'

*Third:* There is no trace of alcohol.

Gettler added: 'All traces of alcohol will not be dissipated from the system until thirty-six hours after the last drink – and that means thirty-six hours of life. If a person dies in the meantime, no matter if it is days before the body is found, the traces of alcohol will be there. They will not be dissipated after death, but will remain in the body. Starr Faithfull had not had a drink for thirty-six hours before she died. That you can count on.'

*Fourth:* There is no trace of any poison.
*Fifth:* The stomach contents contain 150 cubic centimetres of well-digested material. Period of digestion, about 4 hours. The following form elements are present: meat, mushrooms, potatoes, bread, fruit skin.

Gettler added: 'While death usually calls an immediate halt to digestion, there sometimes is a further fermentation of certain stomach juices, but this would cease presently, and it is possible to reach the conclusion that in this case the condition of the food mass within the intestines indicates that the deceased ate a meal from three to four hours before death. It is impossible to know whether the Veronal was taken before or after the meal.'
Schultze did not hear Gettler make a remark that would have confused him if he *had* heard it: that one of the five unequivocal findings still needed to be confirmed. Gettler did not include such a proviso in the report that he afterwards sent to Elvin Edwards.
Leaving the laboratory, Schultze drove to Mineola. On his way there, he probably passed a car taking Martin Littleton and three detectives to Manhattan, in rather excessive response to a phone message from the New York Police Department that a harbour-master had come forward, saying that in the late afternoon of Friday, 29 May, shortly after the *Franconia* had left its moorings, bound for England, a ticketless girl answering a description of Starr Faithfull in one of this morning's papers had been found aboard, and a tug had been sent out to bring her ashore.
Having arrived at Mineola, Schultze was sent from the police

headquarters to the Old Courthouse, where Inspector King was conferring with Elvin Edwards. He remained with them for an hour, till about seven, and then, politely refusing to speak to the same reporters whom he had politely refused to speak to upon his arrival, drove home. As soon as Schultze had left them, Edwards and King each made some phone calls. One of Edwards' calls was to the organiser of a gala dinner that was just about to begin, apologising that he, advertised as the guest of honour, could not come, another to his wife, telling her not to expect him home that night; one of King's calls was to the stenographer, Nathan Birchall, offering him an assignment at short notice for the second night running.

At eight o'clock, catching the reporters unawares, Edwards and King left the Old Courthouse through the tradesmen's entrance, got into a chauffeured car, and were driven away. After picking up Birchall, the driver set off for Manhattan. There may have been some quite sensible reason why, from when the car reached the main road on the western outskirts of Mineola, it was escorted by two motor-cycling policemen.

When the convoy arrived there, St Luke's Place was rouged by a sunset. The reporters – who, a minute before, had been slouched about the stoop of No. 12 – crowded around the car, and then, one or two of them having recognised Edwards from pictures of him that had appeared in their papers during the trial of Two-Gun Crowley, pushed and shoved to get close to him as he alighted from the car and climbed the steps of No.12 and rang the bell, keeping his finger on it after turning to face the photographers. Flash-lights tore the pinkness apart. King told the motor-cyclists to go back to Mineola. There was a shout of 'All right, I'm not deaf' from inside the house, and Edwards took his finger off the bell. Stanley Faithfull opened the door, staying behind it to avoid being photographed, and once Edwards, King and Birchall had entered, closed it. Having been told who and what Birchall was, he led the way up the two flights of wide, uncarpeted stairs on the right-hand side of the house.

At some time during the evening, Faithfull outlined the layout of the apartment to King. Let us assume that he did it now.

Facing the stairs, across the slight landing (above which was the trapdoor to the roof), was the kitchen; inconveniently beyond the kitchen – and at the rear of the building – was the bathroom-cum-lavatory. Making an L with the landing, a passage ran beside the stairs towards the front of the building. The room at the end of the passage was Tucker's; its one window looked out on to the Place, the park. The other front room, the largest room in the apartment, was the living room. The second largest room – at the rear, next to the kitchen and the bathroom – was the master bedroom. Sandwiched between the two large rooms, next to and only slightly wider than the passage, was the room that had been allotted to Starr. It did not, of course, have a window. There were doors in three of its walls: one to the passage, one to the living room (which could also be entered from the passage), and one to the master bedroom (which could also be entered through a side-door there). Starr's room was a dark cell with two too many doors.

Faithfull showed the visitors into the living room. There were no curtains on the windows. Both were wide open at the top, letting in a breeze from the west, salted by the Hudson River. Whenever the bright-striped canvas awnings were dented by the breeze, the iron supports creaked against their sockets. Every so often, there was the sound of a ship's siren. All the time, there was a drifted murmur from the reporters. A light, cupped by a Tiffany shade of green and grey glass, hung from the centre of the ceiling, which was painted white, as were the walls, the doors, the surround of the fireplace. The walls were patched with pictures – water-colours, some so faded that the foxing of the paper was more distinct than the subjects, and heavy-framed portraits in oil that no longer shone. The furniture, all of it old, some pieces old enough to deserve the term antique, rested on a patterned carpet that, being too large for the room, was doubled under at the side by the window-wall. The visible surfaces of the wooden furniture looked often polished, and there was not a speck of dust on the bric-a-brac and easeled pictures that stood on two console tables and on the mantelpiece. Only the ashtrays were grubby.

Faithfull seemed surprised, slightly vexed, when Edwards explained that the main purpose of the visit was to take statements from his wife and remaining step-daughter – each on her own, out of his presence. He left, and a moment later his voice could be heard, coming from Tucker's room. He returned with his wife, helped with the introductions, and walked out, leaving the door open. King closed it. Meanwhile, a scraggy black cat had sidled into the room, clawed itself on to the rose-patterned sofa, and gone to sleep.

Mrs Faithfull was tall and very thin. Her frock drooped from her shoulders as if from a coat-hanger. She had large, obtrusively knuckled hands. The dead-whiteness of her face and neck contrasted with the darkness of her eyes, which were deep-set beneath arched brows, the artificial red on her straight lips, and, particularly, the black of her mop of curly hair. She tended to hold her head to one side, the left, which made her look forlorn.

She sat on the sofa, and while the others found seats, toyed with the cat, talking nervously — saying that the cat's name, given him by Starr, was Peter ... Starr had found him lying injured in the street and brought him home, nursed him, taken him to a vet — who reckoned that he was seventeen — which meant that if Peter were a person, he would be about a hundred and twenty — amazing ... When Starr was small, she had had a dog called Bubbles — she had amused herself one day by coating him with butter ... Dogs were her favourite animals, but she had loved horses too, loved riding them —

Mrs Faithfull broke off. The men were seated by now, Edwards in the only armchair, King on an upright chair by the door, and Birchall, perhaps trying to be unobtrusive, on a Victorian nursery-chair that had Little Miss Muffet and the Spider embroidered on the back. He used his tilted knees as a lectern for his notepad.

Edwards began:

'What was your maiden name?'

'Helen MacGregor Pierce.'

'And your daughter Starr's birthday is when?'

'January 27th.'

'She was born in what year?'

'She was born twenty-five years ago. You can go back better than I can.'

Answering questions about Starr's friends, Mrs Faithfull said: 'I cannot tell you of any in this country. She had no gentlemen-friend in New York. And of late years, she had no intimate girl-friends.

'She had some very good friends in London. I can think of one whose name is Rudolph Haybrook. He is an artist. She corresponded with him.

'She had one friend that she was very fond of — Dr Jameson-Carr. He is British. It is a hyphenated name. He is a surgeon on board the *Franconia*. He is about forty-five, I believe. She went to see him the Friday before last, when the *Franconia* was here. When she came home, she said that the doctor had been terribly annoyed with her. I said, "Starr, you must have had a drink," and she said, "Yes, I did. But everybody drinks and I don't see why I can't ever drink." That was her answer. I understood from her that Dr Carr was not at the party when she had the drink. The party was at another place on board, but she saw him and he was annoyed with her for drinking, and she, in a moment of pique, or whatever it was, said, "Oh, well, I will see somebody else."

'She said that at that moment a man by the name of Hamlin, a cruise director, came along. These were her words – she said he said, "Well, who is Carr, anyway? Come and have a good time. There is a party going on upstairs." So she said she went to the First Officer's stateroom, where there were a number of people, and she said, "I met some very attractive people," and that was all there was to it. I asked her, "Did you meet anyone that you would feel that you could meet again?" She said yes. And I said, "Which of the men are you going to see again?" And she said, "Hamlin."

'During the following week, she told me that she had met Hamlin. The *Franconia* sailed on the Friday – that was the 29th. Wait a moment, I am getting my dates wrong. She spoke of meeting this Hamlin man again on the following Wednesday. I know she didn't meet anyone between the Friday of the *Franconia* sailing and the Wednesday because I know just what she did Saturday and Sunday and Monday and Tuesday. Wednesday she came in, and I was sure she had had a drink. She was not at all tight, but her breath gave perfect evidence that she had had something to drink, and I asked her where she had been and she said, "Oh, I met Mr Hamlin and had a drink." I asked her where and she said, "Oh, he took me to a studio where there was a party going on." Well, I thought that was very strange, but I was beginning to think everything was strange about that time, and I asked her what studio and she gave a name. Now, I know that she was not being truthful, and you don't want me to give the name because it would be just silly to give it.'

*Edwards:* 'Well, give it to us, because it may have some bearing on something else.'

'She said, "I went up to Harry Stoner's studio." He is a very well-known artist in New York, and I know everything about him is absolutely without fault. I don't believe she ever went to Harry Stoner's studio. She did know Mr Stoner. He had helped her to try to find artistic work.

'She drew beautifully, you know. She was terribly bored and longed for something to do, but her education had not been such that she could do any business thing. She went to Rogers Hall School and did the usual things that girls do when they think they are going to lead a life of society. She was frightfully anxious to work in some way and earn some money. At one time about – oh, it was certainly about five years ago – you don't care if I am not exact? – she took an art course in the Winold Reiss studio. I wouldn't say that she was at all art-crazy or anything like that, but she had a very good taste for art, and loved beauty, and I used to go to the Metropolitan Museum with her, and when we were in London we used to go to art galleries – we did that sort of thing a great deal. I don't suppose in this age mothers and daughters are much together, but we were together all the time.'

*Edwards:* 'How many times would you say you had seen her so under the influence of liquor that she might not know what she was doing?'

'Three times.'

'How old was she when she first drank anything – even a cocktail?'

'The first time was when she was, I think, twelve years old. She used to ride horseback a great deal with a gentleman in Boston.'

'Andrew J. Peters?'

'Yes. This is part of the thing which I think Mr Faithfull told you about, do you see? She was supposed to have fallen off her horse. She didn't really have any fall. It was only an excuse. She was taken back to his house and given something to drink. It happened on a day when he was going away for the summer, and nothing more was thought about it. In the following years, all I knew was there was something that was wrong. I mean, I knew it from intuition because of her very nervous condition. We found out about it when she was twenty, after we found out that she had been with this gentleman at the Hotel Astor. I don't think she was particularly fond of Mr Peters. I think she was – well, you see, she was such a baby. He was older than her own father. He had a terrific influence over her – far more than I ever had at that time. In fact, I had no influence over her.

'I think his influence had lessened by the time she was twenty. This is what I feel: that in her own terrible effort to square herself with her own feelings, and her own efforts towards life – and in some strange way to square things for *him* – she longed to get things right, and always felt that they must be right. I mean, somehow rotten things, if you are not rotten yourself, you cannot believe. Do you know what I mean? And so she always was fighting with the idea that rotten things that had happened were not so. For her, liquor was a sort of drowning force. As for her attitude to other men, she liked their companionship but she feared them – feared most of them, that is – feared that what had happened to her in the past might happen again.'

*Edwards:* 'Tell us about last Thursday night and Friday morning, before she left finally.'

'She came in about one o'clock that night. She was perfectly all right. I should not say that she had been drinking. When she had had quite a little to drink, her face relaxed, do you see, and she looked very young. It took the mask off. I asked her what she had done and she said, "Well, I haven't to be ashamed any longer. I have been to a speakeasy." She had never been to a speakeasy. She had never been to any place where she had had anything to drink. I mean, of late years. She thought that was a terrible reflection on her. I had influenced her not to go to speakeasies. My objection to them is on general principles, that you must be frightfully careful of the ones you go to.

'That night, she slept right next to me. Mr Faithfull was away in Boston. He returned next morning. That was the last morning. She got up quite early and was particularly sweet and particularly cheerful. And she got my breakfast and brought it in to me on a tray, and seemed unusually sweet and unusually thoughtful and unusually happy.'

*Edwards:* 'Was she careful about herself?'

'Very. Fearfully careful about her clothes. Her drawers were always in perfect order.'

'Was she a modest girl?'

'Fearfully. She was so careful that she would hardly go around in her bare feet. It was almost an obsession, her modesty.'

'The inference might be drawn that both on the *Franconia* and when she finally disappeared, she might have got tight and thought of committing suicide because she was blue at the world.'

'No, I should say that was the farthest thing from her mind. She never said anything about wanting to commit suicide. She never would have taken liquor to commit suicide because liquor to her was heaven, absolutely. Liquor was a relief. It was happiness for her. She showed that she was blue by being – by just not wanting to talk – by reading a great deal.'

'Did her sister and she get along fairly well?'

'Beautifully. Adored each other. Absolutely loved each other. They didn't often go out together because, you see, there was six years' difference in their ages. And they were of different types. I should say that Tucker has no complexes about things. She meets everyone perfectly easily.'

\*

Edwards thanked Mrs Faithfull for 'the openness of her responses'. At his request, she fetched Tucker.

'For a girl of nineteen,' Edwards remarked later, 'Tucker Faithfull is extremely self-possessed — very definitely her own person.' She appeared to be not quite as tall as her mother, but that impression may have been created by the fullness of her figure. Her jaw was fleshy, and there was already a faint crease, not the kind that comes from smiling, on either side of her lips, which were extraordinarily short, hardly wider than her ordinary nose, but made gaudy by her use of too much lipstick of too bright a red. Less unsubtle with mascara, she used it only on the lashes of her eyes — which were as dark as her mother's but not as deep-set — and, in a chestnut shade, to stress the straightness of her brows and the distance between them. Her forehead was high and rounded. She wore her hair in a simple style, combed from a parting on the left and crimped at the nape of her neck and over her ears. She had let the strange patch of white at the front grow long.

Edwards had expected Mrs Faithfull to bring Tucker in and leave, but he raised no objection when she resumed her place on the sofa and pulled Peter the cat towards her to make space for Tucker at the other end. She stayed silent, though there were times when she must have wanted to interrupt.

After putting a few formal questions to Tucker, Edwards asked: 'Were you and your sister quite fond of each other?'

'Yes, very. I have never known Starr very well, because I have been away at schools, you see, but this past year I have seen a great deal of her, especially last summer, when mother and I were with her in London.'

'This man Hamlin, did she ever tell you anything about him?'

'Never heard her speak of him until just last week. The Friday before, I saw her before she went down to the *Franconia*. Then I went away for the weekend. When I came back on the Monday — a week ago yesterday — I asked her what happened on the *Franconia*, but she did not want to talk about it at all. She just said that this Bill — Dr Carr — would not see her and that she had not had anything to drink before she saw him. Then she went up with the First Officer and there were a lot of people in his cabin, you see, and then she said, "Don't tell mother, but I got rather drunk." So I said no, that I wouldn't — because I knew mother knew it, because mother had told me that when she came back she had been drinking.

'She said that Hamlin had been at the party in the First Officer's cabin. It was sort of irrelevant, but she said that if he were ten years older, he would be just like Stanley. That is my step-father. She said Hamlin is frightfully proper, but he knows everyone in Boston. But then she said, "He is rather fun." That is absolutely all she said about him. But she did say that there was a Mr Jack Greenaway. She said he was tall, dark and handsome. I rather presumed he was not younger than thirty.

'A day or so later − it must have been Wednesday − she said she took Mr Hamlin around to Harry Stoner's; they just dropped in. I have never met Mr Stoner. She had been up to see him before, and he apparently is in love with Miriam Hopkins, the actress, and I don't know whether that is so or not, but Starr said he had a lot of pictures of her around. Starr went up there about one o'clock on the Wednesday afternoon. She thought she would get a job. She wanted to make some money from this Harry Stoner, and he just said she was pretty and he might be able to use her face some time. So she went up there, and he said, "Come on in, there's a party going on," and she said Miriam Hopkins was there, and Mr Greenaway, and a Mr Bruce Winston, an actor, and she said they just sat there drinking. I remember she said that Mr Greenaway was apparently quite crazy about girls. I know I thought he must be rather dumb because she said he said, "Oh, this is my girl," or something like that, before he even met her. She apparently told him she had a sister, because he said he was coming to town again in about two weeks and was going to bring a friend. She said she had had fun and was going to have more fun the next day.

'Mother and I, we were suspicious about this party because of Miriam Hopkins. If I had met a famous actress, I would have made some comment about her. Starr didn't say anything in particular about her.

'I guess it was the next day, Thursday, she was so drunk when she got back in the evening about six. She said she was going out again − going to meet Hamlin again. Wait just a moment, I have remembered something else: that Thursday evening when she came back, mother said, "Where are you going to meet this man Hamlin?" and she said, "I am meeting him at the Savoy Plaza [Hotel, on Fifth Avenue at East Fifty-Eighth Street − facing, across the Avenue, *The* Plaza Hotel]. I met him at the Savoy Plaza early this afternoon − ran into him accidentally." Mother thought that was very funny because she did not think a cruise director could afford to be at a swell place like that. Of course, mother tried to keep her from leaving.

'Well, then I decided that instead of arguing with her, we ought to try to sober her up. So we made some food, and then mother kept saying that she did not think she ought to go out, and Starr started to cry. She went into hysterics, and I took her in the bathroom and she was screaming, so I stuffed a towel in her mouth and threw some water at her. She took off her clothes and put on a pair of pyjamas, and the water soaked the pyjamas. It soaked her hair and everything.

'Well, a little later I said, "Now where are you meeting this man, Starr?" – just as if I didn't suspect anything – and she said, "At 54 West Forty-Fifth Street." I kept asking her as if I had never asked her, because I knew she did not know exactly what she was talking about. A little later I think she said she was meeting him at 45 West Fifty-Fourth Street. I think she got the two addresses mixed. After that, she sort of cried off and on, and I set the clock back. She was supposed to meet this man at 9.45, and I was hoping that if I set the clock back forty minutes, by the time she got up there he would be gone. She must have left here really about 9.30.

'She came back about two in the morning. I think she had had a little bit to drink, but not anywhere near enough to make her tight at all. I can remember vaguely waking up. She said – well, I was terribly sleepy – she said she had had a very good time, that she had been on a long drive to Fordham Road [in the Bronx] with Greenaway and Hamlin.'

*Edwards:* 'Did she say she was going to see them the next day – Friday?'

'No, she didn't mention that. Friday – Friday was the day she disappeared? I will tell you what she said when she went out that morning. She said to mother, "I may not be back until late tonight." She wanted to get out of the house because she knew there would be talk if she didn't. It was about 9.30, and mother said, "You don't want to start out now and stay away all day." Starr said, "I will telephone you," and mother said, "We haven't any telephone, and you have got to come home," and she argued about that and said, "I will send you a telegram," and then mother kept on talking to her and she said, "All right, I will come home."'

*Edwards:* 'Do you think she would commit suicide?'

'Why, I don't know. No, I wouldn't say so.'

'Would you say that when she was tight she might?'

'She might, I suppose. She would act rather foolishly when she was in that state. For instance, she would get up and say, "Tucker is the most marvellous person in the world" – that sort of thing. I know what she said to mother, the night before she drowned or whatever happened, she said, "Tucker is a good investment." '

'When she was sober, would she allow a man to put his arms around her?'

'No, she was the most self-conscious person. She was so modest that she wouldn't get out of bed without putting on mules. That is a fact.'

'In other words, a man would have to give her a couple of drinks if he wanted to pet with her?'

'Exactly. Yes. One time last summer in London, we went to some people's house, and there was a man there that she had known in London before. She had been there so much. He was quite drunk, and she was rather drunk but not very. I mean, she could walk perfectly and all that. The man would put his arms around her, and she would laugh and say, "You look so funny," and things like that. She didn't get at all serious.'

*Edwards:* 'You know about her troubles, don't you?'

'About Mr Peters and all that? Oh, yes.'

'Do you think that anyone had any grudge that they might have wanted to hurt her for?'

'Well, now, this is the weirdest idea. You don't suppose Andrew Peters could have had anything to do with her death?'

'Do you know whether Hamlin knew Peters?'

'He might. Starr said Hamlin knew everyone in Boston.'

'It is a strange thing to me, getting this picture of Starr, that she hadn't any girl-friends that she confided in.'

'Well, I will tell you what the thing was with Starr. I think this all goes back to Andrew Peters too. When she was at school, he used to come out to Rogers Hall, and the other girls would tease her about him. And when she stayed with the Peters family at North Haven, she fell in love with a man named Hamlin − but it was not the same man. I wish I could remember his first name. Paul, it may have been. Yes, I'm sure it was. He tutored the Peters boys, trying to get them into prep school. I saw a picture of him and I sort of remember he was dark and a modern type. Starr had the picture. I think she kept it hidden. Starr was crazy about him, and Andrew spoiled the whole thing. Mrs Choate and Mrs Hallowell were both down there, and there were these yachting races, and they would say to Starr, "Why don't you go with young Hamlin? Why are you with old Mr Peters?" But Andrew would make it so impossible if she didn't go with him. He would hurt her feelings by saying things about her, so she had to go with him. She was very depressed because apparently Hamlin did not fall in love with her at all, and he thought it was very queer about Andrew Peters.'

*Edwards:* 'Is that the only time you ever knew your sister to be in love?'

'Well, no, she was in love with this Dr Carr. She first met him three years ago last August. She took a trip on a boat going from Canada. Dr Carr was the doctor on board. She was drunk – no, she wasn't drunk, she was poisoned by liquor – and they called him in and that's how she met him. She had more or less regard for him ever since. I think he was very much in love with her for a while. When he was with her, she was very happy.

'She was very, very bitter about the way he behaved when she went to see him on the *Franconia*. That was on a Friday, wasn't it? I saw her when I got back on the Sunday night at 8.30. I had been over in Boston, and when I came back she was in bed, and I asked her about the *Franconia* thing, and she said she didn't want to talk about it at all then. But then she told me not to say anything about it, but that she did get very drunk. She wanted me to stick up for her, as she put it, to mother. She said she got on the boat and Dr Carr was at an actor's benefit luncheon. He got on the boat at three o'clock. She said she was sober, which I don't believe, when she went to see him. She opened the door and said, "Hello, how are you?" or something like that. And he said, "I am very angry with you for coming down here." And she said, "Well, that's funny, why?" or "Are you really?" or something like that. She said she didn't let him see how badly he made her feel. He told her that he never wanted to see her again, and she said, "Well, you never will see me again, and go to hell," and banged the door in his face. And then she went up to the officer's room and got drunk. When she told me she had said goodbye to Dr Carr, she said, "I am glad" – but I know that wasn't so because she wrote to him. Mother found pieces of an envelope. So Starr had not put him out of her mind. And she said she thought he would probably come down to see her when he got back again. I guess he will be in London now.'

*Edwards:* 'This trouble that might have been a scar as deep as your mother thinks – '

'You mean the Peters thing?'

'Yes.'

'I will tell you what I think. I think she could look back on it – she really had a very brilliant mind – and I think she could look back and see what she could have been if it had not happened.'

'And you think that might have embittered her, that she took that out in drinking?'

'I think probably yes. The strange part of it was, I don't think she knew very much about drinks. For instance, she wouldn't know cocktails like sidecars or old-fashioneds. A cocktail was a cocktail. It was – well, just something to drink. She couldn't drink anything straight.'

'Now, Miss Faithfull, let us get back to the Peters situation –'

'I think that is at the bottom of it.'

'Well, that is a fair assumption. He was a big man – big in her estimation in view of the glamour and the front page and all that?'

'Well, he was supposed to be very attractive in his way. I mean, in rather a brutal way. I have not seen him for about five years. He seemed very tall and very big, and was a sportsman and rode horseback. I know for a fact he used to give her these Havelock Ellis books, books about the psychology of sex, and make her read them out loud. In fact, he tried to make me read them when I was nine years old. That was his way of getting a thrill.'

'Do you know anything about the identity of the man she was with in a hotel when she was taken to Bellevue Hospital?'

'No. It was said that his name was Joseph Collins. All Starr remembered about that incident was walking down the street, and she remembered being in a taxi, and she said she remembered the lights, the flash of lights, as they probably went up Broadway. She said Collins was small and blond.'

'He might have been big and brunette. She might have wanted to keep away who he really was. Did she ever say anything to indicate that he might have known Peters?'

'No.'

'This is a question maybe I shouldn't ask you, but did you ever see anything in your sister that indicated to you that she had developed any unnatural side, as a result of her experience with Peters?'

'Well, no.'

'Did she ever want children?'

'I think she did, but she was ashamed of it. She never discussed such matters with me. Her modesty went even to that extent.'

'Well, you do know that Peters discussed such matters with her and got her to read books, and so forth?'

'Oh, yes.'

No doubt Edwards would have asked further questions if fewer questions had remained to be asked. There were still many questions to put to Tucker; some of the answers she had already given had raised questions to put to her mother; some answers from Tucker, and some from her mother, had raised questions to put to Stanley Faithfull. Altogether, far too many questions for now, with the time getting on for eleven, if Edward and King were to stick to the schedule they had planned before leaving Mineola. And so the questioning ended in mid-stream.

King and Birchall hurried to the waiting car. Not Edwards, though. Standing on the scoop, he raised a hand, quelling the reporters' babble, said that he had nothing to say at present, and then, when the man from the *New York Times* asked if he thought that Starr Faithfull had committed suicide, said: 'Do you think I'd be working like this if it were a suicide?' Unprompted, he went on to say, speaking at dictation speed, that there was no doubt, none at all, that the girl had drowned in salt water, but that various bruises among the many marks on her body were consistent with the suspicion that she had been 'injured in some manner and then drowned'. His theory, he said, was that two men had beaten up Starr somewhere in Manhattan and driven her to Long Beach, where they had put her on a boat, taken her out to sea, and dumped her, unconscious, overboard. Edwards – himself carried away, out of sight and out of mind of his opening comment – now made his theory sound like a fact by saying that he was 'positive' of the identity of the two murderers. Not yet finished saying nothing, he said, 'One of the men is prominent politically', but then, perhaps suddenly realising that he had said rather more than too much after promising confidentiality, he added, meaning to mislead, 'in New York City.'

The two-part statement, uttered with hardly a pause between the parts, set off a buzz of surmise that the prominent New York politician was the Faithfull's near-neighbour, Gentleman Jim. Understandably, since Edwards was thinking of an *ex*-mayor, Andrew Peters, he looked disconcerted, shifty even, when reporters shouted things like 'Do you mean Mayor Walker?' 'Don't you dare quote me as saying anything about *any* mayor,' he shouted back. 'Now excuse me, please – Inspector King and I are going to Boston.' He escaped into the car.

It travelled north, to a restaurant called the Tudor Romance, close to Grand Central Terminal. Edwards and King having alighted there, the chauffeur drove Nathan Birchall home. Edwards and King had a quick meal, and probably a reviving drink or two, then boarded the 'Owl', the midnight train to Boston.

## 3

The train steamed into Back Bay Station at a quarter to six on the Wednesday morning. As Edwards, dishevelled, and King, spick and span, stepped down to the platform, a crowd of reporters – some for the Boston papers, including the *Christian Science Monitor*, and the rest local correspondents for the New York ones – dashed towards them. And so did an outnumbered crowd of policemen, sent to the station on the orders of the Boston Police Commissioner, Eugene Hultman. The two crowds mingled, jostling, for a minute, then became distinctly two again as the policemen, hand-picked for the assignment on account of their fleetness of foot, sprinted ahead, sorting themselves into two-by-two formation, then made a circle round the men from Mineola, did an about-turn, and marched them bumpily through the crowd of reporters to the exit, where a police car was parked, its engine running, its path ready cleared by other policemen. The whole manoeuvre must have been rehearsed.

The minute the driver had his passengers, he accelerated away, heading west but with no idea where to go till one of them told him to make for the Parker House, a swell-elegant hotel which, being to the east of Boston Common, was in the opposite direction to that which he had taken. Executing a hairpin-turn, and very nearly a jay-walker, he started back, and was spotted as he did so by reporters chasing in cars and cabs. Those vehicles too made U-turns, giving the toppled or cowering jay-walker rather the appearance of a marker-buoy in a yacht-race, but were instantly impeded by a huge van that, having been too suddenly braked by its driver, now shouting rudely at the police car, had stalled. While the reporters shouted quite as rudely at the van, and the recovered jay-walker shouted more rudely at them, the police car shot along Tremont Street, next to the Common, turned right in the vicinity of the Granary Burial Ground, and came to a halt in the tradesmen's alley behind the Parker House. Edwards and King alighted gladly. Not wishing to seem ungrateful for the Boston police's protection of them from the press, they slunk into the hotel by a back way and registered, each for a single room, under assumed names.

In the couple of hours they had to spare, they washed and brushed up and took coffee and Original Parker House Rolls, made to a Pilgrim recipe, in their rooms. King phoned his office and Edwards phoned Martin Littleton. Edwards read the Boston papers. The Starr Faithfull case, reported on all the front pages, was the lead story in many, topping the latest from Rome about a squabble between Pope Pius XI and Benito Mussolini following demonstrations by Fascist students against a lay Catholic organisation that had suggested un-fascist remedies for some of Italy's ills; from Paris about yet another conference of heads of European states, excepting Germany, to work out how Germany might pay its war-debts; from Lima about the exploits of an expedition of American aviators in trying to take snaps of the till-recently-Lost City of the Incas, Macchu Picchu; from somewhere in Connecticut about the first public demonstration, in the hall doorway of the inventor's home, of an electric, pipeless, reedless organ 'with the soul of a robot but the colour of a symphony'; and from lots of places in America about sightings in the sky of 'great balls of fire', probably meteors. The Starr Faithfull stories were essentially similar to those in the first editions of the New York papers that Edwards had bought at Grand Central. Without knowing it, the *Boston Globe* had a sort of scoop, being the first to mention Peters in connection with the case: away from the main story, in a 'filler' column sketching Starr's family tree, the paper noted that 'The dead girl was related by marriage to former Mayor Andrew J. Peters'.

Shortly before eight, Edwards and King left the Parker House – by the back way, not surreptitiously but because the driver of the police car had insisted on waiting for them, and waiting where searching reporters were unlikely to look – and were driven to the Boston police headquarters by a giddying route, almost a complete lap around the Common, taking in the stretch of road skid-marked by the early morning U-turnings. The driver, determined not to be spotted and tailed by any reporters, drove at such breakneck speed that it was still shortly before eight when he pulled up outside the fortress-like building. All of the reporters were there. But so were sufficient policemen to hold a space apart from the kerb to the entrance – which, as the visitors scrambled from the car, was filled by a welcoming party of one, a man who seemed to be smiling from head to toe.

This was Michael Crowley, the sole superintendent of the Boston police since before the strike (which he had tried to avert and, failing, helped to break). Ostentatiously Irish, his brogue as thick as draught Guinness, he had risen through the ranks – swiftly from when, in 1908, then a sergeant, he had received lavish praise from the press for solving a murder case made specially newsworthy by the fact that the murderer, a chubby unsuccessful businessman named Chester Jordan, had packed the separated remains of his victimised wife, once a vaudeville performer under the name of Irene Shannon, in a trunk.[1] Superintendent Crowley's greatest attribute, which made him a treasure to the successive commissioners he directly served, was largely responsible for his worst fault: he was so successful at charming away wrath (it was said that hardly any citizen who came to him with a complaint left without contributing to the Police Benevolent Fund) that he felt perfectly entitled to brag of 'a high level of public satisfaction as evidenced by a low quotient of validated complaints'. He therefore did little towards making the force as satisfactory to the public as it wasn't.

He greeted the visitors, neither of whom he had met before – 'Great to see you, Elvin. You too, Harold' – then bawled at the restrained reporters, 'Now give the gentlemen a break, boys, if you please. I'm positive they'll be talking to you, all in good time', and then shoved the visitors through the entrance, across the marble-floored hall and into a vacant office which, interrupting himself, he told them to treat like home sweet home. Coffee and brownies were brought by a uniformed policeman. He left at once. A minute or two later, a man in plain clothes entered, was introduced by Crowley as Special Officer Mark Morrison, and poured the coffee, including a cup for himself. Once Crowley, munching brownies, was comparatively quiet, Edwards explained the purposes of his and King's visit.

Morrison took notes, but none of them gives the least hint of how Crowley reacted when Edwards first referred to Andrew Peters; or when Edwards spoke of Peters' association with Starr Faithfull, of the payment he had made to keep it secret; or when Edwards stated his belief that Starr Faithfull had been murdered by Peters, aided by Francis Peabody Hamlin, a grandson of a Bostonian almost as eminent as Peters – and with whom Crowley was also well

1. The case – similar in several respects to the Crippen case, starting in London two years later – is entertainingly recounted by Paul Whelton in his article, 'Twelve Parts of a Lady', in *Boston Murders*, edited by John N. Makris (Duell, Sloan and Pearce, New York, 1948).

acquainted. Crowley's strongest reaction would have been dead silence.

Edwards mentioned the phone call received by Peters' lawyer-friend Alexander Whiteside on 1 May from a man, speaking anonymously, claiming to be the representative of a news agency, who had sought confirmation that Peters had paid a large sum to Starr Faithfull in settlement of a claim she had brought against him. Wasn't it likely, Edwards asked, certain of the answer, that Peters, frightened out of his life by what Whiteside had told him, had decided that he had no choice but to eliminate Starr Faithfull?

Crowley demurred, saying that *likely* was too strong: he would accept *possible*.

OK, Edwards said, but what about this? Far more likely than not, Starr had drowned after falling − or being thrown − from a boat. Wasn't Peters an expert sailor? Didn't he own a boat? Mightn't he have sailed his boat to somewhere near Long Beach, and having put it to murderous purpose, sailed away from the scene of the crime?

Crowley knew how to answer the last question. He phoned an old friend, a retired Boston policeman now living on North Haven Island, and asked him to make some inquiries − quickly but, more important, slyly.

Soon afterwards − but still well before nine − Morrison was despatched to Federal Street, within easy walking distance, there to watch unobtrusively for the arrival of Peters at his office. He phoned Crowley at about ten to say that he had just spotted Peters. Crowley ordered him to continue the watch.

With Crowley listening on an extension, Edwards phoned the office. He told the woman who answered only that his name was Edwards and that he wished to speak to Mr Peters privately. The woman asked him to hold on. After a while, a man's voice came on the line. 'Am I speaking to Mr Peters?' Edwards asked. 'No,' the man replied, 'I'm afraid Mr Peters is not in the office at present.' Crowley mouthed: '*It sounds like Peters.*' Lip-reading that, Edwards started to be explicit, but got no farther than giving his whole name and saying that he was District Attorney of Nassau County, speaking from the Boston police headquarters, before the man interrupted, apologised for doing so, advised him to write for an appointment, and, while Edwards was trying to get a word in edgeways, wished him good-day and hung up.

Fewer than ten minutes later, Morrison phoned in again to report that Peters had just hurried from the office block to his car, parked in a nearby lane, and driven away at high speed. Crowley told him to hold on while he spoke to Edwards and King, then gave Morrison another assignment.

Fewer than five minutes later, Edwards received a phone call from Alexander Whiteside, who, speaking brusquely, said that he had 'reason to believe' that Edwards had 'endeavoured by devious means' – 'no, pray do me the courtesy of hearing me out' – to arrange an interview with Andrew Peters 'with regard to a recently deceased person, Starr Faithfull' (whom Edwards had not been given the chance to mention by the man at Peters' office). Sounding as if he were reading from a script, Whiteside went on: 'I am not Mr Peters' counsel. He does not need one. I am acting as his friend. He has assured me that he would be glad to give any evidence he had, but that he has none to give.' Edwards said, 'Yes, but even so ...' – no more than that because Whiteside had only paused for breath before launching into a lecture on an aspect of the federal system, viz. that a few exceptions, none applying in the present instance, proved the rule that a citizen of one state could not be compelled to give evidence in a case within the jurisdiction of another state. Having delivered the lecture, Whiteside snapped, 'I trust you now understand the legal situation,' and rang off.

Whiteside's call was almost immediately followed by a call from Crowley's friend on North Haven Island. He reported that, by chatting over a fence with a part-time gardener at the Peters' house, he had learned that Mrs Martha Peters and some domestic servants had been staying there since the middle of May, preparing the place for full occupancy throughout the summer. Andrew Peters had driven up from Boston late last Thursday and departed on Sunday evening, four days ago; indicating that Peters had slept at the house each night of the long weekend, the gardener had seen him leaving the house early on each of the mornings, dressed in nautical fashion and heading for the harbour. Crowley's friend further reported that, by chatting with old salts in the harbour, he had learned that Peters had messed about on his three-masted yacht, *Malabar VII*, for most of the Friday and the Saturday and from early morning till late afternoon on the Sunday. Peters had once or twice gone out on short spins, none longer than an hour or so, none far from the shore. Crowley's friend said that, rather than risk blowing his cover as a casual nosy parker, he had not tried to find out who had given Peters the help he must have had in sailing the vessel.

Edwards, still smarting from the ticking off by Whiteside, put a bold face on his sadness at the sinking of the Peters' yacht theory.

He had to admit, he said, that the theory had never held water. If Peters had used his yacht in aid of murder, he would have needed, not only one or two accomplices, but also a fair-sized crew of conspirators. But come to think of it, Edwards went on, he should have *expected* Peters to have an alibi. Peters, with a self-protective motive for murder, would surely have tried to protect himself from being suspected of the murder by having it done on his behalf when he was demonstrably elsewhere. Peters' instigation of the crime could only be proved by nailing his proxy and getting him to implicate Peters. Following the call from North Haven, Francis Peabody Hamlin had become – so it appeared to Edwards – a singularly important suspect. And what was more, now that Peters' nauticality seemed immaterial, Hamlin's occupation provided a further reason for suspecting him: as an assistant cruise director, acquainted with any number of professional sailors – Cunard employees, pilots, tugboat men – he was perfectly placed to choose, sound out, and recruit a mariner for a spot of murderous moonlighting.

As if on cue, Morrison returned from his second assignment, which was to visit the Cunard office on Tremont Street and invite Hamlin to the police headquarters, without explaining the reason for the invitation. Morrison had carried out the assignment successfully. Hamlin, saying that he guessed that this had something to do with 'the Starr Faithfull business', had come along at once and was waiting outside.

He was kept waiting a little longer. Meanwhile, Crowley jovially reminded Edwards of Whiteside's lecture on immunity, then called in a stenographer.

Morrison needed to stand aside from the doorway, else Hamlin's entrance would have been impeded. Hamlin was immense: wide-shouldered, barrel-chested, and towering to a height of six foot six in his socks. When he was wearing the light-grey trilby that he was holding in one of his ham-size hands, he took up more than seven vertical feet. The chin of his oval face, become fleshy, lolled over his neck and rested on the soft collar of his white shirt and the small tight knot of his green paisley tie; though the dark hair on his head, parted on the left, was straight, his large eyebrows were unruly. Clearly, he took trouble with the trimming of a moustache, brushed left and right from a scissored gap and shaved at the base so as to leave a line of white flesh above his protruding lips. He had on a dark-grey three-piece suit, the jacket double-breasted, with three buttons on each side. As is often so of large men, but still always unexpected, Hamlin's voice was rather high-pitched; he spoke in imitation of a well-bred Englishman.

Once Hamlin was seated and smoking a cigarette, Crowley, wanting written proof of his observance of the immunity rule, nodded to the stenographer to start writing, and said: 'Mr Francis Peabody Hamlin has been called to Police Headquarters, Boston, at the request of District Attorney Elvin N. Edwards, Nassau County, New York, in reference to investigation of an alleged crime that occurred in the jurisdiction of District Attorney Edwards of Nassau.'

After putting a few formal questions to Hamlin, Edwards asked him, perhaps with greater interest than his conversational tone suggested: 'I wonder if you know Sir Ashley Sparks, the head of the Cunard Steamship Company over here?'

'He knows *about* me.'

'His home is in my county – Nassau.'

'Oh, yes. I have been out to his house at his daughter's wedding.'

'You've read about this Starr Faithfull in the papers this morning?'

'Yes. I heard it over the radio first, and I said, "My gosh!"''

'I understand you met her on one of your working trips for Cunard?'

'I met her first in 1928: January 21st. That was on the *California*, down in the West Indies – a thirty-day cruise.'

'And when did you see Starr Faithfull last?'

Hamlin gave a lengthy answer:

'I saw her on May 29th, the Friday before last. I arrived on the *Franconia*, after a world cruise of five months, on the morning of May 28th, and got through the customs and went and cleaned up on board. And then, in the afternoon, I went to get my car out in New Jersey and drove back to Manhattan and went to a friend's house for cocktails and then I stayed at my aunt's house, 121 East Eighty-First Street, and then I came back to the ship the next day, Friday. It was the day she was to sail, she was to sail at five o'clock, and I went down to the Cunard office in the morning and came back to the *Franconia* about quarter past one. I drove up in my car and went down to the transfer company right next door on the pier to see if my luggage was there, and then went up the pier, No. 56, and I saw this girl standing by the entrance on B deck, pier side, right near the gangway, and I sort of recognised her.

'After I got through with helping an elderly lady aboard, this girl said, "How do you do, Mr Hamlin." She said, "My name is Starr

Faithfull. I made a cruise on the *California* in 1928." I said, "Oh, yes." She said, 'I am waiting for Dr Jameson Carr. He is a friend of mine. I have been told he is not on board." So I said, "I will see you down to his office," and went down to his office and knocked on the door, but there was nobody in. I went down to lunch – I have forgotten who I had lunch with – and when I came up again, she was still waiting. I said, "Haven't you found him yet?" and she said, "No." So I took her down to the doctor's office and knocked on the door. He was there at that time. I was back and forth, trying to help embark the new passengers. I went upstairs a little while later, and she came out of the doctor's office. She was crying. I said, "What is the matter?" and she said, "Well, he won't see me," and I said,"Probably he is busy or something – he may have a patient in there," and I let her have my handkerchief and she seemed kind of upset.'

*Edwards:* 'Had she been drinking at that time, if you know?'

'I don't think so. Not to my knowledge. I couldn't tell. I left her and stayed by the gangway-desk doing my work when new passengers came along, and I was back and forth, showing them to their cabins and trying to straighten out matters as much as I could. Then I saw her again, about three o'clock, and she said, "I feel awfully faint. Could you get me some brandy?" I said, "I don't think so, but I will see what I can do." So I helped her walk down the stairs, and there was one of the stewards there. It was Albert Jones, the chief steward. He said, "I've seen that girl before," and I said, "Yes, her name is Starr Faithfull." He said, "Oh, yes, she was on the *California* cruise with us." I said, "Have you got a drop of brandy? She seems faint." He said, "I will see what I can do." So the whole three of us went into his cabin. The doctor's office was right beside us. She said, "Thank you very much," and I said, "I will see you later," something like that. I saw her later, about 3.30, walking around the deck. She asked me to drive her uptown from the ship. I said, "No, I've got all my luggage, and I'm taking two other people up." That was about an hour and a half before the ship sailed, and I didn't see her again. I mean, I never saw her from that day. I got a letter yesterday from her father. It was posted on Sunday but I didn't get it till yesterday because it was addressed to the wrong address. I replied, apologising that I couldn't throw any light on Miss Faithfull's disappearance.'

*Edwards:* 'When did you leave the *Franconia*?'

'I stayed there until five o'clock, when she sailed.'

'What time did you see Starr Faithfull in the chief steward's room?'

'I would say roughly three o'clock. I didn't keep much track of the time.'

'Was she intoxicated at that time?'

'No, she wasn't when she went in there. She seemed normal in every way except she was upset and sort of faint because the doctor wouldn't see her. One thing I forgot: when I came upstairs — this is probably quite important in a way — she said she was going to jump overboard, or she felt like jumping overboard, or wanted to commit suicide. That was when she was weeping. I didn't take her seriously at all. I said, "Don't be foolish."'

'She was a very beautiful girl, wasn't she?'

'She was quite a handsome girl, yes.'

'What did you do that evening?'

'I was at my aunt's house. She is Mrs Clarence Mitchell. I was going to drive back to Boston in my car that night. It's a Mercedes — you can't miss it. I drove back, I would say, about two o'clock on the Friday night and Saturday morning. I gave a lift to a friend of mine, Harvey Manger, who had been on a cruise to Havana and Manila. I arrived in Boston about eight o'clock, I think, something like that. I went home to breakfast and went out to the Chestnut Hill Show and spent the rest of the day around Boston and Cambridge. I just pottered around on Sunday.'

'And have you been in Boston since that time?'

'Monday in the afternoon I went to the office, then went home for dinner. Then I went down to South Orleans, on Cape Cod, to stop with Mr Stanley Smith. He is a friend of mine. The phone number is Orleans 83, ring 2. I stayed there the rest of the week, until Saturday morning. I didn't do much. There aren't any horses down there. I played golf one day. On Saturday, I left there and spent most of the rest of the weekend with my father at his summer place at Dennis [also on Cape Cod — eight miles east of Centerville].'

'Have you been in New York since May 30th?'

'No, I have not.'

'When you met Starr Faithfull on the *Franconia*, did you introduce her to anyone other than the chief steward, Albert Jones?'

'I did not.'

'Do you know a Jack Greenaway?'

'No.'

'Do you know an actor-fellow named Bruce Winston?'

'No.'

'Do you know an artist named Harry Stoner?'

'No.'

'Do you know an actress, Miriam Hopkins?'

'I don't recall.'

'I will tell you exactly what I am trying to get at so that you will have a familiarity with it because you are going to be threatened a great deal with it, I'm afraid – by the press, I mean. One of the things Starr Faithfull told her parents was that she had been with you on the *Franconia* and at different times during the week following. In addition to that, she said that you had introduced people to her and gone with her to a studio, where there was a party, during that week. She said she went to a speakeasy with you and one or two men. Now, do you say that you have never been in a speakeasy with her?'

'I have never seen her from the day I saw her for a few minutes on the *Franconia*.'

'You are sure that you never took her out to dine, never had her out for a ride in an automobile, never introduced her to any men, never knew of any parties she was going to? You are sure of all that?'

'Absolutely. I will swear to it.'

So as to make one important question appear unimportant, Edwards set it within a series of questions:

'Would you mind if I ask you what your politics are?'

'To tell you the truth, I forgot to register when I was here the last time. I would probably register Republican and vote Democratic.'

'Do you know anybody in public life in Boston?'

'Well, my grandfather is pretty well known. He is General Francis Peabody.'

'Do you know the mayor of the city?'

'I once met Mr Curley when he came in on a ship. He went on the *Franconia* November 18th for a short cruise with Mrs Curley and Miss Curley and the City Treasurer. I met him then. I went up and told him who I was.'

'*Do you know any former mayors of the City of Boston?*'

'My father knew Mayor Peters.'

'Do you know any of the Peters boys?'

'No.'

'Did you ever visit Mr Peters' home?'

'No.'

'Did he ever visit your father's home or your grandfather's home, of your knowledge?'

'I couldn't say.'

'By the way, do you know what Peters' business is? Is he a lawyer?'

'I don't know. I know he was president of the Boston Chamber of Commerce.'

'Did you ever know any of the senators or any of the governors?'

'No. Leverett Saltonstall is my cousin. He is the Speaker of the Massachusetts House of Representatives.'

(Neither Edwards nor King knew that Stanley Faithfull's first wife, 'Miss Butterfield', had worked part-time for the Saltonstalls, usually as a secretary but also as governess of the infant Leverett; see page 27.)

*Edwards:* 'This is where it is embarrassing. Starr Faithfull was beaten up and either thrown overboard or held under water. The circumstances indicate that she was undoubtedly murdered. There was something foul about her passing. The case is of such great importance that if the police themselves didn't do anything, the newspapers would not let this case pass up because it has a tremendous human interest in the mystery part. I think your position is going to be rather uncomfortable for that reason.'

'I see.'

'I believe exactly what you say, but it is just one of those things – like slipping over something and breaking your leg, or have an axle on your automobile break, or breaking your neck. It is just one of those things that happen in life.'

'Yes, sir.'

'Do you know any Paul Hamlin?'

'There are several Hamlins around Boston.'

'There was a Paul Hamlin that Starr Faithfull was in love with about ten years ago. He was employed as a tutor. How much he reciprocated, we don't know, but there was such a man, and we'd like to find out where he is now.'

'I'll go down and ask my father in the stock exchange and my grandfather.'

Edwards, emptied of questions, looked at King to see if he had any. No. Crowley? Yes.

'Now, Mr Hamlin, a fellow on board a boat, in the sort of position you are in, you hear gossip. Who do you think was her best friend? You knew her pretty well? Did you ever hear of anyone that she was very friendly with?'

'No, I never took enough interest in her to find out who her friends were or anything about her. She meant nothing to me. I don't know of a soul.'

The interview ended. At Crowley's suggestion and probably with his help, Hamlin composed a statement for the press, which the stenographer typed and duplicated there and then:

> I have just talked with District Attorney Edwards of Nassau County, and Superintendent Crowley, and have told them all I know about Starr Faithfull, and am ready to co-operate with them in every way. I have told Mr Edwards that if at any time he needs me in New York, I will go to New York immediately. I will do everything in my power to help in any way I can. I knew the girl in a business way, but had no social contacts with her.

The reporters were let into the office. It appears that though they could not have failed to notice Hamlin entering the building with Morrison, an hour or so before, his very visibility had fooled them into disregarding him. Seeing him now, they shouted questions at him. He, 'smiling broadly' but saying nothing, handed out copies of his statement.

Edwards said: 'Mr Hamlin has told us frankly all that he says he knows about the case. He has given us valuable information. There is still considerable work to be done on the case in Boston.'

'Why Boston?' a reporter called out. And another asked: 'Yes, why did you come here, just after saying you suspect a couple of New York politicians?' And another: 'Have you talked to anyone other than Hamlin while you've been in Boston?'

'If I answered those questions,' Edwards said suavely, 'it would prevent the results I am trying to obtain.'

'Are you satisfied that Starr Faithfull was murdered?'

'I am satisfied that she did not commit suicide. Dr Otto Schultze is of the same opinion. Incidentally, I received a long-distance telephone call from Dr Schultze while I was talking to Mr Hamlin. The autopsy evidence indicates that some of the bruises on the girl's body were caused before death, and that the beating occurred within seventy-two hours of her death. Dr Schultze has told me that at no time was she in more than ten feet of water. The large amount of sand in her throat and lungs indicates that she could not have fallen or been thrown from a liner. She was probably held down under water by whoever was interested in her death. Remember, she was an exceptionally good swimmer. She was of a cheerful disposition.'

Saying that he and Inspector King were returning to New York 'to follow certain leads provided by Mr Hamlin', Edwards nodded to the reporters and began chatting with Crowley. Most of the reporters dashed away to phone their papers (all had been taken in by Edwards' pretence of achievement during the morning – none more so than the correspondent for the *New York Herald Tribune*, who had gathered that Edwards was 'leaving Boston laden with fresh clews'); the rest went to the main entrance, waiting to collar Hamlin when he emerged. Edwards, who had thanked Crowley in front of the press, said thanks again, turned down the offer of transport, and having summoned King, who was in discussion with Morrison, walked to the Parker House. There Edwards made one phone call, King another.

Edwards' call was to the manager of the Boston branch of the Burns International Detective Agency, asking him to come to the hotel at once, which he did. Edwards gave him two assignments, stressing that they had to be carried out quickly and quietly, and saying that there would probably be more. (There is no information as to whether or not Edwards had told Crowley that he intended to hire private investigators.) The first assignment was to check Francis Peabody Hamlin's alibi for the previous week; the second was to trace the *Paul* Hamlin whom, according to Tucker Faithfull, Starr had met when he was tutoring some of Peters' sons, and fallen in love with. (The separate inquiries continued – with a report and a tally of expenses being mailed to Edwards each day – till 2 July, when the manager, who signed himself 'X-48', stated that 'Boston Investigator S-55' was sure that the alibi was 'rock-ribbed', and Edwards decided to call off the other inquiry, since none of the score of Paul Hamlins tracked down by 'Boston Investigator L-48' had proved to be the right one.)

King's call was to the detective bureau at Mineola. He gave instructions for a cable to be sent to Scotland Yard (telegraphic address: HANDCUFFS, LONDON), asking for statements to be taken from Dr George Jameson Carr, Albert Jones, the chief steward of the *Franconia*, and other members of the crew who had seen Starr Faithfull in the afternoon of Friday, 29 May. He also asked Mineola if there were any developments at that end, and was told of several but of one in particular – not only the newest, only just heard about in the detective bureau, but also apparently the most important. It caused him to speak to Edwards and then give the order that the Faithfulls were to be collected that evening and driven to Mineola.

An hour or so earlier, around eleven o'clock on this Wednesday morning, Detective Joseph Culkin had arrived at St Luke's Place. You will recall that Culkin was one of the two detectives who had accompanied King to Long Beach following the discovery of the body, two mornings before.

Pushing past the reporters, he mounted the stoop of No.12. The front door was wide open. He pressed the top bell before walking into the hall and up the stairs. Mrs Faithfull was on the landing. She was wearing a frock of grey chiffon which, in the dim light, looked misty. Mistaking Culkin for a reporter, she cried: 'Please go away. My husband and daughter are both out. I have nothing to tell you. You and your kind, you only want to believe lies.'

Culkin showed his badge, and she apologised for her rudeness, excusing it by saying that she was feeling particularly depressed since a reporter had barged into the apartment and asked her to comment on a remark allegedly made by her ex-husband, Frank Wyman, who had arrived in Manhattan from Maine, where he was now working, as a vice-president of a company trying to promote Sugar Island, on Moosehead Lake, as a holiday resort. According to the reporter, Wyman, interviewed at his hotel, the Biltmore, had said, 'There is dementia in my former wife's family.' Mrs Faithfull had shouted at the reporter, 'That is a downright lie.' Repeating that rebuttal to Culkin, she added that Stanley would certainly sue Wyman for slander. (When Wyman heard what he was supposed to have said, he insisted he had said nothing of the sort: 'Of course there is no trace of mental maladjustment in the family line. As for my daughter Starr, she was a perfectly normal girl. I can't believe she killed herself, and can only think that she met with violence. My heart goes out to the family.')

Culkin explained that the purpose of his visit was to examine Starr's room, and Mrs Faithfull indicated the nearest of the three doors to it and wandered away, muttering irritably.

Culkin switched on the only light in the tiny room, a parchment-shaded lamp on a low chest of drawers which, with a mirror hung above, served as a dressing table. The directed lamplight glistened on a few phials of perfume and jars of cosmetics, and on an arranged cluster of pottery items – birds, dogs, horses, elves, and tiny jugs, souvenirs of places visited. Opening the drawers, Culkin found them tidily crammed with blouses, jumpers, underwear. On the floor beneath the chest were two rows of shoes, some in need of mending. On the side of one blue-sateen evening shoe, scuffed at the toes and heels, was what looked like a two-name signature, written with an indelible pencil – 'Vincent-something' was all that Culkin could make of it. A bed-couch, made up and draped with an orange-coloured candlewick spread, took up half the room. Starr had used a tall cupboard as a wardrobe; the frocks and coats were so tight-packed that Culkin, after frisking the pockets (all were empty), had to push and shove to make the door stay shut.

A bookcase stood against the only stretch of wall left that was long enough for it. The four shelves held, besides books, a pile of theatre programmes, a cabinet-clock that had stopped at ten past five, a plate commemorating Lindbergh's solo aeroplane flight, the first, across the Atlantic, more bits of pottery, and a glass globe filled with dried flowers. The books were of several kinds: collections of poems by Milton, Kipling, Tennyson, Christina Rossetti; novels by Galsworthy, Hugh Walpole, Sherwood Anderson; mystery tales; and textbooks, including one by Havelock Ellis (whose name meant nothing to Culkin).

When he sat on the side of the bed, the bookcase was in front of him, the top shelf at his eye-level, and so close that he did not need to lean forward to pick up the theatre programmes. He riffled them, thinking that he might find something tucked away. Perhaps he noticed the titles of some of the shows that Starr had seen – *Wonder Bar, Fifty Million Frenchmen, Earl Carroll's Vanities of 1928, Hello Daddy, The Truth Game* . . . As he slid the programmes back, he noticed that the spines of two books, side by side in a close-fitting line, were chipped at the top, as if both had often been carelessly pulled out. One of the books was a collection of poems by Tennyson, the other a mystery tale, *Behind Locked Doors* by Ernest M. Poate. Culkin pulled them out. He saw, at the back of the space he had made, the top of another book, resting on its spine. He pulled that out, too.

It was a feint-lined notebook, six inches by four, bound in a card cover faced with silk that, originally red, had faded to pink. It had been used as a diary – by Starr, Culkin soon realised as he turned the 32 pages that contained entries.

The diary began on 1 September 1926 with an entry noting that that was the day of Starr's return from her first trip abroad, to the Mediterranean, and continued, with many days unrecorded, till 24 June 1927, which was when she had set sail from Montreal for a group tour of Scotland and England: 'I took a walk and bought some stuff at a drug store. I'm certainly happy right now. Drove to the ship, the Aurania, with Miss Gilbert [an escort]. She's a typical professor*ess* – *ass*. Oh, baby, I'm excited. Got drunk with the Wright boy whose every sentence is "as a matter of fact" & Ed Lillie who keeps saying "I can't handle it". I got horribly drunk.' The dozen following pages were missing, torn raggedly from the binding. Presumably there had been entries on those pages, for the next right-hand page began with an entry for 1 September 1927. From then on, however, the entries were sporadic, often months apart. The last of them, written on 3 January 1929, was the shortest of all:

*'God damn our house.'*

Culkin probably searched to make sure that nothing else was hidden behind the books on the shelves. He may, before leaving the apartment, have told Mrs Faithfull of his find and that he was taking the diary away. Perhaps because he was excited, he neglected to hide his find as he ran down the stoop and towards his car. The reporters, converging on him, shouted questions, progressing from 'What have you found?' to 'Is it a diary?' to 'Is it *Starr's* diary?' to 'It *is* Starr's diary, isn't it?' The absoluteness of Culkin's silence convinced the reporters that they were right. Within a couple of hours, the news that a diary had been found appeared in all of the New York papers that were published, one edition after another, throughout the day. (Although, in the evening, Edwards confirmed the assumed news, he refused – and subsequently stuck by the refusal – to allow any of the diary-entries to be made public. Some reporters decided that since no one knew what was in the diary, it was safe to invent entries; the DA might say that the entries were hogwash, but he could only prove that comment by revealing the entire contents of the diary. Several of the specially sensational inventions cropped up concurrently in different papers, which indicates that they were created collaboratively, on the basis that a shared ersatz scoop was better than none.)

Culkin drove to a call-box and phoned his headquarters. It was during Culkin's return to Mineola that Inspector King phoned from the Parker House and, hearing of Culkin's find, gave the order you know about.

And so: in the early evening, while Edwards and King were being driven from Grand Central to Mineola, another Nassau County police car set off for Manhattan to collect the Faithfulls and deliver them to the DA's office.

Martin Littleton awaited Edwards and King. He too had had a tiring day: he had spent the first part of the morning at Cunard's Manhattan office, gathering information about happenings on and near the *Franconia* before and soon after its departure, and the second part at the Brooklyn Navy Yard, interviewing Coast Guards about currents and tides in the Lower Bay, south of Long Beach. He had then driven to Long Beach, where, in conference with Detective Sergeant Thomas Walsh and other local policemen, he had been told that (1) every hotel, speakeasy and restaurant on the island had been visited but without turning up anyone who claimed to have seen Starr Faithfull at any time, let alone during the three days before the discovery of her body, (2) regular beachcombers had been interviewed, and the southern shore searched from end to end on two occasions, but without finding anything that seemed likely to have belonged to Starr. Even so, Littleton had stowed a sack of beachcombings in his car before driving to Mineola, where he had spoken to Culkin, taken the diary from him, and spent the rest of the afternoon reading it and transcribing certain entries.

Soon after Edwards and King arrived, so did Dr Schultze. It is not clear whether he was expected or simply dropped in on his way home. But he stayed on to listen to the questioning of the Faithfulls (who presumably were given the assurance that he would not reveal anything they said).

Since Edwards had only skip-read the diary by the time they were ushered into his outer office, he told Littleton to do the questioning. He had read enough to know that some of Starr's comments about members of her family would embarrass one or two or all three of them; therefore, he probably said, as if thinking aloud, that Littleton would not, of course, quote such comments – among many others, were these (which, as they were scattered throughout the diary, are given in chronological order but without dates):

I did millions of exercises tonight, in which time I had a fight with Mother who beat me over the head with a towel when my feet were in the air. She lost her little temper.

Stanley did not kiss Mother goodbye this morning. She was frightfully relieved.

This is the dumbest family – row – row. Stanley's pathetic & sick, Mother's pathetic, Tucker's vicious.

Here is a typical Sunday. Get up – breakfast – 'Will you dance with me, Tucker?' 'No.' 'Oh, Stanley, *how* soon are we going driving?' Wait about 5 or 6 hours for Stanley to dust the car and get it out of the garage – start out driving – wait at a gasoline station.

*I hate Mother.* God, and I hate every damn fool in this damn house.

Stanley was dumb this morning. Mother I think can't stand him much longer.

I think Mother is going religious. Her visit to Boston has made her so religious. I have a horrible feeling that she is going to buy me a bible. There is nothing I hate like religion in the conventional sense. I believe I shall go *mad!* Mother is so tense & queer & Stanley is HORRIBLE. I can't bear it !

Stanley's a goof! Mother & Tucker & I were saying his deal at cards was slow & we listened at the door while Mother blew it in to him.

My family get on my nurves [*sic*] tonight – Tucker especially. Stanley is coughing – the poor, weak, helpless fool – and Mother's very irritating . . . This is the most damnable place.

I certainly am a temperamental person. Yesterday I was depressed, & tonight, after a *rough* fight with Mother & lots of nasty Epsom Salts, I am wildly happy. On the way into town today I really thought seriously of taking a job on a ship because Mother was so *dumb*.

Tucker and I don't seem to have a damn thing in common. We act exactly like two frigid people who have known each other a short time & don't like each other.

Oh gosh, how I do hate Stanley! Ugh, pew!!!

Starr's nasty remarks far outnumbered her affectionate ones:

Tucker is a *knockout*. When she is herself she is the sweetest, cutest thing in the world.

Mother is a peach!

Stanley is very nice tonight. I like him now very much.

King left the office, and eventually returned with the Faithfulls. Meanwhile, he asked them to look at the offical beachcombings, which had been laid out on a table. None of the things was Starr's, they said. Tucker turned up her nose at the garments and carelessly declared that Starr 'would not have been seen dead in any of them'.

Littleton began with some general questions. All three of the Faithfulls said they had known that Starr was 'an occasional diarist'; they had not known that she had a hidden diary; she herself must have torn pages from it. Stanley said that he had told the truth the day before: Starr *had* asked him to destroy two diaries, and he had done so uninquisitively. Littleton then made a point: as the hidden diary started in September 1926 and petered out in January 1929, 'one may assume that the diaries consigned to the flames covered periods before or after those dates'. Stanley agreed.

Littleton turned to questions raised by the entries. The time was around half-past seven. The questioning continued till midnight. Yet Littleton's report, written the following day, mentions only three matters about which the Faithfulls gave information.

You know that the diary began on the day of Starr's return from the Mediterranean cruise; you will recall that she had set sail on 1 July 1926, two days after the 'Astor incident'. The first entry contained the sentence, 'Am already missing H.M.' Mrs Faithfull answered Littleton's question: 'H.M.,' she explained, was an Englishman, Herbert Miller, who had been the cruise director. She might be wrong, but it was her understanding that Miller was no longer employed by Cunard and was working somewhere in the Far East (she was proved right: inquiries revealed that he had been a salesman in Bombay since 1929). She said that Starr had 'become quite fond' of Miller during the cruise. Littleton does not seem to have queried the degree of fondness, though subsequent entries indicated that it was considerably higher than quite:

> *2 September 1926.* Oh, God, about tomorrow – I love H.M. like hell. I'm all set to commit suicide if he won't see me. He'll see me – I will see to that BY GOD!!!

> *3 September.* God, what a time! I have been sobbing all morning. At last, after Mother's talking to him and me talking and raging, he said he would meet me. We talked for 2 hours. We have said goodbye forever.

> *22 September.* I hate tonight. Everything is very negative and gloomy and I long so for H.M. Oh, God, if only he lived in N.Y. and wasn't married!!

> *23 October.* I'm in the queerest state! I adore H.M. and I'm beginning to have another crush on Edwin.

Edwin. That name appeared in several previous entries. And it appeared more frequently from now on, lastly on the left-hand page (June 1927) before the gap where a dozen pages had been torn out. While questioning the Faithfulls about Edwin, Littleton quoted some of Starr's references to him; but rather than cause embarrassment, and perhaps provoke a row, even a split, between Stanley and his wife, he steered clear of early references, the first of which was in the very first entry, following 'Am already missing H.M.':

> Was met by Mother, Tucker [who was just fifteen] and Stanley on Pier 54. Then Tucker and I went up to see Edwin. Tucker has a VIOLENT crush on him. So has Mother.

*7 September.* Tucker and I went up to see Edwin. Tucker was frightfully nurvious [*sic*] and kept sending me out. She is desperate over him — God, how I could sympathise with her.

*24 September.* . . . This afternoon I was up at Edwin's. I told him the one thing in the world that I wanted was *love*.

*6 October.* I gave it to Stanley tonight (coming home from the movies in the car). I gave him some dirty digs (I'm afraid that it 'went in one ear and out the other'). I'm advising Mother to have an affair with Edwin to break the monotony of her life. I hope she plays up.

*8 October.* Mother has gone into New York to see Edwin. She looked perfectly wonderful . . .

*15 October.* Such excitement, my dear! It's half past six & Mother, who has gone to Edwin's, just called up & said she mightn't be home for a long, long time & that she was at Edwin's studio. OH, BOY! Stanley made me so damn sick — he spoke to her and said 'Take a taxi right away, dear, and I will meet you'. He's nurvious as a witch. He's so jealous of Edwin.

*16 October.* Poor mother was so desperate last night she nearly committed suicide.

The Faithfulls, all ostensibly unaware of those entries, told Littleton that Edwin's surname was Megargee. He was an artist who specialised in portraits of pet animals, particularly dogs, and more particularly Scotch terriers, a breed which he, as president of the Scotch Terrier Club, judged at many shows, some at Madison Square Garden. Early in 1926, when he was about forty, he had met Starr at a dancing class, she had introduced him to her family, and he had become a family friend (Littleton, hearing that, may have thought that, as family friends went, Megargee had gone farther than most). The friendship had lasted till the start of 1928, since when the Faithfulls had never seen him. But Mrs Faithfull said that, come to think of it, she had an idea that Starr had mentioned him, may even have spoken of having met him, during the week before her disappearance. When the Faithfulls had known him, he lived with his mother and a sister at 16 Garden Place, Brooklyn, and kept a studio at 41 Union Square, east of Greenwich Village.

*Extracts from entries made during the first fortnight of December 1926:* I'm an awful joke because I'm nearly *21* and have no beaux. It's really getting to be almost funny, although not in the least funny to me . . . I'm all unstrung and depressed & nurvious and shivery. I saw Dr Garretson from 10 to 12:15. He said I had an inferiority complex, also that I seemed blasé and world weary ... I am going to see Edwin tomorrow ... I have curious dreads & I get them all of a sudden. Tonight I thought how *horrible* it would be to get old and die. I have decided I shall *never* get old – I am going to be like Mother & Cousin Eliza ... I have reached a crisis in my life! I have written to Edwin a long letter of how much I love him, etc. I met Mother after seeing Dr Garretson and telephoned up to Edwin's. Finally I took the elevated up there. I wasn't wanted ... I drew out $50 for Xmas shopping. Why hasn't Edwin called up?

*15 December.* I'm poignantly crazy over Edwin. I finally went up and stayed about 5 minutes. He was nice and polite, only not a bit the way he used to be. In fact he made me feel rather like an excrescence. The last time he was affectionate was over a month ago. I will get him back or die. Ohh!

*24 December.* I called up Edwin tonight. I thought of our poignant days together last Spring. I'm homesick for last Spring. It was then that he taught me how to kiss.

*17 February 1927.* I haven't written for several days, that is since Edwin has been here. I went from Ned Wayburn's [dancing studio, Manhattan] to Edwin's and we came out here together. When we got here we had cocktails and I got extremely lit. Edwin, *much* to my surprise, refused drinks. Edwin has very *crude* manners. His table manners are very bad, and he didn't, when leaving, say anything about having a pleasant time.

*24 February.* I saw Edwin, who seems to enjoy kissing me once more again. I drink long life to his enjoyment!

*3 March.* Oh God, what a life. I'm *so* fed up with never seeing a damn soul or doing a damn thing. No wonder I'm depressed. I literally thought I'd die after I called Edwin up and he said he couldn't see me.

*17 March.* I went up to see Edwin who looked adorable and was awfully nice. [*Definitely not quoted by Littleton:*] He told me I was a more kissable person than Mother or Tucker. *Quite* thrilling and a subtle compliment.

*29 March.* I wonder when Edwin will call up. If all goes well I'm going to stage an affair with him -- a second one, rather.

*2 April (Saturday).* I went up to Edwin's and I can't repeat the object and result of my call because I'm afraid someone will read this diary. All I will say is I'm looking forward to Thursday.

*3 April.* I told Mother of what happened Sat. Edwin said 'Alright, kid' when I kept offering to stay overnight at his studio & I never would have suggested staying on *all* night if I'd thought he would take me seriously.

God knows what will happen Thurs. Mother said she had no use for Edwin.

*6 April.* Tomorrow is the day, for tomorrow night is when I have my rendez-vous with Edwin.

*7 April.* (Thursday – but written on Friday.) I am sort of dazed, doped & shaky.

*8 April.* I sure do feel jaded now and dizzy & funny. Mother says she's glad it happened and that I was a good sport. I think an awful lot about it, and I have a longing to see Edwin.

*14 April.* Edwin has fallen for me at last *really*. He seemed anxious to spend another night of love.

*20 April.* Mother & I had a talk about babies and how careful one has to be and a lot of blah I don't like to write about.

*27 April.* I told Tucker a little about my times with Edwin, and the result is I feel *furious* with myself for having told her.

*8 June.* I went to Dr Garretson's & cried, which fact seemed to touch him a lot.

*10 June.* . . . I went to lunch, movies & to the Chink restaurant with dear Edwin, who is looking forward to going to a hotel with me.

*17 June (Friday).* Lots of excitement. I'm sailing next Friday from Montreal [on the escorted trip to Scotland and England] & go to Montreal Thursday. I saw Edwin this afternoon and I'm going to see him again tomorrow.

*21 June.* At 6 I saw Edwin . . .

*22 June.* I hope I don't get a reaction. I'm so extraordinarily excited and happy – and *worked up*!! Evening 10 o'clock – I got a reaction today. I never got so morbid & fearful & shuddery in my life. I got an awful fear of everything.

*24 June: The entry beginning 'I took a walk and bought some stuff at a drug store,' and containing the reference to the escorting Miss Gilbert, 'a typical professoress (ass).'*

When Littleton first asked about Starr's sexual relationship with Edwin Megargee, Mrs Faithfull said that it was 'not a true affair', which Littleton took to be an understatement, similar to her estimate of Starr's fondness for Herbert Miller. But he was wrong.

Stanley helped his wife to explain. Tucker was silent. Perhaps the explanation was as surprising to her as it was to Littleton; to

Edwards and King; to Schultze. Perhaps Schultze's surprise blended
into contempt for a doctor named Garretson.

The explanation was this: while Starr was on the Mediterranean
cruise, Mr and Mrs Faithfull had discussed what she had said about
Andrew Peters, and had decided that she needed psychiatric help.
For some reason (which Littleton did not ask them to give), they had
waited till December, more than three months after Starr's return
from the cruise, more than five months after the 'Astor incident',
before arranging for her to see Dr William Van Pelt Garretson –
'one of the most eminent alienists in New York,' said Stanley – at
his office on the corner of East Fifty-Fourth Street and Fifth
Avenue. Following further sessions, Garretson had summoned Mrs
Faithfull to a private meeting and advised that Starr would be best
helped 'by arranging for her to experience a normal sexual relationship'. Acting on that advice, Mr and Mrs Faithfull had approached
Edwin Megargee, who had agreed – if not like a shot, then without
much hesitation – to have intercourse with Starr, deceiving her
away from the slightest suspicion that she was undergoing therapy.

Littleton did not ask Mr and Mrs Faithfull to amplify the
explanation. He may have thought that the bare facts they had given
were enough to be going on with, at least until Dr Garretson and
Edwin Megargee had had their respective says.

So far as one can tell, Littleton did not quote any of a few diary-
entries of the early months of 1927, before Starr's first 'rendezvous' with Megargee, concerning two teachers, one of dancing, the
other of art:

Jack, my instructor at Ned Wayburn's, certainly did *spoon*. He told me
I was delectable and 'sweet' . . . Jack was adorable today. I 'borrowed'
another dollar from him . . . Dancing close with Jack, I could tell that he
was excited.

I got into N.Y. at 9 and started at Art School, which is like the studios
you read of in novels. Mr Reis (spelling wrong, I think) is *very* handsome
& fascinating. If he didn't wear his hair so long I'd have a crush on him
– but I'll probably fall for him in spite of that. My motto from now on
is PLUNGE! When you want some*one* or some*thing*, go for it, with your
mind made up to get it! You're damn right!! You're God damn right –
keep it up! . . . Today Mr Reis was very fascinating. He sat on the arm of
the sofa with his arm around me . . . Mr Weiss talked to me about how
to get drunk without liquor, so to speak. He got quite personal. He looks
like John Barrymore, only more attractive. I am gradually falling for him
. . . I got all dressed up in my huge hat and felt awfully sort of worked up

& went to Mr Reiss's studio. He was there alone and he kissed me passionately.

The diary contained a dozen references to Andrew Peters. Most of them were indirect, mentioning him in the context of the negotiations over the cash settlement. Parts of those entries conflicted, or seemed to conflict, with parts of the account given by Stanley Faithfull the day before; Tucker was shown to have been involved in the efforts to make Peters pay up; Edwin Megargee was shown to have been well informed about both Peters' association with Starr and the progress of the negotiations. Yet there is no indication in Littleton's report that he raised any of those points.

The first reference to Peters appeared in the entry for 22 October 1926 (which, if Stanley's account was accurate, was a few days before Mrs Faithfull unburdened herself to her old Boston friend Mrs Benjamin Russell, who betrayed the confidence):

> I behaved like an ass today. At Russek's [women's clothing store on Fifth Avenue at Thirty-Sixth Street] I was furious with the stupid, ugly saleswoman and the stupid, ugly coats, none of which I bought. I went there with Mother who was all for going to Boston and ripping it into A.J.P. ...

The diary-entry for 4 January, a Tuesday, read:

> Last night Mother got a damnably insulting letter from Mrs Russell about Tucker. Boston is too narrow and stupidly conventional for me. Mother is being criticised, etc., about A.J.P. Mother & I are going to Boston on Thurs. (Later) Everything is horrible. I have been feeling depressed & have decided not to go to Boston. I'm sort of afraid, horribly afraid, of *everything* which is definite, and when I try to get over the feeling I feel sick. Mother is now telling Stanley how much I hate him. I wish I wasn't such a damn fool & such a coward.

The entry for 12 January showed that Starr did accompany her mother to Boston, that Tucker went there too, and that Starr was interviewed by Rowley during the vist:

> I taxied down to Edwin's & had a very nice time with him. I told him about my talk with Mr Rowley about A.J.P. I also talked with him about how, when under the influence of drugs, I used to sort of imagine myself passionate with A.J.P. I almost asked Edwin if he would spend the night with me, but then I didn't dare quite. Mother called up from Boston tonight. Tucker is staying with Miss Frost after all. They & Miss Dow [Emily Dow, an old friend of Mrs Faithfull's] are getting after A.J.P.

*14 January 1927.* This morning I went to Dr Garretson's again & had a horrible time trying to tell him about A.J.P. I didn't seem able to get a word out.

*15 January.* Mother telephoned this morning for Stanley to come over to Boston because more & more complications have arisen about A.J.P.

*18 January.* Saw Dr Garretson. Then I decided to go and see Edwin. We talked for a long time about A.J.P.

*19 January.* The plot is thickening about Andrew. The 'man' Edwin said was in New York was Mr Rowley. He is coming in April again. We are able to prove that Andrew was lying that time when he said all the hotels were full, so I had to stay at his.

*9 June.* I was frightfully logy & depressed some of today. We are going to N.Y. early tomorrow to talk with the lawyers at the Belmont [Hotel, on Park Avenue at Forty-Second Street] about Andrew. Mr Deland [an associate of Alexander Whiteside's] is over, trying to prove Andrew's case – God help him. Tucker's a little nurvious. I will be glad when it's over.

*10 June.* This has been a hectic day & God how hot. We got into the Belmont & first I (quite petrified) was interviewed by Rowley & Deland & convinced them. Then Tucker & Mother went up. It seems Andrew is dying on his feet.

Out of chronological order, in a space on one of the November 1926 pages, was an entry headed 'West Orange again, August 1st, 1927' – the day of Starr's return from the group tour of Scotland and England. The correct place for the entry was among the pages torn out. Perhaps she had copied the original entry at the time of the tearing. It contained the last reference to Peters.

God, some day! Mother & Stanley at the dock to meet me off the California. Stanley looked so well I didn't know him. Everything is unbelievably wonderful! Stanley's tactics have come through, and we get $20,000 out of old A. We'll have another car, and a motor boat 'n' everything. I was so excited & thrilled.
God, how I love Bill!

Bill. There was only that one reference to him in the diary. Littleton asked the Faithfulls if they knew who he was, and Tucker explained that 'Bill' was the nickname of George Jameson Carr, ship's doctor of the *California*, whom Starr had met for the first time during the trip.

The fact that the questioning ended at midnight may mean that it was ended because of the time rather than because Littleton had run out of questions. The Faithfulls were driven back to Manhattan. Littleton and Schultze were the next to leave, 'in animated conversation, oblivious to reporters' pleas for information, as they hastened to their vehicles,' one of the reporters noted. Edwards and King, they most deserving of rest, emerged together but parted immediately. Edwards – who, straightway after arriving from Boston, had told the reporters that he would issue a statement later that night – delayed his departure for as long as it took him to tell those who had waited up: 'There are many people and many circumstances behind the case. There are no additional facts to be given out.' King walked across to the police headquarters, locked the diary in a filing cabinet to which he alone had a key, sat at his desk for a while, sifting through the two piles of papers that had grown there during his absence – the tall one to do with the Starr Faithfull case – and then, at last, drove home.

## 4

Thursday.

Joseph Macken, determined that everything should go off without a hitch, had made all the arrangements himself; had checked and double-checked them. The funeral itself would not show much of a profit – hardly any, in fact, as he had decided to use a de-luxe casket finished in two colours, sycamore-brown on the box, magnolia-white on the lid, and with three handles and a rail, all of simulated brass, on each side, and to charge it at cost-price, in line with Mr Faithfull's request for the cheapest casket he could get – but the publicity would be of untold value to his business. His big worry was that the timing of the operation, quite complicated, might be sent all awry by a single delaying mishap.

None occurred. A fresh-polished limousine, despatched from the morgue at Rockville Centre, arrived in St Luke's Place when it was meant to. Frank Wyman, who had gone up to the Faithfulls' apartment shortly before, came down with them. He was, to look at, very different from Stanley. His body was like a large log of heavy timber; anyone bumping into him would have rebounded. His square face was freckled; he wore pince-nez, the oval lenses of which did not magnify his clear, dark eyes; a moustache, covering all of his upper lip, was briefly red in the middle, grizzled at the sides; his hair was grey, almost white, around the temples, where it was cut short, but still red on top – and made more noticeably so by the way he petalled the red strands in all directions from the centre, rather in the style associated with Nero. He posed for photographs with the Faithfulls (both women all in black, which suited Tucker), stood aside as they entered the limousine, and then undid the tip-up seat between them and the driver and sat uncomfortably on it, out of reach of the door, which Mrs Faithfull, tetchy with him for not having thought to close when he got in, shouted at the most prying reporter to slam. The driver, glancing at his watch all the way to the morgue, arrived there minute-perfectly to schedule, just as the hearse ambled out of the yard and, still extra slowly, allowing the many spectators and the few reporters a good look at the de-luxe casket, began the journey to the Fresh Pond Cemetery in Middle Village, Queens. The slight cortege, hearse and limousine, reached the crematorium dead on time. A bell had begun to toll. The Reverend Carl Nutzhorn was standing at the entrance.

He welcomed the Faithfulls and Wyman, and led them inside, to the front pew. Though they were the only mourners (no one had come from Boston), the other pews were soon filled with reporters and spectators. Macken and his men carried the casket to the sliding bier, bowed in unison, and walked out, two by two and in step. The Reverend Nutzhorn began reading aloud from the prayer book.

All of a sudden, there were noises outside − of a car pulling up, brakes screeching, locked wheels skittering gravel; of crunching footsteps. The double doors, both of them, burst open, and two men entered. Neither removed his hat. One of them stayed by the doors. The other hurried up the aisle, and without even waiting for the Reverend Nutzhorn to get to the end of whichever sentence he, eyes uplifted from the book and staring, was reciting by rote, muttered at him. Meanwhile, there was a stir in the crematorium. The man stood aside, but put a hand on the casket, as if to make sure that it didn't slide away through the crimson curtains. Addressing the mourners, the Reverend Nutzhorn explained that the intruders were detectives − 'the emissaries of the District Attorney of Nassau County' − that 'at Mr Edwards' request', the deceased was to be returned to the morgue, the funeral postponed till the following day.

As the mourners walked out, pushing through the chattering crush in the aisle, the spokesman detective, half-encircled by reporters, persuaded enough of them to give him a hand to carry the casket back to the hearse. There being no sign of the undertakers, other helpful reporters banded together as a search-party, and eventually discovered Macken and his men having a smoke by the door to the furnace-room. The hearse, refilled, set off back to the morgue. Macken sat in the front, trying to look no unhappier than usual. Before Stanley Faithfull and the other mourners returned to the limousine, he told reporters that the last-minute postponement was 'another of Elvin Edwards' dramatic gestures'. He added: 'There is no need for us to attend a second ceremony as the ceremonial objects have been achieved.' (But the Faithfulls did attend the re-arranged funeral, which took place without incident the following afternoon. They were not accompanied by Frank

Wyman, who had had to leave for Sugar Island to keep an appointment with a prospective client.)

The reason for the postponement was this: shortly before, Inspector King had received a phone call from a New York detective, with the exciting news that not just one man, or two, or three, but *four*, believed that they had encountered Starr Faithfull, all in a continuous episode, on the afternoon of either the Thursday-eve of her disappearance or the Friday. Whichever afternoon it was, the episode began in the art-deco lobby of the Chanin Building on East Forty-Second Street, almost opposite Grand Central, when the elevator-starter and a clerk who worked in the building answered an elderly woman's call for help in saving her companion, a pretty girl in her twenties, apparently drunk or drugged, from falling on the marble floor. Once the men had assumed the burden, the elderly woman panted that 'the girl needed to be watched because she had a lot of money on her' – then disappeared through the revolving doors. While one of the men kept hold of the girl, the other called a patrolling constable, who, in turn, called a cab, the driver of which, cleverly comprehending from what the girl slurred that she wanted to be taken to an address in Flushing, the northern part of Queens, took her there, stopping en route at a drug store, where she, supported by the driver, handed over a prescription for medicinal alcohol and enough cash for the purchase of two bottles of Scotch – one of which she practically emptied during the ten minutes or so of the rest of the journey. Upon arrival where the driver believed the girl wanted to be, he dashed into a greengrocer's and bought some lemons 'to straighten her up', then helped her on to the sidewalk, received payment, and watched her as she staggered about, loaded with bottles and lemons, squinting at house-numbers but not seeing them. Worried that she might stagger into the road and be knocked down, the driver half-carried her into a café and left her in the care of a waitress.

Telling the New York detective to hang on, King used another phone to call Edwards, and then, getting back to the New York detective, asked him to arrange for detectives of a Queens precinct to hurry to the Fresh Pond Cemetery and halt the funeral.

In the evening, the four men – elevator-starter, clerk, patrolman, and cab-driver – were transported to the morgue. Unaccountably, no one had thought of enlisting the cab-driver's help in tracing other witnesses: the pharmacist at the drug store (who would surely have remembered the befuddled girl, might have remembered, or been able to tell from his records, when he had served her, and should have been able to produce the filled prescription — which, if he had stuck to the letter of the law, he had got the girl to sign); the greengrocer (who might have remembered the exact day on which he had sold lemons to an agitated cabbie); the waitress (who, perhaps in addition to recalling the day, might have seen where the girl went when she left the café).

The four men viewed the body in the opened casket, and two of them — the patrolman and the cab-driver — almost immediately turned away, saying that there were no more than superficial resemblances between Starr Faithfull and 'their' girl. The others — the pair who had answered the call from the elderly, hastily departing woman — thought there was a strong likeness. Those two were shown Starr's frock. Unless Mrs Faithfull had said that Starr had worn the frock two days running, on the Thursday as well as the Friday (I have come across no such statement from her), the fact that neither the elevator-starter nor the clerk recognised the memorable garment should have been taken only as a possible sign that the incident beginning in the lobby of the Chanin Building occurred on the Thursday — certainly not as a reason for doubting the men's reliability as eye-witnesses. There may have been some other reason for that doubt in the minds of the policemen at the viewing; if so, they kept it quiet. The four men, all thanked for their public-spirited but useless efforts, were transported back to Manhattan. The matter was closed. The magnolia-white lid was screwed back on the casket in readiness for the resumed funeral next day — in the morning of which, at the first of his press-conferences, Edwards smiled and shook his head when asked to comment on Stanley Faithfull's 'dramatic gesture' accusation. He later remarked that 'the police of this county, together with others, the NYPD in particular, are determined, as I am, to establish Starr Faithfull's movements and whereabouts previous to her untimely end. It may be that, as a side-effect of that endeavour, certain persons have been and will be inconvenienced.'

By the time Edwards made those remarks, various investigators had, between them, accounted for a few of Starr's activities — and a few activities of members of her family — during the period from Friday, 29 May. As a result of further investigations, a few of the gaps that remained would be filled. It will make for clarity to combine the facts that came to light during the first fortnight of the case, prior to 22 June, which, as will appear, was a day of special significance.

**Friday, 29 May**

Boiling hot. By noon, the temperature in Manhattan was in the low 80s. About that time, Starr walked down the Cunard Steamship Company's long pier, No. 56, at the foot of West Fourteenth Street, and walked up the gently tilted gangway to the main deck of the liner *Franconia*.[1] She was wearing a small black and white hat, a black and white frock, flesh-coloured silk stockings, black and white shoes with French heels, high and curved. She was carrying a purse and, over her arm, a dark coat.

Sidney Sutherland, the ace crime-reporter for the *New York Daily News*, would paint this picture of the scene:

> The *Franconia*, which had arrived the previous morning from a whoopee cruise, was in the final throes of orderly confusion of preparation for her departure at 5 o'clock for England.
>
> Passengers were beginning to stream up the gangway. Stewards were dashing to and fro, seizing hand luggage and wraps and escorting the arrivals to their cabins.
>
> In the great hatches, fore and aft, gigantic cranes were creaking and grinding as merchandise was lifted from the pier and swung across the rails and dropped swiftly into the gaping caverns below.
>
> Scows on the river side grated against the towering sides of the liner as mountains of coal were hoisted into the mechanical bowels far below.
>
> Master and mates and engineers and office men and head stewards and other officials — blue coated and white capped and brass buttoned and vastly alert and efficient — were everywhere at once, supervising, ordering, smoothing out tangles.
>
> Starr Faithfull, fresh and gorgeously beautiful and wise in the ways of finding herself about the labyrinths of an ocean liner, was only one in a great throng, and few gave her any special heed.

We know what Francis Peabody Hamlin said of his five brief encounters with her, the first at about half-past one, soon after his arrival on board, the last a couple of hours later.[2]

---

1. The second Cunard liner so named (the first *Franconia*, launched from the Swan, Hunter & Wigham Richardson shipyard, Newcastle-upon-Tyne, in 1911, had been requisitioned as a troop-ship soon after the outbreak of the Great War, and on 4 October 1916 been sunk by torpedoes from a German submarine in the Mediterranean, with the loss of twelve crew-members). It was nine years old, having been launched from John Brown & Co's shipyard, Glasgow, in 1922; it measured 625 feet from stem to stern, had two main decks, a shelter deck, and a promenade deck, was able to carry 330 first-class passengers, 420 second-class, and 1500 third-class, and had a crew of 435.
2. Page 113–5.

We also know that a cable was sent to Scotland Yard, asking for certain members of the *Franconia's* crew to be interviewed. By then, the liner was berthed in King George Dock, London, but most of the crew had returned to the home-port of Liverpool. Of those traced, six went to the offices of Hill Dickinson & Co., Cunard's solicitors in Liverpool, and made statements. George Jameson Carr, the ship's doctor, was on a motoring holiday in Belgium, and it was decided that, though that country was small, there was little hope of finding him. An envelope marked EXTREME URGENCY was popped through the letter-box of his London flat to await his return.

One of the crew-members who made statements in Liverpool was Albert Jones, the chief steward. Nothing of what he said dovetailed with anything said by Hamlin, whom he did not mention. According to Hamlin, his fourth encounter with Starr was at about three o'clock, following her rebuff by Carr:

> . . . she said, 'I feel awfully faint. Could you get me some brandy?' I said, 'I don't think so, but I will see what I can do.' So I helped her walk down the stairs, and there was one of the stewards there. It was Albert Jones, the chief steward. He said, 'I've seen that girl before,' and I said, 'Yes, her name is Starr Faithfull.' He said, 'Oh, yes, she was on the *California* cruise with us.' I said, 'Have you got a drop of brandy? She seems faint.' He said, 'I will see what I can do.' So the whole three of us went into his cabin. The doctor's office was right beside us. She said, 'Thank you very much,' and I said, 'I will see you later,' something like that . . .

According to Albert Jones:

> . . . About 3.30 p.m., when passing through B deck square in the course of my duties, I noticed Miss Faithfull sitting in one of the corners. I recognised Miss Faithfull because she had been on the *California*, of which I was chief steward, three years ago. She was a girl of very striking appearance, and on this occasion, as when on the *California*, she was exceedingly well dressed. She was looking on to the floor and did not see me . . .
>
> I next saw her about 4 p.m. I was walking towards my cabin, which is at the end of a short alleyway leading off C deck square. She recognised me. She looked as if she had been crying. I bowed and we shook hands and I asked if she was going with us in the ship. She replied that she was not but that she would like to. She said she wanted to see some friend in the ship and asked me might she leave her coat in my cabin. I said of course, and she just stepped inside my cabin and put her coat on the settee, which is just by the door. She just stepped inside and came out again without her coat. I did not observe where she went after that. That

is the last time on which I saw her. I next went into my cabin about a quarter to five, shortly before sailing time, and Miss Faithfull's coat was no longer there.

Jones's statement was filled with lies. Premeditated lies. If there were inconsistencies only between his statement and Hamlin's, he would deserve the benefit of the doubt – which was the liar? But his mendacity is made incontrovertible by contradictions between his statement and those of two of his colleagues. The charitable explanation for his lying is that he feared that if he told the truth, he, a Cunard employee for twenty-four years, would be sacked before he could celebrate a quarter of a century with the company – because, having told Hamlin that he would 'see what he could do' about getting Starr a drop of brandy, he had provided her with alcohol of some kind, thereby breaking both the US Prohibition Laws and Cunard's rules regarding the provision of alcohol. I think Hamlin was correct in his belief that Starr had not been drinking before he handed her over to Jones; I think she was under the influence of drink whenever it was that she left Jones's cabin, leaving her coat behind.

Here are excerpts from the other statements:

*Alice Davies*, a senior stewardess ('I have been with the Cunard Company since 1919. My husband, who was also with the company, was killed during the War.'):

About midday, I observed a young lady who subsequently proved to be Miss Faithfull sitting in a chair in the square on B deck on the port side, the starboard side being to the quay. I observed that she was still in the same position at about 12.30. As I passed her, she asked me if I knew whether Dr Carr was aboard. She then went on to say, 'I am told that he is not aboard but I know that he is and I am waiting until I see him.' I replied that I really could not tell her whether Dr Carr was aboard or not and that it was a very busy day.

About two o'clock I saw the young lady on B promenade deck, port side, looking over the rail. She was crying and was beating the rail with one of her hands, and it appeared to me that she was hysterical. Just then I met Mr Francis Hamlin, and I told him about the young lady and her state. After Mr Hamlin had been to the young lady, he returned to me, saying that she would be all right, and then I saw him and the young lady going down to C deck. I thought therefore that he must be taking her to Dr Carr.

*Robert Ellis*, the senior second steward ('I have been with the Cunard Company for 22 years.'):

A few minutes before 2 p.m. I was on B deck on the port side in the course of my duties. I observed a young lady who I have subsequently been informed was Miss Faithfull looking over the rail. She seemed to be in a very jumpy state. As I went I met Mrs Alice Davies. She said she had been in conversation with the young lady. Whilst I was speaking to Mrs Davies, Mr Hamlin ... happened to cross the square and, seeing Miss Faithfull, walked over and spoke to her. I knew there would be no need for anyone further to worry as he would know what to do.

The next I saw of Miss Faithfull, she was just inside the doctor's consulting room on C deck square. The door was wide open and the doctor was close to the doorway, speaking to her. It looked to me as if the doctor was edging her out of the consulting room while he spoke.

*Bertram Davies*, the staff captain and chief officer ('I hold a Master Mariner's Certificate. I have been with Cunard for 22 years.'):

About 3 p.m., whilst I was passing through the square on B deck, I saw a young lady whom I have subsequently been informed was Miss Starr Faithfull leaning against one of the pillars and crying bitterly. I went to her and asked if I could do anything for her. She informed me that she had lost her coat and that she had left it in Mr Jones's cabin. I did not know who Mr Jones was but assumed he was one of the passengers. She said she was a visitor and had come to see someone off. I suggested that she should go to the cabin, and she replied that she would do so.

*Alfred Martin*, the senior assistant purser ('I have been with the Cunard Company ashore and afloat for the past 15 years.'):

Whilst I was in my office on C deck square at about 3.30 p.m., I observed a girl standing alone in the middle of the square, alternately crying and laughing and apparently in a state of hysteria. Other passengers were about and the girl was the centre of attraction. I drew the attention of the Purser, Mr Cullum, to her and we both went to see what the trouble was. On getting to the girl, I asked her could I do anything for her and asked her who she was. She did not give me her name, merely telling me that she was a visitor and moaning and saying that she had lost her coat. She said she had left it in Mr Jones's cabin. I asked her could she indicate the cabin as there would be many Mr Joneses in the ship. She could not do this. She then asked me to go away and leave her alone. Having said this, she appeared to pull herself together and walked up the stairs in the direction of B deck. Immediately after this, I passed warning to all concerned that a lady's coat was missing and asked them to keep a sharp lookout for it.

*Alice Davies*:

Between 3.30 p.m. and 4 p.m. I saw Miss Faithfull come from C deck to B deck square and stop and speak to a bell-boy, Arthur Bentley. I was close to and heard her ask him if he could stow her away. The boy appeared to treat this as a joke and seemed quite amused. He replied that of course he could not do so.

*Alfred Martin*:

At 3 minutes to 5 p.m., the ship being due to sail at 5 p.m., I reported in person to Captain Irving on the bridge that all passengers had embarked and that all the papers were aboard and that, as far as I knew, all visitors were ashore. I then made my way to the ship's gangway in case any papers or messages should come aboard at the last minute. None did and the ship sailed at 5 p.m.

Another quote from Sidney Sutherland's article in the *Daily News*:

There were a few hoarse, tympanum-numbing blasts from the *Franconia*'s great whistle; a wild, roaring threshing of the gigantic propellers and a groaning and creaking as the huge steamship began to back slowly into the Hudson River, the rope bumpers of the powerful little tugs alongside edging and hunching the vessel toward midstream.

Commander Irving stood watchfully on the bridge. The liner reached the middle of the river and backed torpidly around. Everything apparently was shipshape and running to schedule. The busy tugs gave a final shove and pulled away. Then, far down below the bridge, there was a sudden scurrying and confusion and excitement . . .

*Alfred Martin*:

At about five minutes past 5 I was informed by Dr Jameson Carr, who was standing just outside the door of his consulting room, that there was a stowaway aboard, viz. the girl who had been seen in the square crying. Immediately I knew, I telephoned to the bridge and was answered by one of the officers. Immediately after this, I sent all available hands to look through the ship with a view to finding the lady.

*Bertram Davies*:

As soon as the gangway was clear I went to the bridge and a minute or two afterwards I received a report from the purser's office that a lady visitor was still aboard. I reported the matter at once to the Commander, Captain Irving.

*Robert Irving* ('I have been Commander of the *Franconia* since 5 January last. I have been with the Cunard Steamship Co. for 28 years and have had command for the past 14 years.'):

I accordingly instructed Staff Captain Davies to telephone aft to the First Officer to hail the Marine Superintendent who was on the pier to send a tug out so that the visitor could be landed. The matter was dealt with thereafter by the Staff Captain.

*Bertram Davies*:

In about ten minutes the tug came out, and as she was approaching I went down on to B deck square to see the visitor safely off the ship. I found the young lady with Mr Hunter, the Chief Inspector of the ship, standing by her. She was more hysterical than before. The Inspector had her gently by the arm and when I came up she besought me not to send her ashore, saying that her father had plenty of money; that in any case she was visiting England in August and that it was most important that she should get there before then. I tried to reason with the girl, pointing out that she had no passport and no ticket and would not be allowed to land in England. She refused to listen, saying that she was determined to stay on the ship, and saying that I did not appreciate what a serious thing it was for me to send her ashore. I told her that I had no option and that if she would not go of her own accord we should have to carry her.

*Robert Ellis*:

Captain Davies asked me to remain by Miss Faithfull whilst he went to see the Commander. Accordingly I took her by the arm and gently edged her towards the bulkhead. She made a rush to go after Captain Davies and I grasped the hand rail with one hand and kept Miss Faithfull imprisoned by my arm. She shouted after Captain Davies, saying that she would do anything to get across to England, even washing dishes. She was stamping and struggling. Inspector Hunter and Stewardess Davies came to my assistance. After Captain Davies's return, I went about my normal duties.

*Alice Davies*:

The Staff Captain, the Inspector, Miss Faithfull and myself went down to D deck. All the way Miss Faithfull was asking that she should not be put ashore and was more hysterical. When we got to D deck, the sea ladder was down.

*Bertram Davies*:

She still would not go, so the Inspector guided her to the shell door under which the tug was lying. The time was then about 5.15. The deck of the tug was less than ten feet below the shell door. The ship was just moving through the water, with the tug alongside, and we dropped the pilot ladder down on to the tug's deck. The girl was obviously in such a state that she could not go down the ladder unassisted and I had a life-line passed round her, under her arms, and we lifted her very gently on to the ladder whilst a member of the crew of the tug came up the ladder and directed her feet on to the rungs as she went down. At the same time the rope was held by those in the ship so that she could not fall and was kept steady. Once she got on to the ladder she ceased resisting, being apparently in a state of collapse and as if she had ceased to care. As soon as she had reached the tug's deck she was assisted into its cabin. Her small handbag was passed to the tug. That was the last I saw of her. I telephoned a message to the Commander, who had slowed the ship so that the visitor could be put ashore in safety, and shortly afterwards we resumed our normal passage towards the bay.

I wish to add that it would have been quite impossible for the young lady to get any alcoholic drink aboard the *Franconia* from members of the crew. The only drink she could get would be such as passengers bring aboard. All the bars and all liquor supplies are under lock and key in port, the keys being in the Commander's safe, to which no one has access but himself.

The tug was called the *Donner*. The name of the man who helped Starr down the pilot-ladder was Peter Hansen. He took her into the cabin, where John Johnson, Cunard's harbour-master, gave her some water. The *Donner* returned to Pier 56, and Johnson handed Starr over to another Cunard employee.

*Police Sergeant Patrick Dugan* (who had been 'the senior officer responsible for patrolling the Cunard Company's dockside premises' for nine years):
I was walking down Pier 56 on the lower level, the freight level, toward the loading bulkhead. I observed a man coming toward me with a tall girl, and she was staggering and he had some difficulty in holding her, so I waited to see how things would work out. I didn't want to rush in. Then I saw he was not able to handle her, she didn't want to go with him. I walked over to her and I said, 'Better come along with the man.'

*Murray Edelman* ('occupation, Taxi Driver; driver's licence No. 025-127'):
I was in the hire line by the Cunard sheds. I saw the young woman when she came out of the freight piers. A man who I thought was the superintendendent of the dock was supporting her. She had her arm round his neck and he was holding her up, but she was walking. They walked in this fashion for about ten feet and then the man put her in a Yellow taxi which was driven by Emanuel Kussoy. Sam Katz, the patrolman on duty at the docks, went over to see what was wrong. He came to me and gave me 25 cents and told me to go into the Munson Lunch, 500 West Fourteenth Street, and get two lemons. I did so. Katz gave the lemons to the woman in the cab and told her to suck on them to brace her up. She was on the dock, I should say, about fifteen minutes, and I heard Frank Flynn, the taxi starter, tell Manny Kussoy to take her to 12 St Luke's Place, but I heard the woman say she wanted to go to an address on Fifth Avenue – No. 5 or No 45 Fifth Avenue. As she sat in the cab I noticed that she was wearing tan stockings, and a scar on her right leg showed plainly through the stocking. The scar was about one inch long.

*Emanuel Kussoy:*

I started to take her to an address on Fifth Avenue, the number of which I cannot remember, but she enquired about the next boat sailing for England. She said, 'I've got to get on it. I've got to get to England.' I told her there would be a ship sailing the next week and doubtless she could catch it. She said, 'All right, then don't take me to Fifth Avenue. Take me to to 12 St Luke's Place.'

We got there about 5.45 or 5.50 p.m. She didn't get out. I went around to the back of the cab and helped her out and up the steps of No. 12. She handed me a key to the vestibule door and I helped her up the stairs to the top-floor apartment. She paid me 65 cents. I left her in the apartment, standing there. Nobody had appeared. I got the impression, as we had made quite a noise coming up, that there was nobody else in the apartment.

When the Anglo-American evidence regarding Starr's visit to and removal from the *Franconia* was imparted to Mr and Mrs Faithfull, they insisted that, while it was true that Starr had gone aboard the liner, meaning to bid adieu to Dr Carr, and had subsequently spoken of Hamlin and of two men, Jack Greenaway and Bruce Winston, whom she had met at a ship-board party, the girl who had given so much trouble to so many people couldn't possibly have been Starr. Stanley said that he recalled, 'as if it were yesterday', hearing the *Franconia*'s whistle blow, glancing at the clock in the living-room, and mentioning to his wife that the time was five exactly. They both swore that Starr returned no more than twenty minutes later. Stanley: 'I think she told me she had come home in a taxi.' They both swore that her clothing was neat; that she was perfectly sober; that she showed no sign of hysteria. Mrs Faithfull: 'I know and recall the time, as well as how she looked, because there was a band playing in the park opposite; the noise was a particularly objectionable feature of the afternoon, and it came to an end soon after five.' Stanley added what he considered the clincher: he was pretty sure that Starr was admitted to the house by Duncan Smith, an artist who lived in the first-floor apartment − 'He is on holiday at the moment, but I can furnish his holiday address, and you can get him to confirm the time of her arrival.'

No official investigator, nor an investigating reporter, seems to have bothered to get in touch with Mr Smith. If the Faithfulls did, they never said so.

**Saturday, 30 May**

Even hotter than the Friday: 89° at 1.30 p.m. — the highest temperature ever recorded in Manhattan on a 30 May.

According to Mr and Mrs Faithfull (not Tucker, who was away for the weekend), as soon as Starr had dressed, she hurried downstairs to see if there was any mail. She left the apartment at about 10 a.m. and returned four hours later, saying that she had been to the movies. Although there was another band-concert in the park in the afternoon — which, Mrs Faithfull said, 'was the source of some annoyance to Starr' — she did not go out again . . . not even for a few minutes to post a letter, the Faithfulls later felt they must insist.

**Sunday, 31 May**

According to Mr and Mrs Faithfull, Starr went out at about ten in the morning and returned five hours later, saying that she had again been to the movies. This time, she specified the cinema: the Roxy, which was at Seventh Avenue and West Fiftieth Street.

(One wonders whether she also outlined the plot of the main feature, *Daddy Long Legs*, starring Janet Gaynor ('Your Darling, more loveable and wistful than ever before,' the advertisements claimed) as the oldest young girl in an orphanage, and Warner Baxter as a middle-aged millionaire trustee of the place. He adopts the girl but keeps his identity secret from her; she refers to him as Daddy Long Legs because she has only seen his elongated shadow; he pays for her further education; at last they meet, and she, not knowing that he is Daddy Long Legs, falls in love with him; she goes to her benefactor to get his blessing for the marriage, and, while still a bit bewildered, accepts his proposal. If Starr really did see the movie, she may have compared the strange but pure relationship between the Gaynor and Baxter characters with the strange relationship between herself and Andrew Peters.)

Mr and Mrs Faithfull said that Starr stayed at home from three in the afternoon.

**Monday, I June**

According to Mr and Mrs Faithfull, as soon as Starr had dressed, she hurried downstairs to look in the mail-box. She left at about ten and returned three hours later (she did not, it seems, say where she had been). After having lunch, she went out again, saying that she was going to stroll to Washington Square and take a ride up Fifth Avenue on the top of a bus; returning at six (by which time Tucker was back from her weekend away), she stayed in for the rest of the evening.

### Tuesday, 2 June

According to all three Faithfulls, as soon as Starr had dressed, she hurried downstairs to look in the mail-box. She left at about ten and returned five hours later (you will soon realise that a comment by Mrs Faithfull in the course of Martin Littleton's questioning about entries in the hidden diary indicates that Starr mentioned where she had been); she did not go out again.

After the Faithfulls had explained some of the diary entries, several persons were interviewed: among them, Dr William Garretson. He confirmed that he had 'treated Miss Faithfull with regard to her emotional problems' on and off for six months or so from December 1926, but claimed that he was forbidden from saying much more because of 'the sanctity of confidential information passed between physician and patient, no matter if the latter is now deceased'. Next, Starr's 'sex tutor', Edwin Megargee, as well as speaking generally about the curriculum, said that she had visited him at his studio in Union Square on the last Tuesday morning of her life.

He had not seen her for many months; was not expecting the visit. The minute she arrived – around eleven, he thought – 'she flung herself on a divan and said, "I need a drink – I need one quick." So I mixed her a weak cocktail. I could see that she wanted to tell me something, but I did not ask. I went on with my work.' He was completing a painting of a blond boy holding a pet rabbit. Though Megargee was white, he bore a resemblance to Duke Ellington:[1] his dark hair was streaked back, he had a moustache, his heavy eyelids made him always look drowsy.

She told him about her 'bad behaviour' on board the *Franconia*. 'I certainly made a holy exhibition of myself,' she said. 'Lord, what a chump I am to drink! I wonder what Carr thinks of me now.'

Painting away, Megargee remarked, 'Well, he probably thinks the same thing of you that you think of yourself. What are you going to do about it?'

---

1. Who had recently given the first performance of his great tune, 'Mood Indigo'.

'I don't know. What should I do? Do you think I ought to write him a letter of apology? I wonder if he's in any danger of losing his job because of the scene I put on. I guess maybe I'd better write a formal apology which he can show to his bosses. What do you think?'

'I think that would be a good idea if that's the way you feel about it,' Megargee replied.

Starr had another drink. She asked Megargee if he could get her some ether. He shook his head. She did not ask again.

She said that she would have succeeded in stowing away on the *Franconia* if she had been sober. 'I wasn't very smart, I fancy. As a matter of fact, I was dumb. You know I can't handle my booze, though I always think I'm pretty smart when I'm pickled. I sneaked into the women's toilet, thinking of hiding there until the ship was so far out to sea that they couldn't back up to put me off. No matter what happened, I'd have had my trip to England and been on the same ship with Carr. But I came out too soon. I felt the ship moving, and after a while I guess I thought we were out a couple of days from land. The truth was, we hadn't even reached the middle of the Hudson when I stepped boldly out. That's what liquor does to me all right. But I'll tell you something: the next time I try to stow away, I'll make it. I positively won't try any such stunts after taking a few drinks. I'll keep my head the next time.'

Megargee 'got her talking about other things, none of much consequence, for example, I showed her a china dog I had just purchased and added to my collection of china animals'. (Far larger than Starr's collection, it was displayed on shelves in the studio.)

She finished her drink and got up from the divan. 'Thanks a lot for listening to my troubles,' she said. 'Goodbye. I may not see you for quite a while.'

'Why, what's up?' Megargee asked.

'I'm going abroad next week, and I may not see you again before I sail. I'm going to England.'

Megargee asked where the money to pay for the trip was coming from.

'Oh, we got quite a sum from mother's accident,' Starr said. (You may need to be reminded that in April, nearly six years after a road-accident in which Mrs Faithfull was injured, the State of Massachusetts paid damages of $4062.) As Starr left, she said, 'Toodle-oo, old pal, until I return. And if I don't see you again – well, bottoms up and happy landings!'

That *was* the last time he saw her, Megargee told the detectives who interviewed him.

### Wednesday, 3 June

According to all three Faithfulls, as soon as Starr had dressed, she hurried downstairs to look in the mail-box. She went out an hour later than usual, at eleven, and was still not home when, in the late afternoon, Stanley set off on a trip to Boston (by bus, he said at first; then said that he travelled by train). According to Mrs Faithfull and Tucker, Starr returned at about six. Mrs Faithfull: 'She was not at all tight, but her breath gave perfect evidence that she had had something to drink.' She said that she had met Francis Hamlin — that he had taken her to a party at the studio of an artist, Harry Stoner, whom she had been acquainted with for some time — that the guests had included Miriam Hopkins, the actress, and two men she had met the Friday before, aboard the *Franconia*: Bruce Winston, who was an actor, and Jack Greenaway. Neither Mrs Faithfull nor Tucker believed her story.[1]

Nor did any of the investigators. They were sure — once Hamlin's alibi was confirmed by the Burns detective agency in Boston — that Starr's last meeting with him was on the *Franconia*. They were sure — once Harry Stoner had been interviewed — that he had not thrown a party on Wednesday, 3 June.

They were less sure, however, that some other parts of Stoner's statement were true — or that it was complete. He was in his mid-forties; still darkly handsome, still a bachelor. His studio was the largest room of his apartment at 18 West Thirty-Seventh Street, just off Fifth Avenue. The detectives who interviewed him observed that a wall of the studio was patched with glossy photographs of Miriam Hopkins — a kind of shrine to the blonde actress. She, though only twenty-eight, had been appearing on Broadway, regularly and in ever more showy parts, since 1921. Stoner, when asked if he was a friend of hers as well as a fan, said: 'Oh, yes. For ages. I sorely miss her.' The explanation for that last remark is that Miriam Hopkins, having signed up with a movie-producer at the start of the year, while playing the part of 'Mimi' in a comedy entitled *Anatol* at the

---

1. For their separate accounts of and attitudes to it, see pages 97 and 101.

Lyceum, had gone to Hollywood on Friday, 5 June.[1] Stoner said that he had not seen Starr on the Wednesday when he had *not* thrown a party – indeed, had not seen her for some months:

'I first met her a couple of years ago when she came to me, seeking modelling work. She was recommended to me by my friend and fellow-artist, Edwin Megargee. I told her I would bear her in mind when I needed a face like hers, but I never used her. She kept calling on me for about six months, then I saw nothing of her for a year. She dropped in on me again about a month ago and asked for work. That was my last sighting of her. I cannot imagine what possessed her to say she came here that Wednesday.'

He said that he knew no one named Winston or Greenaway.

Great efforts were made to trace those two. There was no listing for a Winston (or Winson or Winton), B., in the New York City telephone books. Every single one of the many subscribers with Green etc. surnames and the first initial of J was phoned; those who either didn't reply or, replying, sounded suspiciously evasive were spoken to face-to-face. Hotel registers were searched. Cunard provided lists of passengers and personnel on all of the cruises Starr had taken; also the lists for sailings from New York (including, of course, that of the *Franconia*) during the last week of May and the first week of June.

As Starr had said that Bruce Winston was an actor, inquiries were made at theatrical agencies. One of the agents gave a clue – and the minute the inquirer departed, phoned the clue to just about every newspaper in Manhattan. Consequently, a fifty-two-year-old English actor named Bruce Winston received more attention from crime reporters over the next few days than he had received from drama critics in the twenty years since he had made his debut playing a eunuch – a role that his roly-polyness suited him to – in a farce entitled *The H'Arum Lily* that toured music-halls in the north of England. When not performing, he was noticeably – at that time, outrageously – homosexual. Besides acting, he designed sets and costumes, and, as an untheatrical sideline, fashioned women's hats – occasionally for George V's wife, Queen Mary. In the later summer of 1926, shortly after playing 'La Trémouille' in the first productions of Shaw's *Saint Joan*, starring Sybil Thorndike, he travelled to New York (on the *Franconia*) to play 'Count Orpitch' in

1. One of her first movie-roles was that of 'Ivy Parsons' in the adaptation of *Dr Jekyll and Mr Hyde* in which the eponyms were played by Fredric March (who won the Oscar for his performances).

the Shubert Brothers' production of the musical, *Katja the Dancer*, at the Forty-Fourth Street Theatre. He stayed on after the three months' run, keeping his room at the nearby Hotel Mansfield, and, starting in the following September, appeared as 'Tony Weller' and 'Sergeant Buzfuz' in *Pickwick*, a dramatisation of the Dickens novel, at the Empire, on Broadway at Fortieth Street.

In June 1931, the press cast him as 'The Missing Link in the Starr Faithfull Case' without checking whether he was available. It soon appeared that he was otherwise engaged. Reporters in London found him at the Theatre Royal, Drury Lane, where he had been playing 'Chi-Fu' in *The Land of Smiles*, the play with music by Franz Lehar, since 8 May. 'I never met Miss Faithfull and never heard of her name until I read of her death in the newspapers,' he said. 'I have been in England since March, following a short trip to New York to see friends, so it would have been impossible for me to attend any party with her, had I known her.'

The investigators, the press as well, concluded that though the dramatic Bruce Winston could not have been with Starr at any time during any of the days before her disappearance, he was the man she had had in mind. He had never seen *her*, but she may have seen *him* in *Pickwick* or *Katja the Dancer*. Probably denoting the sudden lack of interest in Bruce Winston, no one thought to ask the Faithfulls if Starr had seen either of those shows, and no one looked to see if programmes of those shows were in the pile in her bookcase.

Jack Greenaway remained mysterious. In a written summary of the search for him – or for an explanation of Starr's choice of the name – Martin Littleton referred to

a man by the name of Jack Greenia who has the reputation of being a ladies' man, enjoying wild parties and frequenting ocean liners. He was made the matter of a thorough investigation which included a check-up of a yacht formerly owned by him and of several yachts owned by his friends, covering the Manhasset Bay area [on the north-western edge of Nassau County] in addition to the New York Yacht Club in the East River. Nothing could be established that associated Greenia with Starr. (In connection with yachts, the Columbia Yacht Club in the Hudson River was also made the subject of some inquiry on the chance that maybe Starr was a guest on some private yacht over her last weekend and slipped or was pushed overboard somewhere near Long Beach.)

**Thursday, 4 June**

According to Mrs Faithfull and Tucker (not Stanley, who was in Boston), Starr was out from eleven in the morning till six in the evening. Intoxicated when she returned, she said that she had met Francis Hamlin in the afternoon at the Savoy Plaza and gone with him to a men's club at 54 West Forty-Fifth Street or 45 West Fifty-Fourth Street; she had arranged to meet him again at the hotel at 9.45. She became hysterical when her mother kept saying that she should not go out again, and Tucker doused her with water, then set the clock back ('I was hoping that if I set the clock back forty minutes, by the time she got up there he [Hamlin] would be gone . . . So . . . she must have left here really about 9.30'). She returned at one or two o'clock in the morning. She appeared to have had 'a little bit to drink'. She said that she had been to a speakeasy near the Times building, Times Square; also that she had taken a drive to Fordham Road, in the Bronx, with Hamlin and Greenaway.[1]

Inquiries at the Savoy Plaza drew a blank; none of the staff recalled ever seeing Starr at the hotel.

There was no men's club, no club of any sort, at 45 West Fifty-Fourth Street – but 54 West Forty-Fifth Street was the address of the Coffee House Club. Two New York detectives went there and, the minute they showed their badges, were hustled out of sight into the office of the chief steward, George Fortescue, who, immaculate in a morning suit, listened impatiently to the reason for their call, and then, having decided how little he should say, said it: 'This club is of a social, artistic and literary nature, and is limited strictly to the membership, which is exclusively male. No ladies are permitted on the premises in the afternoon.' He left the office for a moment, and returned with the guest book, already opened at the page for Thursday, 4 June. 'There is a firm rule,' he said, 'that no guest of either sex may be admitted to the club unless signed in by the accompanying member. The absence of Miss Starr Faithfull's name in the guest book on the day in question is proof positive that she was not here at any time during that day.' He refused to provide a copy of the membership list: 'This is a private club, and therefore, by definition, the identity of the members is also kept private.' He was sure, he said, that Mr Henry Grey, the chairman of the house committee, would say the same. At the detectives' request, he

1. For the separate accounts by Mrs Faithfull and Tucker, see pages 99 and 101–2.

pnoned Mr Grey, a stockbroker, at his office on Wall Street. Replacing the receiver, and not quite managing to seem untriumphant, he said that 'Chairman Grey firmly concurred with him'. The detectives left. Later in the day, a far more senior detective phoned Mr Grey and, in the course of a brief conversation, jokily asked if anything other than coffee was served at the Coffee House Club, and mentioned, only in passing, that he was always being pestered by Prohibition Agents to tell them about places such as private clubs that he suspected were contravening the Volstead Act. Not much later in the day, a messenger delivered a copy of the membership list to the senior detective. None of the private members (several of whom were public figures — judges, politicians, tycoons) had a name that resembled any of those mentioned by Starr. And none of the men known to have been acquainted with her belonged to the club.

An artist, Clive Anderson — young, gangling, minutely moustached, his dark hair of that heavy sort that flops over the forehead — said that Starr called at his studio, which was at 47 Washington Square South, round about midday on the Thursday. 'I only knew her because she had posed for me on one or two occasions in the past. She asked me if I had any work for her to do, that is as a model. She gave me to understand that she was in need of funds. I regretted I could not oblige her. She was, so far as I could observe, alone.'

Between 1 and 2.30 p.m., she turned up at the art school which she had attended in the early months of 1927. The school, at 108 West Sixteenth Street, was run by Winold Reiss (mentioned several times in the hidden diary, his surname sometimes misspelt as 'Reis', sometimes as 'Weiss'). She was met at the entrance by Fritz Windemere, who taught draughtsmanship at the school. He told her that Reiss was engaged and could not come out to see her. 'Reiss is a louse,' she said, then tempered that assessment by adding, 'I mean, a nice kind of louse.' Windemere thought that 'she looked blue as she turned around and walked away'.

Between 2.30 and 3 p.m., she was at Grand Central, twenty-six blocks uptown from Reiss's school. Loretta Fitzgerald, a well-to-do young maiden, spotted her in the concourse:

I knew her well by sight by reason of having been on a Mediterranean cruise with her in 1926 on the steamship *California*. She was carrying a dark coat — black, I think — over her arm. There was nobody with her. She passed right in front of me and I was on the verge of speaking to her, but

152

Long Beach from the West. The cross (center) shows roughly where the body was found.
*Courtesy of the Commissioner of the Nassau County Police Department.*

The body on the Beach.

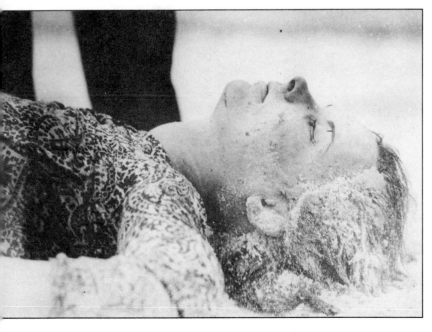

Investigators at the scene.

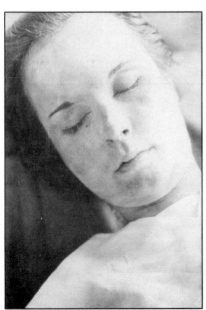

Mid-morning, June 8. Photograph taken by Milton Kruescher in Macken's Morgue. *Nassau County Museum*

Starr Faithfull. *Nassau County Museum*

Starr Faithfull in her late teens.

The remaining Faithfulls in the living room at 12 St. Luke's Place.

District Attorney Edwards and Inspector King

528 Ridgewood Road, West Orange

12 St. Luke's Place

Clive Anderson

Dr Otto Schultze

The paisley frock.
*Courtesy of the Commissioner of the Nassau County Police Department.*

Andrew J. Peters

Frank Wyman

Dr George Jameson Carr, on board the
*Laconia* in Boston Harbor, June 21

Francis Peabody Hamlin

From a set of fifty cards, 'Merchant Ships of the World,' which were inserted in cigarette packets circa 1925. The *Franconia* is at top.

J. V. Haring, handwriting expert, with his comparisons of snippets from Starr Faithfull's letters.

A photograph of Starr Faithfull 'doctored' by a tabloid artist.

I saw that she did not see me, so I let it pass and continued on my way to my residence in New York City, which is 70 East Ninety-Sixth Street.

Anderson, Windemere, Miss Fitzgerald. No one else spoke of seeing Starr between 11 and 6.

And no one at all spoke of seeing her between 9.30, when she went out again, thinking that the time was 8.50, and the early hours of the morning.

A small mystery was added to the large one of how she spent those dark hours. Shortly after the interview with Harry Stoner which seemed to prove that she had made up the story about a party attended by Miriam Hopkins on the Wednesday, it was learned that the actress was the guest of honour at a party on the *Thursday* night, the eve of her departure for Hollywood. Also that Harry Stoner was among the seventy-five ordinary guests. The going-away party, starting at seven and ending around midnight, was given by Bennett Cerf, the thirty-three-year-old founder and president of the Random House publishing company, in his offices at 20 East Fifty-Seventh Street. Cerf, who had inherited a fortune from his French-Jewish maternal grandmother, was

tall, brown-eyed and bespectacled, and flawlessly tailored. [He] looked the dandy, but was saved from foppishness by his boyish, cheerful, unsophisticated manner. He, moreover, was genuinely warm-hearted and likeable and hard-working, and much of his display – his lavish houses, his devotion to Cadillacs, his dining at Toot Shor's, his self-publicity – was forgiven him. He was, after all, Bennett Cerf, and he made very few pretences about his love of pleasure and fun. [1]

Interviewed again, Stoner explained that he had 'not thought to mention previously that there was a real party for Miss Hopkins, as it did not seem material to the questions . . . asked at that time'. He had received the invitation, in the form of a telegram, on Tuesday, 12 June. He agreed that it was 'strange that Starr Faithfull should have referred to a party attended by Miriam Hopkins if she had no prior knowledge of the Cerf party', but stuck to his original statement that he had not seen her for about a month. 'If she heard of the Cerf party, she got the information from somebody other than myself.' He said that she may have gate-crashed that party 'after 9 p.m., which was when I left, long before the end. I should

1. Obituary, *New York Times*, 29 August 1971. (The obituary began on the front page, because Cerf had gained national celebrity as a panellist on the television game-show, *What's My Line?*, between 1951 and 1964.)

certainly have been aware of her presence if she had arrived whilst I was there, but I was not so aware. I left in the company of Mr Harold Allen, a lawyer, and Mr Walter Carnelli, who is an artist. The latter has leased Miss Hopkins' apartment at 108 Waverley Place [Greenwich Village] during her absence. Mr Carnelli and I went on to the Players Club at 16 Gramercy Park [on the east side of Manhattan, between Broadway and Bellevue Hospital], where I signed the guest book, registering Mr Carnelli, and also signed checks for the food for the evening. Our arrival and presence at the Players Club can be confirmed; telephone is Gramercy 5-6116. I met a great many people at the Cerf party, but I do not remember the names of a great many of those I met. The names I do remember are: Miss Lily Cahill, the actress,[1] Mr and Mrs Ramon Buffano of Waverley Place, and Mr Ward Morehouse, dramatic editor for the *New York Evening Sun*.'

By chance, Harold Allen visited Stoner during the second interview. He confirmed that he, Stoner and Carnelli left the party at nine. He said that, as he was Bennett Cerf's lawyer, he 'did not care to mention' whom he knew or met at the party, but gave the address of the apartment where Cerf lived with his father – 13a, 112 East Fifty-Ninth Street – and suggested that the publisher should be asked for the guest-list.

Fifteen years later, Cerf recalled the party and some incidents following and springing from it:[2]

> Since Miriam Hopkins invited all her friends, and I invited all mine, and since almost all of them brought companions unknown to either of us, nobody was quite sure who was there and who was not. To add to the confusion, an impetuous acquaintance from Havana insisted on bringing his twelve-piece rumba band, which played as loudly and continuously as possible. The low ceilings intensified the racket, and everybody poured down cocktails out of sheer self-defence.
>
> The evening ended inexplicably in the swimming pool of the Shelton Hotel, and then Jim Crowder and I went down to the Jersey shore for . . . golf and recuperation. We heard about the discovery of Starr Faithfull's body, but paid very little attention until Jim bought a newspaper at the Elberon station on the way home.
>
> 'Hello,' he said, 'get a load of this headline: "Starr Faithfull Last Seen at Publisher's Orgy"! 'Orgy, hey?' I answered. 'I wonder who the

1. She must have left not much later than 7.30, as she was starring as 'Lucille Lingard' in the successful comedy, *As Husbands Go*, at the Golden Theatre on West Forty-Fifth Street.
2. In his 'Trade Winds' gossip-column in *The Saturday Review*, 30 March 1946.

publisher was.' 'You can stop wondering,' said Jim. 'It was you.'

There were a dozen reporters waiting for me when I arrived home, not to mention my father, who said, 'I told you the office was no place for shenanigans like that. You and your rumba band! Serves you right.'

I put the following sentence in italics for two reasons, one being that it suggests that Harry Stoner told Cerf something that contradicted part of his official statement:

*To this day we have never found one soul who saw Starr Faithfull at the party, although an artist friend remembered mentioning the party to her while she was modelling for him a few days earlier . . .*

Then [Martin Littleton,] an assistant district attorney from Nassau County, very stern, very professional, arrived at the office. 'I'm sure the girl never came here,' he said, 'but I think we'll have to subpoena every guest at the party.' 'That would inconvenience a lot of people,' I pointed out. 'It's a long ride [to Mineola]. And what could they tell you?' 'Nothing,' he conceded glumly, 'but it would show the press we were leaving no stone unturned.' 'One of the stones would be Nelson Doubleday [president of the vast Doubleday publishing corporation],' I said thoughtfully. 'He was here and so were a lot of his friends.' The DA thought it over, then murmured, 'Well, the hell with it.' (Mr Doubleday is one of the biggest taxpayers in Nassau County.)

That about ends the story, except that Miriam Hopkins phoned from California the next day. 'I never heard of Starr Faithfull before,' she said, 'but I guess I can thank her for hitting the front page on my very first day in Hollywood.'

From the *New York Herald Tribune*, 17 June 1931:

When questioned in Hollywood last night, Miss Hopkins ... acknowledged that a farewell party had been given for her on Thursday, June 4. She left afterwards for the Coast on the Twentieth Century Limited [train] ... 'Miss Faithfull may have been at the party and I may even have been introduced to her,' she said, 'but, if so, I do not recall it. I do not know Jack Greenaway or Bruce Winston. For that matter, I don't know any of the persons mentioned in connection with the party Miss Faithfull is said to have attended. I'm beginning to think it was another party.'

The thought that Starr may have attended a different party, perhaps graced by the presence of an actress other than Miriam Hopkins, caused reporters to wonder what a woman presently calling herself Peggy *Hopkins* Joyce was doing on the Thursday night. The Hopkins and Joyce components of the name were mementoes of

155

two of her three annulled marriages (she would be married three times more). Round about 1928, between her second and third matrimonial ventures, she had appeared in some Broadway shows, usually only showing off her blonde and buxom beauty, but once having some lines to say. The third of her husbands, Stanley Joyce, a Chicago lumberman, was said to have given her jewellery valued at a million and a half dollars. Her publicity manager, the most hard-working member of her entourage, told reporters that the night of 4 June was about the only one this year when she had *not* given or gone to a party.

Mrs Faithfull seems to have spent the whole of Thursday at home.

Tucker never publicly admitted it, but she went out during the afternoon. When she left the apartment, she was carrying a coat of imitation leopard-skin over her arm; she was without it when she returned. Meantime, she visited a pawnshop next to the New Yorker Hotel, at Eighth Avenue and Thirty-Fourth Street. Two sailors, Edwin Mansfield and Karl Conjer, attached to the Coast Guard cutter *Upsher*, entered the shop soon after her, and were so intrigued by the sight and sound of 'a beautiful young girl arguing with a hard-boiled shylock' that, a week later, when they saw a picture of Tucker in a paper, they knew for sure that she was the girl. She wanted fifty dollars for the coat, which she insisted was of real leopard-skin. The pawnbroker offered fifteen, saying that the material was 'best-quality hokum'. After considerable haggling, she accepted twenty, then stamped out, muttering anti-semitically.

Stanley was busy in Boston from early in the day till the late afternoon.

The 'primary reason' for his visit, so he afterwards said, 'was to consult with Mr Jordan Marsh, operator of the well-known department store of the same name, respecting Airian pneumatic mattresses'. There is no information as to whether or not he persuaded the operator to stock some. (By the time he spoke of the consultation, George Perry, worried that Stanley's sudden fame might have a depressing effect on the sales of the pneumatic mattresses, had apologetically sacked him.)

A second reason for his visit to Boston was to call on Charles Rowley, at the lawyer's request, made about four weeks before, following the mysterious phoning of Alexander Whiteside by a man claiming to represent a news agency.

The substance of the discussion, together with details of other matters, was divulged by Rowley on 18 June, when he was interviewed by a member of the Burns detective agency, acting on the instruction of Elvin Edwards:

Mr Rowley referred to a cash settlement made to the Faithfull family in 1927 by a man whose identity he hid by speaking of him as 'Mr X'. The matter, he said, had been handled with the utmost discretion by himself, and he did not know that anyone knew anything about it, otherwise than the persons involved, until about May 4 of this year. At that time, he heard from the attorney for Mr X, who said that he had just received a telephone call from a man who stated that he represented the United Press [*sic*] and that he understood that Mr X had been the victim of a shake-down, involving Starr Faithfull and the Faithfull family. Mr X's attorney jumped to the conclusion that Mr Faithfull had been talking. Mr Rowley said that he immediately got in touch with Faithfull, whereupon Faithfull denied positively that he had said anything to anybody. Faithfull repeated that denial at the meeting with Mr Rowley on 4 June . . .

Mr Rowley told me that he was very much averse to going to New York for questioning and, at any event, could not go for two or three weeks as he had been planning for some time to go away with a friend on a private yacht on a salmon fishing trip. He also stated, in a joking way, that he might be seen going to New York, and conferring with the authorities of Nassau County, and if so, and if Starr Faithfull had been murdered, he might be bumped off because of his knowledge concerning the claim that the Faithfull family made against Mr X. He did not make this as a serious statement.

He said that, at the meeting with Faithfull in his own office on June 4, Faithfull, after some round-about conversation, remarked that he had a house somewhere on Cape Cod [Mrs Faithfull's house at Centerville] which he valued at about $25,000, that being the sum that had been offered for it three years ago. Faithfull asked Mr Rowley what he thought the place would be worth today, with the real estate market in its present condition. Mr Rowley told him that if he had been offered $25,000 for it three years ago, he would say its current value would not exceed $12,000.

After further round-about conversation, Faithfull explained that he was in danger of losing the Cape property. He said that actual fore-closure proceedings had been completed early in 1930, but he had prevailed upon Mr Ralph Dunbar, an attorney and former judge who was a long-time friend of his wife's family, to put up $3250 so as to repossess the property on the understanding that he (Faithfull) would meet all interest and carrying charges. Faithfull admitted to Mr Rowley that he had not been able to keep to his promise. Early in 1931, Mr Dunbar had had to put up an additional $200, and had warned Faithfull that he could not carry the place indefinitely and would have to sell. Faithfull further admitted to Mr Rowley that a cheque he had sent to Mr Dunbar had bounced, but that he had afterwards made it good. Faithfull said he had met Mr Dunbar on April 25 of this year, and Mr Dunbar had agreed not to sell the property until May 25, thereby giving Faithfull time to come up with the necessary cash.

Faithfull then said that it was his purpose to obtain a mortgage loan on the house of not less than $15,000 and that he was of the impression that he could obtain a loan of this amount from Mr X, who had previously paid $25,000 to Faithfull to settle his demands. Mr Rowley said he made no comment to this, but that the manner in which this was suggested did not smell good to him, and he was more than ever convinced that Faithfull was a man who would stoop to almost anything to obtain money, if he thought he could get away with it.

As Mr Rowley made no comment, Faithfull then asked his advice as to the best manner of approach to Mr X in order to effect this mortgage loan arrangement. Mr Rowley replied that he did not know how he could go about it, and he preferred not to have anything to do with it. Faithfull at that time spoke about the extreme nervous condition of Starr Faithfull. Faithfull implied that her condition was due to her treatment at the hands of Mr X. He said that the Faithfull family were absolutely without funds, although at one time they had upwards of $50,000, including the money that Mr X had paid, and $30,000 that had come to them in legacies.

Faithfull, Mr Rowley said, was a chemist, and at one time was associated with some Jews in New York in the chemical industry, that he had expected big returns from this connection, but for some reason it blew up as far as Faithfull was concerned, and he was pushed out of the picture.

Mr Rowley has no doubt whatever that Faithfull, just previous to the time of Starr Faithfull's death, had been engaged directly or indirectly in a further attempt to shake down Mr X, and he would not be at all surprised to learn that this was not the only occasion on which Faithfull had attempted to use his step-daughters as a means of blackmail. However, he had no definite knowledge of such attempts beyond what he stated to me.

(Long afterwards, the private eye's report came to Stanley Faithfull's notice. He at once got in touch with Rowley and threatened to sue him if he did not disclaim some of the statements attributed to him. Rowley at once wrote to Stanley, saying that though the subject of the mortgage on the house at Centerville had arisen during their conversation on 4 June, 'both you and I know that you made no suggestion of approaching Peters at all'.)

Stanley's third, and apparently last, appointment in Boston on 4 June was with the lawyer, Charles Walkup, who had represented him and his wife in the action against the State of Massachusetts in regard to their motoring accident. (Supposing that Walkup took twenty per cent of the $4062 awarded to the Faithfulls in April, they were left with $3250. It appears that they used up every cent of that bonanza, either in celebration or to pacify creditors who were threatening legal action against *them*.)

Walkup would be interviewed by a Burns man on 19 June:

> Mr Walkup informed me of certain prior matters relevant to his meeting with Mr Faithfull in the afternoon of June 4, viz. – on April 28 of this year Mr Faithfull got in touch with Mr Walkup about a residential property in Centerville, which he was concerned was to be repossessed, and furthermore stated that Mr Ralph W. Dunbar had put up the necessary funds to save the property but was seeking to recoup his outlay. Mr Walkup subsequently contacted Mr Dunbar and also, in conjunction with his partner, Mr Brooks, perused documents relating to the Centerville property, and on May 19 wrote to Mr Faithfull, stating his opinion that if Mr Faithfull was unable to repay Mr Dunbar, the latter would feel entitled on May 16, immediately following a grace period allowed by Mr Dunbar to Mr Faithfull, to accept an offer of $15,000 he, Mr Dunbar, had received for the house.
>
> Mr Walkup, speaking of his conference with Mr Faithfull on June 4, told me that Mr Faithfull related to him an account of a sexual liaison between Starr Faithfull and Mr Andrew J. Peters, and went on to suggest that Mr Peters might be willing to put up the money needed to save the Centerville property, and wondered whether Mr Walkup could suggest a method of approach.
>
> Mr Walkup then told Mr Faithfull flatly that he would have nothing to do with the proposal, and Mr Faithfull thereupon left, remarking that he had no further business to transact in Boston and was going home.

*How* did he go home? Well, according to Stanley (who, you will remember, first of all said that he travelled *to* Boston on the Wednesday night by bus, then said that he took a train), he made the return journey by sea – on the s.s. *Commonwealth*, one of two vessels (the other the *Priscilla)* of the Fall River Line which plied between the port of Fall River,[1] forty miles south of Boston, and Manhattan. He said that he bought his ticket (which would have cost him $5.50) at the Copley Plaza Hotel, one of sixteen booking-places in Boston for the Fall River Line. The ticket covered the journey on the boat-train from Boston's South Station to Fall River as well as a berth on the *Commonwealth*. Stanley: 'The so-called boat-train leaves Boston at 6 p.m., and I think it takes about an hour and a half to run to Fall River. The purser for the ship assigned me stateroom 504 or 505.'

---

1. Best known to most readers of this kind of book as the setting of the Borden murders, generally attributed to Lizzie Borden, in 1892. Following her acquittal – which meant, among other things, that she was entitled to her share of the estate of her murdered father and step-mother – Lizzie bought a mansion in Fall River and,

For some reason which — whatever it was, indicates the thoroughness of the investigation — a Nassau County detective went to Pier 14, on the south-eastern edge of Manhattan, close to Brooklyn Bridge. The pier was where the Fall River Line steamers docked. The detective asked to see the passenger lists for the *Commonwealth*'s voyage on the night of June 4/5, and was told by the man in charge, whose name was Pusch, that they were kept at the company's head office in New Haven, Connecticut. He phoned the head office, explained what he wanted to know, and was told that the information would be 'despatched expeditiously'. Next day, he received a package of photostats of passenger lists made out at fifteen of the sixteen Boston booking places; an enclosed note expressed apologies for 'the fact that one list, that made out by our agent at the Copley Plaza Hotel, appears to have been mislaid, either while en route to this office from our purser's office at Fall River or since its arrival with those lists located following your request for same'.

Subsequently, the purser was interviewed, his office searched.

The mystery of the missing list — the very one that would have proved or disproved Stanley's statement — was never solved. Rather, it was deepened — by the discovery of the name *G.E. Faithfull* on one of the surviving lists. *That* Faithfull turned out to be a lawyer, 'about 30 years of age, 5ft. 11in., 150 pounds', living and working in Manhattan, who had travelled to Cambridge, across the river from Boston, on 3 June, to attend a reunion of alumni of the Massachusetts Institute of Technology, and who, having booked a place aboard the *Commonwealth* on 4 June, had felt so queasy after the reunion that he had decided not to use his ticket but to return to Manhattan by a mode of transport less likely to make him sick. He 'claimed no known relationship with Stanley Faithfull, although he ventured the opinion that some connection might exist, could the family tree be traced back some years in England'.

There was no name that looked anything like 'Faithfull' on the 'accommodation chart' made out by the purser for the *Commonwealth*'s voyage on 4 June. The space on the chart for Stateroom 504, one of the alternative two mentioned by Stanley, was marked with a symbol meaning 'unallocated'. Stateroom 505

---

sanguine at the gossip about both her axewomanship and her association with certain unconventional persons of her own sex, remained there, insisting on being called Lizbeth, till her death in 1927.

had been allocated to a Mr Gibson — who, a note on the chart showed, had complained that the room was too close to the engines and been transferred to No. 139, leaving No. 505 vacant.

The search for the Copley Plaza list was halted in mid-stream when Stanley, after two visits to Pier 14 while the *Commonwealth* was docked there, on each occasion to examine Stateroom *501*, wrote to the chief executive of the Fall River Line, accusing 'your Mr R.H. Pusch and others of your staff of giving out erroneous information to reporters and the Nassau County District Attorney's office,' and threatening to 'sue the Fall River Line and have slanderous subordinates discharged'. The threat was taken seriously, and, so far as the investigation was concerned, the Line went dead.

What with all the interest in *whether or not* Stanley returned from Boston when and how he said he did, no one thought to ask him *why*, having gone to Boston by bus or train, he had chosen to come home on a ship. It wasn't that there were no buses, no trains, available; the combined rail/sea ticket cost more than a plain train or bus ticket. Perhaps, at some time between his calls on the three Bostonians — Jordan Marsh, Charles Rowley, Donald Walkup — he spotted and was entranced by a placard for 'The Inland Water Route to New York: Sailing on the Sound at dusk is *the surest way to get an enjoyable night of rest*. On famous modern Steamers with orchestras for dancing, and special entertainment each trip. That's the way to travel, these Summer nights.' Or perhaps not.

## Friday, 5 June

The *Commonwealth* docked at Pier 14 between 6.00 and 6.30 a.m.

Anyone disembarking and going on foot to St Luke's Place would probably have proceeded west along Fulton Street, passing City Hall on the right, then north along Church Street, then a bit further north along Seventh Avenue, and then turned left into the Place.

A journey of just under two miles — which, at average walking pace, and allowing for any stumbling till the walker had recovered his land-legs, would have taken about twenty-five minutes.

According to Stanley, and to Mrs Faithfull and Tucker, he arrived in the apartment at half-past eight. He does not seem to have been asked why he had dawdled so.

Still according to all three Faithfulls, Starr went out at half-past nine, saying that she was thinking of having lunch uptown and getting her hair waved; Stanley had given her a couple of dollars.

He stated to a detective that 'he went to the office of the Airian Products Corporation, in the Woolworth Building, soon after 10 a.m., and spent the rest of the day there, with the exception of some two hours during which he discussed a business matter with some wholesale dealer in cloths or materials, whose name he did not remember'.

Tucker stated to the same detective that 'as the weather was warm [70° at 9 a.m., 82° at 3 p.m., 76° at 8 p.m.] and she felt indisposed, she spent the entire day lounging around the apartment reading'.

Mrs Faithfull stated to the same detective that 'she left home shortly before noon, spent the afternoon with her friend, Mrs Foster, at the latter's home in Washington Square, and afterwards went to some tea uptown, not returning home until evening'.

At 11.30 in the morning, Starr bought a paper from Isaac Ginsberg, who sold them from his stand at West Ninth Street and Sixth Avenue, half a mile north of St Luke's Place. He knew her by sight, as she used to buy papers from him when she, her mother and Tucker − not Stanley − were living at 35 West Ninth Street. Idly watching her as she walked away, he saw her descend the steps to the uptown platform of the Hudson tube station.

At noon, Mrs Daisy Wyberg, who had just arrived in town from her home at Mamaroneck, a few miles north of the Bronx, was sitting in the reception area of the Grand Central branch of Carey's, a chain of beauty shops, and chatting with the manager, Mrs Mary Tubeck. A report in the *New York Daily News* of what happened there and then does not differ in detail from the official version:

> Two pretty girls walked into the shop and approached Mrs Tubeck. One of them was a tall, slender brunette, strikingly beautiful, and the other was as fascinating in her blonde charm as the other was in her dark allure. The brunette spoke.
>
> 'I would like to get a wave,' she said.
>
> 'I'm sorry,' replied the manager, 'but we're all booked up. But if you wish, we can probably take care of you in about an hour. Some of the girls may be idle then, and, besides, some of the customers may break their dates.'
>
> 'Very well,' the dark girl nodded. 'What time shall I return?'
>
> 'Let's make it one o'clock,' Mrs Tubeck responded. She reached for her loose-leaf appointment book and a pencil. 'What is the name, please?'
>
> 'My name is Starr Faithfull,' said the slender beauty.
>
> 'My goodness, what a lovely name!' exclaimed the manager, glancing

at Mrs Wyberg, who smiled and nodded — it *was* a charming name.

'All right, Miss Faithfull,' said Mrs Tubeck, writing down the name and the hour. 'I hope you'll be faithful in keeping your appointment.'

All four of the women laughed at this poor pun, and the two young girls went out. Starr never returned.

Written substantiation of this incident is not available, because it is the practice at the shop to destroy the loose-leaves after the check-up is completed each Saturday night.

Mrs Wyberg entertains no doubt as to the day of the week, the day of the month, and the hour of the day; first, because she doesn't often come to the city, and second, because she had an appointment for that time with the shop. Mrs Tubeck confirms her client's memory.

Around about the time when Mary Tubeck was thinking, or even tutting, something about unfaithfulness, Murray Edelman was edging his cab to the front of the queue of cabs at the far western end of Fourteenth Street, opposite the entrance to the Cunard Piers — a good two miles from Grand Central.

We have come across Edelman before. On the previous Friday, he, then some way back in the queue, was sent to buy lemons in aid of the girl thwarted from stowing away on the *Franconia* (page 143).

On this second Friday,

I went to work at six o'clock in the morning and cruised along the docks. I can't be exact about the time, but a little after one o'clock that afternoon I reached the head of the line outside the Cunard piers when this young woman, who I recognised immediately as the person I had seen May 29th in a hysterical condition, came out from the passenger entrance to Pier 53 accompanied by a man wearing a blue suit with brass buttons and striped gold braid across the cuffs. This man was stocky built, about 5ft 7in. tall; seemed to weigh about 150 pounds; wore black shoes and military collar. About 37 years of age. He had no hat. He had black hair, dark eyes, ruddy complexion, and appeared to have been drinking. The name 'Cunard' was lettered on the lapels of his uniform. The brass buttons on it looked extra bright. From the uniform, I judged the man to be a steward, and I guessed he was attached to the Cunard ship at Pier 53 at the time I am speaking of.

(That was the *Mauretania*, which had arrived from Southampton the day before and was due to depart at 5 p.m. on a four-day 'whoopee cruise' to the Bahamas, carrying a crew of 609 and 452 passengers, the latter described by a society columnist in one of the morning papers as 'a glittering assemblage of pleasure seekers of such calibre as the famous Phyllis Haver of the films, Joseph

Schenck, head of United Artists, and Sam Rosoff, the subway builder'. Another Cunard liner, the *Carmania*, which had arrived at Pier 56 from Southampton on Sunday, 31 May, was being made ready to sail back to Southampton on Tuesday, 9 June.)

> The girl's hair was combed pretty. I smelt alcohol on her when she came close to me. She had been drinking but was able to walk. She got into my taxi first and the man in uniform got in on the other side.
>
> He told me to drive to 12 St Luke's Place. He spoke with an English accent. When he gave this address, I recognised it immediately as the address which the same woman had given on Friday, May 29. We drove east on Fourteenth Street, down Hudson Street to St Luke's Place, and I brought the cab up in front of 12 St Luke's Place.
>
> The man and the girl were talking on the way down but I could not overhear what was said. But as she started to get out, she said:
>
> 'I'll see you at the wharf about four o'clock. Bye-bye Brucie.'

*Brucie.* Edelman was sure that was what he had heard. But no one among the crew of the *Mauretania* had the forename of Bruce – or anything like it – or a surname that might have been misheard as Brucie. And no one among the crew had the forename or surname of Winston. There is an irritating note in a report written by Martin Littleton in November 1931: 'Amongst the officers of the *Carmania* appeared a third engineer by the name of Boosey, but this man was apparently in England and could not be questioned.' The use of the word 'apparently', together with the fact that I have come across no other reference to Engineer Boosey, suggests that insufficient efforts were made to trace him. Perhaps the next paragraph of Edelman's statement, which contained implicit support for his belief that the uniformed man worked on the *Mauretania*, and that he was a steward, was seen by the investigators as a reason for turning away from the Boosey lead as soon as it looked like being hard to follow up:

> The man, who seemed anxious to get rid of the girl, said to her: "Don't come back. The passengers will be embarking. I'll be too busy."
>
> The girl got out of the cab and the man remained inside. She started to walk up the steps of 12 St Luke's Place, but at that moment I started my cab back so as to turn around, and when I again looked around, she had disappeared.
>
> The man said: "To hell with her. I have had my pleasure. Take me back to the pier."
>
> I drove him back to the Cunard pier and stopped at the passenger entrance. He paid me $1.25 and then walked to the freight entrance. The

fare each way was 35 cents and there was some waiting time. The $1.25 included a tip.

I remained at the Cunard pier taking my turn in line, and at about two o'clock my cab was again at the head of the line. I was outside of the cab, leaning on the front fender, when I saw this same girl come out of the freight entrance. The same man who was with her before was walking with her, holding her by the arm. I opened the door for them. The man put the girl inside the cab and said to me:

'Take her back to 12 St Luke's Place, and under no circumstances let her come back again.'

Edelman's recollection of this incident was partially corroborated by another cabbie, Samuel Weiss, who hailed from Brooklyn: 'About 2 p.m. that Friday I was near the Cunard piers, waiting my turn, when I saw a ship's officer and a girl leave the freight gate, and I saw Murray Edelman put her in his taxi. The girl looked drunk to me. I have been shown photographs of Starr Faithfull, and I am sure she was the girl I saw.' Back to Edelman:

I started to drive east on Fourteenth Street, but before reaching Tenth Avenue, when directly in front of the Munson Lunch, there was a truck in front of me and I had to stop my cab. At that moment the girl said:

'I have only got ten cents. I'll have to get out.'

Before I could say anything the girl opened the door on the right side of the cab, next to the Munson Lunch, and got out. She walked a few feet to the corner of Fourteenth Street and Tenth Avenue, and turned south on Tenth Avenue. I pulled my cab up to the corner and watched her. She walked down to the next corner and then turned right, walking towards the piers. That is the last I saw of her.

My trip record (*produced*) shows one trip to St Luke's Place [but no house number] and back to the pier, and the second trip as far as Fourteenth and Tenth. [He had not recorded the times.]

I thought nothing further about the girl until I saw a picture of Starr Faithfull in a morning newspaper and recognised her at once. I told this to Sam Katz, the patrolman, and he reported it to his precinct. Ever since, I am hounded by the police and reporters. This week I did not get to do a day and a half's work the whole week. This affair has cost me dear.

Murray protested too much. Several reporters paid him for quotes, and he received a specially handsome reward, well in excess of a week's earnings from hacking, for talking to the city editor of the *New York American* for three and a half hours one evening, when he wouldn't have been working anyway.

\*

Thirty-three-year-old Mrs Anita Valentine, an alumna of the posh Wellesley College, near Boston, was a freelance writer. Though she and her husband Allard were separated, they were still good friends, and every so often she journeyed from her apartment to his, which was on the third floor of 52 Morton Street, to tidy it up. She did so on Friday, 5 June, arriving around midday and staying till four.

Morton Street is the next thoroughfare to the north of St Luke's Place. The rear of Allard Valentine's apartment was directly opposite the rear of the Faithfulls'; twenty yards away, across the two back-gardens.

Allard would have to do all of his chores for himself for the next few weeks, as Anita was leaving the following day for a vacation at Provincetown, at the very tip of Cape Cod.

According to Martin Littleton's report of what she told him when she got back to Manhattan,

> Between 3 and 4 p.m. that Friday, she heard piercing screams coming from the Faithfull apartment and another woman's voice saying, 'She mustn't do that. She must stop it.' Suddenly the shrieks ended as abruptly as they had started. She also heard the other woman, or another woman, talking in a loud voice. Mrs Valentine looked out the rear window to see if she could see anything, and she saw the Faithfull windows were open and what appeared to be several rugs hung over them, but she could see no signs of activity.
>
> So impressed by this event was Mrs Valentine that she noted the fact of its occurrence in her diary under the date, June 5. The notation was made the next day, Saturday, June 6. She did not read of the finding of Starr Faithfull's body until some days after it was first reported, and it was even later that she learned that the Faithfulls lived directly behind her husband's home. Mrs Valentine has been interrogated several times whilst she has been at Provincetown. She entertains no doubt whatever about the occurrence and has furnished an affidavit to that effect.

Detectives conducted a house-to-house inquiry in both Morton Street and St Luke's Place, but found no one else who had heard screams on the Friday afternoon. Mrs Faithfull said: 'If there were any untoward sounds in the vicinity of our apartment at that time, I would not have heard them, for I was away during the whole period from noon until evening.' Tucker said: 'Yes, I was home all day, alone during the afternoon. I was asleep some of the time, and I was never disturbed by the slightest sound, certainly not of screaming.' Stanley, who had already said that he was out all day from 10 a.m., said: 'There was no argument between any members of my family at any time that Friday ... We never hang rugs over the windows. Some time during the day − I have no idea *what* time − I did take a pneumatic mattress and place it on the roof to air and eliminate any odours which might have been present in the rubber. After putting it there, it disappeared mysteriously, and I am still wondering what happened to it.' Stanley made those comments to the press shortly after being sacked by George Perry − who, when he read them, may have suspected that the ones about the stinking pneumatic mattress that vanished into thin air were intended as reprisal against himself.

There was a sudden shower of rain on downtown Manhattan on the Friday night, starting at 10.20. Police Sergeant Patrick Dugan had been sheltering under an awning opposite the Cunard piers for five minutes when he saw

> a young woman and a stocky man come through the gate to Pier 56. I did not know the man, but I guessed he was connected with some ship. I recognised the woman as the same woman who I had seen on Friday, May 29, after she was ejected from the s.s. *Franconia* [page 143]. I had the opinion that she was now intoxicated. I overheard no conversation. They stood at the gate for a few moments and then a green taxi drove up and the man put the woman in the taxi and she was driven off. Having seen photographs of Starr Faithfull, I am convinced she was the woman I saw.

In darkness, even darkness diminished by artificial lights, it is hard to tell one dark colour from others. Dugan may have assumed that the cab was green − the colour of many of the minority of New York cabs that were not yellow − for the simple reason that it was not the light colour of the majority of cabs. However, a police report indicates that Dugan's statement was accepted as being accurate, colour and all:

> Because Starr Faithfull was seen entering a green cab, investigation was made of the Parmelee Taxicab System, who are the largest operators of green taxis in the City of New York. Their records for the date of June 5 respecting the fares carried by their green taxis were subjected to a thorough scrutiny but failed to reveal that any fare was carried from Pier 56 at any time during that day.

The fact that there is no mention in Dugan's statement of the direction taken by the hired cab must mean that he, asked about that, could not remember.

Starr Faithfull was driven away from Pier 56.
Whoever the driver was, he never admitted it.


## Saturday, 6 June

According to Mrs Faithfull, she, Stanley and Tucker 'were terribly concerned at breakfast, wondering what had become of Starr'. During the morning, Stanley walked to the Woolworth Building and expressed his anxiety to George Perry, who advised him to report Starr's disappearance to the police, and Tucker went away for the weekend.

When Stanley returned to the apartment, he began typing a letter for his wife to sign. Both of them afterwards said that he typed from her dictation; but that was shown to be a lie by the discovery of a draft of the letter in his handwriting on Airian Products Corporation notepaper. It appears likely that he had composed the letter the day before, while he was at the office. As he dated the letter 'June 5th, 1931', which was what he had written at the top of the draft, he seems to have been so satisfied with his composition that he copy-typed unthinkingly. The letter was to William Phillips, Martha Peters' elder brother:

My dear William:

I am sure that you must have heard something relative to an episode which involved Andrew Peters and Bamby. The affair in itself was horrible and the consequences to Bamby were worse than death. I am going to give you a brief account of the happenings from the year Bamby went to boarding school until now.

You will probably remember that you and other members of your family were kind enough to contribute the needed money for her school expenses and Andrew made the disbursements, thereby establishing a close contact between him and Bamby. In response to a telegram from Andrew, Bamby met him at the Biltmore Hotel in New York on June 29th, 1926. He telephoned me saying that he was taking Bamby to the theatre and had engaged a room for her at the Biltmore, where he was also staying. I met him the next morning at the Biltmore but Bamby had returned to [West] Orange, and I did not see her until my return home. I then found her hysterical and dazed and after questioning her for hours drew from her the story of the past years. Beginning when she was only a young child Andrew had forced his attentions on her and at many hotels where he had stopped with her on trips to North Haven and New York he had falsely registered her. On the previous night he had not been at the Biltmore but had registered her as his wife at the Astor Hotel, the reputation of which must be known to you. After hearing Bamby's story

Mr Faithfull went to the Astor and verified this registration.

I found it difficult to make up my mind what to do about such a grave matter. To present it to the District Attorney and have Andrew prosecuted under the Mann Act[1] would have hurt us all too much and my affection for your Mother was always so tremendously strong. So I did nothing.

Although I did not know the cause of Bamby's nervous condition we had been worried about her for some time and had arranged a cruise for her to the Mediterranean Sea. Hoping that an absolute change of scene might help her we let her go. Upon her return I realised that her condition was, if anything, worse and then placed her in the hands of an alienist specialist, as I feared for her sanity.

Later I went to Boston to place Tucker in school and saw Mrs Benjamin Russell of Brookline, a friend of Martha's as well as mine. She took me to task very seriously for not letting Martha know that Tucker was to be in Boston and said that if I did not, she would speak to Martha. She also wanted to know all about Bamby and why she did not keep up with the contacts with girls she formerly knew. I felt it was necessary to tell her the story about Andrew but cautioned her not to repeat it. She did, however, talk it over with her husband and the next day Mr Russell urged me to let him tell the story to his attorney, Mr Charles F. Rowley.

On my next trip to Boston I had a request from Mr Rowley to see him. He said he could not believe my story and that if I could not prove my statement I had done a very serious thing. We then employed detectives and submitted the evidence to Mr Rowley, such as a photostatic copy of the registration of Andrew with Bamby (which was false) at a third-class hotel in New York, proof of the registration at the Astor, etc. Andrew's explanation of his taking Bamby to the Richmond Hotel in New York and there registering her falsely was that he could not find any room in any first-class hotel. Investigation at the Hotel Association showed that first-class hotels were particularly empty that night. The evidence was so conclusive that Mr Rowley then interviewed the doctor who had charge of Bamby and then said he felt I should be reimbursed for at least the actual money I had spent on Bamby's case. Mr Rowley finally collected $20,000 for me. This is only a fraction of the amount which Mr Faithfull and I have had to spend for Bamby. No money can alleviate the suffering, even now, we are going through on account of Andrew's behaviour.

Bamby's case seemed to settle into one of nervous depression which could only be relieved by a change of scene, motion, travel. All the money from Andrew was used for Bamby in a desperate effort to restore a normal reaction towards life. At least once a year and sometimes twice a year we have planned a trip for her. My only reason for going abroad

---

1. A federal law (passed in 1910 through the efforts of James Robert Mann) forbidding the transportation of girls or women from state to state for immoral purposes.

last summer was to be with Bamby as I could not arrange any chaperone for her last year. You can see what a terrific financial drain this has been. This year we have been unable to plan any trip for her and her depression is so great I am more than ever worried.

To provide the money needed for her trip two years ago, I had to place a second mortgage on my house on Cape Cod. When this mortgage came due, it was impossible to renew it on account of the stock market crash and Mr Faithfull's business failed for the same reason. A friend in Boston advanced the money, but he now needs the money and if we cannot raise it within a very few days the house in which I have spent my summers for over thirty years I must lose. I have in the past had many offers of $25,000 and even today, at a forced sale, an offer has been made of $15,000. The first mortgage is $6000, of which $500 has been called, leaving a balance of $5500. The additional mortgage I need is $4500, to make the total mortgage $10,000. Last year I rented it for $1400, and this year we hope to get $1500. The net income from the house I want to use for the payment of interest and reduction of the mortgage.

As I have mentioned Mrs Russell and Mr Rowley in this letter, I am sending a copy to them.

For the time being, Mrs Faithfull did not sign the letter. The last sheet of it was left in the typewriter. Something might need to be added.

Around 10 p.m., Stanley left the apartment and walked to the police station on Charles Street to report the disappearance of his step-daughter Starr.

### Sunday, 7 June

During the morning or early afternoon, Stanley added the following to the letter to William Phillips:

Sunday, June 7th, 1931

Since writing this letter Bamby had disappeared and we can find no trace of her. Friday morning she left to take a walk and has not returned. We have enquired of every place where she might be found and nobody has seen her. Yesterday afternoon, Mr Faithfull went to Police Headquarters and listed her among the missing. Later the police were asked to send out a general alarm but we requested no publicity, such as newspapers, and still no word. All records of the hospitals and accidents have been examined but no clew. We are in a terrible predicament. If we give the information needed for a public search it would probably result in a lot of undesirable notoriety, involving perfectly innocent people. This is the one thing I have tried to avoid. We must find Bamby, and yet I do not see how I can do it privately. Can you help?

If you only knew how I regret having to write this letter to you, but I feel that your co-operation could help. Will you?

Mrs Faithfull signed herself 'Sincerely yours, Helen,' and some time before five, Stanley went out to post that letter (presumably, also the copies to Mrs Russell and Charles Rowley) and the one, signed as well as written by himself, to Francis Peabody Hamlin.

I cannot make out how the investigators learnt about the letter to William Phillips. It seems unlikely that the information came from Phillips or from Rowley. Perhaps Mrs Russell, or her husband, handed over her copy. Or perhaps Stanley's draft, or his retained copy, came to light when, in his absence from the apartment on a day towards the end of the first week of the investigation, Inspector King went there and, despite Mrs Faithfull's protests, rummaged around in Stanley's desk. (As soon as Stanley heard of King's warrantless search, he wrote to Elvin Edwards, accusing him of being 'an accessory to a wanton act of burglary'. Edwards wrote back that 'a stringent inquiry of the Inspector reveals that he in no way acted improperly'.)

However the letter to Phillips was discovered, Martin Littleton considered that, 'in itself, and by virtue of the fact that it was written and mailed in the period between Starr's disappearance and the finding of her dead body, together with other equivocal or more or less suspicious details in regard to Mr and Mrs Faithfull, Mr Faithfull in particular, the "Dear William" letter raises strong doubts as to whether the Faithfulls have been sincere and honest when speaking to us of matters directly or indirectly associated with Starr'.

Littleton arranged for a senior policeman, Lieutenant George MacGovern, to collect Mrs Faithfull, her alone, and bring her to his memento-lined office. He kept her waiting outside – partly, no doubt, in the hope that she, not knowing why he wanted to see her, would become tense, and partly because he needed a few minutes to clear his desk of everything except a photostat of the 'Dear William' letter and his much-thumbed copy of the New York State Penal Code, open at Section 2, which explained the penalties for withholding facts from public authorities during the course of a criminal investigation. Long afterwards, he needed to insist that 'nothing in the illumination of the office could have led Mrs Faithfull to feel that she was being subjected to a third-degree grilling: there was only a chandelier containing four lights of about

NEW YORK WORLD-TELEGRA

## Artists' Sketches of Central Figures

Stanley E. Faithfull.

Starr Faithfull.

50-watt capacity, and they were shining right down from the top – nothing of a blinding nature'.

The interview did not go according to plan. Mrs Faithfull – shown into the office by Lieutenant MacGovern, who straightway departed, leaving her alone with Littleton – appeared to be perfectly at ease:

172

in City's Most Mysterious Tradegy

Mrs. Stanley E. Faithfull.    Elizabeth Tucker Faithfull.

She sat down in the visitor's chair and, before I had the chance to state my purpose in summoning her, proceeded to tell me that she knew my father and was glad now that we had an opportunity to sit and talk like a lady and gentleman about the case; that we ought to be able to understand each other — meaning, I suppose, that we were removed from the police. I told her that the fact that she had met my father didn't interest me, and that personalities were not involved in this thing, and that I had asked her to come to talk with me about a matter that was somewhat delicate and difficult for me to put to her.

She said that I must think that she and her husband were queer people, strange people. I said, what I thought had no bearing on the case whatever – that it would be much better if we left that alone. But she was persistent in asking what I thought. She kept after the question of wanting to know what I thought and why I thought they were queer people.

At last, realising that she would not let up on the question, I told her that I indeed thought they were queer. I told her that I had never encountered anybody quite like them. She requested me to continue, so I told her that I thought they were queer because of the relationship that had existed between Andrew Peters and her own daughter from the time Starr was eleven years of age, and she, Mrs Faithfull, had never detected such a thing; the fact of her daughter, only a child, being allowed to go around touring the country with this comparatively elderly and rather remote relative, and indulge in the practices which had been described by Faithfull, without manifesting any outward sign of having gone through these ordeals. And I thought it was also queer that, as she and her husband claimed, on the occasion of Starr's first normal sexual experience with Peters, the girl should become hysterical and excited and overwrought at the age of twenty. None of that sounded very sensible. I told her what I thought about people who had told us that a girl was modest to the point of not putting her foot out of bed without a slipper, and what I thought about something Tucker had said, that she had never seen Starr nude. Those statements were almost beyond belief. Finally, there was the procurement of a man to come into their home as a guest and give him the opportunity of sexual relations with the daughter – that was, to me, an arrangement which was almost beyond belief. I was referring to Edwin Megargee.

When that part of why I thought the Faithfulls were queer people came up, she said about Megargee that it was done at the advice of a doctor, or it was considered essential for the health and welfare of the child, and that was about all she had to say.

Having been side-tracked from my purpose in having her brought to my office, I commented upon the 'Dear William' letter. In that connection I read to her Section 2 of the Penal Code. Because of suspicions that had developed in my mind, I commented in particular upon the significance of the letter in the light of that section of the Penal Code. She said that the letter was written because they were having trouble holding on to the Centerville property. She had written Phillips for assistance in carrying that property. She said that the letter, dated June 5 but continued on June 7, was written on a typewriter because she was indisposed with arthritis.

I told her that I was suspicious concerning the frankness of her husband, and that my suspicion was stimulated by the 'Dear William' letter. Referring to the continuation of the letter on June 7, two days after Starr's disappearance from home, I characterised those paragraphs as a 'poisonous addenda'. I said, or implied, that the letter, particularly the 'poisonous addenda', sounded to me like an obvious 'touch', an attempt to coerce Mr Phillips into parting with money.

She said that there was nothing at all 'poisonous' in the letter. She said that Mr Faithfull was not a relative of 'Dear William', and that was the reason or the propriety of the situation that required her to put her signature to the letter; she signed it because she was the relative asking for a favour.

She said little more than that. Most of the time, she just listened, because I was talking rather fast and voluble, and after a while I could see that she was getting annoyed. I was kind of run out of 'soap', and I guess she felt she had heard all she wanted to hear.

In the end, she stood up and said, 'I am not accustomed to being talked to this way.' That broke up the interview. I could see that I could not get any further with her. I called Lieutenant MacGovern in and asked him to drive Mrs Faithfull home. If she had stayed on, I would have asked her more about the timing and writing of the 'Dear William' letter. I tend to think, however, that I would not have got any reliable explanations from her. Like her husband, she was difficult to pin down on subjects that, for reasons of her own, she was not inclined to discuss. The 'Dear William' letter, with its 'poisonous addenda', was such a subject.

**Monday, 8 June**

One can be no more exact than this: several hours after the body was found at Long Beach, but still a few hours before Stanley identified it, Tucker came home.

Where had she spent the weekend? With whom?

During the following days, reporters kept on putting those questions to the remaining Faithfulls, and they, all three of them, refused to say more than what one of them, Stanley, said: 'None of your ____ business! A person's social activities are his or her private concern.' Then a stringer in the seaside town of Providence, Rhode Island, came up with the news that, early on the Monday morning, Tucker 'registered at the Biltmore Hotel here but without taking a room, and after smoking cigarettes in an agitated manner for about ten mintues, approached an assistant manager and began negotiations for a loan of $5. After some deliberation on the part of the assistant manager, she received the money and signed a note in acknowledgment, giving her name as "Sylvia Faithfull", and appending the New York address of her family. She left shortly thereafter.'

Till that report appeared, none of the official investigators had shown the slightest interest in Tucker's absences from home over the past *two* weekends. Now, however, the leading investigators, those privy to the confidential information about Andrew Peters, were very much interested indeed – the reason being that the Biltmore, Providence, was one of the hotels where Starr and Peters had stayed during their motoring tour in the summer of 1923 (the itinerary of which Starr had subsequently noted in her scrapbook).

Tucker was immediately interviewed by Elvin Edwards, who promised her that nothing she said about her weekends away would be passed on to the press. She told him that she had spent both weekends in Providence, most of the time in the company of a local businessman, J.D.K. Jones, Junior, whom she had known for some months, having been introduced to him 'at a select social gathering in New York'. She had had to pawn her imitation leopard-skin coat so as to afford the fare to Providence on Saturday, 6 June. It was a complete coincidence that she had visited the hotel where her sister had stayed for one night eight years before. She would not have needed to go there if Mr Jones 'had not turned out to be only half a gentleman' and refused to give her the money for her fare home.

Edwards kept his promise, and the papers continued to print at least one paragraph per edition about the 'mystery' or 'puzzle' or 'conundrum' or 'enigma of Tucker's weekend whereabouts'. Thus becoming as celebrated as Stanley, and far more so than her mother, Tucker received piles of mail, including offers of marriage and of non-speaking engagements, in night-clubs, theatres, circuses, fairground booths, and, as a 'featured guest-star', in low-budget movies. Stanley described the offers as 'barbarous', adding that his own enlarged mail was 'mostly from cranks and lunatics – spiritual mediums and suchlike – and not even deserving my contempt'. Tucker said:

'I, of course, take one look at the communications of a romantic nature and treat them as garbage. As for the commercial offers that appear to be respectable, I don't think I can avail myself of any of them. I suppose, when everything is settled down, I'll have to go to work to keep occupied, but that is out of the question at present.

There are too many worries and distractions for myself and my family. No one seems to see our side of things, just because we don't keep emoting all over the place.'

## 5

**W**arned by Dr Otto Schultze that if he didn't take a short rest, he would be forced to take a long one, Elvin Edwards – who *did* look 'exhausted', 'haggard', 'careworn', when he talked to the Mineola-based reporters ('around eighty or a hundred of them,' by Inspector King's reckoning) on Friday, 12 June – set off that night to spend the weekend at his country house near Riverhead, facing Great Peconic Bay at the eastern end of Long Island.

Next morning, the *New York Times* published a witty but not quite accurate editorial headed **A Model Prosecutor**:

> Once upon a time there was a District Attorney who enjoyed publicity. He got much attention from the metropolitan newspapers. But the items about him were often brief and were placed on inside pages. Life was beginning to seem dull, when in rushed an assistant with the news that the unidentified body of a girl had been found floating in the waters which washed the prosecutor's district. 'Let us investigate at once and bring the culprits to justice,' said he. 'And be sure to tell me when the reporters arrive.'
>
> The reporters arrived, but the District Attorney was away investigating. They had not long to wait, for the considerate prosecutor was kind enough to telephone to them as they sat in his office. Although the county medical examiner had given the cause of death as drowning, the District Attorney announced on the telephone that the girl had been murdered by two men, one of whom was prominent in politics. The corpse, he said, had been taken to the waterside by motor and then thrown out from a small boat. This made what is known as a Good Story, and the District Attorney's name decorated all the first pages. The next day he had a new explanation which he obligingly made public. The girl had been beaten into unconsciousness and then thrown from a boat, whereupon, being unconscious, she drowned. Two men had done this. 'Was one of them the prominent politician?' 'No, the politician has been practically eliminated from the case.' This made another Good Story. On the third day the prosecutor said that he had summoned prominent witnesses to tell the grand jury what they knew. 'Just watch who comes

to my office,' he said; 'you will see how prominent they are.' And he was good enough to add that the dead girl's diary contained very interesting reading. That made still another Good Story, although it got matters no nearer to solution.

Of course, none of this could have happened in the United States, least of all around New York City, where, as everyone knows, public prosecutors are more intent on preparing their cases than giving out piece-meal and contradictory information while in the throes of preparation. Because of this scorn for publicity, all mysteries in this neighbourhood are solved with dignity and despatch.

First thing on Monday, Edwards — looking 'greatly refreshed' and 'exhibiting no sign of the slight laryngitis which was evident prior to his brief sojourn by the sea' — invited a few reporters, none from the *Times*, into his office and read out a long statement, presumably written while he should have been resting, which ended:

> I would feel myself derelict in my duty, no matter what the criticism is, unless we ran down every clew, because it is quite evident that Starr Faithfull dead lessens the danger to certain people than if she remained alive to talk.

Over the weekend, reporters other than those at Mineola or in St Luke's Place had run down clues — some deciphered from equivocal comments by Edwards, some from remarks that Stanley Faithfull had, perhaps unguardedly, let slip — to the identity of the 'prominent politician' and to that of the man who had paid for the Faithfulls' silence about something or other involving himself and Starr. By Sunday evening, at the latest, many editors knew that the politician and the payer were one and the same: Andrew J. Peters. The editors talked with their lawyers, who told them what they had expected to hear, that, no matter how sure they were of the Peters connection, no matter that an unequivocal reporting of it would send circulation figures sky-rocketing, until there was a far slighter danger of Peters suing for libel, of winning colossal damages, references to him had to be distanced, just by a sentence or so, from references to the politician, the payer. Readers might — or rather, to be unpublicly frank, certainly would — read between the lines, but no newspaper with artful re-write men could be held responsible for such astigmatism. The lawyers may have added that, though the Freedom of the Press did not extend to the hounding of interesting parties, the maximum fines that could be imposed for offences committed in the normal course of hounding were so moderate that they could be paid out of the petty cash.

Each of the editors despatched reporters to Peters' home in Jamaica Plain, Boston. Each contingent of reporters had similar instructions to 'offer Peters the opportunity to comment on unconfirmed rumours associating him with Starr Faithfull' – and, whether he accepted that offer or not, to keep watch outside the house and follow him if and when he went out.

Peters, apparently thinking that if he gave the horde of reporters a few quotes, they would all go away, came to the front door and told them: 'I am very much interested in the Starr Faithfull case. Although the relationship between the girl and my wife was rather distant, I used to know the family well. When they lived in Boston, they were frequent visitors. I haven't seen the girls or their mother for five years, and I don't believe I've ever met the girls' step-father. I haven't been to New York for many weeks. The last time I was there, I was with my wife, and we attended a funeral. I'm utterly at a loss to understand why my name should be dragged into the case.'

Shaking his head at the ragged chorus of questions that broke out, he turned back to the door, then glanced over his shoulder. Looking 'distressed' or 'angry' as he realised that the reporters intended to stay, he snapped, 'That really *is* all, gentlemen,' before slamming the door. There was the sound of a bolt being rammed into its keep.

Around noon on the Monday, the *New York World-Telegram* came out with the first instalment of a series 'revealing the Faithfull family's intimate insights into the life of Starr Faithfull'. The series, bought from the United Press, was written by one of that news agency's staff correspondents, Carl Groat. The first instalment, which was headlined **STEPFATHER BLAMES GIRL'S WOES ON CHILDHOOD AFFAIR WITH PROMINENT MAN**, quoted the Faithfulls as saying that some of the things that had appeared in the press about Starr's 'victimisation by the prominent man in question' were true; but the instalment ended with a complaint from Mrs Faithfull that there had been 'many fantastic and grotesque reports that Starr knew an inordinate number of men': 'I have been with her every single evening. Stories of "wild night life" are without a shred of foundation. She knew only a few men, and these men were of good standing.'

(It is reasonable to assume that Edwards, Littleton and King, who had needed to promise Stanley Faithfull that they would not breathe a word about Peters, were taken aback when they learned that the Faithfulls had talked about Peters to Carl Groat. Bits and pieces of the story behind the Groat story did not come to light till long afterwards. The undoubted facts are as follows. On the

Saturday before the Monday when the series started to appear in the *World-Telegram*, Stanley had visited the Manhattan offices of the International News Service and, during a meeting lasting two or three hours with Barry Farris, the vice-president of the news agency, and Fred Goodfellow, the assistant general manager, offered 'a story of the Faithfull tragedy, of Starr Faithfull's life', saying that 'there would be a very heavy expense involved. He did not, in so many words, ask for a direct offer ... he said that he had no funds and he thought that [his expenses] would have to be financed to the extent that he could send Mrs Faithfull and his step-daughter Tucker away, and required money for that ...' Farris and Goodfellow 'were not very greatly impressed' as they 'did not think Mr Faithfull had anything new to tell that had not been told, or matter that [they] could carry on the wires, matter fit for publication'. Stanley had left. Later in the day, he had spoken to a reporter for the United Press, and, as a result, Carl Groat and a colleague had visited the Faithfulls at their home. Groat: 'Mrs Faithfull came into the room ... and Mr Faithfull left the room, and she talked with my colleague in my presence and said that the family had some difficulties ... about rent and food, and said they did not even have enough funds for mourning clothes at the time ... and finally my colleague said, "Well, just what do you suggest in this matter?" and Mrs Faithfull said she did not know what to suggest, and finally my colleague said he did not see any reason that there could not be some money given to the Faithfulls if they were in these circumstances, and also that he did not see any reason why Miss Tucker should not be put on our payroll for a few weeks. And Mr Faithfull came back about that time and we finally agreed that she [Tucker] should be put on our payroll at a hundred dollars a week for eight weeks.' Straightway, Groat had begun to question the Faithfulls, who 'confided in him, fully, for publication, the story of Starr's life'. The questioning had continued the next day, and, at the end of it, Stanley had given Groat a bundle of documents. Stanley claimed: 'I gave the United Press a bundle containing documents ... with the understanding that these were to be kept in their safekeeping overnight, and not to be opened. I did not know what was in that bundle at the time.' Tucker was paid the hundred dollars a week, in cash, for eight weeks: not bad wages considering that she never did a stroke of work for the United Press – did not even need to go to the offices, as Stanley collected the cash on her behalf. There is no indication that he or Mrs Faithfull received any payment from the agency.)

The second instalment of the Groat story appeared in the

*World-Telegram* on Tuesday, 16 June: mostly excerpts from letters that Starr had written to her mother during stays in London. One of several accompanying reports on the case was a despatch from Boston, sent that morning, which lied:

## RICH BOSTONIAN AGREES TO TALK
### 'At Proper Time' Announces Man
### Accused of Mistreating Starr as Child

The prominent Bostonian who is said to have taught Starr Faithfull erotic practices ... and who later gave her $20,000 or more in an effort to rehabilitate her, will have a complete explanation when the time comes. He is silent now, it is said, because he does not want to add to the distress of his family. He is prepared to charge that the girl suffered delusions which caused her to imagine that various men were in love with her and had been intimate with her. He will claim that it was because of this delusion that the girl believed he had treated her improperly when she was a child and had many clandestine engagements with her as she grew to womanhood ...

Between when that despatch was sent and when it was published, Alexander Whiteside issued a statement to the press:

Andrew J. Peters ... has today, through a friend in New York [the friend was John W. Davis, the Democratic Presidential Candidate defeated by Calvin Coolidge in 1924], communicated with Mr Edwards, District Attorney of Nassau County, that if he had any information or evidence which would be of the slightest assistance to District Attorney Edwards in the investigation he is making of the so-called Starr Faithfull case, he would gladly give it to him, but he has no evidence whatever which has any bearing on the death of this unfortunate girl. The girl was a distant cousin of Mr Peters' wife. Mr Peters had told me that never in his life did he have any improper relations with her in any way whatsoever. The foregoing is the only statement Mr Peters cares to issue.

Shortly before or just after Whiteside issued that statement, Charles Rowley was ferreted out by a reporter for the *Boston Globe*:

Mr Rowley admitted that a wealthy man had made a big cash settlement on Starr five years ago. He admitted that he had reached the settlement. The *New York American* said today that the girl's family had received $79,000 in three payments. Mr Faithfull has denied this amount was correct. Mr Rowley declined to name the sum, but said that, 'If Faithfull said it was $20,000 or any other sum, I'll leave it at that'.

182

On Wednesday, the third instalment of the Groat story was illustrated with a facsimile of a page of handwriting in Starr's scrapbook; references to an individual had been blanked out. (Stanley had not told the investigators that the scrapbook was extant. Perhaps he was unaware that it was. Perhaps he was unaware that it was in the bundle of documents he had given Groat. After all, he, so he said, 'did not know what was in that bundle at the time'.) A reporter for the *World-Telegram* described the scrapbook as 'a wholesale collection of trivialities', and went on:

> Sandwiched between harmless recital programmes, 'team' pictures, a dance card or two, [school] demerit slips, &c., appears a matter-of-fact recital (reproduced above) in what the Faithfull family assert to be Starr's handwriting, of two motor journeys she said she took with the middle-aged, highly-placed family man the girl's relatives swear ruined her at 11, the individual who, in 1927, paid $20,000 in settlement to the Faithfulls. One trip led to Quebec, the second to New York., One took place in July, the other in August, 1927. Starr, champion swimmer and sprinter, hockey player and, judging from group photographs, the prettiest girl in school, listed ten hotels at which she stopped with her companion . . .
>
> On the page alongside the penned story of the perambulations Starr had pasted three ticket stubs – one for a matinee at Tex Austin's rodeo current at Madison Square Garden that August; a night show at the Astor Theatre, and a matinee at the Palace.

The penned story of the perambulations was not connected with the Groat instalment, which told 'the story of the [early] childhood of Starr Faithfull . . . as related by Mrs Helen Faithfull, with a few points contributed by Mr Faithfull and his stepdaughter Tucker'. Presumably, the piece was set in type before Alexander Whiteside issued his statement and was published without alteration, for it ended:

> When the time came for Starr to enter a higher school, Mrs Faithfull's cousins arranged a fund for her education. This fund was entrusted to Andrew J. Peters, of Boston, who has been a Congressman and Mayor of Boston.

At 10 p.m. on the Wednesday, Peters was visited by his doctor, Roger Lee, who had to push through reporters to get to the door. Emerging from the house at midnight, the doctor was again surrounded by reporters, most of them shouting, 'Has Peters suffered a nervous breakdown?' 'I will neither confirm not deny that,' he said. 'I cannot discuss my patient.'

Next morning, Peters was admitted to the Faulkner Hospital in Boston.

(There were other casualties of the case that day. The Nassau County detective, Joseph Culkin (discoverer of the 'hidden diary'), had to take to his bed, for he was suffering from physical and mental exhaustion. And, as wired by the Associated Press to the thousand or so papers, at home and abroad, that subscribed to its news-gathering service, 'Peter, the 17-year-old cat which was Starr Faithfull's pet, died in a veterinary hospital this afternoon. The animal refused to eat after Starr vanished, and developed indigestion and auto-intoxication. The body is to be cremated by order of Starr's step-father.')

On Friday, the *World-Telegram* published the final instalment of the Groat Story: **STARR DIDN'T CAROUSE IN GREENWICH VILLAGE, SAY PARENTS**. Several papers, grown venturesome, *stated* that Peters was the rich Bostonian who was *said* to have seduced Starr and who was *alleged* to have paid the Faithfulls to keep quiet about it. And, in the evening, Peters was driven to his country place on North Haven Island.

A few days later, according to a report in the *New York Daily News* on 26 July,

> Peters collapsed completely, his nerves a wreck as the ghosts of his past, the ghosts of his sordid affair with Starr, came crowding in on his memories . . .
>
> With his family, the former Mayor of Boston is still in seclusion at North Haven . . . There he lies, broken, disconsolate and inaccessible.

It must have been some time during the second week of the case, the Damnation of Peters one, when Morris Markey, the 'Reporter at Large' for *The New Yorker* magazine, visited 12 St Luke's Place:[1]

> There were many lounging figures on the stoop when we [journalistic plural] arrived, which was just after a heavy dusk had settled, but our movement to join them was a little diffident, for a policeman in uniform passed slowly back and forth. Then we recognised the loungers as newspapermen. The policeman turned his back on us and paced away.
>
> We said to the reporters: 'How do you get upstairs to see the Faithfulls?'

1. The following is a combination of extracts from two similar retrospective articles by Markey, one in his book *Manhattan Reporter* (Dodge Publishing, New York, 1935), the other in the excellent anthology *The Aspirin Age* (edited by Isabel Leighton; The Bodley Head, London, 1950). Both articles contain many inaccuracies about the Starr Faithfull case.

One of them said: 'You can walk, can't you? But it's as hot as hell up there.'

Mr Faithfull was standing thoughtfully in the doorway of his living-room, a big pipe in one hand and a volume of the *Encyclopaedia Britannica* in the other.

'Come in,' he said. 'I'm trying to get something positive on the weight of the normal human liver. That might give us a definite knowledge of the amount of Veronal they found at the autopsy. Do you know how to translate grammes into pounds and ounces?'

A very large photograph of Starr stood in a leather frame on a table, with a vase of peonies drooping over it. On the table, too, were books: *The Way of All Flesh*, *The Story of Philosophy*, *Diana of the Crossways*, *Imperial Palace*, *Cyrano de Bergerac*, and several volumes on criminology and anatomy.

Faithfull murmured figures to himself, recalling after a moment's thought the number of grammes to a pound, turned pages hurriedly now and then, worked out little sums on a pad of yellow foolscap.

Mrs Faithfull came in, a worn woman with nerves drawn to high tension. But one felt that this was a permanent characteristic with her: the fluttering hospitality, the rapid speech, the darting gestures.

We asked if we might be presented to Tucker, and she led us through to where the girl was propped up in bed, altogether poised and without a trace of the weariness one might have expected.

Without the least rancour or excitement, Tucker began to talk about the newspapers: 'One of them said today that we were pals with [the gangster] Legs Diamond. I never heard of the man except in headlines. And at least half of what they print about Starr is perfectly ridiculous. Do they really just make it up?'

Within the next hour, our talk fell quite away from the mystery and the dead girl who was the centre of it – about books, about Europe and travel in general, about the theatre.

'How did you like *Wonder Bar*?' Mrs Faithfull asked.

We confessed that we had found it dull.

'Well, now,' she exclaimed brightly. 'Isn't that interesting? It was the last show Starr saw, and she told us she thought it terrible.'

Tucker asked, 'What's going to happen to all of us when the excitement dies down? Will they let us alone? Will we take up living again just like we lived before?'

Mrs Faithfull said, 'There's one thing you can say for all the excitement. It keeps you so worked up, you don't have much time to think that Starr is really gone, and isn't coming back.'

Tucker looked up with a peculiar expression.

'Starr!' she said. And she did not smile.

It was past two o'clock when we wished the Faithfull family good night and left. The jabbering of voices was still constant in the living room, where four or five reporters leaned back in their seats, puffing pipes and offering theories.

If the Faithfulls were moved by no tearing grief over the odd death of their daughter, the papers had told us enough to make that understandable. If they made mistakes with everybody in the country staring at them, that too could be understood. There is no chapter in the etiquette book with the heading: 'How to Behave When There's a Murder in the Family.'

These Faithfulls – they were quite pleasant people to sit around and talk with. Their lives contained, no doubt, the customary hidden passages. All of us would look a little sinister if the tabloids began to tell our private secrets (getting them not quite right).

Those last comments chime with a comment attributed to Al Capone:[1] 'There is a little larceny in all of us.' In suggesting that the Faithfulls were a perfectly ordinary family, Morris Markey seems to have overlooked some facts about them which the press had unearthed and reported accurately. For instance:

At the time of Starr's disappearance, a dozen legal actions were in progress or pending against Mr or Mrs Faithfull for alleged non-payment of bills submitted over and over again by as many clothing or department stores, including Lord & Taylor, Franklin Simon & Co., Russeks, Inc., and James McCreery & Co. (all on Fifth Avenue), Vera Sanville, Inc. (on Madison Avenue), and L. Bamberger & Co. of Newark, New Jersey. The amounts of the claims ranged from a mere $64.65 to $1710.99. Among the items listed on the writ from Vera Sanville were $359.50 for six frocks and $21.50 for four pairs of garters. The earliest of the unpaid bills was one from Bamberger's for clothes supplied to Starr in April 1929. Stanley's reckoning of his business income in recent years was '... for 1929, $1325; 1930, $3000; up until June 5, 1931, my income was nothing'. He added: 'On June 5, 1931, I had a total indebtedness in the vicinity of ten thousand dollars, which indebtedness was giving me no cause for worry because of the contract I had with the Airian Products, Inc., and from which I had

1. During the first fortnight of June 1931, a federal grand jury in Chicago indicted Capone on charges of income tax evasion and of conspiracy to violate the Prohibition Laws. On the East Coast, at any rate, newspaper reports of the latter indictment, handed down on the 12th, were given second billing below the latest on the Starr Faithfull case. In October, Capone was found guilty of several of the charges of tax evasion, and of contempt of court, and was sentenced to eleven years' imprisonment and ordered to pay fines aggregating $50,000 and court costs of $30,000; the indictment for violation of the Prohibition Laws was not pursued.

every reason to believe I could liquidate this indebtedness without any embarrassment to my family, and in a perfectly amicable arrangement with my creditors, who were not in the least unfriendly.' As he can hardly have counted the dozen suers among the creditors who were not in the least unfriendly, his total indebtedness must have been considerably more than ten thousand dollars.

The librarian of the *Boston Post* came up with two bundles of faded clippings. One bundle, the smaller, showed that in September 1923, some two years after Stanley's lactic-producing companies at Mansfield went bust, he was indicted by a federal grand jury on the charge of using the mail in a scheme to defraud. The indictment charged that, in literature and letters seeking investment in one of the dead companies, Lactic Chemical, he had lied that he was the originator of the first known process for producing edible lactic in large quantities; that Lactic Chemical was selling huge quantities of chrome alum to the Eastman Kodak photographic corporation, and that he owned a factory covering two and a half acres at Trenton, New Jersey. In October 1923, he stood trial before a judge and jury – and was acquitted. The report of that outcome did not say whether the judge, after discharging the defendant, ordered that the members of the jury were to be discharged, or banned, from further service.

The other bundle of clippings related to a murder case.

On the morning of Saturday, 1 September 1917, Harold Whitman, the thirty-one-year-old chemist of the lactic-producing companies at Mansfield, came into Boston. He left a suitcase at the Essex Hotel, saying that he would collect it in an hour or so, on his way to the North Station to catch the 1.15 train to East Auburn, Maine, and then visited Stanley – who, so he stated to a detective next day, cashed a cheque for him. At 3 p.m., Whitman bumped into a friend, Frank White, in the lobby of the Copley Plaza; he told White that 'he was bound for East Auburn to spend the weekend with his parents. He said he had missed the 1.15 train and was going to get the four o'clock train at the North Station. He was not carrying any luggage.' Early next morning, a tramp found Whitman lying unconscious amid debris on the Mystic River Marsh at Somerville, across the Charles River from Boston. He was wearing his bowler hat, which was undamaged. When the hat was taken off by an ambulanceman, it was seen that Whitman's skull had been fractured by blows from a blunt instrument. Apparently, the assailant had delivered the blows to Whitman's bare head and then, being tidy-minded, replaced the bowler. Whitman was taken to the Somerville Hospital, where, on the following day, he died without having recovered consciousness. By then, the police had collected the suitcase from the Essex Hotel (it contained 'a few personal effects such as any man might carry for a short trip') and interviewed friends of Whitman (who were 'unanimous in the belief that he was not a man who would have given up his life without making a determined fight, provided he knew, or even suspected, that he was in danger'). Inspector Thomas Damery, the head of the Somerville detective bureau, had spoken to Whitman's boss. Over the next few days, Damery interviewed Stanley Faithfull several times – sometimes at Faithfull's home in Brookline, sometimes at his factory in Mansfield, and at least once at the Somerville police headquarters. Faithfull said that 'Harold was working on a secret formula for a dye' and that he himself was convinced that 'enemy agents, aware of the value of the product to the German war effort, had lured Harold into an automobile in an effort to procure the formula and, failing in their intention, crushed his skull and driven him to the dump-heap in Somerville'. Impressed by that theory, the police questioned many German-born Bostonians. None became a suspect. After a few weeks, the investigation petered out. The murder of Harold Whitman remained (and remains) a complete mystery.

In 1864, Franz Müller, a German working in London, committed the first murder on a British train (pinching the top hat of his victim, an elderly banker named Thomas Briggs, and leaving his own bowler in the carriage). In 1910, Dr Hawley Harvey Crippen, an American working in London, became the first person, so far as is known, to use the drug hyoscine for murder (of his wife, generally called Belle Elmore, her stage-name as a singer, whose body he cut into portions, most of which he buried in the cellar of their home). Chiefly because both Müller and Crippen tried to escape justice by sailing to places in North America (respectively New York and Quebec), the Müller and Crippen cases received almost as much press coverage in America as in Britain. I believe that in 1931 those cases were inimitable in that respect.

Vice versa – with the sensible exception of murders and attempted murders of some American politicians – the Starr Faithfull mystery received more press coverage in Britain than any previous American case of undoubted or suspected murder.

At first, British interest in the far-away mystery was whetted by its British associations: Starr's eviction from the *Franconia*, an English liner bound for England; her anglophilia, manifested by her several trips to London during the past five years. Then the ship's Scottish surgeon, George Jameson Carr, was named as a missing link in the mystery – and, though only for a few editions, so was the English actor, Bruce Winston. Feeling that there *had* to be a 'London end of the investigation', the popular press invented one, saying, for instance, that 'senior Scotland Yard officers are working round the clock in an endeavour to establish how and with whom the dead heiress occupied herself whilst in London'. On the first Sunday, the *Dispatch* ('The Best of the Batch') went so far as to say that under-cover detectives were shadowing drug-dealers in Limehouse, the Chinese quarter near the London docks, in the hope of corroborating a theory that Starr had financed her transatlantic trips by acting as a courier for an international drug-ring. In fact, all that Scotland Yard was asked to do, and did, was to arrange with the Cunard Company for certain members of the crew of the *Franconia* to give statements.

The *Daily Mail* published the longest reports on the case, usually starting at or near the top of the front page. And, nine times out of ten, it was the *Mail* that found or, more likely, was approached by London acquaintances of Starr, most of whom insisted upon being quoted anonymously. For instance, under the sub-heading **BEAUTY AND BRAINS**, 'A Friend of the Dead Girl' (whether male or female is indeterminable) provided both a pen-portrait and a psycho-analysis of Starr:

[She] was only in some ways a typical example of modern young New York. She had such flawless beauty that the average girl of her circle was put in the shade when she was there. She danced to perfection, she was never at a loss for a word, and she would [figuratively, it subsequently becomes clear] drain her glasses to the dregs. So far, she was typical.

But her intelligence was far and away above the average. Intellectual men found it difficult to keep pace with her in conversation. She could speak fluently on most subjects.

One had the impression, when talking to her, that real happiness seemed to have gone out of her life. She seemed already to have lived too long, to have sought something dynamic in a social circle which she knew, in a few whirling years, to be static.

It has been said that Starr Faithfull was a drug addict. I do not believe it. She showed no ordinary signs of drugs. She drank more than most, but she was not a dipsomaniac. Drink itself, when I knew her, held no fascination for her. The fascination was in rubbing the rough edges from life that she at last found tragically boring. It may be that in time that habit grew so strongly on her that she could not tear it off, and that for that reason men fought shy of her after brief acquaintance.

By arrangement with the United Press, the *Mail* published Groat-quoted extracts from letters on Savoy Hotel notepaper that Starr had written to her mother during her stay in London in the summer of 1929:

I am all settled in the new house, namely the Commodore Hotel, 4 Pembroke Square [off Earls Court Road, Kensington]. I told you about D.B. [Dennis Barnett, a wealthy young man about London town]. He is buying a car and is really trying so hard to make up for being 'nasty to Susie' that she has forgiven him practically. Cheerioski. [The 'signature' was a drawing of a star.]

Have you bobbed the big bush? [referring to Mrs Faithfull's mop of hair] ... If Mr S[tacpoole, the manager of the Greyfriars private hotel, 31 Pembroke Square, where she had been put up for a few days – and from which, with other young American tourists, she had been evicted because of 'rowdiness'] was better looking I would heap coals of fire on his head by asking him to dinner at the Commodore. He looks exactly like a match before it is lit ... Really, you know, London pubs are a study in themselves. They have the variety of ships or people. About my amours, I have none at present, as I am going through a very platonic phase starting after my row with D.B. The last I saw him, he looked like a plump bird with big wondering eyes. I am having him to dinner tonight and afterwards drive in his new car. My other loves [that word ringed with dashes, to give a glittering effect] are away. D.B. is too fragile to appeal to me. R.H., the artist [whose identity will soon be revealed], was a bit too rough. When a person is beastly I get that way myself, and the result was too damn noisy so that the landlord complained ... The English look upon the Americans as being crude, loud and with horrible accents. The word 'bloody' to an Englishman is comparable to profanity to the American ... A man named Lord Brendon [or calling himself that; there *was* no Lord Brendon] wanted me to go to Budapest. (How the hell do you spell it?) D.B. begs I go to live with him in a new flat. As I told you, I have become very platonic. It is a great state to be in.

'A peer's son' told a *Mail* reporter that he had seen less of Starr during her last stay in London, between June and November 1930, than of her mother and sister, who were visiting the city for the first time:

On several occasions I was compelled to assist Mrs Faithfull and Sylvia [Tucker] financially. I actually had to buy food for them, although Starr always seemed to have plenty of money. She always was a mystery, even to her mother and sister. Neither of them knew where Starr was living in London. Starr always was extremely well dressed. She had the appearance of affluence, while the mother and sister were literally starving after the Wall Street crash [a long time after: the crash was in October 1929]. They lived at an artist's flat in Chelsea. Starr would come round once a week to the flat, but she never would tell her mother and sister where she was staying or what she was doing. I know Mrs Faithfull was terribly worried about her. Starr did not assist them in any way.

Last November I was asked if I would telephone or cable to Mr Faithfull in New York asking for money. Sylvia told me her mother was dangerously ill and they had no money. The cable which I agreed to send and for which I had to pay read: 'Mother dangerously ill. Cable money for expenses, hospital.' The address of a West End banker was given and two days later I discovered that Mrs Faithfull was not ill and that $5000 had been sent to the bankers. Immediately afterwards, Mrs Faithfull, with Sylvia and Starr, left for New York, and until this tragedy I heard nothing more of them.

A thirty-year-old artist, Rudolph Haybrook, slightly built and goatee-bearded, supplied so much material that the *Mail* decided to publish it in dribs and drabs, over several issues. Either Haybrook was the sort of person who said one thing one minute and something else the next or he was occasionally misreported. Three versions of how and when he had come to meet Starr were attributed to him: (1) 'I met her in England for the first time, quite by chance, in 1928, when she was making her third voyage.' (2) 'I first met Starr two years ago, when I went to meet friends arriving on the *Mauretania*, who introduced me.' (3) 'I met her in August 1929, when she was brought to my studio in Gower Street, Bloomsbury, by a friend who had met her in Piccadilly. She discovered I knew a man she had been chasing for more than a year, and thereafter she haunted my studio.'

But perhaps none of those versions was correct. Haybrook's stories, wired to New York by the United Press, included the information that he had once been engaged to Tucker. A day after Stanley Faithfull had vehemently denied that Tucker had been engaged to Haybrook ('or anybody else, for that matter'), Tucker contradicted Stanley – and, in so doing, contradicted all of Haybrook's versions of how and when he had become acquainted with Starr: 'She and I were formally introduced to Mr Haybrook at the Albert Hall last summer. He became very attentive to me, and before we returned to America last fall our engagement was announced in London. We corresponded for about three months after I got back to New York, and, although I like him very much,

I decided we were not temperamentally suited to each other, and the engagement was broken off.'

Meanwhile, back in London, Haybrook was pestered by reporters other than for the *Mail*. Having identified him as the R.H. in one of Starr's letters to her mother, they asked him to comment on her criticism that he was 'a bit too rough'. How roughly had he treated her? Had he heard about the pseudonymous Joseph Collins who, in March 1930, had beaten her up so badly that she had needed hospital treatment? Trying to sound righteously indignant rather than threateningly angry, Haybrook replied: 'Those words, "a bit too rough", obviously were used by Starr to extenuate her own conduct when the landlord complained of the noise. This . . . can be substantiated by my landlord and my secretary. I have nothing to add.' Then he closed his studio door, taking care not to slam it roughly on the reporters' faces.

His contention that Starr had been guilty of unladylike conduct was a little difficult to reconcile with his description of her as

> a charming girl, athletic and fond of reading, who particularly enjoyed analysing problems of life in discussion. She did not go to any parties over here. She was reserved in that way. She went to the theatre once or twice, but the very fact that she was in England was sufficient enjoyment for her. She was far from fond of America and never was happier than when she was in England. Yet she had extremely few friends here.

Nostalgia for London − a kind of inverted homesickness − was a recurrent theme of letters that Starr had written to Haybrook from America. None of the letters was dated; but the invariable heading, '12 St Luke's Place, N.Y.C.' showed that they had been written during the six months or so following the female Faithfulls' return from England at the start of December 1930. At least one of the letters, the first of those quoted below, appears to have been written before Tucker broke off her engagement to Haybrook:

> . . . You have no conception of how much you are missed. Everything is deadly stupid without you . . . Even the outlook is loathsome. We are somewhere between Seventh and Eighth Avenues − not a very polite part of town. Our front room looks out on a city playground filled with God's horrid little creatures. If ever you see a play called 'Street Scene',[1] you will know our environment . . .
> I wish I could feel more kindly about —. He seems to me a sort of

1. By Elmer Rice. It opened on Broadway, at the Playhouse, in January 1929, and ran for nearly eighteen months.

living symbol of futility − or the unimportance of being earnest. If it is true that nothing succeeds like success, it is also true that nothing fails so completely as a failure. I am certainly far from being one to talk − but I can't help it . . .

I am more and more bored by my native land. If I were a man I would join the Foreign Legion and forget my past.

I am living on tea and tomatoes, and day by day the scale creaks less as my (not so elephantine) physique bears down on it. When you see the new figure it will positively explode with grace. It won't be long either! Yeah, sez me!!

Yesterday I swear I was completely overcome by depression. New York seemed like a huge graveyard, and the skyline didn't thrill me a bit.[1] It just looked like a lot of elongated dominoes and perfectly ridiculous.

Everything here seems like a most awful anti-climax. I realise that my depressed attitude is far from admirable, but if I 'made an effort' I think it would be like bursting a blood vessel mentally.

. . . In practically every letter you say 'Be good'. You should just see how damnably good I've become . . .

*Never, never* again shall I be the worse for drink, or anything else one swallows or inhales. I want to go on a terrific, wild and champagny 'bender' . . . Being good is all very well when one is fat − but now I'm thin, we shall see. This spring, in London, we will all look in the opposite direction from Heaven for a change, and discard wings, halos, etc.

From a letter written on stationery of the Astor Hotel, Manhattan:

. . . Not that it is frightfully interesting, *but* − I have lost twenty-five pounds! Gone is the bloated ox, swollen whale, elephant, or what have you which used to trot so eagerly to Woods [grocers in Chelsea, London] after Bourbon biscuits or to the Cadogan Arms [Chelsea] for beer. We did consume some beer last summer. I dread to think what would happen if I should live in Berlin . . .

. . . I am so anxious to cheer you up − and yet I can't think of much except that we are all only living in the FUTURE − that is, when we sail for dear old London, and see darling old you . . .

Don't worry about Tucker. When we are nineteen we say all sorts of things. I have an old diary which proves that!

I value your peace of mind, happiness, whatever you choose to call it,

---

1. The second part of this sentence sounds very like the line after 'I get no kick from champagne' − *'Mere alcohol doesn't thrill me at all'* − in Cole Porter's song, 'I Get a Kick Out of You,' which was first performed at the end of 1934 (by Ethel Merman in the musical comedy *Anything Goes*).

as much as I do my own. It is one of the few *un*selfish feelings I've ever had for anyone ...

... Life is most depressing. I wish I were starving without a shilling for gas in Limerston Street [towards the western end of King's Road, Chelsea], with the roof falling in and rain pouring in — anything but this.

Do you know where I wish I was at this moment? I wish I were having a nice, long, double whisky with you at the Six Bells [in Kings Road]. Please button up your overcoat, be careful crossing streets, and in every way take good care of yourself. [1] At present I can't believe that anyone like your charming, brilliant self ever existed. You are so far removed from this maelstrom and all its low-down inhabitants ...

Rudolph Haybrook said that he received this letter early in May 1931:

How does the old busy bee improve his hour these days and is he having fun? Let me know.

I have ['have' double-underlined] my passage booked on the Franconia, sailing from N.Y. May 30th. A friend of mine is sailing on that boat, which explains my decision.

Tucker will undoubtedly sail before this. After the boat has passed the Statue of Liberty I shall believe in God, fairies, Santa Claus, and so on. Oh Yeah? Yeah!

In the first of the Haybrook features — which appeared in the *Mail* on Friday, 12 June (before there was any mention in the press of Andrew Peters' payment of $25,000 to the Faithfulls in 1927) — Haybrook was quoted as saying, 'Starr never committed suicide. I am absolutely certain of that. She may have ... got into the hands of people with good cause to have her out of the way.' And he was reported as saying that he believed she was murdered because she was to be the principal witness in a $25,000 settlement case which would have caused a sensation when it came to court.

Three days later, by which time the press knew about the Peters payment, Haybrook issued a statement: 'I emphatically deny the story in the British press that I mentioned anything regarding a $25,000 settlement case in which Starr was involved. I cannot understand the origin of the story.'

If that was true, then the *Mail* man who put together the first

1. The sentence is a paraphrase of the opening lines of a hit-song from the musical comedy *Follow Thru* — music by Ray Henderson, lyrics by B.G. DeSylva and Lew Brown — which opened at the Forty-Sixth Street Theatre in January 1929 and ran there till the end of that year.

*12 St. Lukes Place*
*U.4.C.*

*Dear Strongers —*

*How does the old busy bee improve his hour these days and is he having fun? Let me know.*

*I have my passage booked on the Francouio, sailing from U.4. May 30th. A friend of mine is sailing on that boat, which explains my decision. Starr*

*Part of Starr Faithfull's last letter to Rudolph Haybrook.*

Haybrook feature *invented* the forthcoming $25,000 settlement case – invented it completely, out of thin air, unassisted by the faintest idea that Starr had already been involved in a $25,000 settlement case. Uncanny!

*

Starr's letters — the few published in the Groat series, the several published in the Haybrook features (which, with New York five hours behind London, appeared, complete or in part, in American papers on the same days as they appeared in the London *Daily Mail*) — were analysed by American reporters who fancied themselves as psychologists. Readers of more than one paper, already muddled by the difference between the Faithfulls' description of Starr and that being pieced together by the press, were further muddled by the psychological analyses, as contradictory as horoscopes.

Inspector King, scanning all the papers 'in case some journalist gave written information which tied in with evidence which we [the official investigators] were in possession of', seems to have let his eyes wander from the news to the psychology. At any rate, it was he who conceived the notion of 'engaging a proper expert to peruse Miss Faithfull's writings, including the diary': 'I suppose I was responsible for that,' he felt impelled to admit. 'I suggested it to the District Attorney. We thought we might get something of Starr Faithfull's character and characteristics from the handwriting through Louise Rice, who is known as a graphologist, and she was brought out here, and she had the diary in her possession for three-quarters of an hour to an hour, while she was sitting in the office of one of the assistant district attorneys.' She submitted a report, by special messenger, the next day — by which time, apparently, King had lost interest in her divinings: 'I don't think I ever read the report, to tell you the truth.'

Louise Rice was the founder and president of the Graphological Institute of America, an organisation which, going by its premises, part of Ms Rice's apartment on West Twelfth Street, was rather less impressive than its title. Miffed that she did not even receive an acknowledgement of her report, she sold a censored version of the findings to the *New York World-Telegram*:

> Starr wrote seven different scripts. Normal people usually employ two at different moments; very stable people may write an unvarying hand. When at peace, she used an upright, light-pressure script, refined and distinguished. But in her most erotic moods she wrote a forward-leaning, heavy-pressure, ugly, muddy script. At those moments she seems to have got a vicarious thrill out of telling her reactions to sex experiences ...
>
> Introduced prematurely to sex, to alcohol, tobacco and other influences commonly held to be subversive to the young, she lost permanently her emotional and moral balance. Even without that experience, but with proper care, and otherwise normal life, she would have been a borderline case, a problem to her family and teachers. But

she was extremely intelligent and imaginative, and she might have become a writer or an artist except for that complete moral breakdⱬwn. Starr was really a mental type, not sensual – but she fell into sensual hands at an early age. She drank to find release and I doubt, from reading her diary, that she was sober except for brief intervals during the last seven or eight years. When drunk, she was entirely different, wholly irresponsible.

Many of the erotic stories and wildly fantastic tales going about are absolutely not true. I find no hint of various unnatural practices. The diary has been misunderstood because read by persons not equipped to make out its meanings. The story that the family hired a man to coach Starr in normal sex practices seems to me to be unbelievable hokum ...

She was not a Narcissus type, not vain. Indeed, she suffered from a grave inferiority complex. She had no self-confidence and was torn by doubts and fears of her conduct, charm, beauty, intelligence, etc.

She made many depressed entries in the diary, along with gay and pleasant ones, and while to the casual eye they might point to suicide, more complete study reveals to me four or five situations which might supply motives for her murder.

Mrs Faithfull 'laughed sharply' at those findings. Referring to Louise Rice as if she were the entire membership of the Graphological Institute of America (which was probably not far wrong), she spoke of 'handwriting experts hired by those ridiculous detectives, the ridiculous Mr Edwards,' and, letting out another sharp laugh, suggested that 'the expertise of the experts can be gathered from the fact that one of them discovered that Starr had seven distinct personalities, all rolled into one'.

Tucker did not find the findings amusing. Asked what she thought of them, she uttered a word or words too rude to be reported, then cried out: 'Starr must be happier now. *We* are. I know *we* are.' While Mr and Mrs Faithfull hovered sheepishly, the former muttering something about last straws, Tucker elaborated on her outburst – revealing, according to one of the scribbling reporters, the man from the *Herald Tribune*, that 'her older sister had been a termagant at home, and had bullied and abused her family. Her temper was so explosive that she would not wait a second for a meal if it were not ready at the moment she wanted it. She would pinch her mother and sister and slap her step-father. Even when the sisters were out shopping together, her temper would get the better of her and she would grip Tucker's arm so savagely that bruises showed for days afterwards. She ruled the family with a rod of iron, and even dictated where they should live.' Having shouted her say, Tucker ran from the room. Stanley again muttered something about last straws; but the reporters, not wanting to hear a diminishment of Tucker's remarks, were already on their way out of the apartment.

Tucker's turncoat tirade cannot have come as a surprise to those who read reports of it. For in the past few days the Faithfulls' portrait of Starr as a kin-dependent homebody, rarely undemure, had been defaced with all sorts of revelations from all sorts of people.

*Item*. Texas Guinan — the undisputed Queen of the Speakeasies, whose bellowed greeting, 'Hello, Suckers!', had become a national catch-phrase — was on the high seas when the Starr Faithfull case began. Having sailed to France with a dozen of her show-girls, intending to open a licensed club in Paris, she and they, declared undesirable aliens by the prudish authorities, had been refused permission to tread on French soil other than that between where their ship had docked and where another was being prepared for the return journey. The day after she got back, meanwhile having read reports of her heroine's welcome at the French Line's Pier 57 (next to Cunard's three) and noted that those reports were squeezed off the front pages by the latest on Starr Faithfull, she announced that 'the glamorous Tucker' would be 'an added attraction in her next fun-filled show'. Soon after Tucker denied that she would be any such thing, Texas told reporters that Starr and Andrew Peters had, 'frequently and always together', been among the suckers she had greeted at a hostelry in Lynbrook — the small town just to the west of Rockville Centre.

If that was true, then the Faithfulls' assertion that Starr had never been to Nassau County was incorrect. Texas did not say, or was not reported as saying, *when* she had seen Starr and Peters. During the first seven years of Prohibition (1920–26), she worked constantly in Manhattan. Her first appearance in Lynbrook, at the Blossom Heath Inn, was in 1927; her only other appearance there prior to mid-1931 was for a month or so from 17 November 1930, at the Show Place (an advertisement said that she and her 'Mob of Adorable Kids' — '20 Beautiful Girls 20' — were doing two shows a night, at 8.30 and 12).[1] And so, *if* she saw Starr and Peters in

---

1. Arthur Mattson, the historian of Lynbrook, believes that the Show Place was the Blossom Heath Inn under a different name. In a letter, he writes: 'The old-timers I spoke to could not help except to say that they had always associated Guinan with the Blossom. They had never heard of the Show Place ... Lynbrook

Lynbrook, it was while Charles Rowley and Alexander Whiteside were arguing over the amount of the cash settlement, or shortly after Peters paid the $25,000, or three and a half years later than that. Strangely, no one seems to have noticed the implication of Texas Guinan's comment − or if they did, made no effort to learn whether or not she had suckered the press.

*Item.* The Montclair Hotel, presumably named after the town in New Jersey where Starr had spent part of her childhood, was in Manhattan, at Lexington Avenue and East Forty-Ninth Street (close to where the Waldorf-Astoria now stands). John Cunningham, a night officer of the Montclair, said that, at about two in the morning of 20 February 1930, a Thursday, he had received a complaint 'about noise and boisterous talking' in one of the rooms:

> I knocked on the door and there were two women and a man in the room. The older and prettier of the women was Starr Faithfull; the other was a young blonde girl about eighteen or twenty whose name I do not know. The three of them had been drinking quite heavily, and I told the man, 'You have to break this party up,' and he said he would.
>
> About two weeks later, I was going through the hotel on my rounds, and I heard a woman scream. That was on the fourth floor. I knocked at the door and the [man inside] refused to open the door ... I took my pass-key and opened the door and went in, and a man and a woman were standing up, and he had a suit of underwear and she had nothing on ...

---

joined the rest of the country in finding numerous ways to circumvent Prohibition. Only 33 minutes from midtown Manhattan on the Long Island Railroad, or an hour's drive on Merrick Road, and with only a handful of policemen to worry about or to bribe, Lynbrook became an attractive location for some of New York City's gangsters to set up shop. Many of Lynbrook's respectable hotels were converted to roadhouses and gambling halls. Also, some stores were modified for illicit booze operations.' He refers to three local speakeasies in addition to the Blossom Heath Inn: the Castillion Gardens Hotel, the Fountain Inn, and Nick's Place.

Whittaker Chambers (who in 1948, having renounced Communism and given up spying for the Russians, accused Alger Hiss, a State Department official, of being a fellow conspirator) was brought up in Lynbrook. In his autobiography, *Witness*, (André Deutsch, London, 1953), Chambers speaks of visits to Nick's Place in the mid-1920s, accompanying his brother, a heavier drinker than himself:

'My brother's evenings usually began at a little store with the lower half of the show windows painted or blinded. Behind the store was a backroom. Here a mousy Greek, with greying hair, served a home-brewed wine ... Nick's Place (I never heard the proprietor called anything but Nick) was friendly, and the wine was cheap and not nearly so harmful as the villainous whisky sold at the bars.'

I told her she would have to get dressed, and she was fighting and claimed that this man promised her some money which he would not give her, and I asked him and he said, 'No, get her the hell out of here,' and I took her downstairs and out through the front door, and I came back to the desk, and then I went upstairs for half an hour, and when I came down I got a call from the same room to come back, and there was the girl, the same one, trying to get back. She said she wanted the money that this man promised her, and I threatened to take her to the Fifty-First Street police station and have her arrested.

I took her downstairs and she was quite drunk. I put her in a freight elevator and dropped her to the basement and took her out through the Fiftieth Street entrance so that nobody could see her. She was battling, and I called a cab. She had a little postcard and a letter with her name on, 'Miss Faithfull', and some address down in Greenwich Village. I gave the taxi-driver a dollar and told him to take her home [or rather, to the *address*, for the Faithfulls were still living at West Orange in February 1930].

There was no corroboration of Cunningham's account of the first incident'; but there was hearsay corroboration of the incidents a fortnight later from the manager of the Montclair, Oscar Richards, who said that he 'distinctly remembered' that Cunningham had reported the facts to him before clocking off. Whether or not Cunningham had mentioned to Richards that the girl was a Miss Faithfull is not clear.

*Item.* Rex Fairbanks looked exactly how one expects someone called Rex Fairbanks to look. Tall and slim and elegantly tailored; his dark hair brushed immaculately back from a parting on the left. Like all the romantic male characters in short stories by Scott Fitzgerald. Going by press photographs of him, he was never off the phone, and always stood at the phone, legs crossed, the unsupporting one on tiptoe. He was thirty. According to some reports, he wa a clerk for the Brooklyn Edison Company; according to others, which seem more credible, he had worked for that electricity supplier till six years before, when he had inherited two million dollars from an uncle in California whom he had never met. Separated from ' a former show-girl wife', he lived in a 'palatial suite' on Washington Avenue, Brooklyn, overlooking the Botanical Gardens, 'his sole permanent companion a uniformed butler of English lineage'.

Early reports – for instance, in the *New York Daily Mirror* – said that he had first met Starr in October 1930; but when it was pointed out that she was in England then, the date was amended to

December, soon after her return.

I became acquainted with Starr during a dinner-dance in the Grill at the Hotel Pennsylvania [opposite the railway station; it was the largest hotel in Manhattan − 2200 rooms, all with baths]. She was sitting at the next table with a middle-aged woman and a middle-aged chap. We were introduced by the woman, a mutual friend of both of us, and Starr immediately became infatuated with a platinum wrist-watch and its Roman-lettered silver chain which I was wearing. We danced and had a few more drinks, and then I asked could I call her or would she call me, and she said she would do the calling. She said it was her policy to do the calling, that she would keep her life in front of her, and I thought that was kind of mysterious.

She was a crackerjack of a good sport, a little inclined to 'go places and do things' − that was her favourite expression.

She called me the latter part of December and asked me what I was going to give her for Christmas, and I told her, owing to the fact that I did not know her so well, I would not give her anything, and she said, 'All right, farewell.' She called me immediately after Christmas for New Year's ... The first week, I think, in January, I met her and she came over to my apartment. We had a party there.

Nothing transpired that night. We just had drinks, with the exception that the chap who was temporarily sharing the apartment with me, his side-line is as an artist, drew her picture on the wall in the nude. I mean, she posed for it in the nude. First she started with her dress. She had taken her scarf off. She started in her step-ins, and then she took those off, and then there was some remark, and she stood on the piano-stool. A couple of the other girls in the party proceeded to undress. The men were partly nude: down to step-ins − underwear, running trunks, shirt. Some of the couples had intercourse that night. No one had intercourse with Starr. I called a taxi for her and sent her home ...

About the third week in January, Starr telephoned me. We went down to the Village, a place called the Fairies' Paradise [on Bleecker Street], where all the fairies hang out. It is a high-class speakeasy. And we got liquored up, and I think we went taxi-dancing after that, at about ten. The taxi-dance was at the Venice [Dancing Studios, on East Fourteenth Street]. She spoke of it; that was the first time I was in it. Well, then we went back to Brooklyn and went up to my apartment, and she stayed all night and left the next morning about five o'clock. I had intercourse with her. I hesitate in saying that [because] I have a certain amount of principle.

After this first experience, Starr phoned me frequently. Sometimes she would phone after midnight, when she was polluted − I could tell that by the way she talked and the way she carried on. And she would come over, quite liquored up, to the apartment, and she told me that she had a birthday. This was the beginning of March. She asked me what I would give her as a birthday present, and I bought her a dinner ring. It was a small ring, and I paid, I believe, around $175 for it. Then, later on, I found out that I did not think March was her birthday. I gave her several little gifts after that. I gave her a little chain with her name printed on it and had a star printed on it.

We went to several parties here and there and continued to talk about sex, and in fact we indulged in it quite frequently, and she expressed her view on sex, and I felt that she had been a girl that something horrible had happened to in her life. I could not quite understand her. And then I thought, she is just like the ordinary girl, she is a wild girl and likes fun, and she is all mixed up as to desire of sex. She was not sex-mad in a normal way, but it was not repulsive to her or anything of that kind. She enjoyed it.

Oft-times, she would appear depressed. She wanted to marry someone she loved and have a love-nest all of her own. There was never any question of love between us, however. We were merely good friends. She was a good girl – morally. A little daring, perhaps, and with a wild desire to travel and see the whole world. She wanted to know life. The best description I can give of her is that she was a highly educated girl who lived in a dream world all of her own. She used to tell me that she hated most men because 'men are sex-crazy'. She was an entirely different person from the one represented since her dead body was found at Long Beach.

She showed me wrist-watches and a ring that she said she had been given as presents. She had a cheque once, and she asked me would I cash it, and this cheque was for two hundred dollars. I asked about the cheque and she told me she was called by an agency as a party girl or words to that effect, and she gave me an idea about what the party was like. The guests were men ranging anywhere from forty-five up to sixty or seventy. They had dinner served, and from the line of conversation I imagine there must have been at least eight or nine or ten couples there, and with the dinner they had music and then they kept on drinking. They had some kind of another orchestra around midnight, and they were here and there, and the next morning they had breakfast served, and there were barbers and manicurists. That leads up to the cheque. At dinner, the girls were given one sort of napkin, the men another, and around the ladies' napkin was a slip of paper, and on this slip of paper was the cheque unsigned, and on this slip of paper was written as to the girls that stayed over until the party was terminated, the cheque would be signed on the way out. So I asked her, 'Did you get your cheque signed?' And she said, 'Yes.' I asked, 'Did everybody stay?' And she said, 'I did not see anybody leave.'

One time, I decided to give a little party for Starr in my apartment. Along about midnight I decided that as this was a Sunday night and the next day was business, everybody should leave early. I told Starr I would call a machine for her and send her home, and she embarrassed me quite a lot by declaring she would not go home. Being a little intoxicated, we started to pow-pow – a little argument, pro and con, here and there.

Other guests ran out and I had quite a little argument with her in the bedroom, and she would not leave, and I threatened to have her locked up if she did not leave and tried to frighten her to get her to leave, and she was intoxicated, and so was I. She crawled under the bed and I went after her, and she threw pillows at me and I threw over chairs, and we went to bed, and she slept and went out the next morning. It was just a repetition of the same thing.

The last occasion I saw her was early in May. I heard from her last on May 26 [the Tuesday before the Friday when the *Franconia* sailed].

She telephoned and asked me to attend a party with her. I had another engagement and was unable to accept her invitation. Now I wish I had been able to.

*Item.* Remember the pair of blue-sateen evening shoes, one apparently autographed, that Detective Joseph Culkin noticed during his search of Starr's room, ending with the discovery of her diary? The fact that the shoes were not listed in any press inventory of Starr's belongings can be taken as proof positive of the truth of a story told by Vincent Lopez, a well-known band leader. The story was this:

In November 1928, the Vincent Lopez Orchestra was playing music for dancing at Joe Pani's Woodmansten Inn, a roadhouse on the border between the Bronx and Westchester County, a dozen miles north of Manhattan. The inn was popular among 'Broadway's fugitives' – Manhattan socialites deterred from drinking in local watering-holes by the fear of being caught in a raid by Prohibition agents. Years later, Vincent Lopez recalled: 'Out in the country, among the singing locusts and the weeping willows, they danced to the muffled strains of name bands, which had begun to blossom in the mid-twenties, but of which there were comparatively few. You bought set-ups, although you were theoretically supposed to have brought along your own neutral spirits. But of course you bought the charged apple cider which the places pushed upon you as champagne; or slugged yourself with rye fresh from the fusel farms [fusel oil = an acrid oily liquid, consisting chiefly of amyl alcohol]; or Scotch that tasted like reformed carbolic acid. Tuxedoed gorillas and their molls fronted the ringside tables along with Broadway celebrities. And here and there some visiting butter-and-egg man [rich businessman] boasted, boozed, and basked.'

On the 4th, which was a Sunday, Mayor James J. Walker and his girl-friend, Betty 'Monk' Compton, were among the customers. Walker, drunk on arrival, became more so. Towards midnight, Betty dragged him on to the dance-floor. 'Just a few steps,' he said, 'then Cinderella must go home.' And she said something like 'My slippers may not be glass, but they're killing me.' When they got close to the band-stand, Betty took off her shoes. She held them up to Lopez and asked him to autograph them, which he did. As Walker and Betty staggered away, other dancers, presumably only women, beseeched Lopez to autograph *their* shoes. One of the shoes he signed was Starr Faithfull's.

It is understandable that her name lodged in his memory − but how did he come to hear it in the first place? Perhaps, when she handed up her shoe, she told Lopez her name, hoping for an inscription rather than a plain autograph. Discarding the idea that she went to the Woodmansten Inn alone, one wonders who she was with. As the Faithfulls were then living in New Jersey, where did she spend the rest of the night? Other questions readily come to mind.

*Item*. Compared with Texas Guinan, Vivian Denton was a small-fry 'speakeasy madame'. All such women were. She said that she had first met Starr in 1929, when she was running The Rubaiyat, a 'restaurant' on Bleecker Street, south of Washington Square: 'A regular customer introduced us. At the time I laughed, thinking her name was kind of fantastic, and I said, 'Yes, and I am Miss Moonbeam,' or words to that effect.' Even so, Starr also became a regular customer, often dining with men − and, on occasion, with 'a little girl . . . in mannish clothes, dressed in collar and tie'. After closing The Rubaiyat − 'because it had become a hang-out for homosexuals of both sexes'[1] Vivian did something of an unspecified nature on the vaudeville stage and then, in January 1931, opened, or re-opened, the Green Club (on Prince Street, two blocks south of Bleecker Street and about a quarter of a mile south-east of St Luke's Place):

> Miss Faithfull was one of the guests on opening night. She came in accompanied by a blonde girl of sixteen or seventeen whom she introduced as Iona. The minute Miss Faithfull saw me there, she asked me to accompany her to the ladies' rest room, which I did, and she said, 'I don't want you to tell anybody I am Starr Faithfull. I am known here'

1. The possibility that Starr had lesbian romances seems to have been mooted by Martin Littleton when he interviewed Constance Little, the girl she was intending to go out with on the day when she actually met, and was beaten up by, 'Joseph Collins'. I can see no other explanation for a word in a sentence of the report of the interview: 'Miss Little did not think Starr exhibited Elizabethan tendencies [but] said she frequently indulged in conversations about sex matters.'

– evidently the place was operating before I went there – 'I am known here as Fair and sometimes as Sally.' She said, 'I have got myself a new daddy and he has furnished up a lovely apartment uptown in the Seventies and I don't want him to know my right name.' She referred to this man only as Dud. She said, 'You know, I go to clubs and places every night and he sees me in the daytime. [She said that] she stayed with her parents at night. She told them that she was modelling, posing for artists. She told me that her father [sic] was driving her crazy and her mother was a nervous wreck.

According to Vivian, Starr often came to the club, sometimes with a young man known as Gigolo Spike:

She had given him a ring and a new suit . . . I was sitting at their table when he . . . pulled out his hand and he showed this gorgeous ring, this little-finger ring with a diamond in it, and [he was wearing] a brand-new suit of clothes. He was a good-looking boy of nineteen, only a kid. He showed the suit and pulled out his pocket with money in it, and she made a remark: 'I wonder what my old sugar-daddy would think of that.' He said, 'Look at this, folks,' and he held out his hand – 'Look what my baby bought me.'

The next time I saw Miss Faithfull was on a Saturday night, and the place was packed. She was accompanied this time by Iona again. She came in and she was dressed in evening clothes. Her evening cape was hanging halfway off her shoulder. She was obviously intoxicated. I took her into the ladies' room and arranged her hair and powdered her nose, and she said she would sit down at a table . . .

She got up and went over to the piano. I think she gave the piano-player a few dollars, and he played her some ditty, and she sang. The number was called 'My Daddy Rocks Me With a Steady Roll'. Several people walked out while she was singing, and after she got through she took her dress off and danced. She lifted the evening dress right off her shoulder. She had a little brassiere and girdle and panties on. She started to do a cootch dance, one of those wiggle dances that the burlesque dancers do. One lady objected terribly, and I picked up the dress and grabbed her and rushed her through the kitchen with her dress on again.

Vivian's story of Starr's impromptu cootch dance was corroborated by a man who had not objected terribly to it. Neither Iona nor Gigolo Spike was ever traced.

---

(Constance Little also said that 'Starr frequently commented upon suicide. She described this as in her opinion being an effort at the dramatic and that Starr never had any intention of committing suicide, that she was dearly fond of life, always desiring to get the most out of it, and was in dread and fear of death. It was her opinion that Starr did not and would not commit suicide.')

*Items*. By the middle of the second week of the case, more than five hundred letters about it had been received at the Nassau County police headquarters; almost as many had been delivered at the DA's office. Many of the letters were from cranks or people who simply enjoyed writing letters; there were offers of help or actual solutions from clairvoyants, spiritualists, water-diviners, authors of whodunits, and people who had been given ouija boards for Christmas; there were confessions, all patently bogus, most from people who often confessed to much-publicised crimes (of those people, one, a lay-preacher on Staten Island, was so keen to take the blame for the sins of fellow-mortals that he had duplicated a form-letter and merely filled in the spaces). And there were tip-off letters that gave names or nicknames of individuals who were said to have been acquainted with Starr.

Of course, the papers received tip-offs too. (Later on, the *Daily* and *Sunday News* offered a reward of $5000 'for exclusive information which will solve the mysterious death of Starr Faithfull', claiming that 'District Attorney Edwards has made the extraordinary offer of immunity to the informer, if he were involved in the murder, but was not the master mind or the actual killer'; the response, described as 'overwhelming', seems to have literally overwhelmed the *News*, for after a few days, the publisher, Colonel Joseph M. Patterson, phoned Edwards with the suggestion that the sacks of 'reward mail' should be redirected to Mineola — to which Edwards said thanks but no, thanks.) The tabloids, while viewing all tip-offs with an equal degree of unsuspicion, took care to publish them questioningly. Like this, which is from the *Daily Mirror*:

Who is 'Gigolo Mike'? [Probable answer: A variation on the 'Gigolo Spike' in Vivian Denton's story.] . . . Was he Starr's escort at many nocturnal orgies in night clubs and hotels? Does a well-known East Side gangster, who formerly ran a 'dive' in Greenwich Village, which was frequented by Starr, her girl-friends, 'Dawn' and 'Billy James', now own a similar place in or near Flushing? Who is 'Dawn'? Who is 'Billy James'? Was Starr known as 'Fayre' or 'Faire' at the 'Black Cat' in Greenwich Village? At the 'Open Door'? At the 'Three Fives'? Was she acquainted with Jean Malin, famous female impersonator? With Faith Bacon?

There was no need to say who or what Faith Bacon was. Everyone had heard of her, and many had seen much of her. Coy only about her age — which, to give her the benefit of considerable doubt, was twenty-two in 1931 — she was a sort of cross between

Isadora Duncan and Gypsy Rose Lee: an artistic dancer who included stripping in the choreography. No one seems to have disputed her claim that she invented the fan-dance. She appeared, very much so, in the stage extravaganzas, respectively *Follies, Scandals* and *Vanities*, of Florenz Ziegfeld, George White and Earl Carroll, and all three of those showmen, when asked to choose The Most Beautiful Girl on Broadway, unhesitatingly plumped for Faith. The publicity stunts she devised were as artistic as the new routines they publicised. On one occasion, during rehearsals at the Edison Hotel, off Times Square, for a show in which she was to dance to Debussy's *L'Après-midi d'un faune*, shedding all but one of the leaves of an eight-leaf costume as she did so, and while two stags, 'hired to impart realism', chewed straw in the background, she caused a traffic jam, in part because, never minding the briskness of the April day, she emerged through the revolving doors 'attired in the strikingly flimsy garb of a Grecian dancer', and in lesser part because she was walking a fawn — which, flustered by all the fuss, dropped pellets all over the sidewalk, in contravention of a street-cleanliness ordinance. She, the fawn and the press photographers were arrested and carted off to a police station where, after the photographers had been released and she had enquired, 'Can't I even walk my baby round the block?', she was charged with several slight offences. The charges were dismissed when she appeared in court, conventionally dressed to the nines and without the fawn, next day. On 15 June 1931, when the *Mirror* posed the sly question about Faith Bacon, she was in Pittsburgh, Pennsylvania, starring in the latest — and, as it transpired, last — *Zeigfeld Follies*, which was being tried out before opening on Broadway. If the question was not put to Faith, she must have volunteered the answer. As the answer was not published in any of the tabloids, it must have been unsensationally negative.[1]

Unaided by tip-offs, the tabloids amended 'Joseph Collins' to suit their purpose, which was to make readers think that he was Andrew Peters. More suddenly even than the picture of Dorian Gray, the

---

1. In the 1940s, Faith Bacon's career, her life, went on the skids. Surprising some of those who suspected that she was a lesbian, she married a businessman of Buffalo; they soon separated. In September 1956, she travelled from her drab home in Erie, Pennsylvania, to Chicago, hoping to find a job, willing to accept any offer. She shared a room on the third floor of a fleabag hotel with a young woman. On the 26th, she committed suicide by throwing herself out of the window. The American Guild of Variety Artists paid the funeral expenses.

man who had attacked Starr at the St Paul's Hotel perceptibly decayed. Described only as middle-aged in the Bellevue Hospital report, he became, by 15 June, 'a man of advanced years'; by the following day he was 'bald-headed', and by the 20th he did not merely *look* 'distinguished' but *was*: 'He was certainly somebody pretty important,' said the *News*, and sought to bolster that guess with another: '. . . for the detective on the beat [in the vicinity of the St Paul's, readers were expected to assume] said "Collins is so prominent in his community that he is able to build a stone wall around him to keep out publicity".' Given a few more days, no doubt some specially venturesome reporter would have created a clinching clue – perhaps from an of-course-anonymous bell-boy, disclosing that Joseph Collins's overnight bag bore the monogram AJP.

But, from 22 June, a Monday, unreliable tip-offs, inspired guesses and downright lies were spiked by sub-editors, needing every inch of space for stories concerning and emanating from the ship's surgeon, Dr George Jameson Carr.

# 6

He still had some holiday left when he returned home from his motoring tour of Belgium; but as soon as he read the message that 'the legal authorities of Nassau County, New York State, would be obliged for assistance in regard to investigations into the death of a Miss Starr Faithfull', he arranged to take the place of the doctor scheduled to be aboard the next Cunard liner bound for America, which was the *Laconia*, leaving Liverpool on 13 June.

During the voyage, he received wireless calls from New York papers. All of his responses were discreet – which led one of the calling reporters to assume that he was 'a reticent Hibernian'. Speaking of himself, he said that he was forty-six, a native of Edinburgh (he was born on 26 October 1884 at 30 Pilrig Street, the son of George Bobie Carr, Minister of the Colston Street United Presbyterian Church, and Jane Carr, *née* Jameson). After graduating (as a Bachelor of Medicine and of Surgery) from Edinburgh University in 1910, he had 'spent several years in the valley of the Amazon, helping to clean up a yellow-fever district', and had joined Cunard in 1921. Speaking of Starr, he said that she was 'a beautiful, striking, attractive girl, alert of mind'. He confirmed a rumour that she had written three letters to him shortly before her disappearance, and that he had the letters with him.

The *Laconia* touched at Boston, only to disembark a comparative few of the passengers, on Sunday, the 21st. Reporters and photographers went aboard, and, according to the *New York Herald Tribune*,

found Dr Carr reclining in a deck chair, dressed in a tan tweed golf suit ... He is a tall, bronzed Scot ... lean and fit, with searching brown eyes and a powdering of grey hair above his ears ... When pressed to give his own opinion on the value of the information which he brings, and whether he considered it of vital importance in a possible solution to the mystery, he answered good-temperedly, 'If I didn't, I wouldn't have sailed across the ocean, using up my hard-earned leave of absence.'

How long had you known Miss Faithfull? When did you first meet her? These were among the questions put to the surgeon.

'I met her when I was the surgeon on the *Aurania* in June 1927, during a trip from Montreal to Glasgow,'[1] he replied. 'At that time I met her professionally. I treated her.'

Asked the nature of the illness for which he had treated Miss Faithfull, Dr Carr explained that that was a service within the scope of his profession, and he, therefore, could not discuss it. 'Most of my dealings with the girl,' he said, 'were of a professional nature.' . . .

Dr Carr said he last saw Miss Faithfull on the *Franconia* on May 29, just before the vessel sailed. He did not see a great deal of her on that occasion, he said; but he admitted that he was aware that she was taken off the ship and lowered to a harbour tug after the *Franconia* had sailed . . . He denied that he had ever met the girl socially ashore, all the meetings being aboard transatlantic liners . . .

Dr Carr evaded all questions and requests for comments upon the report that Miss Faithfull was at one time 'madly in love with him'. He produced a number of clippings from English newspapers, and pointed to the reproduction of a letter Miss Faithfull had written to a friend in which she said, 'Everything in New York is anti-climax to me now. I can't even get a thrill from the New York skyline any more.' 'That shows me how she felt,' commented Dr Carr. 'Anyone who cannot get a thrill from the New York skyline is pretty far gone.'[2]

It was on the basis of this single statement that some of Dr Carr's interviewers inclined to the belief that he supported the suicide theory, but he refused point-blank to commit himself publicly upon any theory about the case.

In the course of the interview, Dr Carr repeatedly refused to give any inkling of the contents of the three letters which he carried from Miss Faithfull.

After reporters finally left, Dr Carr retired to his cabin.


The *Laconia* sailed on to Manhattan, arriving at Pier 54 on the Monday night. Other reporters, far more of them, went aboard. During the day, the tabloids had regaled their readers with stuff like this, which is from the *Daily News*:

1. The group tourists, Starr among them, travelled to Glasgow on the *Aurania* – and, having toured Scotland and England by charabanc, returned, from Southampton, on the *California*.
2. Reminiscent of Dr Johnson's remark to Boswell: 'When a man is tired of London he is tired of life.'

On her ocean voyages Starr met many men, and on shore she revived those friendships. Dr George Jameson Carr, surgeon of the Cunard line vessels, was an intimate ... The relationship continued until exactly seven days before Starr walked out of her house and down the steps into eternity.

Jameson Carr is a bachelor, a middle-aged, somewhat fascinating voyageur. Doctors know a lot about women. And doctors on board a vessel know even more. Starr seems to have become madly infatuated with the suave, understanding, profoundly wise physician of the vasty deep ...

He had called at her home, and had taken her out, and the girl's starved heart found surcease from its deadly home routine and daily struggles in the soothing balm and comprehending nod and smiling eyes of the Scottish surgeon ...

Having read such things, and therefore felt concern that the physician of the vasty deep needed protection from the reporters for the gutter press, a famous corporate attorney, Samuel Untermyer, went aboard the *Laconia* ahead of the pack of New York newsmen. By the time they located Carr, he had gratefully accepted Untermyer's offer to stand by him, literally as well as advisingly. Untermyer explained that he was repaying a debt: 'In 1928 I fell desperately ill while crossing on the *Aquitania*, and the doctor attended me, accompanied me to London, and continued to treat me until I sailed back for the United States, and I have never ceased to remember his skill and kindness.' Unknowingly paraphrasing words spoken by Alexander Whiteside, he added: 'I am not acting in behalf of Dr Jameson Carr in a legal capacity, but as a friend. The doctor does not need a lawyer.'

Untermyer insisted that questions 'had to be restricted to non-personal matters', and the reporters seem to have obeyed. Carr parried some questions, and replied flippantly to others:

Would he say that Starr had a suicidal temperament?

'I don't know what temperament one has to have to commit suicide.'

Was it true that he had described Starr as charming and beautiful?

'All ladies are.'

Had Starr's death surprised him?

'It is forty years since I was surprised.'

If Starr had jumped or been thrown from a liner heading eastward in the Ambrose Channel between Long Island and New Jersey, did he think, from his knowledge of the sea, that the body might have washed up at Long Beach within a couple of days?

'Not having fallen off a ship in those waters, I cannot say.'

Wasn't it likely that a propeller would have caught her?

'I haven't the faintest idea. All I know is that I shouldn't like to be caught by a propeller.'

After half an hour or so, at 9.30, Untermyer brought the questioning to an end. Reporters who lingered on the pier spotted the doctor and the lawyer leaving the ship and being driven away in the latter's chauffeured limousine.

During the next two days, Tuesday and Wednesday, Carr paid two visits to Mineola, both times chaperoned by Untermyer − to talk with Edwards, Littleton and King, and to testify before the grand jury examining the case of 'The People v. John Doe and Richard Doe[1] (Death of Starr Faithfull)' − and the press learned much of what he said, supposedly in secret, to the grand jury, and all about the exhibits he produced before them, supposedly for their eyes only. But those events did not happen quite in that order. Somehow or other, the press got the grand jury information before the grand jury did. Almost certainly, the leak sprang from one of five men; but there are no indications as to which of them was the culprit, nor as to whether he acted independently or was in cahoots with one, some or all of the others, nor as to his, or their, motive.

It is best, I think, to ignore the various reportings of Carr's testimony, and to use instead a deposition that he made later:

> ... In June 1927, shortly after the *Aurania* sailed from Montreal, I was called by my nurse to deal with an emergency in one of the third-class tourist cabins. Starr Faithfull, whom I had not met before, was in the cabin. There was a young man in the cabin with her, also intoxicated. Both persons were fully clothed. She was comatose; in fact, I thought she was dead. But he was making love to her. She, naturally, had no response at this stage. I arranged for the young man to be placed under surveillance until, after I had used a stomach-pump, Starr Faithfull regained consciousness.

(In the two days between his appearance before the grand jury and his return to England aboard the *Laconia*, Carr snapped at the umpteenth reporter to ask if his relationship with Starr had been romantic. 'You don't become romantic about a girl on whom you used a stomach-pump the first time you saw her.')

---

1. Names used in legal proceedings when the true names are unknown.

A day or so after my first meeting with Starr, I was called to see her and tried to persuade her to leave the smoking room of the *Aurania* at about eleven o'clock in the morning, where she was drinking with several other passengers and had become hysterical ... She was insulting to the hostess who had called me. She made reference to the obesity of the hostess, which was never disputed as regards the fact of her obesity, but it was said in a manner which was insulting ...

I met her on a number of further occasions ... and she spoke of confidential matters. I learned of her experiences with Mr Peters. She also told me, and subsequently mentioned in letters to me, about taking ether and hypnotic drugs. She said she got an enormous kick out of ether, and it made her forget her past. When I expressed surprise that she could procure ether, she said that it was a very common thing for young ladies in New York, as they could buy ether for eighteen cents for two cones at any drug store.

(Extracts from a police report: 'A thorough check has been made of all drug stores within the vicinity of 12 St Luke's Place as well as those near the family's former home at Ridgewood Road in West Orange, New Jersey. The result of this inquiry reveals that Lind's Drug Store on Ridgewood Road, West Orange, was the source of supply of hypnotics to Starr in the period of time she resided in the locality. The clerk of this drug store states that Starr was a very frequent purchaser of the hypnotics, Veronal and Luminol. He had no available records to show. He says that when the Faithfulls moved, they owed a bill, which is still unpaid ... H. Grimm, drug store located on Hudson Street, between Morton and Leroy Streets, Manhattan, is the only known drug store patronised by the Faithfulls since their arrival in St Luke's Place. Mr Grimm states that Mr Faithfull frequently came into his store and made small purchases, principally soap and cigarettes. He also states that Mr Faithfull bought a great many postage stamps, and remarked that he must be a wonderful letter writer; he believed that Mr Faithfull in all probability bought soap and cigarettes to give him a chance to make a few cents profit because there is no profit for him in the purchase of postage stamps. He states he did not know Starr and had not sold her any hypnotics and that it was necessary to have a prescription for hypnotics in the Greater City of New York ... As no prescription is required outside the Greater City of New York, a search in the neighbourhood of Long Beach would be fruitless because of the fact that druggists are not required to keep a record of these sales. Inquiry from the immediate family as to the possible source of drugs was not productive of any information.')

*Dr Carr's deposition continued*: I knew Starr more by her letters than any other way. They were charming and amusing. In fact, she was brilliant, so much so that I said, 'Why don't you get on *The New Yorker*?' I tried to persuade her that that was her metier. I don't know whether she was the originator of the saying, 'Fifth Avenue is the place where you meet low-bred women and high-bred dogs.'...

I observed that she showed a distinct liking for men when she took alcohol, or I should say an apparent liking ... Upon the occasion of her being in the smoking room of the *Aurania*, she was throwing her arms around the necks of men who had given her liquor. But she told me that she had the most appalling contempt for men; she hated them ...

In August 1928, I was ship's surgeon of the *Aquitania*. We docked in New York after a world cruise, and I spent the night in Mineola, and on my return to the ship the next morning I was met by my assistant, Dr Raymond Lancaster. He met me on the gangway and said, 'There is a girl who says she knows you.'

I said, 'Who is she?'

He said, 'Miss Faithfull.'

I said, 'Really?'

He said, 'She is in my cabin.'

He took me down to see her. I found Miss Faithfull completely intoxicated, shrieking at the top of her voice, making a tremendous hubbub, and she was too intoxicated even to recognise me.

I said, 'How did this occur?'

He told me she had come aboard and she had been taking intoxicants. He had given her more intoxicants, and this was the condition in which she had become, and he did not know what to do with her.

I said, 'I cannot help you in this matter. It is your case.'

I left the ship immediately and did not return till she sailed.

On a later occasion, she told me that she was devoted to Dr Lancaster. She told me that they had shared a room in the Astor Hotel as husband and wife.

In September 1928 I was the doctor aboard the *Laconia*, which was then waiting to sail to New York from Liverpool. Five minutes before sailing time, I received a summons to my consulting room. I found Miss Faithfull there with a Cunard official and she was in a state of hysteria again. She told me that she had run away from home at the suggestion of Dr Lancaster, and had come to London on the *Franconia* third-class. That Dr Lancaster had seen her in London and turned her down. That she stayed at the Cecil Hotel, could not pay her bills, and then was kicked out and had gone to a small hotel opposite, where, after having finally appealed to her father and mother for funds through the American consul, and they not being forthcoming, the hotel had kicked her out, retaining her baggage. That she had looked up some steamship going to Boston, and had discovered the *Laconia*, had sneaked on to the train and made her way to Liverpool, where she enquired as to who was on the

*Laconia*, and amongst other officers, she discovered I was there. She appealed to me to do something to get her back to her family, because if it could not be done, she would immediately jump overboard.

At this time, she was on her knees. The situation demanded immediate attention. I went to the purser and asked what he could do about it, and he said that they could take her as a last passenger, if they could get somebody to guarantee that they would be repaid. I immediately said that I would guarantee the passage, as I knew Mrs Faithfull. I did not know Mr Faithfull then; but I knew they appeared to be in very comfortable circumstances, and thought nothing more about it ... She had no handbag, no toilet articles, no money, no extras of any kind. She was just as she stood.

When the *Laconia* docked at Boston, Miss Faithfull was met at the pier by her step-father. I later wrote to Mrs Faithfull, enclosing an itemised bill of what I had paid out; it came to about $169. I got a letter from Mrs Faithfull, expressing her appreciation of the assistance given to her daughter in returning to the United States, and saying that she hoped soon to be able to settle the bill; at present, due to monetary difficulties, it couldn't be done. I subsequently saw both Mrs and Mr Faithfull ... There was an opportunity of mentioning the bill on many occasions if they were inclined to pay the money ... The money has never been repaid. Carr's account of incidents aboard the *Franconia* on the afternoon of Friday 29 May 1931, can be omitted, as it added nothing important to the account pieced together from statements made by members of the crew.

The doctor had brought three letters with him. Letters from Starr that had reached him after her death. He believed that the letters – or rather, two of them – went far towards explaining her death. Throughout the *Laconia's* voyage from Liverpool to Manhattan, via Boston, and till shortly before he, with Samuel Untermyer, went to Mineola to talk with Edwards, Littleton and King, he had kept the letters in the chief purser's safe.

None of the letters was dated, but the doctor had kept each of them in its envelope, which was clearly postmarked, showing the date and approximate time of posting, and the area of Manhattan in which it had been posted. The notepaper and envelope of each letter was of the customers' stationery of one of three commercial establishments in Manhattan – which, as some visitors to those establishments took such stationery away with them, did not mean that the letters had been written on the commercial premises.

The first-posted letter, using Hotel Plaza stationery, had been posted in the late afternoon of Saturday, 30 May – some time before 6 p.m. – in District 6, the collection district between West Fourth and West Fifty-First Streets (well south of the Plaza). The envelope was marked 'for BERENGARIA' — the next mail-carrying ship leaving for England. There was no salutation at the start of the letter.

I am going (definitely now — I've been thinking of it for a long time) to end my worthless, disorderly bore of an existence — before I ruin anyone else's life as well. I certainly have made a sordid, futureless mess of it all. I am dead, dead sick of it. It is no one's fault but my own — I hate everything so — life is HORRIBLE. [That word was double-underlined.]

Being a sane person you may not understand — I take dope to forget and drink to try and like people but it is no use. I am mad and insane over you. I hold my breath to try to stand it — take allonal in the hope of waking happier but that *homesick* feeling never leaves me. I have, strangely enough, more of a feeling of peace or whatever you call it now that I know it will soon be over. The half hour before I die will, I imagine, be quite blissful.

You promised to come and see me. I realise ABSOLUTELY that it will be the one and only time. There is no earthly reason why you should come. If you do, it will be what I call an act of marvellous generosity and kindness.

What I did yesterday was horrible. Although I don't see how you could lose your job as it must have been clearly seen what a nuisance you thought me.

If I don't see you again — goodbye. Sorry to so lose all sense of humour. But I am suffering so that all I want is to have it over with. It's become a hell such as I couldn't have imagined.

If you come to see me when you are in this time you will be a sport — you are assured by this letter of no more bother from me.

My dear,
STARR

12 St Luke's Place,
New York City

The second-posted letter, using Hotel Pennsylvania stationery, had been posted in the early evening of Tuesday, 2 June — some time before 8 p.m. — in District 11, the collection district overlapping the east of District 6. The envelope was marked 'for BERENGARIA', leaving next day for Liverpool. The letter was short, not quite covering one side of a single sheet.

Dear Dr Carr:

I want to apologise and to tell you how deeply I regret my conduct on the *Franconia* last Friday. I had come down hoping to renew our acquaintance but I fear I only made a fool of myself and that it was very disagreeable for you. I had brought some drinks on to the boat with me, and drank them too fast. I become utterly irrational when I drink, and I

No ether, alcohol, or window jumping.
I don't want to be maimed. I want
oblivion. If there is an after life
it would be a dirty trick - but
I'm sure fifty million priests are
wrong. That is one of those things
one knows. Nothing makes any
difference now. I love to eat and
can have one delicious meal with no
worry over gaining. I adore music
and I am going to hear some good
music. I believe I love music more
than anything. I am going to
drink slowly keeping AWARE
every second. Also I am going
to enjoy my last cigarettes. -
I won't worry because men
flirt with me in the streets. I
shall encourage them. I don't
care who they are. I will

*The last letter: second page.*

should I you!. But its more than I can cope with this feeling I have for you. I have tried to pose as clever and intellectual thereby to attract you, but it was not successful and I couldn't go on writing those long, studied letters. I don't have to worry, because there are no words in which to describe this feeling I have for you. The words lover, adore, worship have become meaningless. — There is nothing I can do but what I am going to do. I shall never see you again. That is extraordinary! Although I can comprehend it, as more than I can comprehend the words "always". or "time": they produce a very merciful numbness.

Starr.

want you to know how deeply sorry I am for the embarrissment [*sic*] I must have caused you.

Very Sincerely,
STARR FAITHFULL

12 St Luke's Place,
New York City

The third-posted letter, using stationery of the Lord & Taylor department store, had been posted in the mid-afternoon of Thursday, 4 June – some time before 4 p.m. – at the post office's Grand Central annexe. The envelope was marked 'for S.S. OLYMPIC'.

Hello Bill Old Thing:
It's all up with me now. This is something I am GOING to put through. The only thing that bothers me about it, the only thing I dread is being outwitted and prevented from doing this – which is the only possible thing for me to do. If one wants to get away with murder one has to jolly well keep one's wits about one. It's the same way with suicide. If I don't watch out I will wake up in a psychopathic ward, but I intend to watch out and accomplish my end this time.

No ether, allonal or window jumping. I don't want to be maimed. I want oblivion. If there is an after life it would be a dirty trick – but I'm sure fifty millions priests ARE wrong. That is one of the things one *knows*. Nothing makes any difference now. I love to eat and can have one delicious meal with no worry over gaining. I adore music and I am going to hear some good music. I believe I love music more than anything. I am going to drink <u>slowly</u> keeping AWARE every second. Also I am going to enjoy my last cigarettes – I won't worry because men flirt with me in the streets – I shall encourage them – I don't care who they are. I wish I got more pleasure sleeping with men. I'm afraid I've always been a rotten 'sleeper'. It's the preliminaries that count with me. It doesn't matter though.

It's a great life when one has 24 hours to live. I can be rude to people – I can tell them they are too fat or that I don't like their clothes, and I don't have to dread being a lonely old woman, or poverty, obscurity, or boredom. I don't have to dread living on without ever seeing you, or hearing rumours such as 'The women all fall for him' – and 'he entertains charmingly'. Why in hell shouldn't you! – But it's more than I can cope with – this feeling I have for you. I have tried to pose as clever and intellectual thereby to attract you, but it was not successful and I couldn't go on writing those long, studied letters. I don't have to worry because there are no words in which to describe this feeling I have for you. The words Love, admire, worship have become meaningless. – There is nothing I can do but what I am going to do. I shall never see you again.

**219**

That is extraordinary. Although I can't comprehend it any more than I can comprehend the words — 'always' or 'time'. They produce a very merciful numbness.

STARR

*Starr Faithfull*
A drawing by Rudolph Haybrook

## 7

*That*, most people thought, was *that*. Starr Faithfull had written of committing suicide – first, on the day after her disgraceful exhibition aboard the *Franconia* (provoked. it seemed, by her doctor-friend's refusal to have anything to do with her); second, and with greater determination, on the day before her disappearance. Ergo, she *had* committed suicide. Probably, having learned lessons from her unsuccessful attempt to stow away on the *Franconia*, she had managed to do so on some other Europe-bound liner, probably the *Ile de France*, which had departed from the French Line's pier late on the night of Friday, 5 June. Probably, having dosed herself with Veronal, she had emerged from wherever she had hidden and flung herself overboard as the liner had slowed to drop off the pilot near the lightship marking the eastern end of Ambrose Channel, at the opening to New York Harbour, ten miles east of Sandy Hook, New Jersey, and about the same distance south of Long Beach.

But – and you will not be surprised at this – Stanley Faithfull insisted that the *that* of the letters did not equal the *that* of suicide. 'The letters are forgeries!' he cried (and, not for the first time, Mrs Faithfull, worried about his blood pressure, embarrassed by his vehemence, muttered, 'Now, Stanley ...'). He had not seen the letters when he first cried forgery. Cooling down a bit, he explained that Starr could not have posted the first two letters, therefore could not have written them, as she had been in the apartment, had never left it, not for a minute, during the periods when they were posted. If two of the letters were forgeries, all of them were. The letters were the devilish invention of her murderer, whom he, Stanley, had named in a letter he had written to Inspector King on the very day of Dr Carr's arrival in Manhattan. No, he would certainly not name the culprit in public. It was up to King, or some other chump out in Mineola, to get subordinate chumps working on the leads he had provided in his letter. (As you will have guessed, Stanley had named Andrew Peters.) His voice rising again, he said that he expected

Elvin Edwards to submit the letters received by Dr Carr to a hand-writing expert. Oh and by the way, he already had a long list of 'legal reasons for complaint' against certain newspapers, and if any of those papers, or any of the few so-far-unoffending ones, dared to call the letters suicide notes, instances of 'such misnomering' would be added to the list. ('Now, Stanley. . . .' Mrs Faithfull muttered.)

The minute Louise Rice heard that Stanley expected Edwards to submit the letters to a handwriting expert, she told the press that the letters had already been submitted to her (who else?), and the minute Edwards heard what Louisa had said, he emphatically denied it. But as, by then, Stanley's expectation had become a press conclusion, Edwards added that, 'needless to say, of course, a handwriting examination is in hand'. The letters had been, or hurriedly would be, sent to Albert Osborn, who, though not a member of Louisa's Graphological Institute of America, was reckoned to be the doyen of examiners of questioned documents.[1] In his office near the foot of Broadway, Osborne made two piles of confetti, one lot snipped from facsimiles of the letters, the other from facsimiles of pages in Starr's diary, then compared words and parts of words that cropped up in both. He reported that 'meticulous scientific perusal of the missives in question [the letters to Carr] as compared with the provided sample leaves no doubt whatsoever that the two sets of scripts emanated from the same hand; I am prepared to swear so'. Meanwhile, Stanley had approached, or been approached by, another handwriting examiner, J. Vreeland Haring. As soon as Osborn's finding was announced by Edwards, who stressed that 'the threat of suicide contained in two of the letters is not valid proof of suicide itself', Stanley introduced the press to Haring, who said that all three letters were forgeries – 'among the cleverest, most cunning, I have ever seen, understandably fooling even the most trained pair of eyes, but forgeries nonetheless'. It turned out that his opinion was based on comparison of a facsimile of the first of the letters with letters that Starr had written to her mother from London. When Edwards was told of Haring's contradiction of Osborn, he smiled and said, 'My long courtroom experience has taught me the invariable rule that if one expert says white, sure

1. He was best known to the general public as the examiner of love-letters found strewn around the bodies of the writers of them, the Reverend Edward Hall and his leading choir-singer, Mrs Eleanor Mills, in the shade of a crab apple tree in De Russey's Lane, near the New Jersey town of New Brunswick, the clergyman's living, in 1922. The widow and her two brothers were accused of the murders but, after two trials, acquitted. The Hall-Mills case remains unsolved.

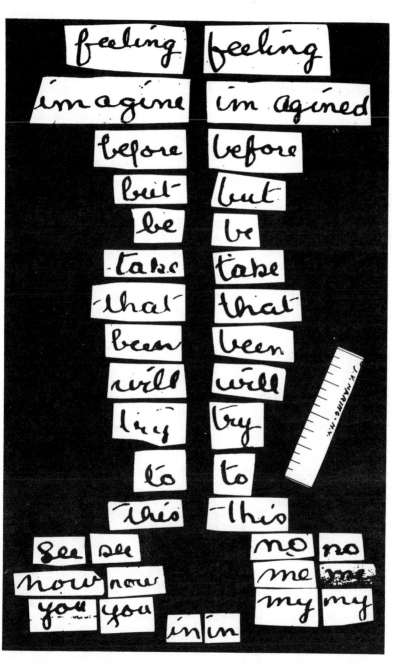

*Clippings from* (left) *letters from Starr to her mother,* (right) *the first of her three letters to Dr Carr.*

enough he will be countered by an expert saying black. That does not mean, of course, that every second-guessing expert's testimony is contaminated by a desire for fame or a wish to please his master.'[1]

Not quite as suddenly as the Starr Faithfull case had taken over the front pages, it disappeared from them. St Luke's Place became its old self, quiet except on Friday and Saturday afternoons, when the band played in the park. In Mineola, the lawns between the police headquarters and the Old Courthouse grew immaculately green again, recovered from the scuffing and pocking by newsmen, sightseers, and peddlers of ice-cream.

Stanley worked hard to keep the story running. He phoned editors with offers of what he called scoops, arranged press conferences at which fewer and fewer reporters turned up, and issued written statements. The trouble, one of the troubles, with Stanley was that he continued to say things that he had said at the start of the case and which had long since been proved false. He still insisted, for instance, that the girl who had caused all the trouble on the *Franconia* was a Starr look-alike — but that Starr *had* been aboard the liner, undemonstratively enjoying herself at a going-away party during which Francis Peabody Hamlin had enveigled her into the company of 'agents employed by somebody whose security and peace of mind were threatened by the very fact that Starr was alive, somebody whose interest, public and social and domestic, would be vitally served by her silence — or death'.

Every so often, the tabloids extracted juicy quotes like that from Stanley's written statements, topped or tailed them with 'information from a reliable source', that the investigators were 'floundering in the choppy waters of a sea of uncertainty' or 'confident of an imminent break-through', and used the result to fill a gap on an inside page, inconspicuous in proximity to heavier-headlined reports that, for instance, a woman calling herself Princess Anastasia, and claiming to be a daughter of the murdered Czar of Russia, was 'facing the bugaboo of deportation' from America; that Thomas Alva Edison was 'waging a cheerful fight against death' at his home in West Orange; that the recently-former wife of the film director Josef von Sternberg was suing Marlene Dietrich for 'love theft'; that the newish wife of the prize-fighter

1. In 1934, Osborn and Haring, separately working for one prosecutorial master, helped towards proving that, two years before, Bruno Richard Hauptmann had kidnapped Charles A. Lindbergh, Junior, the baby son of the aviator, from his home at Hopewell, twenty miles south-west of New Brunswick, and murdered him.

Gene Tunney was 'not on the list of that bird of happy omen, Doctor Stork,' but was merely indisposed by a muscle pulled while her husband was not training.

Towards the end of July, Stanley at last, and for the last time, managed to get the case back on the front pages. On the morning of Friday the 25th, he told the press that he had issued an ultimatum: 'If the police of New York City, in whose jurisdiction my daughter was kidnapped, and the authorities of Nassau County, in whose jurisdiction she was criminally drowned, do not, by noon this day, pledge to me their efforts to solve her death, I shall immediately take steps to remove the conduct of the case from their incompetent hands and place it in the hands of authorities able and disposed to act.' Asked if he suspected Andrew Peters of being 'in any way involved in Starr's death', he replied, slowly selecting his words: 'I think it is perfectly logical to assume that Peters might be mixed up in this crime. But please quote me correctly.'

The *New York Daily News*:

Stanley E. Faithfull held his watch in his hand and saw the hour and minute hands become one as they reached the Roman figure XII on the dial.

It was exactly 12 o'clock – the deadline he had set ...

Faithfull's teeth clicked almost as audibly as the cover on his watch snapped when he returned the timepiece to his pocket. His lips tightened to a thin white line.

Nothing had happened. Neither Police Commissioner Mulrooney nor District Attorney Edwards had answered Faithfull's challenge ... In the New York police headquarters nobody in authority was prepared to comment on the unique situation brought about by Faithfull's sudden re-emergence on the front pages of the metropolitan press. And in Mineola, District Attorney Edwards shrugged and observed:

'This case isn't closed. I am still investigating, and I'd like it known that I am sincere in my statement. I will welcome any information that will help solve the death of that poor child. Whenever Mr Faithfull gives me something tangible to work on, something that is not merely suggestion and innuendo that can't be used as evidence in any court, I will be glad to investigate whatever leads he points out.'

But far away in the North the repercussions from Faithfull's latest indignant outburst against the mystery that shrouds Starr's death were felt with terrific impact.

Andrew J. Peters, millionaire aristocrat and Massachusetts politician, felt the full force of the publicity and notoriety now whirling about his head ... For the second time, Peters has broken down and been placed under a doctor's care since the grey dawn of Monday, June 8, when a beachcomber early abroad stumbled on the huddled corpse of Starr

Faithfull on the spray-drenched sands of Long Beach. The sins ye do by two and two, as Kipling says, ye must pay for one by one ...

Following the high noon challenge, Stanley Faithfull appealed to Governor Franklin Roosevelt for help ... He sent a letter and a carbon-copy, both special delivery, to the State Executive, one to his Manhattan residence, 49 East Sixty-Fifth Street, and one to Canoe Place Inn at Hampton Bays, [near the eastern end of] Long Island, where he is spending the weekend.

The weekend passed. And so did Monday, when Roosevelt returned to the state capital, Albany. Whenever he was shown Stanley's letter, he must have been at least a little upset by its accusations against Andrew Peters, his friend since they had both served as Assistant Secretaries in the Woodrow Wilson administration – the Massachusetts Democrat who next year, all being well, would organise the collection of funds for his, Roosevelt's, campaign for the Presidency. On Tuesday, his press secretary confirmed that the letter had been received, and said that the Governor, 'without committing himself, has decided to grant Mr Faithfull a hearing by his legal adviser, Samuel L. Rosenman'.

The hearing, at Rosenman's office, 20 Exchange Place, a block south of Wall Street, lasted most of Thursday morning. Stanley 'looked sour' when he emerged. He had nothing to say, he said. Soon afterwards, Rosenman announced that he would not be advising the Governor that 'it was behoveful to pursue the complaint'. He was 'confident, on a number of bases, that the investigation of the death of Miss Starr Faithfull is being conducted as vigorously at the present time, and will be, as it undoubtedly has been conducted'.

His confidence was slightly misplaced. Only slightly, in regard to manpower, man-hours. Around the time of George Jameson Carr's visit, Edwards, needing to catch up on a backlog of other work, had put Martin Littleton in charge of the investigation. For a similar reason, King, while insisting that he still wanted to see copies of all 'SF reports', had gradually handed over the case to two of his subordinates, Sergeant Robert McLaren and Acting Sergeant Jesse Mayforth, and had reduced the number of detective constables working on the case full-time to half a dozen. From their respective back-seats, Edwards and King continued to act as spokesmen whenever reporters phoned, asking if there were any developments in the Starr Faithfull case.

That suited Littleton, who felt that 'the over-sensationalising of certain areas of the investigation in its formative stages may well have mitigated against complete efficiency ... If further progress was to be forthcoming, our efforts should be, as far as possible, out of the public gaze.'

Reading the day-by-day reports of the Littleton-McLaren-Mayforth team, one is struck by the fact that they *were* a team – unlike Edwards and King, who, as well as disliking each other, held opposing views on the case, Edwards having decided, long before deciding was sensible, that Starr had been murdered, King having felt that he could only explain away the unruly start of the investigation by saying that he was convinced that Starr had not been murdered. One is not merely struck but amazed by the team's doggedness – by their refusal to let disappointments, dozens of them, lessen their commitment. Working quietly, sometimes secretly, they were the unsung heroes of the case. In December, upon Littleton's recommendations, which do not seem to have been supported by King, Robert McLaren was promoted to lieutenant, and Jesse Mayforth was given the substantive rank of sergeant. Even if I had the space to chronicle the team's activities, I should not do so, for nearly all of the leads they followed either fizzled out or landed them in blind alleys. Take what happened, among other things, in September, as recounted by Jesse Mayforth:

*8 September.* A man named Charles Memberson, a resident of Long Beach, has told a Daily News reporter named Dick Lee that he has a friend, Miss Claire Maher, who knows that the owner of a speakeasy named Tim Hunter knows how Starr Faithfull met her death. Memberson says that on the night of Friday, June 5, 1931, Starr was in Tim Hunter's speakeasy at Long Beach with two men, one named *Greene*, a cruise director for the Cunard S.S. Line, and the second man unknown. The trio were under the influence of the liquor they had taken. Starr got nasty, and in a row that occurred, one of the men, either Greene or the unknown, gave her a push or a blow, and she fell to the floor unconscious. The two men believed that Starr was dead, and were greatly in fear of being involved, so they made up their minds to carry the body out to the beach and lay it on the sands, close to the incoming tide....

Memberson's information appears to be of great value. With what is known of the death of Starr, it may supply us with the missing links that to date have been unexplained. Starr's parents allege that, in the week before her disappearance, she said she was introduced to a man named *Greenaway*. Greene resides at Long Beach and it may be assumed that he brought her there. The information places her in a speakeasy in proximity to the beach; the positive facts that her body was found near the alleged speakeasy, and that she had died in shallow water, as evidenced by the sand in her lungs, make Memberson's story sound very plausible. Further credence is given to the information by the bruises on the deceased, which could be connected with blows struck by Greene or the other man – and further, Starr's reaction to intoxicating liquors made her get out of control.

It has been decided by Mr Littleton, McLaren and I to carefully check over all details of this lead, without arousing the suspicions of the principals named. We have ascertained that Howard L. Greene, a cruise director for Cunard, resides in a bungalow on Louisiana Avenue, Long Beach, 3 blocks west of Minnesota Avenue, at the foot of which the body was found. We have ascertained through the local telephone directory, the post office at Long Beach, and the Queensboro Gas & Light Co., that there is only one person named Timothy Hunter residing at or in business at Long Beach.... [As the information about this man] does not fit the description of the Tim Hunter named by Memberson, it has been decided that Dick Lee should be asked to meet with Memberson again and get a more definite location of the alleged speakeasy.

*12 September.* Again checked up at Long Beach with the purpose of locating a speakeasy owner with a name similar to Tim Hunter. Located a man named Jack Hunt who operates a restaurant and lodging house on the seaward corner of New York Avenue, approx. ⅓ mile east of where the body of Starr Faithfull was discovered. He was served with a forthwith subpoena to Mr Littleton's office, and was examined at great length, but the results were negative.

*14 September.* Arrangements were made to bring Claire Maher out to Mineola from New York City, for the purpose of having her point out the place she believed was Tim Hunter's speakeasy. During the late afternoon Miss Maher, accompanied by McLaren and [Detective John] Fogarty, drove to Long Beach. They went to West Beach Street, close to Minnesota Avenue, and Miss Maher pointed out an alleged speakeasy which she stated was owned by Tim Hunter. The place she indicated was the Old Tavern, operated by one Bob Selesky. Miss Maher was returned to Mr Littleton's office, where she was interrogated. After considerable questioning, all concerned and present were satisfied that Miss Maher had been romancing when she said she knew about a Tim Hunter speakeasy.

Up to this date, Charles Memberson had been left to Dick Lee for fear of frightening him into silence, but it was now decided that nothing was to be gained by further delay. Therefore Mr Littleton communicated with Memberson and arranged to meet him at Long Beach at 12.20 a.m. midnight, this date – or rather, tomorrow.

*15 September.* Mr Littleton, with detectives, I among them, met Memberson in front of his home at the appointed time. He was

**228**

questioned until 3 a.m. He is white, about 35 years of age, a Hebrew, and resides at 461 East Front Street, Long Beach, with his mother. He is in the renting business, with offices in New York City. He was questioned in regard to the information he had given, and he denied that he had said anything of the kind. He said that his information was as follows: That one morning, some time after the finding of Starr Faithfull's body, he was en route to New York from Long Beach in a L.I.R.R. train, seated in rear of two men who were talking very loud. He heard one of these men say to the other that he knew a speakeasy proprietor named Tim Hunter who had told him that two men were in his place on the night of June 5 with Starr Faithfull. The man in the train, who said he knew Hunter, continued on to give the story as related in my report of Sept. 8. Memberson informed us that he did not know the men on the train, and had not seen them since that morning. In spite of the lack of weight for Memberson's story, he was requested to keep a sharp watch for the two men he had heard talking, and if he saw them, to find out where they went and immediately communicate with Mr Littleton or any other member of the group.

*16 September.* ... It was agreed upon that there would be nothing gained by delaying the interrogation of Howard L. Greene. McLaren proceeded to Long Beach and located Greene at the bungalow where he resides and served a forthwith subpoena upon him. Accordingly, he brought Greene to Mr Littleton's office at 8.15 p.m. Greene was carefully and persistently questioned from 8.30 p.m. until about 3 a.m....

He has been married about 12 years. Has no children. Has sub-let his own home in Long Beach for the summer, and he and his wife live with a Miss Lesbia Collins at 101 Louisiana Avenue. States that he never met Starr Faithfull.... He states that he was on the *Franconia* on May 29 in the a.m. and also in the afternoon, arranging matters about the disembarkation of some passenger who had died on the incoming trip of the Franconia. He may have seen Starr but does not remember her. Says he saw Dr Jameson Carr relative to the death certificate and official papers. Says he saw Francis Peabody Hamlin but did not talk to him. Never was on a cruise with Starr to his knowledge. Claims he left the Franconia about 4 p.m. Does not know a speakeasy owner named Tim Hunter. States that he was kidded a good deal by some of his friends at Long Beach about being the man that did away with Starr – because of his connection with the Cunard Line. He remembers an occasion when he entered a speakeasy and some fellow said 'Hello Starr' and laughed, and he said he did not find the remark funny.

*17 September.* The results of the preceding night's interrogation of Greene were talked over in Mr Littleton's office. There was unanimous agreement that no statement made by Greene indicated guilt on his part. We are of the firm opinion that Memberson's story was invented in the

**229**

hope of gaining the $5000 reward offered by the Daily News.

Others of our group continued working on other information that has come to hand, but I had to be temporarily absent as I had been ordered by Inspector King to be on duty at the auto races at the Mineola Fair Grounds.

Early in October, while McLaren and Mayforth were away in West Orange, talking to residents and business people who had had dealings with the Faithfulls, Ben Greve, one of the detective constables assigned to the Starr team, was put in touch (I have no idea by whom) with two men of Jamaica, the central part of Queens. Straightway after meeting them, he spoke to Littleton, who told him to 'pursue their acquaintance'.

Before quoting excerpts from Greve's reports, I must explain that Island Park is the slight peninsula from the mainland of Nassau County, separated from Long Beach by Reynolds Channel but linked to it by a roadbridge and the bridge of the Long Island Rail Road, both of which lead into the centre of Long Beach, about a mile east of the State-named thoroughfares of which Minnesota Avenue is one.

Greve's second meeting with the men was on the night of 7 October, a Wednesday: '... I proceeded to Jamaica, using my automobile, where I met my informants, Perone and Bruno, in a speakeasy. Together we had several drinks of whisky and again I was informed that Starr Faithfull was in Tappe's Hotel on the south waterfront of Island Park just prior to her death.

'I also learned that a man by the name of A.C. French, also known as Kriss, and a woman by the name of Pearl Bishop, also known as Bitler, were the proprietors of Tappe's Hotel. I also learned that George Kriss, a son of French's, works at the hotel. I also learned that Hiram Levitt puts on the show and also acts as bartender, and that a man named Gay, who most often works as a bartender for Barberi[1] at the Show Place[2] in Lynbrook, sometimes acts as bartender at Tappe's Hotel. This man Gay is considered a gunman, and so are Hiram Levitt, George Kriss, and Max Simone, who sometimes appears in the shows, doing conjuring tricks. A man called Mike has charge of the coat room and cigar stand. A Mr Berg,

1. Frank Barberi was one of the leading criminal residents of Long Beach, where he ran both a real-estate agency and a speakeasy, the Lafayette Hotel. He openly boasted that 'he could do anything he liked in Long Beach — he had brought the mayor and the chief of police and everybody right on down'.
2. See page 198.

one of the proprietors of the Wheel Restaurant at 22 Warren Street, New York City, has the restaurant concession at Tappe's Hotel. This hotel is a favourite rendezvous for gangsters such as Bill Dwyer, Vannie Higgins, Ferrara, Dutch Schultz, Mannie Kessler, and Nick the Greek.[1]

'On October 8, I again proceeded to the speakeasy in Jamaica, where I met my informants and learned that Bob Case was the

---

1. *William Vincent Dwyer*: an ex-stevedore whose sobriquet of 'Big Bill' referred not to his physique but to the scope of his illegal operations. John Kobler writes (in his excellent book, *Ardent Spirits: The Rise and Fall of Prohibition*, Michael Joseph, London, 1974):

'From two Broadway office suites ... Dwyer presided over a complex of different enterprises. In addition to heading a rum-running syndicate, he secured part or full ownership of two hotels, several nightclubs, the biggest brewery in Manhattan – the Phoenix Cereal Beverage Company at Twenty-Fifth Street and Tenth Avenue, which netted about $7,000,000 a year – two Miami Beach gambling casinos, race-tracks in Florida, New Hampshire, Ohio and Quebec, the Brooklyn Dodgers football club and, after introducing professional ice hockey to the city, the New York and the American Hockey clubs. The latter acquired Mayor James J. Walker as one of its directors.... Dwyer entertained regally at the suburban estate in Belle Harbour [Nassau County: five miles west of the western end of Long Beach] which he shared with his wife and five children.... Dwyer sometimes augmented his seaborne stocks with liquor hijacked ashore. For such plunder he relied on *Charles "Vannie" Higgins....*'

*Frank Ferrara*: a rum-runner associated with, among other criminals, Vannie Higgins and Frank Barberi. In April 1931, Ferrara, Barberi, and fourteen other men, eight of whom were Long Beach policemen, were prosecuted by Elvin Edwards on a conspiracy charge involving the smuggling of liquor into Long Beach. All sixteen defendants were acquitted. (During the trial, it was proved that Vannie Higgins – who was not among the defendants – had a direct telephone line from his home at Atlantic Beach, Brooklyn, to the home of a Long Beach police sergeant, Thomas Moore.)

*Dutch Schultz*, whose real name was Arthur Flegenheimer, was a psychopathic bootlegger and mass-murderer. He was the best customer, and a partner in various undertakings, of Big Bill Dwyer.

During the early years of Prohibition, *Emmanuel 'Mannie' Kessler*, then in his twenties, had acquired the title of 'King of the Bootleggers' in Manhattan and Brooklyn. He had since lost the title and much of his fortune (reputedly of ten million dollars in 1925) but he remained an influential gangster. Time and again, he and his partner, Morris Sweetwood, had been arrested by federal agents and almost always either released without being charged or given nominal sentences. There are strong reasons for believing that Mannie and Morris told tales to the federal authorities in return for leniency. In April 1931, Mannie had been arrested for not paying a cent of income tax for the previous six years – but although agents of the Department of Internal Revenue had proved that he had deposited large sums in pseudonymous bank-accounts, the charges had been dropped.

*Nick the Greek* ran a speakeasy in Lynbrook. All references to him that I have seen refer to him only by his nickname.

master of ceremonies at Tappe's Hotel and that he formerly worked for Rothstein[1] and also A.C. French when French ran the Chateau Shanley speakeasy in New York City; that a woman known as Margy Williams was one of the girls who acted as a hostess; that the gangsters Dominic Sacco and Ferdy Grafolla of Island Park hang out in this place.

'A Mr Gadney and his wife also live at the hotel and they run the speedboat rides right opposite the hotel.

'All of these people were working and residing at the hotel up to the time Starr Faithfull was found at Long Beach.

'At this place a great many things have happened and no one would know what took place unless they were in on the racket. They charge 75c and $1.00 for a bottle of beer or a glass of whisky, and when people get somewhat intoxicated, they pad their checks and charge them double. They will rent a room with or without baggage and they do not care whether you register or not as they register you themselves. Max Simone is the strong-arm man as well as a musician and entertainer, and he is one of the men that if you refuse to pay your bill or kick about the prices charged, he will place a gun in your side and compel you to pay. On one occasion, when a man by the name of Peterson, a carpenter who did some work for French, came to collect his bill, they refused to pay and they hit him over the head with a bottle and then threw him out.

1. Arnold Rothstein − variously known as The Brain, The Big Bankroll, The Man Uptown, The Fixer, and simply A.R. − was the leading financier of East Coast criminals for some fifteen years till 4 November 1928, when he was shot to death in his suite at the Park Central Hotel, Manhattan. Officially, the crime was never solved.

According to Gene Fowler, a biographer of James J. Walker (*Beau James*, Viking Press, New York, 1949), recounts incidents on the night of Rothstein's death which I have referred to on page 204 when during a visit by Walker and Betty Compton, and by Starr, to the rural Woodmansten Inn, first Betty, then, among others, Starr had their dancing shoes autographed by the band-leader, Vincent Lopez were followed, 'some time after midnight, by a noticeable stir at one of the ringside tables, where several men allied with underworld activities were sitting with women companions. A man unknown to Lopez went to the Walker table and whispered something in Jim's ear. The Mayor seemed disturbed. He paid his check. . . . Lopez handed his baton to a member of the band and went with Jim and Betty to the cloakroom. Betty excused herself to go to the powder room. While Jim was waiting, with her fur wrap in his hands, Lopez said, "Something's happened, Jim. I noticed the 'boys' were acting funny."

'"Rothstein has just been shot, Vince. And that means trouble from here in."' (Presumably Walker was worried that pretenders to Rothstein's crown would start a small war.)

'Again I was informed that Starr Faithfull was at Tappe's Hotel just prior to her body being found at Long Beach, and that there had been a quarrel between Starr Faithfull and a gentleman friend, but what caused same my informants did not know.

'After leaving my informants, I reported to Mr Littleton at Mineola, and after leaving there, I went to Rockville Centre and procured a young lady of my acquaintance to accompany me to Tappe's Hotel, aiding my intention to visit the place incognito. The young lady and myself entered the hotel at about 9 p.m., following two men who I later learned were from the Lincoln speakeasy in Oceanside [a small town just south of Rockville Centre]. We had altogether sixteen drinks of whisky and two steak sandwiches. The drinks were $1.00 and the sandwiches $1.50. I observed while there that the place was a dive, as nothing but gangsters were in the place and the sky was the limit. I was told by A.C. French and Mrs Bishop, who spoke to me while my companion was in the ladies' room, that if I wanted to use an upstairs room at any time, it was O.K. When we left they asked me to return and hoped that I was treated all right.

'On October 9, I conferred with Mr Littleton, and upon leaving, proceeded to Jamaica, where I again joined my informants, but could not learn anything new. After supper, I proceeded to Island Park, and through a regular informant I learned that Chief [Alexander] Rosenswaicke and Lieutenant [Harry] Yale [of the five-man Island Park Police Force — which, like the Long Beach force, was autonomous] were very friendly with French and Mrs Pearl Bishop and the rest of the employees, as they would go there and have dinner and drinks free of charge; that different complaints have been made to them about Tappe's Hotel, but no action has been taken by them.

'I learned that, about the 6th of June, a woman who was with a man and who answered the description of Starr Faithfull was left by her gentleman friend who went upstairs, and Mrs Bishop and one or two other men and this woman sat drinking together, waiting for the return of the gentleman friend, and these men asked this young woman, who was well under the influence, to accompany them. She refused at first, but owing to her condition, they prevailed upon her to go with them and they took her up to Sacco and Grafolla's speakeasy in Island Park.

'When the gentleman friend came downstairs, he wanted to know where his lady friend was, and he was informed that she had departed with a couple of men. He then raised an awful fuss and

**233**

threatened to call in police from outside Island Park. Mrs Bishop became alarmed and sent two of the men in charge of the parking space up to Sacco and Grafolla's, and when these men returned they had received quite a beating; what became of the woman and of her gentleman friend, it has been impossible to ascertain. However, on a later date, something similar happened, and they took a woman out of Tappe's Hotel and took her to Sacco and Grafolla's, where men assaulted her; when others in the woman's party wanted to know what had happened to her, Mrs Bishop again became alarmed and sent two men up who were taking care of the parking space, and they were beaten unmercifully. The parking men made a complaint before Judge Pearl, and their assailants were held, but when it became time for the complainants to testify against their assailants, the complainants had disappeared and were living in the City of Boston, Massachusetts, and failed to appear before the grand jury, because they were told that if they did, they would be taken for their last ride.

'After leaving my informants at Jamaica, I went to Lynbrook and endeavoured to meet another informant who used to frequent Tappe's Hotel and was there on the night Starr Faithfull was said to be there, but he had left for parts unknown. I then went to Tappe's Hotel and held same under surveillance. I observed the same gang that was in the place the night previous. I observed one of the gang leaving and joined him, acting casual. He told me that during the month of June he had been up in Canada running beer for Vannie Higgins' mob, but he would not talk about the Starr Faithfull case, saying he did not know anything about it and would not say he had heard anything as to her being at Tappe's Hotel or not. Later I entered the hotel and was joined by Mr French, Mrs Bishop and Max Simone, the entertainer, bouncer and all-round strong-arm man in the place. We had twelve bottles of beer between us and six whiskys. I learned that liquor was landed there and that the place was receiving protection from the Island Park Chief of Police, who came there this very night, that fights were not uncommon and that when they got too bad the fighters were usually thrown out after getting a real trimming.

'On October 10, I conferred with Mr Littleton, and then proceeded to Jamaica, but did not receive any new information from my informants. I proceeded to Long Beach to endeavour to locate the former bartender for Barberi named Gay, but did not meet with any success. I proceeded to Island Park, where I met another informant who informed me that Jackie Mayo and others

234

from the Show Place at Lynbrook came to Tappe's Hotel late at night and had parties and that the women entertained men in the upstairs rooms. Margy Williams, one of the girls in the revue, entertains men privately in her room, and when she has them drunk enough, she rolls them for their money. A dog-faced girl at Long Beach whose friend was shot at Long Beach this past summer, but of which the local police have no record as far as we know, could also tell that Starr Faithfull was at the hotel as she, the dog-faced girl, was there on the 5th, 6th and 7th of June, when Starr Faithfull stayed at Tappe's.

'On October 11, I proceeded to New York City, but because it was Sunday could not locate Mr Berg, who has the restaurant concession at Tappe's Hotel. I then joined my informants at Jamaica, and they told me that Hiram Levitt, who puts on the show, books the girls from an office above the Roseland dance hall on Broadway, New York City, and that he was at the hotel when Starr Faithfull was there. I also learned that Vannie Higgins, Bill Dwyer and Dutch Schultz frequently have parties at the hotel and that rum is loaded at Tappe's Hotel dock; that on one occasion, Vannie Higgins and two other men and three women were drinking together, and two of the women left between two and three in the morning and that Vannie Higgins and his gangster friends assaulted this woman who had remained and tore her clothes and then threw her out of the place. I also learned that Al Joslin, a chef who was employed by Mr Berg, left the employ as he considered there was too much gun-play at this place.

'After eating supper, I went to Island Park, but Tappe's Hotel was deserted except for three of the regular crowd, and up to the time the place closed, no one entered except the Chief of Police of Island Park and he stayed only fifteen minutes, arriving there at 10.00 p.m. and leaving at 10.15.

'On October 12, I interviewed Mr Berg at 22 Warren Street, New York City. I showed him pictures of Starr Faithfull without naming her, and he stated that he had seen her at Tappe's Hotel but could not recall when or under what circumstances. He also stated that there had been a near-drowning at the hotel around the 6th of June but would not state that it was the woman whose pictures I had shown to him. He was positive that she had been there and when I told him later that it was Starr Faithfull, he said he did not recall her by that name, but was positive that the woman had been at Tappe's Hotel prior to June 7, but that he did not want to swear that it was the same woman unless he could see her in person.

'I then proceeded to Jamaica, but did not get any new information from my informants, and went on to Island Park to ascertain, if possible, the automobile licence numbers of those who visited Tappe's Hotel. I also learned that Natalie Cardevi, who formerly worked for Al Capone in Chicago, works as an entertainer and hostess at the hotel. A former waiter, Abe Lamont, says that Vannie Higgins was down at the hotel almost every night as they ran in liquor there, and that the sky was the limit as to the parties they had with the different women and his men friends. I went into the hotel and had six bottles of beer at 75c per bottle. I held a conversation with Max Simone and two other men and failed to learn anything of importance. These men are of the mobs who are gangsters and rum-runners and are most reluctant to talk except on the general topics of the day, such as fights, wrestling matches, etc. After leaving, I endeavoured to get some information from several of the taxi drivers, but they said that they would not say a word because they were afraid that the mob would learn that they talked and it would mean the end of the line for them.

'On October 13, I again interviewed Mr Berg. His partner, Mr Hymie Horowitz, was there, and also a woman, and they said to Mr Berg, "You do not want to get mixed up in a murder scandal." Mr Berg then said, "Well, that is indubitably true. I am positive that the woman was there, but I would not swear to it. I would be no use in the case." I asked him if he was afraid of Vannie Higgins and others, and he said of course he did not fear them. He then gave me the addresses of agencies that he thought he had booked diferent waiters and chefs through, and I then proceeded to call at the agencies but did not meet with any success as the names Mr Berg had given me were not the proper names.

'On October 14, Detective [Chester] Evans and I reported to Mr Littleton, then proceeded to Island Park in our separate cars. We observed Mr French and Mrs Bishop and another woman board Mrs Bishop's car. Evans and I held them under surveillance and they proceeded through New York City, where they and we had dinner, and carried on to New Jersey. They arrived at Sparta, New Jersey, and stopped at an old hotel of wooden structure, off the main highway. Here they remained for the night and we held it under surveillance.

'On October 15, Evans and I observed French and Mrs Bishop board their car at about 4.00 p.m. They went to New York City and had supper, then returned to Island Park. We were unable to hold them under surveillance in the City of New York, losing them through a red light, but we proceeded to Island Park later and found their car there.

'On October 16, Evans and I conferred with Mr Littleton and others, and then proceeded to the City of New York. We visited numerous employment agencies and waiters' clubs as well as head waiters' clubs, but did not meet with any success in locating waiters named by Mr Berg.

'On October 17, Evans and I proceeded to New York and located William Olsen of the Elite Head Waiters' Association and served him with a request subpoena to appear in Mineola on Monday, October 19. We also located another waiter, Edward Trainer, whose address is the Mills Hotel. Upon questioning him, he positively identified the pictures of Starr Faithfull and described the dress she had on when he had seen her at Tappe's Hotel, without our leading him as to the description of the dress. We then told him it was Starr Faithfull. He said, "I can't help it if it is Starr Faithfull. That girl was there." We asked him about the newspaper pictures. He stated that he had read about the Starr Faithfull case, but at the time did not connect the newspaper pictures with the woman he had seen. He recalled that a near-drowning took place either at the hotel or in Long Beach.

'On October 18, Evans and I proceeded to Rockville Centre to locate Margy Williams, the showgirl, and finally did locate the address where she formerly resided and learned that she had just left there after resigning her position at Tappe's Hotel, where she received $50 a week and was permitted to increase her incomings as she liked; that is where all her mail is forwarded to. We joined Eddie Trainer at the Mills Hotel, New York City, and we then located Joe Sapolla, another waiter, at the Cabin Grill on Broadway. We gave them a subpoena to appear at Mineola on October 19. We again interviewed Mr Berg, who stated that while walking on the beach near Tappe's Hotel he found a lady's wristwatch, the make Elgin, of seven jewels, but same had no strap on it. This can be had at any time. We located the carpenter, Olaf Peterson, but we did not subpoena him on account of first wanting to question the waiters on Monday.

'We drove to Island Park. Evans entered Tappe's Hotel, pretending that he was not a detective, and found everything very quiet, only four men in the place besides the employees and the proprietors. He drank beer with Max Simone, and from his conversation with him gathered that all was not well and that none of the gangsters were around. Simone said, "Things are not so good.

237

The boys are all staying in New York for the present, and when the gang isn't here, this place is dead as mutton."

'On October 19, Evans and I conferred with Mr Littleton, and we then interrogated the three waiters. We returned to the District Attorney's office at 8.00 p.m. and later joined Mr Littleton and Detectives McLaren and Mayforth. It was decided that nothing further was likely to be learned about Tappe's Hotel from other sources, and therefore the place should be raided.

'We immediately proceeded in separate cars to Island Park, where we raided the hotel, which was only dimly lighted. We found a quantity of liquor and some papers, which were taken by Mr Littleton, McLaren and Mayforth. We placed A.C. French under arrest and questioned the employees and two patrons. While we were there, a Miss Madeline Bates called the hotel by telephone and conversed with Mr Littleton. It emerged that she was one of the three women visitors to the hotel, two of whom had left by taxi before the third, who had then been assaulted by Vannie Higgins; Miss Bates, who is now residing at 7 Ella Street, Lynbrook, stated that Max Simone, the magician, introduced her and her companions to Vannie Higgins on the occasion referred to. She claimed she did not know the names of the other two women and that she had never seen either of them before the incident or since, and failed to explain how she knew that the third woman had been assaulted. We questioned the two waiters, one Sam Fox or Fisher or Francis and the other Ambrose Crippen, who had been there throughout the summer, and they denied knowing anything about the place that was wrong except that they did sell liquor once in a very great while. Max Simone also denied that he had seen anything wrong going on and he denied knowing Vannie Higgins or any gangsters mentioned as being frequenters.

'While we were there, all the while being fairly inconspicuous, an Island Park police officer entered and wanted to give a message to Mr French from one of his superior officers. He was ushered to the presence of Mr Littleton, who was conversing with French in an upstairs room, and who interrogated the officer closely. While he was doing so, Chief Rosenswaicke and Lieutenant Yale of the Island Park Police, both in civilian clothes, entered the hotel and wanted to see Mr French. They were informed that Mr French was upstairs and for them to go along up, which they did. They were ushered into the room where Mr French and the subordinate officer were in the presence of Mr Littleton, and were considerably surprised.

'Upon leaving the hotel, we separated, and Evans and I, upon the instructions received from Mr Littleton, discontinued. McLaren and Mayforth returned with Mr Littleton to the District Attorney's office to talk over the significance, if any, of Tappe's Hotel to the Starr Faithfull case.

'On October 20, Evans and I were informed by Mr Littleton that he, McLaren and Mayforth were of the opinion that there was little hope of obtaining further substantive information about Tappe's Hotel in regard to Starr Faithfull. We were thanked for what we had done in that regard and given other assignments to perform.'

On 10 November − five months to the day since Edwards, having rushed to Boston with King, had been given a legal brush-off by Peters' friend Alexander Whiteside − he received a long-distance phone call from Richard Keating, a partner in Peters' law firm, who said, without explanation, that Peters was prepared to talk to him or his representative.[1] While Edwards was still trying to seem unsurprised, unperplexed, by the belated change of mind, Keating stipulated the arrangements: the date, time, maximum duration, and place − adding that the arrangements would be nullified by the least breath of prior publicity.

In the early morning of Wednesday the 18th, Littleton, McLaren and Mayforth drove to Boston, and while they were having breakfast at the Parker House, were spotted by a reporter for the *Boston Globe*. The spotting may have been serendipitous, but one suspects a leak. Littleton, staying magnificently calm, denied that he and his companions were investigating the Starr Faithfull case. The reporter, who just happened to have Edwards' home phone number on his person, dashed to the lobby and, watching the entrance to the restaurant the while, put through a call to Edwards − who told him, 'I have sent Mr Littleton to Boston to check over all the evidence uncovered up there. The Starr Faithfull case has never been closed. I still believe she was murdered.' The reporter went back to the restaurant, meaning to confront Littleton with his lie, and found that Littleton and the detectives had escaped through the kitchen.

They reached their rendezvous, Peters' office at 1 Federal Street, unseen and on time. They were intercepted in the outer office by Richard Keating, who at first said that only Littleton could go inside, but then compromised, saying that one of the detectives

---

1. Perhaps coincidentally, Mrs Faithfull and Tucker had been in Boston the week before, reportedly 'bent on trying [but in vain] to save a relic of happier days, a cottage owned by the family at Centerville, Cape Cod'.

would be admitted, as long as he promised to remain mute and still throughout the meeting. McLaren having been chosen, Keating tucked Mayforth out of sight in an ante-room.

The reducing of the Nassau County numbers may have been necessitated by a shortage of space in Peters' office. There was little of it left after Littleton and McLaren had entered, and Keating, following, had closed the door and dropped the latch. Peters sat at his desk (he had lost about two stone since the middle of June, but his midriff was artificially paunched by a swathing of crepe bandage, support for his spine, which he had injured in a fall down a flight of stairs during the last of his nervous breakdowns). Flanking him and distributed on chairs facing away from the front of his desk were a dozen eminent Bostonians – among them, Alexander Whiteside, Martha Peters' brother William Phillips, and a leading lawyer who, able to write shorthand, had agreed to use that skill from the very start to the very end of the meeting, protecting Peters from the risk of being misquoted afterwards.

At the end of the two hours that Keating had stipulated as the maximum duration of the meeting, Littleton and McLaren – the latter leg-weary from standing throughout – remained completely in the dark as to why the meeting had been arranged. Next day, back in Mineola, Littleton told Edwards that

the arduous excursion by myself and the detectives proved an absolute waste of time.... At the outset of the meeting with Mr Peters, he expressed the desire to co-operate and to shed what light on the Starr Faithfull situation he could, but said that he doubted very much that there was anything he could say which would be of any help. However, his whole conversation, which was given in a very nervous and anxious manner, was of no value and entirely negative, on occasion so much so as to give me cause to wonder whether I was hearing things: in particular, he went so far as to very vigorously assert – on three occasions – that, contrary to well established facts, at no time were his relations with Starr anything but of the highest order. He wished it definitely understood, he insisted, that he had not had any immoral relations with the girl and that she had always been very dear to him and his wife and he thought very highly of her. He said he felt that it would not have been very long before she would have denounced the whole situation herself, but that now, unfortunately, it was too late because she could not speak.... Despite Mr Peters' occasional lapses from complete honesty, I know that I speak also for Sergeant McLaren when I say that I gathered that Mr Peters' association with Starr Faithfull in no way indicates that he was knowingly responsible for her premature death.

*

I cannot make out why there was such a long delay – till Monday, 7 December – before the investigators talked to a Cunard ship's surgeon named Charles Young Roberts. He had recently been transferred from the *Carmania* to the *Carinthia*, which had arrived from England on the 6th. He had been the *Carmania's* surgeon from early in 1930 and had been attached to that liner during its return-voyage in the early summer of 1931, docking at Pier 56 on the morning of Sunday, 31 May (two days after the *Franconia's* departure from the same pier), and leaving, en route to Southampton, Le Havre and London, on Tuesday 9 June (the day after the discovery of Starr Faithfull's body). Since then, he had accompanied the *Carmania* on four other return-voyages across the Atlantic, yet had not been approached by the investigators during the stop-overs, each of at least a week, in Manhattan. It is far easier to understand why Dr Roberts had not volunteered information than why nobody had asked him if he had any. One can only suppose that Littleton and his team, working quietly but zealously on local leads, fell into the trap of confusing motion with action, and did not stop for a minute to think about priorities.

George Jameson Carr had mentioned Dr Roberts when he, 'minded' by Samuel Untermyer, had met Edwards, Littleton and King, chiefly for the purpose of handing over the letters from Starr, on 23 June: 'I have heard from others in the Cunard company that Miss Faithfull was at a party in Dr Roberts's cabin on the *Carmania* until late on the Friday night of her disappearance; that she had been on the *Mauretania* until some time before 5 p.m., and that Dr Roberts had then taken her to the *Carmania*, which was lying on the other side of Cunard's dock, and that she remained there until approximately 11.30 o'clock at night at this party.'

In the late afternoon of 7 December, Detective John Fogarty collected Dr Roberts from the *Carinthia* and drove him to Mineola – not to the district attorney's office but to Gino's Restaurant, where he, Fogarty, McLaren and Mayforth were treated to dinner by Littleton. There were two reasons for the dinner: as well as hoping to put Roberts at ease before questioning him, Littleton wanted to express his gratitude to the detectives, for today was the last day of the investigation. At the end of the previous week, the decision had been taken by Edwards and King, over-ruling Littleton, that the investigation was to be terminated after exactly six months.

Leaving the restaurant at nine o'clock, the men adjourned to Littleton's office. Nathan Birchall, the stenographer, was waiting there.

Roberts was in his late twenties, of medium height but stocky. He brushed his dark hair straight back from his tall forehead; his caterpillar-like eyebrows dwindled together over his nose, which was wide-bridged at the top, globular at the end. Though his Yorkshire accent would have seemed slight to other Englishmen, Birchall was occasionally confused by it, and needed to get him to repeat parts of some of his answers to Littleton's questions.

Asked when he had first met Starr, he said, 'I think it would be about June 1930, I think, as far as I can recollect. She was on the *Carmania*, travelling to England with her mother and her sister . . . I did not need to render professional services to her, but as ship's surgeon one meets all of the passengers during the course of one's duties. . . . Her conduct was not always exemplary − I mean, she was given to over-drinking, and on occasion was quite intoxicated. . . . I cannot recall her sister at all. Nor the mother. . . .

'The next time I saw her was in March of this year. She was down on the ship seeing some people go off one night. She joined a big party in the main square of the ship.'

His next comment almost certainly solved one of the small riddles of the case: Where had Starr got the name 'Bruce Winston' from, supposing that she had not met anyone of that name during the week or so before her disappearance?

'The party in the square was not really a party − just a big number of friends who were seeing off an actor, an English actor, Bruce Winston, and Starr Faithfull was there. I don't know if she knew Bruce Winston or was, as it were, a trespasser on the gathering. I didn't see her talking to Bruce Winston, but I know she was one of those who were all more or less together in the square. I don't know who else was in the party. I can only recollect that it was for Bruce Winston because I knew him before, having sailed with him, and I naturally recognised him again, as he is the sort of person, a homosexual, who is once seen and never forgotten. Starr Faithfull saw me looking on, and she said "Good evening" or something − we just said "How do you do?" It just happened that she recognised me from the trip before − the trip to England in 1930, I mean.'

*Littleton*: 'Were you at this time, if you know, one of the victims of her frequent crushes?'

'I hope not. I don't think I was.'

'According to your best recollection, Doctor, when did you next see her?'

'The next time was when we arrived in New York at the end of May. I'm afraid I can't remember dates.'

'If I told you it appears from the Cunard records that the *Carmania* arrived at 9.10 a.m. on May 31st, which was a Sunday – '

'Well, then, it would be the Monday morning. It was then that I had a phone call from her, saying that she wanted to see me as she was contemplating going over to Europe and wondered would I see her. I made an appointment. I think it was at eleven o'clock that morning at the Pennsylvania Hotel. We stayed there talking, well, probably ten minutes. She said that she had heard that the *Carmania* was going over at such a time as would fit in with her plans, and she would like to make the trip with us. She wanted to know if it could be arranged, and I said, "I think the ship is pretty full" if she was thinking of the forthcoming trip because we had a big party of Rotarians.

'I asked her to lunch on the ship, and we went there immediately from the Pennsylvania. We actually had lunch and tea on board. She stayed until about six o'clock.'

(If that was true, then the account given by Mr and Mrs Faithfull of Starr's movements on the Monday was not. They had said that she left the apartment at about ten, *returned three hours later, had lunch, went out again, saying that she was going to stroll to Washington Square and take a ride up Fifth Avenue on the top of a bus*, returned at six, and stayed in for the rest of the evening.)

*Littleton*: 'Now, Doctor, I am not trying to pry into any purely personal matters that went between you and herself – whatever they may have been, or if there were any – while you were entertaining her on the *Carmania* that day. I do not particularly care about such things. But I am particularly interested in what she said to you regarding her plans, her future, her hopes, and what she contemplated.'

'Well, she was very undecided. She talked about this Europe trip. I think it was in relation to a French woman in Paris – or I don't know whether it was a French woman, but she said she had a friend in Paris. She never mentioned the woman's name. She was just talking about some woman there in Paris who was going to leave her some money.... As a matter of fact, I felt that she was absolutely uncertain in her mind. I remember we had some cocktails, and she kept on sort of begging for a drink, and if I should give her one, it would go down like *that*' (indicating) 'and then another went down bang. And then she got sort of weepy, you know.... She said she could not get work anywhere. That remark was part of her general sort of fed-upness. She mentioned that she had been out to see artists, trying to get work. She said, "Even artists

243

cannot afford to pay models nowadays." She mentioned about her sister — that she did not like her sister, that she was jealous of her.... The only person she mentioned by name was Dr Jameson Carr. She said she was in love with him.... When she left at around six o'clock that Monday evening, I escorted her to a taxi. I just took her to the taxi, and that's all I know.'

'Now, then, after that meeting when did you see her again, Doctor, or hear from her?'

'On the Thursday, I think it was.'

'Thursday was June 4th, the day before she left home for the last time. I know you don't remember that, but it's a fact. Now, how did you meet her on that day?'

'As far as I can recollect, it was a phone call, and she wanted to see me at the Roosevelt Hotel [on Madison Avenue at Forty-Fifth Street] at ten o'clock that night. It was appertaining to this Europe trip she had talked about before. I think it was taken for granted that if she did make this trip, I would do what I could for her, perhaps get her better accommodations than she had picked. I think it was in the late afternoon, about five o'clock, when she phoned me.'

'Did you know while in New York anyone by the name of Miriam Hopkins, Harry Stoner, or Bennett Cerf? I ask because, according only to what she told her mother and sister, on that Thursday evening she went to a party where those people were present.'

'No, I don't know any of them.... I met Starr Faithfull in the lobby of the Roosevelt at ten. I was with the fellow I had been dining with, a fellow called Hart. I don't know his first name. We had dined at some speakeasy. He had been a passenger on this last trip from England. I had treated him for a minor thing, a tummy-ache, and he appreciated what I had done and had arranged this little friendly party. We walked from the speakeasy to the Roosevelt, I introduced him to Starr Faithfull, and we practically went right back to the speakeasy. All three of us had one drink each. Then Mr Hart said he was busy, he wanted to work, and we went out, and Mr Hart went back to wherever he was staying.

'Then Starr Faithfull and I got in a taxi and went for a drive. We went north along — I think it is Riverside Drive, beside the Hudson River. I don't know where we went from there. We came back down Broadway or Fifth Avenue, or whatever it is. The drive took about three-quarters of an hour, I should think. We had left Mr Hart about half-past ten or twenty to eleven, so the drive ended at about half-past eleven. She wanted the taxi to be stopped at — this is all memory, but it was the Fifth Avenue Hotel, as far as I can recollect. It was near the foot of Fifth Avenue – near Greenwich Village somewhere. She just sort of said, "Pull up here," see? She didn't go into the hotel, or wherever we stopped outside, but she walked around the machine and walked away. I went back to the ship.'

*Littleton*: 'Now, then, during the course of that drive, eliminating personal conversations which I am not interested in, what did she have to say about her plans and aspirations?'

'She talked very little about her plans that night. I don't think she said anything about going abroad on that occasion. She talked about Dr Jameson Carr. She was very infatuated with him.'

'You had never been to her home?'

'No, I didn't know where she lived.'

'Did you see her again after that Thursday night?'

'Yes. On the Friday afternoon. I had not arranged to see her. She just came on board the *Carmania* unbeknown to me, or uninvited. I was on the *Mauretania* at the time, helping out with preparations for its departure at five o'clock on a short cruise to the Bahamas. She came down at about 3.30, I think. My steward came over to the *Mauretania* to say that a lady was waiting for me, and I sent word back that I would probably be late, and to say not to wait. When I returned to the *Carmania*, it was about half-past five, and she was still waiting. She stayed until about 10.30.'

'And this was on the Friday?'

'This was on the Friday.'

'How did she appear at that time?'

'She seemed much the same as usual. She was always sort of – what shall I say – unhappy. I think her affair with Jameson Carr was rather in the back of her mind. She kept talking about him, saying that she was very keen on him, in love with him. She sought solace from me – commiseration, sort of.'

'Now, then, on this Friday did she talk about going abroad?'

'Yes, she went on again about this woman in Paris. She was full of talk about money the woman was going to leave her. I think it was in a year's time she was expecting this woman to leave her some money and make her independent. That seemed to mean that this woman was expecting to die. It seemed funny to me, but I did not pursue the question. She was anxious to go to Paris.'

'If she was so bent on going to Paris, why did she talk about taking passage on the *Carmania*? That did not go to Paris, did it?'

'It went to Havre. The trip is New York – Southampton – Havre – then London. Going to Havre would be the shortest way

**245**

of getting to Paris. All the big British ships more or less call at Havre
or Cherbourg — the *Berengaria*, *Mauretania* and *Aquitania*.'

'Did she say anything about any other place she wanted to go to?'

'Calcutta. She said she had a friend there, but again she did not
mention a name. I think it was a male friend. She was keen to go to
Calcutta, I know. I think her desire to go to Paris was more or less
fifty-fifty.'

Littleton recalled the entries in Starr's diary referring to her
infatuation for Herbert Miller, the cruise director of the
Mediterranean cruise she had taken in the summer of 1926.
Knowing that Miller had left Cunard and was working in Bombay —
not *too* far from Calcutta — he asked Dr Roberts, 'As to Calcutta,
did Starr say anything about a man named Herbert Miller?'

'Not that I recall.'

'Did she mention any place other than Calcutta and Paris?'

'Now that I think of it, she did mention that she was going to
Montreal for the weekend. She didn't say why or with whom.'

'Do you know of any Cunard ships that ply between New York
and Montreal?'

'No.'

'Did she say that by going to Montreal she might get cheap or free
or easy passage across the Atlantic?'

'No. The Cunard ships on the transatlantic routes that go to
Montreal are the A's — like the *Ascania*, the *Alaunia*, the *Aurania*.
In the summer-time. Coming from England, the ones I mean leave
from either Liverpool or London, and go to Queenstown, in
Ireland, and then to Montreal. In the winter-time they come straight
across to Halifax, Nova Scotia.'

'Now, Doctor, in looking back — I know it is hard — did she ever
make any suggestion that you might assist her in stowing away?'

'Oh, no, no, not at all.'

'Is there anything else you recollect of this Friday conversation?'

'She mentioned about the *Ile de France*. I wasn't quite sure, but
since thinking it over, I am sure she had a date at ten o'clock on the
*Ile de France*. She was going to a party on board. The *Ile de France*
was sailing that night — to Havre, I think. They would probably call
at Plymouth or Southampton and then go straight to Havre. That is
the French Line's home-port.'

'How was she dressed on this Friday, if you can remember?'

'She had a frock on. A frock and a coat. I think the coat was black
with fur around the collar. I think she had a hat — black, a tight-
fitting thing, such as they call a cloche. I think she had a black

handbag. I don't remember if she had gloves. The frock had unusual sleeves. They were sort of ruffled, with little bell things of different colours.'

'Doctor, I am going to show you a photograph of the dress Starr Faithfull had on when her body was found at Long Beach. Tell me whether that is the dress she wore on the Friday night that you saw her.'

'I'm sure it is, yes.'

'Now, then, going back to this engagement she had on the *Ile de France*, Doctor – she did say she had an appointment on board around ten o'clock?'

'I'm sure. It was either a party or friends who were sailing.'

'Did her comment about the *Ile de France* just come up as she was leaving?'

'No, no. It was fairly early on, I think. Because she stayed on so as to make this appointment on the *Ile de France*. That was it.'

'Did she say anything about being in a hurry to keep the appointment?'

'No, no. She mentioned it was a ten o'clock appointment, but I don't think she knew the time. As far as I knew, it was after ten when she left. But my watch was on the blink. As far as I know, she left to go to the *Ile de France*, which sailed at midnight that night.'

'What did you have for dinner, Doctor, that night?'

'We had boiled eggs and ham sandwiches and either milk or coffee. That was at about half-past eight. You see, in port we don't have set suppers or anything. My steward just brought up the eggs and sandwiches.'

'No meats or mushrooms or potatoes – no fruit?'

'No.'

'A fearfully personal question, but impelled by necessity, and put in a perfectly good spirit: At any time on this Friday, for any reason, either by reason of her sitting down with her legs crossed or whatnot, did you notice by any chance whether she had any undergarments on?'

'No.'

'Did you ever get the opportunity to make any such observation?'

'Certainly not.'

'Another question, and this also impelled by necessity: Would you say from your observation of her that night – and we are able to tell, any man is, from a cursory examination of a woman, particularly with a sheer dress on – whether she might have worn such a thing as a brassiere? As a matter of record, she was rather well developed in the bust.'

'No, there was nothing apparent, I am sure, because I noticed nothing like that. I am sure she had a brassiere because there was nothing noticeable about them. She had rather a sort of figure then.'

'Your impression was that she did have a brassiere on?'

'Yes. I would never have suspected that she was heavily laden that way.'

'Was she apparently influenced by some drug when she left you?'

'Not that I observed, no. But she was more or less dopey. I don't think she was under the influence of drink. She had a very stony stare. Her eyes were funny. At one time, she asked me if I could give her a prescription for Veronal. I, of course, said I couldn't. She wanted to know if she could get Allonal in New Jersey, I think it was. She thought she could without a doctor's prescription. I said, "No, no, I am sure you can't."'

'Did she say she had any drugs with her?'

'No. And, as far as I saw, she didn't take any.'

'Now, upon her leave-taking, you escorted her to a taxi?'

'Yes. As we were going down, she wanted a dollar, and I gave her four quarters in silver for the taxi. It was raining, or had been raining and was wet. There was a taxi waiting, and she went right into the taxi and I came right back. I did not give any address to the driver, and I did not hear what she said to him. That is the last I ever saw of her. I am sure that it was in her mind to go to the *Ile de France*.'

'Did you notice the direction taken by the taxi?'

'No.'

'Do you recall the type of taxi?'

'I cannot actually, but usually it was a yellow taxi waiting outside there. I'm only going by what usually happened. I'm not sure.'

'If I told you it was a green taxi, would that —'

'That wouldn't convey anything.'

'You returned to the ship?'

'Yes. And later that night, I sat up on deck on my own and watched the *Ile de France* go by, all lit up. She went out at midnight, as far as I can remember.'

'Now, I want you to take this next question in the spirit in which it is given, Doctor. During the times you saw Starr Faithfull in that last week of her life, did she not make any proposition that, as an officer in the Cunard Steamship Company, you might think improper or of such a nature as would embarrass you in your official duties – something that you might hesitate in telling us about?'

'No, no, not at all. Veronal was the only thing.'

'Doctor, I now show you a photograph, and I will ask you whether you recognise that to be Starr Faithfull.'

'Oh, yes, that is her right enough.'

It was a minute past midnight – a minute after the last day of the Starr Faithfull investigation – when Dr Charles Young Roberts got into Detective Fogarty's car for the drive back to Manhattan. Nathan Birchall – who had taken shorthand notes of evidence on and off throughout the six months of the case, right from the very first day – had just gone home. Martin Littleton and his friends, John McLaren and Jesse Mayforth, all of them exhausted, all of them euphoric, strolled from the silent centre of Mineola, back to Gino's Restaurant, where, it is reasonable to guess, they contravened the Prohibition Laws. They were certain that, just in time, they had solved the mystery.

They believed that what had happened was this: that Starr had gone aboard the *Ile de France* – had stowed away – had emerged from her hiding place as the liner, approaching the Ambrose Lightship (the nearest it got to Long Beach), slackened speed to let the pilot off – had jumped or fallen overboard.

They were wrong, but it is good that they were sure that they were right. They deserved the feeling of triumph.

For some reason (maybe because Dr Roberts, before agreeing to talk, had extracted a promise of confidentiality), the Littleton team's solution was kept secret. If it *had* been publicised, someone surely would have noticed a disproving defect.

The press learned nothing about the doctor's testimony.

Nor did the Faithfulls.

Around about this time, the family moved from 12 St Luke's Place. Duncan Smith, occupier of the first floor and owner of the whole house, having received no rent for the top apartment since May, though he had often requested some and always been assured by Stanley that the arrears would be reduced forthwith, had offered to rescind the mounted debt if only the Faithfulls would go away forthwith, allowing him what by now seemed the luxury of having paying tenants. Stanley, having asked for a little while to consider the offer, had popped round to see George Perry – who, already of the opinion that Stanley had 'become more or less crazy since the finding of the body of his step-daughter', had advised him to get out while the going was good, before Smith had second, ungenerous thoughts. When Stanley had hesitated, wondering aloud whether Smith might be persuaded to pay him a 'leaving fee', had lost his patience and roared that if he didn't leave the Place of his own accord, and quickly, he might leave feet-first, beaten up by one of the neighbours, 'all of whom think that if Starr met her end by foul play, you are the guilty party'.

And so the Faithfulls moved − out of the Place, out of Manhattan. To a tiny apartment at 141 Nixon Avenue, in the district called Tompkinsville on the part of Staten Island closest to the Ambrose Channel. Their mail, much of it re-addressed to them by the kindly Duncan Smith, consisted mainly of statements of accounts long overdue, letters from creditors or creditors' lawyers. Smith also re-directed servers of summonses. If not on New Year's Eve, then in the first post of 1932, Stanley received an umpteenth letter from Joseph Macken, who, characteristically writing in sorrow, not in anger, regretted that the bill for Starr's funeral remained unpaid − and, in a postscript, said that if he didn't soon receive instructions regarding the despatch or disposal of the can of her ashes, he would feel quite entitled to distribute the contents, while retaining the can, which was of some value.

## 8

**A** romantic picture. The young English ship's surgeon, far from home, sitting solitarily on the deck of the *Carmania* at midnight, his face gilded by the myriad lights of the *Ile de France* as it glided past, making for the harbour, the Ambrose Lightship, the wide Atlantic, ports not all that far from his home.

The picture is made differently romantic by the fact that an important component of it was based on a wrong assumption made by Dr Roberts and accepted by the investigators of how Starr Faithfull came to die.

The doctor told the Littleton team that Starr stayed late with him on the night of Friday, 5 June, so as to fill in time before joining a party aboard the *Ile de France* at about ten. His watch was on the blink, but he believed that it was after ten when she left: 'It was raining, or had been raining and was wet,' when he escorted her off the *Carmania*, along Pier 56, and into the street, to a waiting taxi.

The time *was* after ten — about half an hour after. We know that because a shower of rain, the first of the day, began pattering across downtown Manhattan at 10.20, and about five minutes later, Police Sergeant Patrick Dugan, sheltering under an awning opposite the Cunard piers, saw two persons emerge through the gate to Pier 56: 'a stocky man' who he assumed 'was connected with some ship' and a young woman whom he had good reason to recognise as Starr Faithfull, having seen her after she was ejected from the *Franconia* a week before. Dugan watched as 'a green [*sic*] taxi drove up and the man put the woman in the taxi and she was driven off'.[1]

About 10.25.

The *Ile de France* had left its moorings, bound for Plymouth and Le Havre, at 10 p.m.

Of course, when Starr said good-night to Dr Roberts, she may not have realised that she had missed the ship. And she may not have

1. Page 167.

known (it does seem odd that Dr Roberts didn't) that the French Line's only New York berth was at Pier 57, the next one north from Pier 56. The two piers were no more than a hundred yards apart, 57 at the foot of West Fifteenth Street, 56 at the foot of West Fourteenth. If the taxi she got into was already facing north, and the driver took off before she told him where she wanted to go, she was already at or even past her destination by the time she completed the instruction — *if* that was to take her to the French Line's pier. She would have arrived at her intended journey's end — and the driver would no doubt have started swearing at her — before Dr Roberts had gone back through the gate to Pier 56. And Sergeant Dugan would have wondered whether he had just witnessed — or, having blinked from a raindrop in the eye, missed seeing — the shortest taxi-ride ever.

Starr may have thought of attending a party aboard the *Ile de France* — thought of it before she met Dr Roberts in the late afternoon, occasionally during the five hours she spent with him in his cabin, and for a little while afterwards — but, if so, she was disappointed. By the time she left Pier 56, all of the non-passenger party-goers had been back on America's officially dry land for at least forty minutes. Even the most conscientiously sentimental of them had stopped waving and walked away from Pier 57 about twenty minutes before. The *Ile de France* was, if not out of sight, no bigger to the eye than a bit of phosphorescent plankton.

If Dr Roberts' romantic picture was not altogether romantic, then the ship that he saw passing in the night was the White Star Line's *Olympic*, which left Pier 59, one of the five adjacent 'communal' piers used by lines of the International Mercantile Marine that could not afford piers of their own, at midnight, bound for Cherbourg and its homeport of Southampton.

Of course, maybe Starr went aboard the *Olympic* — illicitly stayed aboard till somewhere near the Ambrose Lightship. But there is no reason to suppose that she did. The only reason why the Littleton team thought they knew that the *Ile de France* was her final walking place was that she had told Dr Roberts that she was going aboard that ship. The fact that that ship was not there for her to board cannot be seen as evidence that she went aboard the only other transatlantic ship leaving New York that night — or, indeed, until eleven o'clock next morning, when the Atlantic Transport Line's *Minnewaska* left the 'communal' Pier 58, bound for Cherbourg and London. (The *Minnewaska* was the least splendid of three liners that sailed on the Saturday. Half an hour later, at 11.30, the White Star

Line's *Britannic* left Pier 60, bound for Queenstown and Liverpool, and half an hour afterwards, at noon, the Anchor Line's *Transylvania* left Pier 64, bound for Londonderry and Glasgow.)

Starr certainly did not fall or throw herself off the *Ile de France*, and there are strong (I think conclusive) reasons for believing that she did not fall or throw herself off one of the liners sailing later, the *Olympic*, the *Minnewaska*, the *Britannic*, or the *Transylvania*.

The Littleton team's *Ile de France* 'solution' was a particular form of the theory that was easily the most popular of those advanced by investigators, journalists and opinionative newspaper-readers who believed that Starr's death was either accidental or suicidal. The theory (which is still the favourite among students of the case who have discarded the idea that Starr was murdered) was of the history-repeating-itself variety: she tried unsuccessfully to stow away aboard the *Franconia* on the afternoon of Friday, 29 May – she tried again, this time successfully, on one or other of the transatlantic liners that left New York on the following Friday or the day after. Then came the variations on the theory.

Those who favoured the *suicide variation* suggested that it was bolstered by her several suicide threats (in her diary, in two of the three letters she had written to George Jameson Carr during the last week of her life, etc.) and, generally speaking, by the indications that she – harum-scarum, up one minute and down the next, bordering on what psychiatrists called manic-depression – was a 'suicidal type'. Ergo, she stowed away aboard a liner with the intention of throwing herself overboard after taking a stupefying dose of Veronal – this to ensure that she, a strong swimmer, should not be able to try and save herself if, post-plunge, she changed her mind about wanting to die. (The suicide variation required a pooh-poohing of parts of Starr's last letter to Dr Carr: '. . . If one wants to get away with murder one has to jolly well keep one's wits about one. It's the same with suicide . . . *No ether, allonal* [author's italics] or window jumping . . .')

The *accident variation* was, if anything, more reliant on Starr's unsuccessful attempt to stow away aboard the *Franconia*. Or rather, it relied upon an excerpt from what she had said to Edwin Megargee in his studio on Tuesday, 2 June:[1] '. . . I sneaked into the women's toilet [on the *Franconia*], thinking of hiding there until the ship was so far out to sea that they couldn't back up to put me off. No matter what happened, I'd have had my trip to England and been on the same ship with Carr. But I came out too soon. I felt the ship moving and after a while I guess I thought we were out a couple of days from

[1] Page 147.

land. The truth was, we hadn't even reached the middle of the Hudson when I stepped boldly out. That's what liquor does to me all right. What a chump I was. But I'll tell you something: the next time I try to stow away, I'll make it ...' Ergo, Starr − such an Anglophile, so desperate to get across to England, so desperate to see Carr (supposing that she could get across to England before he set off on another voyage back to New York) − had stowed away aboard a liner that had left on the following Friday or Saturday ... and had made much the same mistake again. Stupefied by the drug she had taken, she had stumbled across the deck, hoping to sight water stretching uninterruptedly to the horizon (which would mean that the ship was so far out to sea that 'they couldn't back up to put her off'), and had not merely lurched against the rail but had banged into it, lost her already unsteady balance, and toppled overboard.

The two-variation theory got a mite of support from an experiment that had been carried out by marine scientists of the New York Bureau of Geodetic Survey in the summer of 1929. Fifty green bottles, each with a request-message corked inside, were dropped from the Ambrose Lightship. The scientists received reports that two of the bottles drifted south to the Bahamas, one farther south to Puerto Rico, one a long way east to the west coast of England, two seven nautical miles south to New Jersey − and one 7½ nautical miles north to Long Beach. The other forty-three bottles either sank without trace or were found by people who couldn't understand the message or couldn't be bothered to reply to it. The scientists were interested only in the direction of the currents, not in their speed, and so they did not log the dates when the seven bottles washed ashore. Applied to the Starr Faithfull case, the experiment seemed to show that there was considerably less than a 1-7 chance that an object dropped into the sea near the Ambrose Lightship would end up at Long Beach. But still, there *was* a chance: the idea that Starr had fallen from a liner, and her drowned body drifted on to the shore of Long Beach, was possible.

In the early days of the investigation, the Bureau of Geodetic Survey provided Littleton with information that was more or less specific to the case. He also received help from the Weather Bureau, situated in the Whitehall Building, Manhattan, and from Coast Guards at the Brooklyn Navy Yard. In a report, he summarised the information from the three sources:

> The general consensus of scientific and expert opinion is that there is little likelihood that a body entering the water outside of New York

Harbour (that is to say, to the east of the Ambrose Lightship, which marks the entrance of the harbour) would tend to drift to the shoreline of Long Beach. From data accumulated for several years, it may be said that, as a rule, the bodies of persons lost from ships in the vicinity of the lightship are washed ashore in Jamaica Bay [south-east of Brooklyn and south of Queens – its entrance about seven miles west of where the body of Starr Faithfull was found[1]] ...

General tide conditions and currents within New York Harbour run from east to west. However, on Sunday night, June 7th, there was a violent storm and a very heavy sea with a south-westerly breeze prevailing over the greater portion of the time – which might, perhaps, have increased the possibility that a body of a person drowned at an earlier time near the Ambrose Lightship could be washed ashore at Long Beach.

The phrase 'at an earlier time' begs the question: How *much* earlier?

If Starr fell or jumped from a liner, it was from one of four:

The *Olympic*, which left Manhattan at midnight on Friday, 5 June.

The *Minnewaska* – 11 a.m. on Saturday, 6 June.

The *Britannic* – half an hour later, at 11.30.

The *Transylvania* –half an hour later, at noon.

The distance from the piers to the Ambrose Lightship is about twenty-five miles. The sailing time was about two hours.

Though none of the Coast Guards consulted by Littleton would commit himself, they all expressed strong doubt that the body of a person drowned near the lightship in the early afternoon of the Saturday would float the 7½ nautical miles to Long Beach within thirty-six hours, arriving there on the high tide in the early morning of Monday the 8th. Sensibly, they refused to hazard a guess as to what the average time for such a trip might be – but they gave instances, not unusual ones, of bodies taking weeks, even months, to travel like distances. In any event, it seems inconceivable that Starr could have stowed away aboard any of the Saturday-departing liners and that – in the broad daylight of the early afternoon, when the decks were crowded with some of the hundreds of passengers, the hundreds of members of the crew – she found an unoccupied section of rail, and clambered or toppled over it without a single person noticing. To answer a question that may have occurred to you: the port-holes below the decks of the liners were too small for an adult to climb through.

1. Nowadays, the John F. Kennedy International Airport extends along the north-eastern shore of Jamaica Bay.

Virtually certainly, then, if Starr went aboard and then overboard from a liner, that vessel was the *Olympic*.

But also virtually certainly, it was not.

The reasons for that statement come from the report by Dr Alexander Gettler, the toxicologist. [1]

Before explaining them, I must tell you that part of the report was wrong — was admitted to be wrong by Gettler himself, in a letter marked STRICTLY CONFIDENTIAL which he wrote to Elvin Edwards on 1 July, three weeks after the submission of the report (and, perhaps unconnectedly, a week after the publication in the press of the full texts of Starr's letters to George Jameson Carr, the last of them containing the reference to Allonal). Gettler's letter has never been made public until now.

> In my report to you on the analysis of the Starr Faithfull case, I reported the presence of Veronal. However, the Veronal group of drugs has several members ... all of which have very similar chemical properties, and give the same chemical reactions.... Since reporting to you, I have been constantly engaged in purifying the crystals isolated from the organs, the purpose being to get them 100% pure, so that a melting-point determination could be done. It is only by the melting point that they can be definitely differentiated.
>
> The following are the melting points of the four members of the Veronal group: Veronal 191, Luminal 170-172, Proponal 145, Dial 170.5.
>
> The pure crystals which I isolated from the organs melted at 171. This indicates that the drug in the organs is Luminal.
>
> Since there was present about 10 grains in the whole body, and as Luminal is a much more powerful hypnotic than Veronal, I can with reasonable certainty say that the deceased was deeply under the influence when she reached the water.
>
> Purification experiments such as these take days to weeks, and since a report was needed as soon as possible, and having proven the drug to be of the Veronal group, I at that time reported Veronal.

A present-day toxicologist, Peter Minty of the Department of Forensic Medicine & Toxicology at the Charing Cross and Westminster Medical School (University of London), comments that 'the melting points given in Dr Gettler's letter differ from those published in recent years. For instance, phenobarbitone or Luminal's melting point is $176-178°C$, and allobarbitone (Dial) about $173°C$; hence the melting point the distinguished Dr Gettler measured ($171°C$) could have come from an impure standard of

1. Pages 92–3.

either. I also doubt whether the method is accurate to 0.5°C. With regard to the dose, 10 grains is equivalent to 650 mg. Fatal doses of phenobarbitone are in excess of 1500 mg, and of allobarbitone, 2000 mg. Hence this level could represent a considerable amount taken, certainly sufficient to make a naive user pretty drowsy; however, tolerance could influence the matter. It is open to speculation as to the method used by Dr Gettler to calculate the 10 grains found in the body.'

All that can safely be said is that, shortly before Starr's death, she took – or was given – a large dose of Luminal (phenobarbitone) or Dial (allobarbitone). So far as Dr Roberts was aware, she did not take any drug during the five hours she spent with him on the Friday evening. Her request to him for a prescription for Veronal (which he refused) and her question to him as to whether she could get Allonal in New Jersey without a prescription (to which he replied, 'No, no, I am sure you can't'), suggest – no more than suggest – that she did not have any drug on her. Her cadging of a dollar for the taxi suggests – no more than suggests – that she did not have the cash to buy a drug from a New York chemist open at all hours and willing to break the law by supplying drugs to prescriptionless customers.

Gettler made no other amendment to his report – one of the firm findings of which was that Starr had not drunk any alcohol in the thirty-six hours before her death, whenever that had occurred.

Littleton neglected to ask Dr Roberts whether or not he had provided Starr with alcoholic refreshment during the five hours she spent in his cabin on the Friday evening. It seems reasonable to assume that she did have something stronger to drink than a glass of the milk or a cup of the coffee that accompanied the hard-boiled eggs and ham sandwiches that the doctor's steward brought in on a tray at half-past eight. Surely, when she 'kept talking' about Carr, 'seeking solace – commiseration, sort of,' from Roberts, he strengthened whatever solace he gave with a liquid stiffener of some kind?

But put those assumptions aside. If one accepts the evidence of the taxi-driver, Murray Edelman, at about one o'clock on the Friday afternoon, when he drove Starr from the Cunard piers to 12 St Luke's Place, 'she had been drinking but was able to walk'.[1] And shortly after ten o'clock the previous night, she took a drink in the company of Dr Roberts and his friend Mr Hart at a speakeasy near the Roosevelt Hotel.[2]

1. Page 164.
2. Page 244.

She *had* drunk alcohol in the thirty-six hours before two o'clock on the morning of Saturday, 6 June, when the *Olympic*, having left Pier 59 at midnight, was off the Ambrose Lightship. (And, going by Edelman's evidence, she had drunk alcohol in the thirty-six hours before the last of the three Saturday-departing liners got close to the lightship.)

Another of Gettler's firm findings: Starr had eaten a meal consisting of meat, mushrooms, potatoes, bread and fruit (skin and all), within three or four hours of her death, whenever that had occurred.

A sitting-down-to-eat, cutlery-requiring meal, by the sound of it. Considerably more filling than the snack she shared with Dr Roberts at half-past eight on the Friday evening. Not at all like the nibble-with-a-drink titbits that might have been provided at a going-away party aboard the *Olympic* which Starr might have gate-crashed (and at which, if she did attend such a party, and if one accepts Gettler's no-drink finding, she must have passed up any of the proffered drinks.)

Does it seem at all likely that Starr, having eaten hard-boiled eggs or ham sandwiches, or both, at 8.30 p.m., would have sat down to a hearty last supper, including a fruit dessert, between about twenty to eleven and a quarter to midnight, when she would have had to be aboard the *Olympic* if she intended to stow away on that vessel? Or that she would have gone aboard the *Olympic* and, successfully pretending to be a fare-paid passenger, sat down to a last supper in one of the restaurants, remained at the table till the liner was well past the Statue of Liberty, and then, her pretence still intact, walked out on to the deck, taken a post-prandial stroll around, and then, accidentally or deliberately gone over the side into those waters that, because of the closeness of the Ambrose Lightship, were one minute glistening like quicksilver, the next naturally coffin-dark?

If you believe, as I do, that neither of those notions is plausible, you must conclude that Starr did not set foot on OR OFF the *Olympic* that night. And if you are of the opinion that she did not set foot on OR OFF any of the three Saturday-departing liners, you accept that the whole falling-or-jumping-off-a-liner theory is rubbish.

You will have wondered, I expect, how the theorists got round the fact that, at the second autopsy, Dr Otto Schultze discovered sand in the trachea and lungs, indicating that Starr had drowned in shallow water. Well, all but one of the theorists ignored the indicative sand. Exceptionally, Inspector Harold King, the truest of the true disbelievers that Starr was the victim of a murderer, tried to explain away the sand by telling lies about it. He did not tell the lies till the case was, he believed, so far in the past that he stood a good chance of getting away with them, some of those persons who could have shown him up as a liar having died, others, surviving, being unlikely to see his lies in print − or, if they did, to be too upset to take the trouble to put the record straight.

Some time in the early 1950s, King, interviewed by a journalist, Fred J. Cook,[1] said that 'the quantity of sand in Starr's trachea [was] coarse. This was entirely different from the very fine, white sand we have on the Long Island coast. There was fine sand in the lungs, but the coarse, darker sand in the trachea was too heavy-grained to penetrate to the lungs. And it was far different in texture than our sand, indicating that Starr did not drown at Long Beach' − but (as Cook only reported King as saying) in the Ambrose Channel, ten miles south of Long Beach, into which 'Starr Faithfull went overboard from the huge French liner *Ile de France* ... the triple screws of which must [*sic*] have churned up the water so that it was filled with fine particles of sand [from the sea-bed, 75 − 90 feet below the surface]'. Cook also reported King as saying that 'On one occasion [he] swam far out to sea, then turned and floated, his body as motionless as a corpse. Bobbing up and down on the waves, he drifted slowly, surely towards the Long Beach shore in a vivid demonstration that proved Starr *could* have floated there after going overboard at sea in the steamer channel.'

Perhaps King really did do the bobbing-up-and-down experiment − though, unless he began it in the vicinity of the Ambrose Lightship, not at some point within a mile of Long Beach (which is suggested by his saying that he swam out to the experiment's starting point), the fact that he floated back towards the Long Beach shore went nowhere near proving his conviction that Starr had accidentally or suicidally gone overboard in the steamer channel.

There is no doubt that King lied when he said that the sand in the trachea was coarser, darker, heavier-grained than the sand in the lungs. Dr Schultze did not notice any difference, did not take samples of the sand, did not remove the lungs or the trachea. During the autopsy, King sat with the other witnesses − several feet from The Triple Miracle, his eyes roughly on the same level as the side of the body when it was lying flat. He could not, from that distance,

---

1. Author of *The Girl on the Lonely Beach*, the only previous book on the Starr Faithfull case, published in 1954 by Fawcett Publications, New York, as one of a series of paperbacks. The titles all began 'The Girl ...' or 'The Girls ...'.

from that level, have seen the sand, let alone been able to detect a difference between the sand contained in the light-coloured froth within the bronchi of the lungs and that which was caked to the sides of the trachea. Supposing that he stood up while Schultze was examining the trachea, he may have glimpsed sand that, because it was damp, was dark — but he could not have told, without touching the caked sand, what type it was, and nor could he have compared it with the grains in the light-coloured froth.

Schultze did not give an estimate of the time of Starr's death in his autopsy report. Subsequently, however, when pestered by reporters, he hazarded a guess that she had been dead for about two days when her body was found. In other words, that she had died some time between midnight on the Friday and mid-day on the Saturday.

That *was* only a guess. He claimed that it was 'based primarily upon the evidence of rigor mortis'. The speed of the development and of the disappearance of rigor, and the length of the period between, varies a great deal, as it is affected by many factors: for instance, the surrounding temperature, the person's age, the muscularity of the body, the amount of exercise taken shortly before death. The immersion of a body in cold water usually accelerates the onset (2 – 3 hours) and development (5 – 7 hours) of rigor, and often causes it to remain longer (sometimes for up to 2 – 4 days) than is often the case with bodies that have stayed dry. Rigor usually appears first in the face and neck, spreads to the arms, trunk, and legs, and disappears in the same order.

If Schultze was correct in his belief that rigor was *disappearing* from Starr Faithfull's body when he began the autopsy at half-past eight on the Monday evening, then all one can say is that the rigor behaved very oddly indeed. He noted that it was not in the arms (excepting the fingers of the right hand, where it was 'disappearing') but that it was 'still' well developed in the jaw and in both legs. And yet 5½ hours before, at 3.15 p.m., Dr Algernon Warinner had noted that there was no rigor in the arms or neck but that it was present in the hips and knees.

A present-day forensic scientist, Dr Bernard Knight,[1] considers that 'the length of time that a corpse has been immersed in water is ... a difficult question to answer, due to great variables in water temperature and contamination — *very often, an experienced river policeman or "longshoreman" may be more accurate in guessing this than a pathologist'*.

1. The author, under the pseudonym of 'Bernard Picton', of *Murder, Suicide or Accident: The Forensic Pathologist at Work* (Robert Hale & Co., London, 1971).

I have put the end of that quotation in italics because it gives some validity to the opinions expressed by several people who saw Starr Faithfull's body on the beach and who were therefore surprised to read Dr Schultze's guess as to the time of her death. The opinions were published in the *New York World-Telegram* of Monday, 15 June, exactly a week after the discovery.

Towards the end of that week, according to the reporter, Inspector King, who visited the beach [at 9.30 a.m.], voiced the opinion that she [Starr Faithfull] had been alive ten hours before – that is, till late on the Sunday night. The inspector subsequently revised that opinion – and drastically, by the addition of about forty-five hours, so as to coincide with his stated belief, based on the mistaken belief that the *Ile de France* had departed at midnight on the Friday, that Starr had gone overboard from that liner near the Ambrose Lightship at about two o'clock on the Saturday morning.

Of the people of Long Beach interviewed by the reporter, Dr Nathan Ginsberg had most to say. He arrived on the beach a few minutes after nine o'clock on the Monday morning, having been phoned to go there by the local police.

Dr Ginsberg declares that he thought the girl had then been dead not more than ten to fifteen hours. 'We can all make mistakes,' Dr Ginsberg has told the World-Telegram, 'but I do not believe that Starr Faithfull died more than twenty-four hours before I saw her. I believe it was a great deal less. The only discoloration I noticed was a redness in the corner of the eyes. It seems impossible to me that her body could have been as white and firm as it was. After one or two days in the water, all human bodies are generally swollen and badly discoloured. There was no sign of violence except the bruises, which might easily be explained by the driftwood. If she had been in the water for two days, and particularly in the violent storm of Sunday night, the body would have been cut to pieces.

Thomas Cusick, a veteran lifeguard at Long Beach, was of the same opinion. And so was Sergeant Thomas Walsh, of the Long Beach police, who stressed that 'there was no bloat, always apparent after twenty-four hours'. And so was Mrs Constance Callaway, who may have been the early-morning dog-walker who phoned the police station on behalf of the first policeman to arrive, Patrolman O'Connor, and who was certainly a retired nurse. She thought that 'the condition of the girl's body proved conclusively that she could not have been in the water very long. The girl's finger-nails were still highly polished. There was no sign of rigor mortis . . . and there was no sign of discoloration.' One of earliest of the spectators, Abraham

261

Rosenthal, a grocer in Long Beach, was especially struck by the fact that 'there was still a curl left in Starr Faithfull's hair' – proving, it seemed to him, that she 'had not been in the water very long'. The curl was commented upon by other eye-witnesses, all of whom drew the same conclusion from it.

Longer able to observe the body than any of the above, Joseph Macken also contradicted Schultze's guess, not publicly but in a letter to Elvin Edwards, who may or may not have asked for his views. Macken began by saying that he had the greatest respect for Dr Schultze, 'under whom I studied at Bellevue Hospital', but that he was 'nevertheless of the certain opinion that the doctor made a grave error in his estimate of the time of Miss Faithfull's passing':

> I have taken care of all the drowning cases in Long Beach for the last ten years. . . . Miss Faithfull had not been in the water 10 hours when her body was found, if as long as that. The fingernails were still heavy with rouge, and only the pads were shrunken. I can answer scientifically about the question of her inflamed eyes. She was not unconscious when she struck the water. The eyes were inflamed from the salt water, a condition which I could prove would not have occurred after death. . . . There was oil and sand in her hair. . . . That means that she was drowned on the beach, or in shallow water. Further proof of this is indicated by the finding that when she was found the beach was covered with crude oil. [That was a considerable overstatement: there were some patches of oil on the beach, none stretching far. (But maybe some of the sand in Starr's trachea and lungs was darkened by oil.)]

I have left till last in this section a point that seems to me to be clinching evidence that Starr did not go overboard from a liner, did not enter the water before the storm on the Sunday evening, did not drown far from the beach. Less surely, it indicates that at least some of the injuries to Starr's legs were caused before she entered the water.

The point is this: when her stockings, removed by the undertakers as soon as her body was at the morgue, were examined next day, two slight ladders were noticed – one in each of the stockings, each of the ladders leaning to the seam. According to King, the stockings 'were in good shape. There was just one or two tiny runs starting, but they were almost perfect. . . . We mounted them on [dressmaker's] forms just as we did the dress.' Either the two tiny runs were present when the body was found or one or both appeared as the result of the removal of the stockings by the undertakers, who were interested only in baring the body, not in preserving the integrity of items of clothing that might be of evidential value.

The stockings were of sheer silk − indeed, 'decidedly sheer', in Littleton's estimation. 'Sheer', in the hosier's sense, means 'of very thin and transparent material'. I have discussed silk stockings with women who were of adolescent age or older in pre-nylon days, and they all have told me of the care that was needed to prevent laddering. One of them recalled that she, her mother too, put on rubber gloves, sheathing her finger-nails, and removed any rings before rinsing silk stockings. Another said that 'even a harsh skirt rubbing on them could make the blessed things run'. Another would bet that 'before nylons came along, there were more women with ladders and snags in their stockings than women without any runs at all'. They were unanimous in believing that, as one of them put it, 'if a woman wearing silk stockings − stockings of any sort, for that matter, but sheer silk ones especially − swam [or floated] in the sea for any length of time, occasionally being struck or grazed by driftwood and suchlike, the stockings would finish up like fishnet, with more holes than hose'.

The fact that Starr's stockings were marred only by two small runs, either or both of which may have been made after her body was found, proves to my mind that Schultze's guess was wildly wrong − that Starr did not go into the sea and drown there much before a quarter past ten on the Sunday night, when the great storm which had chopped and churned the debris-littered water since eight o'clock began to diminish.

The two runs may well have been present when the body was found − and they may have been present before Starr entered the water. The stockings may even have been laddered when Starr dressed on the Friday morning. It would be interesting to know whether there were *any* perfect stockings among the things she left behind in her bedroom; in Detective Culkin's inventory, the contents of the drawers of the dressing-table are lumped together as 'misc. small items of ladies' wearing apparel, etc.'

There may have been *no* damage to the stockings while the body was in the water, but let us say that the *most* damage was the two small runs. How does one reconcile that slight damage to the stockings with the *sixteen* injuries to the legs that were observed by Schultze?[1] Unless one believes that only a couple of the blows that caused the injuries also punctured the stockings, one must believe

1. Page 49.

that most of the injuries were caused when Starr was alive – at some time when she was not wearing stockings.

Similarly, the complete lack of damage to her frock of soft untwilled silk indicates that some of the injuries to her trunk and arms were caused when she was not wearing the frock.

At different times after the autopsy, Schultze gave different estimates of the number of ante-mortem injuries; the estimates ranged between six and fifteen. So far as I can tell, Schultze never specified which of the injuries he was referring to. All the investigators and all the writers on the case seem to have assumed that as Schultze had identified up to fifteen such injuries, the rest – eighty-five or so – were caused after death, mostly while the body was in the water encountering floating debris, some of it heavy and jagged, and the remainder while the body was lying on the beach, still being toppled to and fro over the gritty, trash-strewn sand by the waves that had brought it ashore.

That is a false assumption. When Schultze spoke of a number – or rather, of numbers – of injuries which, in his opinion, were definitely ante-mortem, he was not saying that all of the others were definitely post-mortem. Many of the latter lacked distinctive signs by which to class them. Some of the injuries that appeared to Schultze distinctively post-mortem may have been ante-mortem. And vice versa. He may have been misled into believing that injuries caused while the body was in the water or on the shore, or even later, as the result of rough handling by Macken's men or by still rougher probing, piercing, pulling and pushing by Dr Warinner, were inflicted before death. He may have fallen into the trap of associating bruising solely with blood *pressure* while the heart is pumping – although bruising can occur after death, from an injury that tears dead vessels and opens tissue spaces into which blood seeps passively. Such post-mortem bruising is especially possible in areas of hypostasis, the lividity produced by the gravitational settling of the blood. After reading Schultze's report, Dr David Bowen, presently Professor of Forensic Medicine at the Charing Cross and Westminster Medical School (University of London), commented: 'It does not appear that hypostasis was entirely recognised at autopsy, although it should have been well defined if the body had been lying in a supine position on the shore at Long Beach.' Professor Bowen added: 'The marks on Starr Faithfull's limbs were clearly some form of bruising, but I wouldn't like to say how or when they were caused.' Referring to Schultze's observation that 'there are six depressions in the middle of the back along the left side of the lower spine,' Professor Bowen commented that the depressions 'sound very much like indentations made by a row of buttons on the back of a dress, pressing into the skin beside the spine of a woman lying supine'. That suggestion conforms with the fact, not known to Professor Bowen, that there *was* a row of small knobby buttons at the back of Starr's dress. This supports my feeling that Schultze's powers of reasoning were not great – nowhere near good enough to make one confident of the rightness of his opinions.

Turn now once more to the 'overboard from a liner' theory. In the book on the case by Fred J. Cook, the author says:

> According to the veteran detective, Inspector King ... the second vital angle [the first vital angle being the 'presence' of non-Long Beach sand in the trachea] was the absence of any bruise on Starr's body corresponding to the location of six transverse tears of the liver beneath. 'Dr Schultze himself didn't see the significance of this until I pointed it out to him,' King remarks, with a touch of pardonable pride. 'But the point is that, for the liver underneath to be ruptured without a bruise appearing on the skin, the body would have had to fall from a considerable height into some relatively yielding substance, like water or hay. The shock then might produce those internal tears without leaving an external trace. That's the only way it could happen, and that was what led us [*sic*] to conclude that Starr must have fallen into the sea from the deck of a liner.'

Schultze was dead by the time King talked to Cook. Had he been so impressed by the 'liver angle' that he would agree that Starr *must* have fallen into the sea from the deck of a liner? If he *was* so impressed, that is another reason to question his judgment. His autopsy finding regarding the liver (page 51) contains the salient sentence: 'Over the posterior superior part of the right lobe there are six transverse tears through the [enclosing] capsule and running about one-eighth of an inch into the liver tissue, without hemorrhage.' According to Professor Bowen, the absence of haemorrhage strongly indicates that the tears were a post-mortem trauma, most likely to have been caused by pressure – rather than sudden impact – upon the back of the *corpse*.

The only garments on the body were the silk stockings, the girdle that suspended them, and the paisley frock of untwilled silk. According to Dr Roberts, on the Friday night Starr was wearing the same frock and had a coat ('black with fur around the collar,' he thought). He also thought she had a hat ('black, a tight-fitting thing, such as they call a cloche') and a black handbag. He could not remember if she had gloves. He told Littleton that he had 'certainly not' had the opportunity to notice whether she was wearing underclothes – but he felt sure that she was wearing a brassiere (because 'there was nothing noticeable about [her breasts]'; he would 'never have suspected that she was [as] heavily laden' as Littleton had just told him that she was).

Neither the coat nor any of the things she presumably wore ever turned up.

In the first couple of days of the investigation, the southern shore of Long Beach was twice searched from end to end; the regular beachcombers were interviewed; none of them admitted having found anything that might have belonged to Starr. They were asked to watch out for, and to hand over, anything that they thought might have belonged to her. There were subsequent searches – not only at Long Beach but also along other south shores of Long Island; the combers of those latter places were interviewed and asked for help. The press reported what the investigators were looking for. Littleton noted in his 'final report' that 'a thorough investigation was made at the Long Island Rail Road stations, bath houses, and other public places maintaining public check rooms or storage lockers; a similar check was made of the public check rooms and storage lockers in the Grand Central and the Pennsylvania Stations, New York City . . . but there were no results. In addition, the contractors for the refuse for Long Beach, Ameli Bros., were questioned and were requested to keep a watch-out . . . but the result again was negative.' All sorts of stuff from all sorts of places was handed in – eventually a small roomful of it at the police headquarters. Some of the stuff was shown to the Faithfulls, who invariably shook their hastily averted heads, and sometimes stated or implied that the shoddiness of the goods was indication enough of their irrelevance to Starr.

I can see no significance in the fact that Starr, who was wearing her coat on the last Friday of her life, wore it on the penultimate Friday – and, after getting Chief Steward Albert Jones's permission to leave it in his cabin on the *Franconia*, became almost as distressed by her inability to find the cabin and collect the coat as she was by Dr Carr's refusal to talk to her. She found her way back to the cabin at some time before a quarter to five, when Jones returned there and saw that the coat was gone. If, on the last Friday, she had absent-mindedly left her coat in Dr Roberts's cabin on the *Carmania*, he would have held on to it, expecting her to return for it before the liner sailed; if, she not returning, he had thrown or given away the coat, he would surely have told Littleton so.

Probably rather than possibly, between shortly after Starr said goodnight to Dr Roberts and shortly before she went into the water, she left her coat (and any other missing things) in some indoor place — a private dwelling, perhaps, or a hotel — and an occupant or employee subsequently destroyed those evidences of her stay. If the coat had been dropped out of doors, or if it had gone into the water with her — though not, of course, *on* her — the likelihood is that it would have been found and, as the fur collar was such a strong indication that it was Starr's, handed over to the police.

Apart from Dr Roberts's belief that Starr was wearing a brassiere, there is no evidence that she was. Actually, he did not say that he believed she was wearing a brassiere six months earlier, but that he did not recall any indication that she *wasn't*. That is an important difference. Though she was, in Littleton's words, 'rather well developed in the bust,' her breasts were firm. If they were bra-less that night, the tight-fitting bodice of her frock gave them some support. Since the night was warm and the small cabin probably warmer, her nipples would have been soft and shallow, hardly perceptible to an onlooker even if her frock had been unpatterned, and made virtually invisible by the paisley design. I think that Dr Roberts's belief should be discounted; strong negative evidence can be as strong as the strong positive sort, but what he remembered *not* seeing does not deserve to be described as evidence. In any case, though Littleton had done his best to put the doctor at ease, and had put his question about Starr's breasts as a man-to-man parenthesis, Roberts may well have felt it wise to say nothing that might suggest he had tried, or been tempted to try, some hanky-panky with Starr in the privacy of his cabin. The same applies to his response, 'Certainly not', when Littleton delicately asked if he had looked up Starr's skirt and noticed whether or not she was wearing panties.

I think Starr was not wearing underclothes — unless a stocking girdle can be classed as such: no brassiere, no panties. The absence of those garments on her dead body is hard to explain otherwise. If she was wearing underclothes on the Friday night, then she later undressed — or was undressed by someone else. The undressing was not necessarily complete: the top of the frock had to be unbuttoned and pulled down, away from her chest and off her arms, else the shoulder-strapped brassiere could not have been removed; the girdle and the stockings may not have been taken off. But if, some time later, she went into the sea of her own accord, why on earth had she either removed her underclothes in preparation for drowning or, having removed the underclothes for a reason unconnected with her intention to kill herself, neglected to put them back on (presumably leaving them in a pile with her coat and any other belongings)? If she was dumped in the sea, almost certainly the person responsible had transported her to a shore or a boat from wherever her underclothes were. Why on earth had he not forced or persuaded her to get completely dressed – or completely dressed her himself – though it must have occurred to him that the dead body of a woman without brassiere or panties was more likely to arouse suspicion of foul play than the dead body of a woman with the conventional minimum amount of underwear, and though a complete dressing would reduce the number of evidences of the crime that had to be destroyed or hidden? Supposing that she was naked or near-naked when he determined to drown her (or, if she was by then so affected by a drug that he believed that she was already dead, to dispose of a corpse in the sea), why did he not superintend her complete dressing – or, if she was too far gone (or, as he thought, dead), completely dress her himself? It would have taken him less time to roll her panties up her legs and fasten her brassiere over her breasts than to get her back in her dress and, a fiddly job, do up every single one of the little knobby buttons.

The upshot of those questions and answers is that I don't believe Starr Faithfull committed suicide or drowned by accident.

The possibility that she drowned by accident would be less remote if she had stowed away on a transatlantic liner, fallen from one, drowned in the Ambrose Channel, and floated to Long Beach. That notion (so dear to Inspector King that he invented support for it; accepted by Martin Littleton, solely because he believed, after talking to Roberts, that Starr had boarded the *Ile de France*, which she couldn't have boarded, for the simple reason that the ship had sailed) is contradicted by a surfeit of facts. Starr drowned near Long Beach: certainly not in the early hours of the Saturday, probably not in any of the Saturday hours, but most likely on the Sunday evening, towards the end of or soon after the great storm. She could have drowned by accident only if for an inexplicable reason she had travelled to a shore along the south of Nassau County (an area that seems to have been unknown to her) and (1) become unconscious from drugs (which somehow she, though apparently penniless and without a prescription, had acquired) and been engulfed by a tide; (2) staggered, drug-blind, into the sea; (3) unhitched a moored boat, clambered aboard before it drifted, and a short while later, by then fuzzy from drugs, either fallen off the uncontrolled boat or, vaguely thinking that the only possible way out of the predicament she had put herself in was to try to swim back to the shore, jumped overboard. No one recalled seeing Starr, or any girl resembling her, travelling to the south of Nassau County. How could she, apparently penniless, have got there? She didn't have the money for the bus or train fare, let alone the hiring of a cab or a hire-car. No one admitted giving her a hitch-hike. No one admitted treating her to the cooked meal she ate some time after she left Dr Roberts. How did she pay for it? Where did she eat it? No one recalled seeing a girl staggering along any shore, lying unconscious on one, or walking into the sea from one. There were reports that boats had been tugged from their moorings by the storm, but no report that, between early on Saturday and late on Sunday, a boat had been set adrift by a person. And nothing that had belonged to Starr was found, dry above the high-tide mark or wet below, on any shore.

With slight variations on some of them, all of those anti-accident points are also anti-suicide points.

In the first and third of the three letters that Starr wrote to Dr Carr during the week before her disappearance, she said that she was going to commit suicide. In the first of the letters (page 216), she began by saying, 'I am going (definitely now — I've been thinking of it for a long time) to end my worthless, disorderly bore of an existence ...,' but blunted the threat — or rather, indicated that there was no cause for immediate concern — by filling much of the end of the letter with expressions of hope that the doctor would 'come and see' her when he returned to New York. The very fact that she, having posted that letter on Saturday, 30 May, was able to post the other letter (page 219) on Thursday, 4 June, would have made the doctor think that the suicide threats in that other letter were not to be taken seriously.

Had he received similar letters from her in the past? Had any of her other 'crushes'? — Herbert Miller, for instance (part of her diary-entry for 2 September 1926: '... I love H.M. like hell. I'm all set to commit suicide if he won't see me ...').

How often do suicide threats precede suicide attempts? Statistics don't give much help towards an answer; the only fairly reliable data concern the successful attempts. In his book *Suicide and Attempted Suicide* (Penguin, London, 1964), Erwin Stengel, a professor of psychiatry, speaks of surveys which suggest that

> in the United Kingdom and in the United States the number of suicidal attempts is six to eight times that of the suicides, at least in urban

**269**

communities. (At Basle, Switzerland, the number of suicidal attempts per annum was recently found to be ten to fifteen times that of the suicides.) This means that an English city of half a million inhabitants with a suicide rate of thirteen per 100,000, which is above the national average of eleven, would have 390–520 suicidal attempts per year. The number of suicidal attempts in Metropolitan London, with a population of over eight million, would be in the region of 7500–9000.

As it is reasonable to assume that many, if not most, incidents classed as unsuccessful attempts at suicide are sham attempts, and that many of those are preceded by suicide threats, and that many people who threaten suicide never even pretend an attempt, their words being only disguised 'cries for help' (attention, sympathy), it is safe to say that thousands and thousands of people who threaten suicide take such uninterruptedly good care of themselves that they live to a ripe old age.

Though Starr told a good many lies to her family about where she had been and where was going, she seems to have been usually truthful to friends and acquaintances – not so much telling downright lies as embroidering memories and speaking of mere hopes for the future as if they were certainties. One can see no reason why she should have lied to Dr Roberts about her desire to go to Paris 'in relation to ... some woman there who was going to leave her some money', her 'keenness ... on going to Calcutta' (in the hope of seeing Herbert Miller?), her intention of 'going to Montreal for the weekend'. Far from giving any indication that she meant to commit suicide before the weekend was over, she spoke as if she had no idea that she had but a short time to live.

If she did commit suicide, parts of the prelude to the act differed from intentions expressed in her last letter: 'No ... allonal' – 'I am going to drink slowly keeping AWARE every second.'

She also said in that letter: 'I won't worry because men flirt with me in the streets – I shall encourage them – I don't care who they are. I wish I got more pleasure sleeping with men. I'm afraid I've always been a rotten "sleeper". It's the preliminaries that count with me. It doesn't matter though.'

In 1971, when all that I knew about the Starr Faithfull case was from Fred J. Cook's paperback and a few articles, most of them based on Cook's account, I wrote a short piece about it,[1] ending with the suggestion that, bearing in mind the 'Joseph Collins'

[1] As a chapter in *Posts-Mortem: The Correspondence of Murder*, David & Charles, Newton Abbot.

incident and Starr's criticism of Rudolph Haybrook, the London artist, as being 'a bit too rough' (I did not know about the statement of John Cunningham, the night officer of the Montclair Hotel [pages 199–200]), perhaps there was a clue to her death in her last letter, which I have just quoted: perhaps a man she encouraged to flirt with her became so frustrated, so angry, when he discovered that she was a 'rotten "sleeper"' that he beat her up, and, thinking that he had killed her (a misconception that may have been created by her being comatose from drugs), disposed of her 'corpse' in the sea.

That suggestion was at least based on a *few* facts, which is more than can be said for most of the murder theories put forward in the press during the first weeks of the case. For instance, in the *New York World-Telegram* of 15 June, a staff writer named Lou Wedemar listed 'speculations which [so he claimed] have been advanced by the authorities, the public, and the family of Starr Faithfull, to account for her being found drowned at Long Beach a week ago this morning':

> *Starr Faithfull was murdered in an international plot to obtain a chemical secret of her step-father's.* When her step-father was manager of the Atlantic Chemical Works in Mansfield, Mass., in 1917, Harold A. Whitman, chief chemist, was murdered. German spies were suspected, and Faithfull preserved much the same mysterious attitude as he has after the death of his step-daughter. He still works on chemical formulae about which he will not speak.
>
> *She was murdered by gangsters.* . . . . Inspector King has found no proof of this.
>
> *She was murdered by someone of whom she had made demands of marriage.*
>
> *She was murdered by someone of whom she demanded money.* Her . . . lack of money might be regarded as support of this theory.
>
> *She was murdered by a bored wooer who had tired of her.* Her occasional outbursts of temper might have made her unpleasant to him.
>
> *She was murdered by a jealous woman.* Her beauty might have made her a capable rival.
>
> *She was murdered by an insane man.*
>
> *She may have been struck by a hit-and-run-driver, who threw her into the sea to hide evidence of the crime.*
>
> *She was shanghaied by a ship's crew, attacked and thrown overboard.*
>
> *Some relative killed her.* Silence of her family on many facts about her life has suggested this theory.

\*

271

Until Dr Roberts's evidence changed Martin Littleton's mind, he believed that Starr had been murdered. And he suspected that Stanley Faithfull was in some way involved in the murder. He also suspected that Mrs Faithfull and Tucker knew how Stanley was involved.

A week before 7 December 1931, the last day of the investigation – and, as it happened, the day when Dr Roberts was interviewed – Littleton prepared the 'final report'. Under the heading INVESTIGATION OF THE FAITHFULLS, he wrote:

> By reason of their peculiar conduct and inconsistent statements, particularly on the part of Faithfull himself, their conduct preceding the death of Starr was made the matter of careful scrutiny. The inquiry entailed a very lengthy and careful examination of all of their activities, particularly that of Faithfull.
>
> This inquiry looked closely into the Peters relationship and financial settlement of $25,000 by Peters; the fact that Faithfull was at almost all stages of his life impecunious; the fact that while living in West Orange, New Jersey, the family were unable to meet their obligations and that they left that locality owing practically everyone in town, and many of the debts are still unsettled. An attempt to confirm Faithfull's statements was made, . . . with the result that in more cases than one it was established that Faithfull has been far from consistent in his utterances.
>
> Since a date during the first week of the investigation, all mail delivered to the family has first been intercepted and carefully examined, but without result. As there was no telephone in the Faithfull home, the assistance of both Western Union and the postal telegraph companies was enlisted in obtaining copies of all telegrams delivered at the Faithfull home at 12 St Luke's Place from June 1 to June 8 inclusive, but there were none of any significance.
>
> Faithfull's attitude throughout the inquiry has been of such a character as to not only not furnish any material aid but rather on the other hand seriously to impede any constructive progress. . . . For the above reasons, natural suspicion was aroused concerning Faithfull, his wife, and Tucker. It must be stated that Faithfull's attitude is problematical at this time and cannot be explained.

In other parts of the 'final report', Littleton referred to incidents which, in his opinion, went towards justifying his belief that Stanley Faithfull was somehow mixed up in Starr's murder:

> Whilst in Boston on Thursday, June 4, the day preceding Starr's disappearance from her home, Faithfull met with Charles Rowley and another attorney [Charles Walkup], ostensibly to discuss matters relating to the mortgage on the Centerville property belonging to Mrs Faithfull

and a number of Faithfull's own financial problems, and obliquely suggested a further shake-down of Peters, which both attorneys state they would have nothing to do with. (*Pages 157–9.*)

A thorough and careful check-up of the Boston steamship line which operates the steamship *Commonwealth* failed to confirm Faithfull's statement that he was a passenger on that vessel, arriving at New York City early on the morning of June 5. The present status is, therefore, that there is no available evidence showing that he did in fact take this boat. (*Pages 159–61.*)

On Monday, June 8, Sergeant Gannon of the Missing Persons Bureau of the Police Department of New York City interviewed Faithfull respecting the disappearance of Starr. Gannon states that he was very much impressed with the virtue and high character of the girl, as given to him by Faithfull. In the early afternoon, upon leaving Bellevue Hospital with Gannon, Faithfull, apropos of nothing, asked how long it took a dead body to float.... Gannon was impressed by this enquiry – especially later, when it developed that the girl had died by drowning. (*Pages 37–8.*)

On Saturday, June 6, Faithfull composed a letter, as if from his wife, to a relative of Peters, and next day, after reporting the disappearance of Starr to the police, added a long postscript, clearly an attempt to extort money, which I have characterised elsewhere as 'the poisonous addenda'. (*Pages 168–71.*)

Littleton also referred to the phone call received by Alexander Whiteside on Monday, 4 May, from a man who, claiming to represent a news agency but refusing to give his name, sought confirmation of a rumour he said he had heard that Whiteside's friend Andrew Peters had paid a large sum to Starr Faithfull in settlement of a claim she had brought against him. From the placing of the reference between references to Stanley Faithfull, it is plain that Littleton believed that the mystery caller was Stanley, preparing the ground for the attempt to extract more money from Peters – which, just over a month later, at his meetings with Rowley and Walkup, he made clear was an intention that had been in his mind for some time.[1]

---

1. Though Rudolph Haybrook denied that he had told a reporter for the London *Daily Mail* that Starr had told him that she was *to be* 'the principal witness in a $25,000 settlement case which would have caused a sensation when it came to court' (page 194), there is a strong indication (the appearance of the report before the publication in London of rumours about the 1927 cash-settlement) that he was reported accurately. If so, it appears that, before the summer of 1930, when Starr, with her mother and sister, visited London, the Faithfulls, all or some of them, had begun considering ways and means of getting more money from Peters.

I believe that Littleton was wrong in thinking that the call was made by Stanley.

I believe that the caller really *was* a journalist: not a journalist representing a news agency but a man named George Benwell, who was employed full-time by the daily *Boston American*, and who greatly increased his income by working on a freelance basis, covertly, for racketeers in both Boston and New York City, reporting to them items of information that, for various reasons, either could not be reported in any newspaper or were, he consoled his slight conscience by thinking, unlikely to appeal to the editor of his own paper. Each of the several Benwell-retaining racketeers was under the impression that he was Benwell's sole extra-mural master. Actually, to give Benwell the only credit which other moles, no one else, may think he deserves, he rarely passed the same information to more than one racketeer, but, to remove part of that small credit, he rarely came up with information that he could sell twice over. Mostly, he provided warnings; and most of the warnings were of raids that were planned by policemen or Prohibition agents or drug-enforcement officers and of arrests that such law-enforcers were contemplating. In the course of his full-time employment, he heard plenty of tittle-tattle, some of it about skeletons in the cupboards of persons who were rich or famous or influential. But hardly any of that was retailable to the racketeers − for hardly any of it was the stuff of blackmail, few of the alleged dark secrets being of the shock-horror kind, few of the subjects of the tales being of such unblemished reputation that they might be willing to give money or favours, or both, to keep the dark secrets opaque.

I am not changing the subject when I say that, between the end of June and the middle of September 1931, different investigators of the Starr Faithfull case were told one story by three narks, none of whom appears to have known either of the others; two of the informers lived and committed crimes in New York City, the third in Boston. This is Detective John Fogarty's outline of the story:

'Mr Andrew J. Peters of Boston was shook down for $30,000 in a room at the Astor Hotel, Manhattan, on a date during the first or second week of May 1931. This shake-down is said to have been done by a gang from Boston. The $30,000 is supposed to have been given up by Mr Peters as "hush" money so that the story of the so-called degenerate acts that happened between Starr Faithfull and this man Peters would not be publicly divulged. It is also said that later on, after the blackmailers received the $30,000 from Mr Peters, they drove back to Boston on the Post Road and met with the organisers of the shake-down in a room at the Essex Hotel in that city, and while there was discussion going on concerning the splitting of the money, some racketeers from New York came into the hotel room, stuck them up, and took from them the money received from Mr Peters, and made their getaway.'

Only one of the narks named names. He said that, shortly before the shake-down at the Astor, *George Benwell* had received the information about Peters from *Joseph Lyons*; that Benwell had passed the information to *Charles Solomon* and *Dan Carroll*, who, between them, had organised the shake-down; that the armed robbery of the blackmailers at the Essex Hotel was carried out by members of *Vannie Higgins*'s gang.[1]

This story from the three narks does not seem to have created much of a stir among the investigators. The only apparent reference to it in Littleton's 'final report' comes at the end of the section dealing with the long-delayed interviewing of Peters on 18 November:

> He [Peters] was asked directly if at any time prior to Starr's death he had been approached by any individual or individuals who attempted to blackmail him or extort money from him by reason of his alleged impropriety with Starr. He vigorously denied this and stated that at no time had anybody ever approached him in this vein.

There is an undated report by Detective Fogarty which shows that he took the story seriously enough to check whether the Bostonian Dan Carroll was related to a couple of criminal Carrolls of New York City:

> After visiting the NYC post office authorities with regard to the tracing of mail delivered to the Faithfulls, I called at the East 67th Street Station House and learned that the result of the inquiry concerning Dan Carroll

---

1. Such an exploit would have been, for them, a variation on their frequent hijackings of rival rum-runners' cargoes. John Kobler notes that 'liquor unloaded on Long Island normally travelled in a truck convoy, led by a scout car, along Route 25, running 150 miles from the eastern tip of the island into New York City. Vannie Higgins would set up an ambush with gunmen waiting by the roadside in parked cars, behind trees and buildings. Unless the convoy belonged to the "Big Bill" Dwyer syndicate or had paid for protection, two cars would shoot out from opposite sides of the highway, blocking the scout car. As the trucks ground to a halt behind it, the Higgins gang would enfilade them with tommy-gun fire, then, dumping the dead and wounded, drive the trucks to Dwyer's scattered New York City drops.'

was that there is no known connection between him and Michael and Thomas Carroll who now run speakeasies at 312 West 43rd Street and 21 Grand Avenue, Bronx, and have been operating speakeasies in New York a long time prior to them having their present places. They once had a place at 38th Street and 7th Avenue.

Towards the end of September, following the third rendering of the story, Littleton hired the assistant manager (known as 'X-42') of the Boston branch of the Burns Detective Agency to gather information about the Bostonians named by one of the narks. The following potted biographies are made up of quotations from X-42's report, marked CONFIDENTIAL AND FOR YOUR ATTENTION ONLY, and material from other sources.

### Joseph T. Lyons

X-42: 'Lyons is known as "10% Joe". He is thick-set man with a bull neck and florid complexion. This man would have participated in such a thing as a shake-down of Peters and he also would have been in possession of the information. When Peters was elected Mayor of Boston in 1918, Lyons posed as a "bag man" for Peters and collected 10% on many contracts that the city made, but Peters never saw any of the money as Peters was considered to be honest in this respect. Since that time, Lyons has lived by similar activities, but with Peters out of office it has been impossible for him to make much money in this way as he is only known to be identified with Peters although Peters has no particular use for him. Nobody seems to know exactly what he is doing now but during the Peters regime he was very well known.'

If you are experiencing a feeling of déjà vu, it is probably because '10% Joe' Lyons was referred to, though not by name, on page 70 in the quotation from the recollections of Peters' term as mayor by the Boston newspaper reporter, Joseph Dineen:

> In an anteroom adjoining Peters' office there was a 'bag man' who would deal, dicker or negotiate for almost anything.... Jobs and promotions had price tags on them. Political affiliation meant nothing. Anybody could buy almost anything at the bargain counter. All that was needed was the price....

The mystery of why 'Honest Andrew' Peters allowed Lyons to pose as his bag-man is best explained by the assumption that Lyons had a hold over him − that Lyons knew something which Peters was desperate to keep secret. An only slightly less reasonable assumption is that Lyons knew about Peters' sexual intimacy with a little girl named Starr Wyman – an intimacy that had begun during the year before Peters' election, when Starr was eleven.

Lyons, who was slightly older than Peters, was an alumnus of Boston College, where he had excelled athletically, being a star of both the baseball and the football teams, but shown no great scholastic ability. Till he was about forty, he worked in real estate and dabbled in politics; meanwhile, he became friendly with Peters. In 1916, Peters, then Assistant Secretary of the Treasury in charge of Customs, appointed Lyons as Chief Appraiser of the Port of Boston. In 1917, 'Lyons was one of the most active campaigners for the election of Mayor Peters' (*Boston Globe*); following Peters' election, 'Lyons became one of the mayor's most confidential advisers' (*Boston Globe*) and 'a powerful figure at City Hall' (*Boston Herald*). In January 1921, the start of Peters' last year as mayor, the *Boston Herald* reported:

> The special committee appointed by Mayor Peters to investigate the local garbage situation has discovered that Joseph T. Lyons is a $2500-a-year employee of the Boston Development & Sanitary Company....
>
> The company recently threatened to break its 10-year garbage disposal contract with the city unless the mayor would authorise payment to the company of $25,000 a month more than the contract price.... Mayor Peters rejected the proposition and the company has so far failed to carry out its threat....
>
> According to information received by the special committee, Lyons has been on the company's payroll for several years as a 'dump locater'. It is not known exactly what the duties of a 'dump locater' are. With the exception of the East Boston dump, those that the company uses were selected at the time the contract was signed in 1912.... For nearly a year, Lyons has not often been seen at City Hall.

One wonders whether the garbage company had promised '10% Joe' Lyons a raise from $2500 a year to $2500 a month if the contract price went up by $25,000 a month. One also wonders whether the company continued to pay him to locate dumps that they didn't need once his presence on the payroll was revealed. Probably not, for in February 1921 Lyons announced that he was 'giving up public service activities to pursue real estate and building contract business'. He seems to have received only one subsequent mention in the press: that was in 1928, when he served on a committee to decide the best way of enlarging the Suffolk County (Boston area) courthouse. He died at the age of seventy-one in April 1947.

**Charles Solomon**

X-42: 'This man, whose nickname is "King", is of Jewish extraction. He has resided in Boston for many years, of late years spending a great deal of his time in New York City. He first became well-known ten or fifteen years ago, when it was said that he was engaged in drug traffic. Some time after this [in January 1923], he was sentenced to five years in Atlanta Penitentiary [for subornation of perjury and obstruction of justice]. After remaining there a month or so, he was brought back to Boston; the case was heard in court again and he pleaded guilty and was only fined. Inquiries on that case have failed to disclose just why this unusual procedure should have taken place. Since that time he has never been arrested. For some time after this episode, nothing was heard of him. He then became friendly with one Dan Carroll. He and Carroll were said to be engaged in the drug and liquor business.... Solomon has become the much bigger man of the two in gangster circles and is said to be a partner of Owney Madden.[1]

'It is said that he has been seen in recent times with three men, the two Devaney gangster brothers and Vannie Higgins, with the idea of opening a new beer racket in Boston. He has as his secretary the wife of Charles Ponzi, who is now in the Plymouth Jail.[2] Solomon has a financial interest in many of the night clubs in Boston and owns the Cocoanut Grove night club in Boston which is run in his brother's name.[3]

1. From *The Mafia Encyclopedia* by Carl Sifakis (Facts on File, New York, 1987): 'Madden (1892-1965) came to New York in 1903 from his native Liverpool, England, [and] joined the Gophers, one of the major gangs of the day.... When he was released from Sing Sing prison in 1923 [after serving eight years for the murder of 'Little Patsy' Doyle, who had threatened his leadership of the Gophers], Owney ... formed a new gang and went into rum-running and rackets involving laundry services and coal deliveries. He was such a steady producer that Tammany's Jimmy Hines provided him protection. Madden now moved as an equal among such criminals as Lucky Luciano [and] Frank Costello....'
2. Where he was serving the second of two sentences for a gigantic investment swindle that had been uncovered by the *Boston Post*; thousands of small investors, many of them Italian-American residents of Boston, like himself, had been victimised. (Following his release in 1934, Ponzi was deported to Italy, where, according to some reports, Mussolini hired him as a financial adviser. Shortly before the Second World War, he emigrated to Brazil; he became almost blind, partially paralysed, and quite destitute, and died in a charity ward in 1949, aged seventy-one.)
3. In the space of twelve minutes on the night of Saturday, 28 November 1942, a fire swept through the Cocoanut Grove, on Piedmont Street, causing the death of at least 490 customers and employees. Officially, the club was no longer owned by any member of the Solomon family. The title to the premises had passed to Barnett

'I found, by interviewing various informants, that it is absolutely out of the question that Solomon would have played any visible part in a shake-down of ex-Mayor Peters or that he would have had anything to do with interviewing Starr Faithfull herself. I am of the opinion that Solomon has interests that are too large to bother with such a thing as a shake-down in person.'

That Charles 'King' Solomon was an even more powerful underworld figure than X-42 made him out to be is signified by the fact that he was the Boston delegate to a conference of leading criminals from far and wide which was held at Atlantic City in May 1929, the main purpose being to discuss the establishment of a national crime syndicate. Among the delegates (more than a dozen, though the conference has become known as The Meeting of the Big Seven) were Al Capone and Jake 'Greasy Thumb' Guzik from Chicago, Abe Bernstein, leader of the Purple Gang of Detroit, and Charles 'Lucky' Luciano, Meyer Lansky, Dutch Schultz and Joe Adonis, all from New York.

Solomon was murdered in the early hours of 24 January 1933, a Tuesday, at the Cotton Club, at the western end of Tremont Street, Boston. A moment after he went into the Gents, four men got up from their table and followed him. Four shots rang out and the four men left the club — unhurriedly, seemingly unconcerned about the large number of patrons and waiters, to say nothing of the now-silent negro jazz band, ostentatiously pretending not to be watching them. Solomon staggered out of the Gents and collapsed at the edge of the dance floor. The crime was never solved.[1]

From the *Boston Evening Globe* of the day of the murder:

> Law enforcement officers ... today frankly credited Solomon with being ... the Al Capone of the East ... But for the report that he was 'rubbed out' with .32 calibre bullets, the Government agents declare they would be satisfied he was 'put on the spot' by killers, gunmen, from either Detroit or New York.... Solomon was to have been in the Federal

---

Welansky, who had been one of Charles Solomon's lawyers till January 1933. There was no record that Welansky had paid for the title.

1. It resembles, in style and setting, the shooting of Dutch Schultz (et alios) on 23 October 1935; Schultz died two days later, having said, among many other strange and strangely poetic things, 'A boy has never wept nor dashed a thousand kim.' (The transcript of his ramblings is included in my anthology, *The Pleasures of Murder*, Allison & Busby, London, 1983, and Sphere, London, 1986.)

Court tomorrow morning for a hearing on his removal to Brooklyn, where he had been indicted by a Federal Grand Jury in the rum-smuggling racket with others of his associates. . . . Federal agents say the slain man got his 'cut' from many sources – that it was death to oppose him and deny him his cut in the proceeds. . . . During recent years, Solomon lived at 193 Fuller Street, Brookline, although in the indictment his address was given as the Hotel Essex, Boston.

Solomon was born about 47 years ago in Russia and moved to Salem when a small boy. Early in life he was known as 'Sly Boots'. . . .

He managed, according to Federal agents, to make contracts with some high-grade citizens through connections made at his night clubs, and he was indisputably becoming 'high-hat'. This fact did not increase his personal popularity with his former associates. . . . Tall, suave, slightly drooped, a flashing smile always on his dark features, he found it a tremendously expensive task to carry on his narcotic drug business by the old-time methods because he had to 'take care' of so many persons. Authorities claim he was feeding a small army of 'hop-heads', 'gun-killers' and pedlers. . . .

Superintendent of Police Michael Crowley declared that . . . Solomon had much influence in certain places, but he emphasised that Solomon had no influence with the Boston police. He added that he believed Solomon would interest himself in anything that meant money.

From the *Boston Herald* of 27 January 1933:

Among those who entered the Solomon home for the funeral service were Dan Carroll, manager of Jimmy Maloney and other fighters; David 'Beano' Breen; Matt McGrath, Boston attorney . . . Herbert Callahan and Thomas Creed, lawyers; Johnny Wilson, former middleweight champion, Joseph 'Little Corky' Stein . . . 'Big Hymie' Gold . . .

The six room flat on the second floor of the duplex was . . . tightly packed with mourners. . . . An old man, bearded and stooped, cracked his knuckles one by one as he listened to the sermon, and while tears ran down his face he said again and again, 'Nothing but trouble. Nothing but trouble.'

So many and varied were the flowers that they filled the six rooms, flowed out on to an upper porch and finally became so profuse that a large section of the front yard was hidden by them. As the funeral cortege began its eight mile journey to the United Hand-in-Hand cemetery, Dedham, behind came the mourners, perhaps as varied a group as ever followed a coffin to the grave. Night club girls and stout Jewish matrons, 'strong-arm' men and jazz musicians, vaudeville artists and gangsters, 'sports' and lawyers, dancers and doctors, feminine men and masculine women, immigrants and Bostonians, the powerful and the hangers-on. . . . The services at the grave were over within 15 minutes. The crowd, chilled by the cold, slipped swiftly away. Two small boys remained . . . and danced about the grave of the 'King' while they shouted some derisive rigmarole about 'Solomon was bad and he got shot'.

And that was the end of Solomon.


## Daniel J. Carroll

X-42: 'Dan Carroll, known as "Large Dan", was a police officer until he went out on strike during the famous Boston Police Strike in 1919. Not much was heard of him for some time after other than that he was interested in fights and fighters and was prominent in the liquor business. Carroll, as well as Solomon since his one and only arrest, never actually handles any liquor himself. Both of these men in late years are considered to be the greatest powers in Boston in the underworld.'

All of the immediately following quotations are from Boston papers published between January 1929 (when Carroll was alleged to have contributed to a slush-fund for the purpose of bribing members of the state legislature to push through a bill legalising professional sporting events on Sundays) and the summer of 1931:

The Boston police strike made Dan Carroll, as it did Calvin Coolidge. The then Governor of Massachusetts might never have reached the White House but for that occurrence. As for Daniel, he would probably still be pounding the pavements if he had not, after eight and a half years in the police service, been discharged. He secured a job as an investigator for the Joseph Walsh law firm, and after a short time decided to capitalise on his love and knowledge of boxing. He became the first licensed referee until the present boxing law. One night he gave a decision to the right man and the crowd told him to get another job. Dan took their advice and became a matchmaker for the Faneuil Athletic Club.

But energetic Dan was not wholly satisfied with this life. As a real vocation he went into the trucking business. Dan put the same amount of steam back of his trucks as he has in bringing Honey-Boy Finnegan, the uncrowned junior lightweight, Jim Maloney, and other prize fighters to the front rank under his management.[1] Dan still had spare time that he was anxious to fill. He opened restaurants which all paid from the time the doors were opened.

He merits his nickname of 'Large Dan'. Fine black hair, with a tendency to curl as it parts in the centre of his head, crowns a florid countenance. Inquisitive eyes hide beneath dark eyebrows.

He does a great deal of walking to keep down to his weight of 230 pounds, and finds surcease from the grind by smoking 30 cigars a day.

'Who IS Dan Carroll?'
'Sh-h-h!' advises the night club habitué.
'Sh-h-h!' cautions the follower of sports.
'Sh-h-h!' warn 'the boys'.
'Sh-h-h!' moans the politician.
'Sh-h-h!' sighs the policeman.
Around Dan Carroll swirl winds from all strata and directions in Boston. When his nimble fingers flex, it is said they pull the strings that move puppets in high and low positions.

Most of the press references to Carroll between the summer of 1931 and that of 1949, when he died, aged sixty-six, refer only to his activities as a boxing manager. In its obituary of him, the *Boston Herald* noted that 'he had been a friend of Charles "King" Solomon, murdered racketeer, and at one time also was associated with Barnett Welansky,[2] owner of the ill-fated Cocoanut Grove night-club . . . Although during the past year he limited his activities largely to his trucking firm, he was held in awe during the height of his power by politicians, policemen and night-club habitues alike.'

**George Benwell** was twice 'liquored up and pumped' by X-42. On the first occasion, X-42 'got the impression that Benwell said that before Peters had ever had his name appear in the papers after the finding of Starr Faithfull's body, he, Benwell, had been interviewed as to his knowledge of the case by a fellow reporter from the *Boston American* office'. On the second occasion, 'Benwell said that he never heard of Starr Faithfull previous to her death, and the only thing he ever heard about Peters was when Peters withdrew from the mayoralty after his first term; it was noised about in political circles that he withdrew because of information in the hands of his opponents regarding his affairs with a woman. At that time, Benwell stated to me confidentially, he called an attorney on the phone (by the name of William G. Kelly) who is said to have participated in shake-downs. Kelly was a great friend of the late Billy Fallon.[3] When Benwell asked Kelly if he had heard anything

1. Jim Maloney, a contender for the world heavyweight title, was one of the many persons grilled by the investigators of the murder of Charles Solomon at the Cotton Club on 24 January 1933. (Though Dan Carroll owned the Cotton Club – pretending that he didn't by using a clerk in Joseph Walsh's law firm as a 'front' – the investigators did not ask him for assistance with their inquiries.)
2. In 1940, a judge ordered Carroll and Welansky to pay $44,134 to an investment trust for 'failing to keep promises made'.

about Peters and his woman affairs, he told Benwell that he hadn't until recently but he wished he had known about it before. After telling me of the above incidents, ten years in the past, Benwell lapsed into silence.'

I believe that George Benwell did learn, in the spring of 1931, of Andrew Peters' illicit relationship with Starr, of Peters' payment to the Faithfulls, from '10% Joe' Lyons; that, seeking to confirm the information, he phoned Alexander Whiteside, his reporter's ears straining to detect nuances of meaning in whatever noncommittal reply Whiteside made before hanging up; that, satisfied that Lyons's tale was true, he passed it on to Charles 'King' Solomon or 'Large Dan' Carroll, or the two of them together, and subsequently heard from one or both of them of the arrangements made for a shake-down of Peters.

(At first sight, the story given to the Starr Faithfull investigators appears to be made less credible by the setting of the shake-down of a Bostonian by gangsters of that city in a room at the Astor Hotel, *Manhattan*: why in Manhattan? Why not, conveniently to shakers and shaken, in their home-city? In fact, when one comes to think about it, the setting actually adds to the story's credibility. Why, if the story was invented by the three informants, did they complicate the plot with geographical details that might raise listeners' eyebrows questioningly? There are several possible reasons for the Hotel Astor setting: Peters may have been in Manhattan, staying at another hotel, when the gangsters learned his secret; he or they may have insisted on an away-from-Boston rendezvous, thereby reducing the risk that someone who knew him and any of them would observe the coming-together or the parting; the gangster who first got in touch with Peters may, wishing to imply rather than state the grounds for blackmail, have ordered him to the Astor Hotel – a choice of venue that showed that he knew about the incident that, so the Faithfulls said, sparked off their claim against Peters.)

Either because Benwell was just plain greedy, or because he was dissatisfied with his reward for the Peters information I am, you

---

3. William J. Fallon (1886-1927): probably the most successfully crooked of the criminal lawyers practising in New York City in the dozen years before his death from alcoholism. Of the hundred or so persons he defended on the charge of murder, about sixty were acquitted, and the rest got off with light sentences. Many, if not most, of his courtroom successes were the result of his bribing of jurors. Many of his clients were never brought to trial, he having arranged for prosecution witnesses or documents to disappear.

understand, still surmising), he sold advance details of the shake-down to Vannie Higgins or one of Higgins's lieutenants. The biters, having returned to Boston, and gathered with others in Charles Solomon's room at the Essex Hotel for the sharing out of the $30,000, were bit.

Solomon and Carroll, to say nothing of the underlings who had done all the shake-down work, were most upset. When they had calmed down enough to be able to think coherently, constructively, they wondered how the armed robbers had known that there would be sufficient cash in the room to make an armed robbery worth while; they wondered if George Benwell had any idea; they may have asked him. They wondered whether or not Peters should be told what had happened – should be asked to make good their loss or, at any rate, to pay the second instalment at once rather than when they had planned to ask him. And they may have discussed a matter beside the point of the robbery: how long they should wait before putting the squeeze on Peters to do favours for them or to seek favours from his powerful political friends on their behalf, favours that would assist them in their present criminal endeavours and open up opportunities for diversification.

Long before Solomon and Carroll may have discussed that last topic, the robbers were back, safe and sound, in New York and may even have already celebrated the coup with their master, Vannie Higgins, and received from him their cuts of the $30,000. Even before his men had set off for Boston, perhaps following the Boston gangsters' car along the Post Road, Higgins had given less thought to the amount of the loot than to the loot's intrinsic value: conclusive evidence that *all* of the information sold to him by George Benwell was true – that Andrew J. Peters, once Mayor of Boston, subsequently president of the Boston Chamber of Commerce, still powerful and with powerful friends in Massachusetts, and likely to have far wider power if his friend Franklin Delano Roosevelt won the next Presidential election, was blackmailable on account of his association with some girl called, would you believe it, Starr Faithfull. It would not be surprising if Vannie Higgins slobbered at the implications. He would have worried that those implications had occurred to Charles Solomon, with whom he had done many deals since the start of Prohibition, and with whom he, together with the Devaney brothers, was planning 'to open a new beer racket in Boston'. He had heard the saying that knowledge was power, but he had never imagined, not in his wildest dreams, that he would get hold of the sort of knowledge that could make him as powerful as any criminal anywhere, in the same league as Al Capone (whom he felt sure, like everyone else, would get off lightly from the convictions for tax evasion), 'Lucky' Luciano, and James J. Hines, the czar of Tammany Hall who, as such, was Franklin Delano Roosevelt's patronage dispenser in New York City.

In the few weeks following the shake-down of Peters, the robbing of the Boston blackmailers, Vannie Higgins gave much of his spare thinking time to the questions of how he could and, far more important, how he should use his knowledge about Peters; he discussed the questions with his lieutenants, his lawyers; he may have got in touch with George Benwell, offering him a seemingly generous bonus if he could ferret out specific facts, evidence confirming them.

By the first week of June, having learned little, if anything, towards putting Peters in his pocket, Higgins came up with an idea that struck him as being so obvious, so obviously excellent, that he became dangerously angry that none of the people he employed to think on his behalf had come up with it. He might have given the idea a second, questioning thought, might have been less angry with his thinkers, might have asked one or other of them what they thought of the idea, but for his worry that if he didn't act decisively and soon, Charles Solomon might have the very same idea and act decisively and sooner, putting Peters in his own pocket.

The idea was this: to find out everything that was worth knowing about Peters' relationship with Starr Faithfull from the one person who had every scrap of the information − Starr Faithfull herself.

From half-past nine on the morning of Friday, 5 June, when Starr left home, till mid-afternoon, when she went aboard the *Carmania*, she was followed around Manhattan by at least two of Higgins's men − men whom he had hand-picked for the assignment by a process of elimination of those who were as rash, as impatient, as psychopathic, as he was himself. It was as well that he had chosen the men carefully. He had told them that they were only to carry out the purpose of the assignment when they were sure they were unobserved: after dark, probably. That entailed a long wait, close to the Cunard piers. They waited, confident that the girl who had gone in through one of the gates had to come out through one of them; there were no back or side-exits to worry about. They took turns, surely, to visit the café opposite the piers which, though called the Munson Lunch, was open all hours. They waited till 10.25, saw the girl emerging through the gate of Pier 56, escorted by a man they did not know was Dr Charles Young Roberts and saw that she was looking for a taxi.

There is a slight possibility that one of the men was on his own in one car, the other or others in another − that the man on his own decided, on the spur of the moment, to pretend that he was a taxi-driver, his car a taxi. Nearly all of the taxis in New York City were shown to be such by being painted yellow; particularly at night, some of the rest, painted in dark colours, looked little different from private cars − and vice versa. The lone driver could have driven to where Starr was standing with Dr Roberts; if either of them had commented that his car didn't look at all like a cab, he could have said that he was a hire-car driver − or simply a good samaritan, offering a free lift on a rainy night. The possibility of the pretence is made less slight by the fact that no taxi-driver ever came forward, saying that he was *the* driver − despite repeated, much-publicised pleas from the investigators, and then the official offer of a reward of $100 'for positive information as to the route and destination of a female passenger entering a taxicab at Pier 56 . . .', and then the offer by the *New York Daily News* of a reward of $5000 'for exclusive information which will solve the mysterious death of Starr Faithfull' (or, presumably, a slice of $5000 for information that helped towards the solution).

Whichever: from the sidewalk by the gate to Pier 56 or from near where Starr alighted from a licensed taxi − *she was abducted* . . .

*driven to Island Park, Nassau County* −

*to Tappe's Hotel*, the favourite watering place of the Vannie Higgins gang − favoured by them for several reasons, one being that they could do what they liked there, safe in the knowledge that the place was protected by the Island Park police, who were as corrupt as they themselves were criminals.

Things didn't go as Vannie had planned. (No − *planned* is not the word. He wasn't up to much as a planner; he tended to get carried away with ideas that he considered bright, giving little thought to what nowadays are called scenarios. Let us say that things didn't go as Vannie had hoped.)

Starr was treated quite well at first. She was given a meal; perhaps more than one. The meal, or the last of the meals, was of, among other ingredients, meat and mushrooms and potatoes, raw or stewed fruit for dessert. If she was offered a drink, she said no. Supposing that, as Dr Roberts's testimony suggests, she possessed no calming drugs, she asked for some, and was provided with Allonal − stronger than Veronal, which she was used to taking.

# $100 REWARD

for <u>positive</u> information as to the route and destination of a female passenger entering a taxicab at Pier 56, foot of West 14th Street, North River, (Chelsea Piers), at about 10:25 P. M. on the night of June 5, 1931.

*Communicate with*

## Harold R. King,

**Inspector, Nassau County Police,**
**Detective Division, Mineola, L. I.**

*('North River' is another name for the Hudson)*
*Courtesy of the Commissioner of the Nassau County Police Department*

She was told that she had no need to be frightened. Once she had dished the dirt, every speck, on Andrew Peters, she would be driven back to Manhattan; she might even be given a present, a little something as a gesture of gratitude for her co-operation, of regret for the inconvenience she had been caused, of appreciation for her promise that she would invent a reason for her absence from home.

She talked – said everything she remembered about her relationship with Andrew Peters.

But Vannie Higgins was not satisfied. There must have been more to it than that, he insisted. Did she expect him to believe that the relationship had gone on for nearly ten years before, one night at the Astor Hotel, Peters had had sex with her? Never before? Never again? Just that one and only time? It made no sort of sense. Why the hell, then, had Peters paid out $55,000 – $25,000 to the Faithfulls, $30,000 to Charles Solomon's men? One way or the other: either she was holding something back or Peters had paid far, far above the odds to keep such a relationship secret. Even $25,000 – even that was out of proportion. But more than twice as much? That made Peters out to be stupid. Peters wasn't stupid. Therefore, Starr must think that he, Vannie Higgins, was stupid. She would have to be taught that she was mistaken . . .

And so Vannie Higgins – perhaps aided by a couple of his goons, working turn and turn about, enjoyably – tried to beat the truth out of Starr.

She had no more truth to tell.

She may, in desperation, have puffed up her story with lies. But she was not a good liar; never had been. The lies made Vannie furious.

She was left alone for a while, told that she had only herself to blame for the bruises on her body, that she would suffer further injury, worse injury, if she remained obstinate. She took another dose of Allonal, all that was left.

Vannie Higgins, returning, found her unconscious. He may already have decided that she could not be allowed to live. Now, perhaps, he concluded that the beating had been too brutal, that if she was not yet dead, she was dying.

He made arrangements to dispose of her, to give her death the look of an accident.

Tappe's Hotel was nicely suited to those related purposes, being on the southern waterfront of Island Park, and having its own little dock, which, apart from being used nocturnally as a landing-place for liquor, was the berth for the speedboats hired out by a Mr Gadney and his wife, who lived at the hotel.

Starr Faithfull was carried to one of the Gadneys' speedboats. The driver had been given a negative instruction – to drive out of Reynolds Channel, the strip of water separating Island Park from Long Beach, before dumping the cargo. It didn't matter where the cargo was dumped, as long as there was no chance of its drifting back into the channel and coming ashore anywhere near Tappe's Hotel.

The speedboat travelled west to the nearer end of the channel, a distance of four miles, and curved south and then east around the western headland of Long Beach. After a mile or so – just to make certain of being away from the currents into the channel – the driver shut off the engine, checked that the lights along the shore of Long Beach were indistinct, and that there were no other boats around, tipped the cargo overboard, re-started the engine, and drove back to the little dock of Tappe's Hotel.

That is what I think happened. I may be wrong, of course. I rather hope that I am. I have become, in a sort of way, fond of Starr Faithfull, and would prefer to think that for once in her life, in the last few hours of it, she was content.

**9**

**R**eal life makes coincidences that would be considered far-fetched in fiction. On 10 April, which was Good Friday, 1936, Nancy Titterton, a young married woman (her husband, a radio executive, was working that day) who had had short stories published and was writing a novel, was raped and strangled with pieces of the clothes torn from her body in her apartment on the fourth floor of 22 Beekman Place, a quiet and fashionable street in Manhattan, close to where the United Nations Headquarters now stands. The police eventually proved that the murderer was John Fiorenza, an upholsterer's assistant who had first met Mrs Titterton on the afternoon before the crime, when he had called to collect a love seat for repair. But in the early hours of the investigation, the police wondered whether this case was somehow linked with the death of Starr Faithfull. They had found a note scribbled on a pad beside the phone in the apartment: directions on how to get to 12 St Luke's Place. It turned out that a married couple named Mansbridge, friends of the Tittertons, now lived at the Faithfulls' old address, and had invited the Tittertons round to celebrate a wedding anniversary. Mrs Titterton had phoned Mrs Mansbridge on the Good Friday morning, asking how to get to St Luke's Place by subway.

There appears to be another coincidence. In 1935, John O'Hara published a novel inspired by the Starr Faithfull case; he called it *BUtterfield 8*, explaining in an introductory note that that was the name of a New York City telephone exchange. He and his publishers, nervously aware that Stanley Faithfull was eagle-eyed for the slightest possible hint of libel, had taken care to ensure that no part of the novel specifically indicated its source. O'Hara cannot have known – or rather, perhaps, cannot have realised that he had read and subconsciously remembered – that Stanley's first wife was called Miss Butterfield, both before and, in business, during their marriage.[1]

For almost exactly six years, till the late summer of 1937, Stanley seems to have devoted all of his energies to the prosecution of legal actions. Neither during that time nor ever afterwards, so far as I can tell, did he do a stroke of non-legal work. Presumably his lawyers acted on a contingency-fee basis — no payment unless damages were awarded, and then a percentage of those. Even so, he must somehow have managed to get money from somewhere, someone, else he, and his wife and Tucker, neither of them working, would have become destitute in no time at all after Tucker's 'employment' by the United Press from mid-June till mid-August of 1931. I have suggested a solution to the Starr Faithfull mystery, but I am completely foxed by the question of how Starr's remaining kin kept a roof over their heads, never mind how they kept a large pack of wolves from their door.

First, in August 1931, in the Manhattan Magistrates' Court, Stanley brought an action for criminal libel against Colonel Joseph M. Patterson, editor and publisher of the *New York Daily News*, and Sidney Sutherland, author of a series of articles on the Starr Faithfull case that had appeared in that paper. The hearings dragged on till December, when the magistrate deemed that there was no case to answer. Upset but undeterred, Stanley brought an action for civil libel against Patterson and Sutherland in the Staten Island Supreme Court, claiming damages of $350,000. After several weeks, the case went to the jury, who found in favour of the defendants. Meanwhile and subsequently, Stanley pursued an out-of-court action, instigated before Starr's death, against Jay Leo Rothschild, representing the Dunbar Molasses Company, from whom he claimed $75,000 for alleged breach of contract. The action seems to have become inactive some time after December 1932. Having failed to punish and profit from the *News*, Stanley set about the *New York Daily Mirror*. Again, he claimed damages of $350,000. Again, a jury found against him. That was towards the end of May 1936. The trade-journal, *Editor & Publisher*, gave this account of the six-week trial:

1. There have been many editions of *BUtterfield 8*; my copy is of the edition published by Barrie & Rockliff, London, in 1951. In 1960, Elizabeth Taylor won the best-actress Oscar for her portrayal of the Starr-like 'Gloria Wandrous' in a screen adaptation of the novel. The most satisfactory of other novels inspired by the Starr Faithfull case is *Some Unknown Person* by Sandra Scoppettone (Putnam, New York, 1977).

Mr Faithfull claimed that he had been accused of blackmail, implication in the disappearance of his step-daughter, suppression of evidence, and various other charges, such as mortgaging his wife's property without her knowledge....

The *Daily Mirror* contended that Mr Faithfull had given many false and inconsistent accounts of the life, characteristics and demeanour of his deceased step-daughter....

Manheim Rosenzweig, attorney for the *Daily Mirror*, commented on the efforts of the plaintiff to have certain officers and writers of the *Daily News* held for indictment. According to Mr Rosenzweig, the testimony given by the plaintiff on that occasion was so false and malicious that he did not dare submit himself to cross-examination in this trial with respect to it....

In his summation, Mr Rosenzweig said that the *Daily Mirror* had truthfully reported incidents revealed by the investigation into the death of Miss Faithfull. He argued to the jury that the *Daily Mirror* had never accused Mr Faithfull of being a blackmailer, but that if he desired to assume that role, the evidence before the court provided abundant proof that he had in fact occupied himself in that manner.

A year later, *Mrs* Faithfull was the plaintiff in a libel action against the *Mirror*. She was represented by a young attorney who was enjoying a phenomenal run of successes in jury cases on Staten Island. On 30 June 1937, Stanley's stubbornness seemed to have paid off: a jury granted his wife damages of $45,000. But it was a false dawn. Manheim Rosenzweig insisted that the judgment was against the weight of the evidence, also that the amount of damages was excessive, and a judge, agreeing on the latter point, reduced the award to $5000. Soon afterwards, Mrs Faithfull's attorney was disbarred, for the secret of his success in jury cases had been revealed as being largely attributable to his success, almost as phenomenal as that of the late, more generous William Fallon, in striking up friendships with jurors.

Whatever remained of the $5000 after the attorney had subtracted his agreed cut and any juror-bribing expenses he may have incurred, a portion of it may have gone to Tucker as a slightly-belated dowry.

On 14 June, she married Edward A. Hancock, a native of Chicago who was well-educated, being an alumnus of the University of Illinois, Princeton University, and Brooklyn Law School – from which he had graduated and, becoming a member of the New York Bar, joined the legal staff of Rockefeller Center, which was beginning to tower beautifully in midtown Manhattan, on land rented from Columbia University. Tucker (who, some time before – perhaps very recently, from a determination that everything should be perfectly legal – had reverted to her true surname, Wyman) was made Mrs Hancock in Montclair, the New Jersey town where she had spent part of her childhood. Whether the location of the wedding was of her choosing, maybe from sentiment, or of someone else's, I have no idea. The ceremony was performed by the Minister of the Unity Church, Montclair, at the home, nearby, of William Hards, Junior, who was then best known as being the son of William Hards, Senior, a noted journalist and radio commentator (subsequently, editor of *Reader's Digest*). The wedding was a quiet affair, reported in only one paper, and there formally, as one 'society wedding' among several. Tucker said for publication that she was the daughter of the late[1] Frank Wyman, but did not let on about her Faithfull relationships, and claimed collateral descent from General George Reid, a member of George Washington's staff in the Revolutionary War, and General Franklin Pierce, the 14th President of the United States (1853-6). Supposing that the bride's mother and step-father were invited to the wedding, they may have been forced to decline owing to legalistic commitments.

The mystery of how they stayed out of a poor-house or a debtors' prison is made more mystifying by the fact that, between July 1937 and October 1949, they moved back to Manhattan – immediately or eventually to 10 Mitchell Place, a newish apartment block, quite posh, in the small area called Turtle Bay; Mitchell Place and Beekman Place form an L. I would not know that they lived there were it not for this entry in the paid obituary column of the *New York Times*:

> FAITHFULL – Stanley E., at his residence, 10 Mitchell Place, on Oct. 11 [1949], husband of Helen MacGregor Faithfull. Services and interment private. Kindly omit flowers.

In 1951, his widow died or moved or gave up being on the phone or was made phoneless because she was so far behind with the bills. I gather those possibilities from the omission of her name from the Manhattan phone book of 1952.

Having served three terms as District Attorney of Nassau County,

---

1. But for that word, I would not know roughly when Wyman died. In Britain, details of births, marriages and deaths are usually easy to find, as there are only two general register offices, one in London, the other in Edinburgh. In America, however, those events are registered independently in the state in which they take place – which means that if one doesn't know the state, one may have to ask in 49 of them before getting answers to whatever the questions are.

Elvin Edwards did not seek re-election in 1933; he returned to private practice, in partnership with a Mr Froelich and a Mr MacDonough, with offices in Mineola. He died, aged sixty-four, on 16 July 1946, after a long illness. The *New York Times* of the following day noted that he was

> sometimes called 'Nassau's St George'.... Regardless of the size or importance of the case, Nassau residents and New York generally came to expect a good show from the Nassau District Attorney.... His continuous routine work to prevent organised crime from getting a foothold in Nassau was overshadowed by his connection with several of the big headline-making crime cases of the era....
>
> The Republican nominee for Supreme Court Justice in the Second District in 1937, Mr Edwards polled an overwhelming Nassau vote, but his home-county margin was offset by the strength of the Democratic candidates in Kings [Brooklyn] and Queens Counties.... Always active in county affairs, he was at one time a director of the Nassau County Association and served for several terms as president of the Long Island Association. During the recent war he was chairman of the Nassau County National War Fund.

Following Edwards' announcement of his retirement as DA, Martin Littleton was given the Republican nomination for the job. He won the election and served a single term – during which, in 1935, he and Edwards were opposing counsel at the trial of Everett Applegate and Mrs Mary Creighton, of Baldwin, a small town to the north of the eastern end of Long Beach, who were charged with the murder by poison of Applegate's wife Ada, an extremely fat woman who had complained of his sexual relationship, perversely encouraged by Mary Creighton, with the latter's teenaged daughter Ruth. The verdict went Littleton's way, and Edwards' clients were electrocuted at Sing Sing in July 1936. At the end of the following year, Littleton went into partnership with George Morton Levy, a lawyer as forensically flamboyant as himself. Levy's admiration for Littleton (whom he described as 'one of the ablest lawyers I have ever met, and, intellectually, one of the finest men I have ever known') was reciprocated: in 1952, Littleton, with help from a journalist, compiled a book of reminiscences of his then-former partner. That Littleton was highly regarded as a defender, and able to command large fees, is shown by the fact that he appeared on behalf of many racketeers, including Charles Luciano and Frank Costello. In 1946, he defended a man whom he knew very well; I shall refer to that case in a moment. By the end of the 1940s, close to his fiftieth birthday,

Littleton was rich enough to retire; he moved, with his wife Marion and their son and two daughters, to the Big Horn Basin of Wyoming, where he bought a ranch, also a house in Cody;[1] soon tiring of retirement, he opened a general law practice in the town. He died there, aged sixty-eight, on 29 August 1966.

About the case defended by Littleton in 1946: it came to trial in January of that year, in the Nassau County Court, Mineola; the defendant was Harold R. King, formerly the inspector in charge of the detective division of the Nassau County Police Department; he was charged with attempting to bribe and conspiring to bribe a police officer, Sergeant Bert Bedell, the senior detective in the sub-division covering Merrick, the district to the east of Baldwin.

King's resignation from the police department had been offered and accepted on 29 August 1945, a few hours before District Attorney James Gehrig's announcement that 'a secret investigation conducted with the aid of New York State troopers into reports that notorious New York City characters have started big-time gambling operations in Nassau County has uncovered evidence that certain county policemen and other law-enforcing officials are implicated'.

Sergeant Bedell, the star witness for the prosecution, testified[2] that

> King...offered him $50 a week to aid in protecting a gambling establishment at Oceanside...last Aug. 6 as they were driving to Rockville Centre in the inspector's automobile. Bedell said that two days later he ... reported the matter to John M. Beckmann, then an inspector, now Nassau County Police Commissioner. The sergeant declared that had he accepted the protection offer, he would have been required to overlook the gambling carried on first in a tavern and subsequently in the quarters of a bartenders' union.... A code message was arranged to give warning of a raid, the witness said, quoting it as: 'Grandpa will be down in about fifteen minutes. This is Floyd calling.'
>
> Under cross-examination by Martin W. Littleton ... Bedell admitted having made fifty or sixty trips in 1940 to Brooklyn to work on a house he owned, 'signing out' on detective cases after reporting in the morning.... Some of these cases, it was brought out, had been closed for months and still others 'never happened'. Mr Littleton obtained also from Bedell an admission of a 'collusive' divorce in Georgia in 1939.

---

1. The town founded by William 'Buffalo Bill' Cody as an investment; there is a dam called the Buffalo Bill in the nearby Shoshone Canyon.
2. According to the *New York Times*; all of the following are from that source.

The judge accepted Littleton's submission that there was no case to answer on the conspiracy charge, but denied his submission that the remaining charge, of attempted bribery, should be dismissed and the jury directed to acquit.

> Mr King was asked by his counsel whether he had offered . . . any bribe to Bendell.
> 'No, I did not,' the witness replied in a clear voice. . . .
> 'What protection could Bedell give to anyone?'
> 'None whatever,' King replied.
> On cross-examination by District Attorney Gehrig, Mr King defended a proposal he had made to transfer vice investigations from the prosecutor's office to the police, declaring that was where they belonged, as a matter of policy. . . . The prosecutor taxed Mr King with drinking to excess, asserting that 'every District Attorney' was constantly worried about his driving. 'You have drunk so heavily from time to time that you were not fit to drive,' Mr Gehrig declared. This Mr King denied. Questioned concerning an accident during which the car Mr King was driving was wrecked, the former inspector laid the accident to the fact that he had been fifty-two hours without sleep while working on a case.

The jury retired at half-past ten on the morning of 30 January, the eleventh day of the trial.

> Spontaneous applause sounded in Nassau County Court at 3 o'clock when the jury acquitted Mr King. . . . He, a policeman for twenty-six years, tried in vain to suppress his emotion. Tears trickled down his cheeks as he murmured his thanks to the jurors. 'I am intensely gratified,' he said. . . . 'My plans for the immediate future are uncertain.'

On 30 July, he applied for reinstatement, but was turned down by Commissioner Beckmann.
On 15 November,

> the reinstatement of Harold R. King . . . long enough to qualify for retirement was agreed upon in the Supreme Court, Mineola. Marcus Christ, county attorney, said a stipulation to that effect would be acceptable to Commissioner Beckmann. . . . Mr Christ declared that the former inspector, in his previous application to be reinstated, had said nothing about rejoining the force merely long enough to ensure retirement. Mr King would be eligible for an annual [pension] of about $2500.

King received the pension for at least half a dozen years. We know this from the interview by Fred J. Cook about the Starr Faithfull case in the early 1950s. The payments must have been made unnecessary many years ago, for the administration office at the Nassau County Police Headquarters has no record of King's pension; nor of his service, abruptly ended after twenty-seven years plus the minute or so he needed so as to qualify for the pension.

In 1949, Dr George Jameson Carr also became a pensioner – of the Cunard Steam-Ship Company. He was married by then. His wife Margaret had borne him a daughter (who now insists, despite clear evidence to the contrary, that he murdered Starr Faithfull). In 1951, he was made an MBE (Member of the Order of the British Empire).[1]

1. Another of the MBEs appointed in 1951 was Dr Raymond Lancaster, whom Starr had a crush on in the late summer of 1928, when he was Dr Carr's assistant (page 214), and who left Cunard soon afterwards to work as a medical missionary in the province of Kwangtung, China. Starr's other British, mercantile, medical friend, Charles Young Roberts, left Cunard at the start of 1932, married in April of that year, and opened a surgery in Sheffield, Yorkshire; he continued to practise in 'the city of steel' till shortly before his death in the mid-1960s.

Two American doctors, their feet always firm on the ground, who took an interest in Starr respectively before and after her death, became more eminent. William Van Pelt Garretson, as well as treating mentally-disturbed patients privately, found time to be the consultant neuro-psychiatrist of ten hospitals in and around Manhattan, to serve on lunacy commissions, and, in odd moments, to appear as an expert witness at trials for murder alleged to have been committed by persons whose mental status was controversial; he died at the age of sixty-eight in 1948. Alexander Gettler continued to be the chief toxicologist for New York City till 1959, his forty-first year in that office; already laden with honours from medical associations and a university, he was given more during his retirement, till 1968, when he died at the age of eighty-four.

Two of Starr's professionally artistic acquaintances prospered. Harry Stoner, with whom she did not attend a party, had exhibitions in Manhattan and Washington, D.C., of his paintings and sculptures (some of the former of Miriam Hopkins, who, though usually busy in Hollywood till a few years before her death in 1972, made one or two appearances on Broadway and in touring productions – in 1946, eponymously as 'Laura', a character who, at the start of the play, while regarded as a murder-victim, seems almost as mysterious and protean as Starr). Stoner, still a bachelor, died at his place of retirement in New Rochelle, just north of the Bronx, in 1960, when he was eighty. Edwin Megargee, who remained steadfast to the depiction of animals – including, strangely for an animal-lover, cocks fighting each other – and who illustrated several books about dogs, married a woman who gave him a son shortly before divorcing him, and re-married before his death in 1958.

Francis Peabody Hamlin left Cunard in the late 1930s, and at the same time moved from Boston to Manhattan, where he set up a travel agency; he was only fifty-four when he died in 1962.

Bruce Winston often worked, both as an actor and as a designer of sets and costumes, with Dame Sybil Thorndike and her husband Sir Lewis Casson. He played small parts for fat men in several English movies (including *Alf's Button Afloat*, with the Crazy Gang, *The Thief of Baghdad*, with the Indian boy-actor Sabu, *The*

A few years later, the Carrs emigrated to America, and settled in New York State. Carr banked at the branch of Bankers Trust on the corner of Park Avenue and Fifty-Seventh Street, next door to Cunard's Manhattan office. His account was closed in 1971 — which means, I think, that that was when he died (his wife's account had been closed in 1964). He was eighty-six or seven.

Though it is, I suppose, pathetically fallacious to lump a liner with characters in the case, I shall do so. In September 1939, the first month of the Second World War, the *Franconia* was requisitioned by the British Government to be a troop-ship, and in the following year was used for the evacuation of soldiers and civilians from Europe (firstly, and while being attacked by German dive-bombers, from Norway, then from France). In July 1943, she took part in the invasion of Sicily, and in February 1945 was used as the 'headquarters ship' for the Yalta Conference at which Churchill, Roosevelt and Stalin discussed the final phase of the war and agreed to call the first meeting of the United Nations, in San Francisco; by July 1948, when she was returned to Cunard, she had carried 150,000 personnel and travelled 320,000 miles. From 1949, she plied between England and Canada, making her final voyage, back to Liverpool, in the autumn of 1956. Near the end of that year, she was taken to the nautical knacker's yard at Inverkeithing, across the Firth of Forth from Edinburgh.

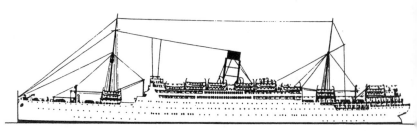

---

*Private Life of Don Juan*, with the ageing Douglas Fairbanks, and *The Private Life of Henry VIII*, with Charles Laughton). Once, having unwittingly shed a stone and a quarter of his 24¾ stones, he fretted to reporters that he was fading away. In 1946, when he was sixty-seven, he set off from England towards New York on the liner *John Ericsson*, but died from a heart attack the day before the docking at Pier 90.

Vannie Higgins spent the night of Friday, 18 June 1932, at Great Meadows Prison, Comstock, New York State – not in a cell but in the cosy quarters of his friend, Joseph W. Wilson, who, though he had run a brewery since Prohibition had made brewing an illegal occupation, had been appointed warden of the prison by Governor Roosevelt. On the following night, Saturday, Higgins attended a 'classical dance recital' in the clubhouse of the Knights of Columbus, at Prospect Park West and Union Street, Brooklyn – not because he was keen on classical dancing but because his seven-year-old daughter Jean was among the performers and he was a devoted family man. The show seems to have over-run, for it did not end till after one o'clock on the Sunday morning. As Higgins and his daughter walked towards his car, some of eight men occupying two other cars fired guns at him. Several of the bullets hit their target; one of the many others nicked one of Jean Higgins's ears. Father and daughter were rushed to the Methodist Episcopal Hospital, where Higgins, questioned by policemen between surgical operations, refused to say more about the gunmen than 'Never mind, I'll pull through from this and attend to them'. But his intention was frustrated by his death before the day was out. The crime was never solved. Crowded at the top of the list of suspects were associates of (*1*) *Dutch Schultz* (Higgins, having fallen out with him over demarcation lines between their respective bootlegging territories, was planning his murder); (*2*) *the late New York gang-leader, Jack 'Legs' Diamond* (members of Higgins's gang were not only strongly suspected of an attempt to kill Diamond in October 1930, but also of his murder in December 1931); (*3*) *Charles 'King' Solomon* (as you know, Solomon – who would himself die from gunshot wounds on 24 January 1933 – had reason to believe that Higgins, his partner in certain criminal enterprises, had double-crossed him on at least one occasion).

If Andrew Peters was at all superstitious, there were times during the last years of his life when he may have wondered whether he, punished enough for what he had done to Starr Faithfull,[1] was being subjected to further punishment, but of a supernatural kind.

---

1. In June 1932, the managing editor of the comparatively staid *Boston Globe*, apparently feeling that Peters deserved a break, circulated a memo among editorial staff:

STARR FAITHFULL
**WARNING!**
Nothing is to be printed about this
person without my express approval.

Early in 1932, still frail from the nervous breakdowns, pretending too hard to be unaware of, or indifferent to, the stares of strangers, the shifty glances of one-time friends, he began working earnestly as a collector of funds towards making assurance double sure that Franklin Delano Roosevelt would succeed Herbert Hoover as President. A few weeks before the election, two of Peters's sons, Alanson and John, were stricken by polio; Alanson died almost at once, John in the following year. In 1935, Peters was one of the arrangers of a birthday ball for President Roosevelt. He was asked to dinner at the White House, and may have gone there hoping that he would be offered a position in government; the occasion turned out to be entirely social. Already a director of several charitable organisations, he joined the boards of others. In 1938, his son Bradford was killed in a motoring accident. In mid-June, close to the seventh anniversary of the passing of Starr Faithfull, he was admitted to the Faulkner Hospital, suffering from pneumonia. He died on the evening of the 26th. He was sixty-six. Next day, most of the proper papers itemised all the main publicised events of his life bar one.

Joseph Macken wrote off the costs he had incurred in having Starr Faithfull cremated. It would be nice to think that when, needing shelf-space or being short of cans, he decided that the gritty remnants of her had to go, he or some sentimental employee, on a business trip to Long Beach, made a detour to the foot of Minnesota Avenue and spilt the ashes on the sand below the high-water mark. But that seems pretty unlikely.

# Acknowledgements

I was especially fortunate in two respects: not only had the Nassau County Police Department retained the foot-tall file on the Starr Faithfull case, but they provided me with photostats of the documents. I wish to thank the Commissioner, Samuel J. Rozzi, and one of his predecessors, Francis B. Looney; also Police Officer Frederic M. Eno. I was helped most of all by Peter A. Matuza ( a sergeant then, now a lieutenant) and Police Officer Howard Burtt. I am very grateful to both of them.

Other Americans I wish to thank are Jacques and Marguerite Barzun; Albert Borowitz; William Cahn, a former District Attorney of Nassau County; John R. Cronin, Librarian of the *Boston Herald*; Michael R. Darby, Assistant Secretary for Economic Policy, Department of the Treasury; Deborah Edel, of the Lesbian History Archives; Harrison J. Edwards; George Flynn and Jane Jensen, of Bankers Trust; Imogen Forster; Mary A. Frisque; Edward Graff, Public Relations Consultant, City of Long Beach; James R. Hubbard, Chief, Tidal Datum, Department of Commerce; Shirley Jobe and William R. Boles, of the library of the *Boston Globe*; Tom, Bea and Innes McDade; Arthur Mattson, Lynbrook Village Historian; Frank Murphy; Robeson Peters; Randy Roberts, Senior Manuscript Specialist, University of Missouri; Angela Rooke-Ley, the present resident of 12 St Luke's Place; the late Francis Russell; Sandra Scoppettone; Peter Benjamin Warren; Richard A. Winsche, Historian, Nassau County Museum Reference Library.

Compatriots to whom I am grateful are David Allen; Richard Boyd-Carpenter; Ivan Butler; Philip Chadwick; Peter Cotes; Leo Harris; David Hodge, of the National Maritime Museum; Peter Jackson; Peter Minty; Colin Naylor, formerly of *Art and Artists*; P.O. Oliver, of the Cunard Steam-Ship Co. plc; Roy Rodwell, of GEC-Marconi Ltd.; Mrs Anne Smith, daughter of the late Dr

Charles Young Roberts; John Foster White; Richard Whittington-Egan; Ian Will. Also these doctors:

Professor David Bowen; David Foster; Lewis Gavin; C.H. Naylor.

I have left till last my thanks to Jeffrey Bloomfield, a young American historian who, while I was writing this book in London, worked on my behalf in and around Manhattan, finding answers to questions that I had forgotten to ask and answering questions that had still not occurred to me. His help was invaluable.

# Index